HEROES, HACKS, AND FOOLS

HEROES, HACKS, AND FOOLS

Memoirs from the Political Inside

Ted Van Dyk

University of Washington Press

Seattle and London

This book is published with the assistance of a grant from the Stroum Book Fund, established through the generosity of Samuel and Althea Stroum.

Printed in the United States of America
Designed by Ted Cotrotsos
12 11 10 09 08 07   5 4 3 2 1

University of Washington Press
PO Box 50096, Seattle, WA 98145
www.washington.edu/uwpress

Library of Congress Cataloging-in-Publication Data

Van Dyk, Ted, 1934–
Heroes, hacks, and fools : memoirs from the political inside / Ted Van Dyk.
p. cm.
"A Samuel and Althea Stroum book."
Includes bibliographical references and index.
ISBN-13: 978-0-295-98751-4 (hbk. : alk. paper)
ISBN-10: 0-295-98751-0 (hbk. : alk. paper)
1. Van Dyk, Ted, 1934–   2. Political consultants—United States—Biography.
3. Political activists—United States—Biography.   4. Democratic Party (U.S.)—
Biography.   5. United States—Politics and government—1945–1989.
6. United States—Politics and government—1989–   7. Political culture—United
States—History—20th century.   8. Presidents—United States—Election—
History—20th century.   9. Political campaigns—United States—History—20th
century.   10. Journalists—United States—Biography.   I. Title.
E840.8.V355A3   2007
324'.4092—dc22   2007020203

The paper used in this publication meets the minimum requirements of American National Standard for Information Sciences—Permanence of Paper for Printed Library Materials, ANSI Z39.48–1984.

CONTENTS

PREFACE

Angry constituent: "Congressman Smith is a liar, a thief,
a womanizer, and irresponsibly lazy."

Political insider: "Quite so. There are millions like him
and they deserve representation."

An enterprising researcher explored in 2005 the backgrounds of a highly selective and well-publicized group. He found that 36 had been accused of spousal abuse; 7 had been arrested for fraud; 19 had been accused of writing bad checks; 117 had directly or indirectly bankrupted at least two businesses; 3 had done time for assault; 71 could not get a credit card because of bad credit; 14 had been arrested on drug-related charges; 8 had been arrested for shoplifting; 21 were current defendants in lawsuits; and 84 had been arrested for drunk driving in the prior year.

No, the data did not relate to the 350 players in the National Basketball Association, but to our 535 elected representatives in the U.S. Senate and House of Representatives.

If comparable data were available for earlier Congresses, they might differ. But they would also show the vast majority of current and prior senators and representatives to be honest, hardworking, and trying to do their best for the home folks—if not always wisely. Ours is a representative government, and our elected representatives generally reflect their constituencies. By the same token, outlooks and conditions in those same constituencies generally are reflected in the content of national policy and politics.

We are at present a red-state, blue-state country, polarized and unable to agree on a wide range of social, economic, and international issues. The moderate middle—where compromises and agreements are found—has shrunk perceptibly. It should not surprise us that relations between White House and Congress, liberals and conservatives, Republicans and Democrats should be in the same condition.

We have passed through such periods before. For large parts of the nineteenth and twentieth centuries we were fractious and had trouble governing ourselves. In the nineteenth century we endured not only civil war but several presidencies that charitably could be called mediocre. Third-party and independent movements have recurred as the Democratic and Republican parties both came to be considered by millions of citizens as incapable of effective governance. The country was polarized and bitterly divided even on the eve of World War II, as Germany and Japan overran Europe and Asia.

The United States is the world's richest and most powerful country. Nonetheless, we are squandering our advantages—at federal, state, and local levels—by spending money we do not have; making promises we cannot keep; overreaching internationally; allowing our education system to deteriorate; tolerating unacceptable inequities in our midst; and postponing policy decisions that will only become more difficult with time. We also have accepted ever-lower public and private ethical standards.

Yet it seems only yesterday that President John F. Kennedy, in his 1961 inaugural address, asked us to consider "not what your country can do for you [but] what you can do for your country" and pledged "to get America moving again." Where there is lethargy, effective leaders can help shake us out of it.

Over a half century, I have seen such leaders make a real difference in the political process. I have had the privilege of working with Jean Monnet, Lyndon Johnson, Hubert Humphrey, the Kennedys, George McGovern, Paul Tsongas, and others who shared two qualities. First, they were moved by purposes larger than themselves. Second, they generated idealism and loyalty among those around them. Although I disagreed with Ronald Reagan's politics, I saw him do the same. I also was privileged to work with countless dedicated leaders and ordinary people in the civil rights and peace movements of the 1960s and 1970s who saw beyond themselves.

Not such a big thing, you might say, except that you should consider which of our current leaders could be so described. Who are they? My own first thought is of our GIs in Iraq and Afghanistan.

This much can be seen in our immediate future:

There will be a new president in 2009. It is far too early to predict which among the Democratic and Republican aspirants will succeed. Some of the leading contenders are sitting senators. Yet only Warren Harding and John F. Kennedy have moved directly from Congress to the White House in the past century. Given present international instability, voters will want someone who is seen as credible on war and peace issues.

Congress will remain closely divided. Democrats regained congressional majorities in 2006, but neither Republicans nor Democrats will be able to gain decisive control over either the U.S. Senate or House of Representatives in the foreseeable future. That will provide a continuing framework for gridlock unless an effective new president proves able to lead across party lines toward consensus policies.

Single-interest and single-issue groups will continue to dominate politics. Both major political parties have ceded power during the past thirty years to willful movements and organizations whose political money and votes go to elected officials and candidates who endorse their narrow agendas.

Difficult issues will remain hard to resolve. Congressional and other leaders simply are unprepared to spell out the public sacrifices necessary to keep Social Security, Medicare, and Medicaid viable. All three are headed for train wrecks, Medicare soonest.

Free trade policies will be hard to sustain. Lacking congressional and interest-group support for global trade liberalization, the Bush administration has been making bilateral deals, country by country, as a substitute. But the once-strong political consensus that supported free movement of goods and capital has eroded steadily.

The chances of a nuclear or similar man-made calamity will increase. There is no end in sight to the attempt by Islamic fundamentalists to seize power in one or more oil-producing Middle East states. Nor is time on our side in our general attempt to keep rogue states or movements from acquiring and using nuclear, biological, or chemical weapons.

We also face, in a globalized economic and financial system, the possibility that a future situation such as the 1994 Mexican peso crisis or the 1997 Asian crisis might not be contained as those were. Domestically, inflation seems less a near-term threat than does the possibility that a burst housing bubble or other dislocation could send the economy into recession. As a nation, we owe too much and have saved too little, counting on rising asset prices to keep us afloat.

As a Depression-born kid, having lived through trying times at home and internationally, I would advise any national political leader to follow the path I learned in my own political generation: Tell the truth to the people. Describe the problems. Explain the sacrifices necessary to solve them. Mobilize support toward a political majority, even if it takes a while. Lead on.

This was the formula employed over several decades by great people in another political time. They risked and gave their lives to make Americans free in their own country and to deter threats from abroad. But the formula seems to have been misplaced in the present low-politics environment, in which safe-seat elected officials of both major political parties are most motivated not by a positive agenda but by fear of retribution from true-believing groups with a media megaphone and political muscle.

Among the present polarizations in the United States is the one between the values of my own Depression-born generation—and the dwindling Greatest Generation that preceded it—and the more numerous baby boomers who now dominate all major institutions. We work-and-save, burn-the-mortgage dinosaurs have long since been supplanted in authority by buy-now, pay-later boomers who have yet to be tested by genuine adversity. The testing time may be coming. Boomer phrases such as "We did nothing wrong," "We made some bad choices," or "Everyone makes mistakes" set Depression kids' teeth on edge.

This book relates what I saw and learned among the great and not-so-great over a half century in an unexpected career of attempted public service. The story is necessarily seen through my eyes. But this book is not meant primarily to tell my story, but rather to help you understand how things really were and are inside the baloney factory where political sausage is made.

My memory, as perhaps yours, holds with great clarity certain moments that made an impression on me at the time. It blurs or buries those things that seem unimportant. I have in this book reproduced a number of events in detail and word for word. Have confidence that these are correctly represented. I have omitted discussion of events of which my memory is unclear. Neither I nor many others in this book will appear in a favorable light at certain times. I have made no attempt to raise or diminish any person's reputation, including my own. I have simply set forth how things were so that you may judge them as you will.

Ted Van Dyk
Seattle, 2007

ACKNOWLEDGMENTS

I postponed writing this book for many years. Beginning in 1969, at the end of the Johnson-Humphrey administration, I began to be approached by agents, publishers, colleagues, and friends suggesting I write a firsthand account about government and politics "as it really was" from the inside. I knew what they meant. Too many books and articles written by former government and campaign figures, it seemed to me, pulled their punches in talking about people and events. Similar accounts by writers and journalists—even those praised as inside accounts—by necessity had to be written from outside vantage points. Real insiders pulled their punches because they might be serving in the future with people whom they otherwise might treat ungently in their accounts—and they feared being treated ungently in return. Even the most skillful journalists and authors, being once removed, had to rely on accounts of others. Too much of what I read did not fully reflect what I personally saw taking place.

I delayed, however, because I had an aversion to accounts, written immediately after campaigns or administrations, in which authors who had participated directly in them related conversations and events that at the time had been private or confidential. I also hesitated to express opinions that were anything less than candid about people who were still active in the political process. Along the way, though, I mentally collected material that I believed could be usefully made part of the historical record.

I have not participated in a national political campaign since 1992. Most of the people I worked with and observed are no longer on the active list. This thus seemed the time to write the book which many had suggested I write over a number of previous years. I wish especially to thank friends and former colleagues who over time have urged me to write this book: John Stewart, Al Eisele, Ken Bode, Richard M. Cohen, Stephen Schlesinger, Jim Dickenson, Win Griffith, Shelby Scates, Milton Gwirtzman, R. W. (John) Apple, Adam Yarmolinsky, Tom McCoy, and Steve Stark, among others. Most have written good books of their own. I owe special thanks to my partner, Jeri Smith-Fornara, whose encouragement and idealism have energized me during the drafting and editing process. She has had her own distinguished career in the consumer, environmental, and women's movements and in the Democratic Party. Her son David and his fiancée, Teresa, have become additions to my family.

On a deeper level I must acknowledge the impulses and experiences that led me to stay in a public arena I entered almost by accident. I have made special note in this book of the values and experiences shared by my Depression-born generation. The popular song of the era, "Brother, Can You Spare a Dime," still brings instant tears to my eyes. The novels of Steinbeck and Dos Passos, the paintings of the Ashcan School, and the remembered voice of Franklin Delano Roosevelt all became part of me and helped me fight through the discouraging times that go with the territory of national politics.

I must acknowledge not only my parents but numerous teachers, coaches, and professors who encouraged me during my growing-up years. Then there are the many people for whom I worked along the way and who were willing to tolerate my independence because they saw some compensating talent in me. They range from Frank Geri, a junior-high coach and teacher, who hired me for my first full-time summer job, to Georg Meyers, a *Seattle Times* sports editor, who hired me for my first full-time daily newspaper job, to such household names as Walter Hallstein, Jean Monnet, Hubert Humphrey, Andrew Cordier, George McGovern, Terry Sanford, Cyrus Vance, and Paul Tsongas, who gave me great latitude to pursue our mutual work as I thought best. Some put their own reputations at risk in doing so.

I owe special acknowledgment to my late wife, Jean, and my four children, who put up with my absences and working hours over the years as I threw myself into causes and pursuits that sometimes did not work out.

I am grateful to the University of Washington Press team that helped bring this volume from rough idea to finished book. They include Michael Duckworth, Mary Ribesky, Anna Eberhard Friedlander, and Beth Fuget. Although I do not know their identities, I wish to thank seven anonymous readers recruited by the UW Press, who raised various questions about my working manuscript as it evolved. I incorporated many of their suggestions. The Humphrey Institute, the University of Minnesota, and the Museum of History and Industry, Seattle, went beyond the call of duty in aiding my search for particular photos. The MOHAI photo of 1930s Hooverville in Seattle is one I have kept in my mind's eye because it represents accurately what I saw with my own eyes as an impressionable child. May I never forget it.

HEROES, HACKS, AND FOOLS

1

DEPRESSION KIDS

I was born at 9 AM, Saturday, October 6, 1934, the only child of Ted and June Ellen Van Dyk, at St. Luke's Hospital, Bellingham, Washington, then a blue-collar town of 30,000 at the north end of Puget Sound. Although I was twenty-four inches long, my birth weight was only six pounds. Few Depression babies were fat. It was unseasonably cold outside and snowing—a rarity for October on Puget Sound.

My family's circumstances were typical of the time. My parents owned no automobile and had no phone service. They brought me home from St. Luke's to 2701 Superior Street, at the edge of town, on a streetcar. They placed me near the kitchen wood stove for warmth. When temperatures neared freezing, our windows quickly iced over on the inside.

My father, born in the Netherlands as Theodorus Johannes Cornelius van Dijk, was an unskilled worker at the Bloedel-Donovan sawmill on the Bellingham waterfront. His daily pay was $1.84. On one occasion a log rolled over his right index finger and crushed it. Dad walked from the mill to a downtown doctor's office, waited his turn in the reception room, and had the finger amputated. He was back at work the following day. For three years during the 1930s he and his fellow workers went on strike until they won the right to unionize the mill. The strike was straight out of a John Dos Passos novel. My father spent time in the jail in the basement of city hall after leveling with a folding chair three strikebreakers who had invaded the Labor Temple, where he was on duty alone. There were far more violent incidents than that. Once, my father related, strikebreakers had driven a full load of lumber out of the Bloedel-Donovan mill through his union's picket line. He and others had followed the strikebreakers out onto the Mt. Baker highway, pulled them from their truck, and then pushed both the truck and its load down the mountainside. From my fifth birthday onward I went with my dad every Saturday morning to meet his mill buddies for shots and beers at the Up and Up Tavern in downtown Bellingham, then to the Labor Temple for a brief meeting. They were my heroes in work shirts.

Both my parents had come to Bellingham from prior lives not untypical of their own generation. My father was born the second of seven children in The Hague. His formal schooling ended at age seven. His family migrated to South Africa, where his father and uncles supervised a railroad-building project in the Transvaal. When the Boer War broke out, my father, his mother, and his siblings were interned in a schoolhouse that also served as a barracks for British Tommies. His father and uncles took to the hills to join the uprising. My father would sit in the laps of the Tommies each evening and polish their uniform buttons. Some would be missing the next evening; when he asked about them, he would be told that they had been "killed by the bloody Boers" (perhaps, he thought, his father and uncles). When the Boers recaptured the territory he saw Winston Churchill led down the street a war prisoner, his hands cuffed behind his back. His childhood experience in the Transvaal stuck with him. He expressed horror at the lashings and beatings he had seen inflicted on the black construction workers by their white supervisors. He never came to terms with his own father's cruelty at the time.

After the war the van Dijk family migrated to a Dutch-German farming colony in Southern Chile and then, when my father was seventeen, migrated again to a wheat-farming region near Gull Lake, Saskatchewan. Because he was in a vital occupation as a wheat farmer, Dad was rejected for World War I service in the Canadian Army. In Gull Lake he met my mother, June Ellen Williams, the youngest of thirteen children in a family that had emigrated to Saskatchewan from their farm in Christian County, Missouri. She was the teacher in the town's one-room school. Her fiancé had been accepted for army service and had been killed in Flanders by a bullet through his heart. It passed through a letter from her which he carried in his vest pocket; the army returned it to her with the bullet hole and bloodstains.

My mother was drawn to my father, she later said, by his rough-edged goodness. Throughout my childhood I saw him work tirelessly but always without complaint and with a buoyant optimism. There was a kindness that shone from his face; as a child I sometimes imagined it to be an aura.

When hard times hit the Canadian prairies, my father headed south to work, drilling wells in Montana, picking fruit in eastern Washington, and then hopping a freight train to the Puget Sound area. Arriving in the middle of the night in the Everett, Washington, freight yard, he was undecided whether to jump another train south, toward Seattle, or one headed north toward Canada. To decide, he spun his Jackie Coogan cap. He would go in whatever direction the bill pointed. It pointed north. So he crawled onto a freight car headed for Vancouver, British Columbia. When the train reached Bellingham, twenty miles south of the Canadian border, he saw a Help Wanted sign at the gate to a sawmill near the tracks. He jumped off the train, was hired at the mill, and sent for my mother in Saskatchewan. A few years later he would become a naturalized American citizen, changing his name legally to Ted Van Dyk. That is how I came to be Ted Van Dyk Jr., an American.

Radio was our channel to the outside world. My mother, listening to Orson Welles's 1938 Mercury Theater radio production of *War of the Worlds*, believed, as millions of others did, that the broadcast reports of an alien invasion were real. She broke into inconsolable tears. Dad, in a stab at reassurance, told her: "Better the Martians than Hitler." We and our neighbors sat by our table-model Philco to listen to Adolf Hitler's rants, via shortwave from Europe, and to President Franklin Delano Roosevelt's inspiring fireside chats. It is hard to imagine now the extent of FDR's hold on the American people in his time. Many homes, including ours, had several Roosevelt photographs mounted on the walls. "President Roosevelt" normally was uttered as a single word. (I consider it a special honor that for many years I have been a board member of the Roosevelt Institute, associated with the Roosevelt library at Hyde Park, New York.) I cast my first vote at age six, when my father took me into a voting booth in the Bellingham High School library in 1940 and I pulled the lever for FDR and a straight Democratic ticket.

A year later the Japanese bombed Pearl Harbor, we were at war, and Bellingham kids were being killed in the Pacific and other war theaters. Both my father and mother, now a bookkeeper and secretary, worked six-day, nine-hours-a-day workweeks—as did everyone else not in uniform. Our First Christian Church at A Street and Girard became a barracks for soldiers. Beaches were closed, blackouts instituted, and sand and shovels distributed to households in case of air-raid fires. A big political shift also took place. World War II had broken the Depression, as the New Deal had failed to do, and political discourse moved from sometimes strident class rhetoric to ways in which a unified America could defeat international totalitarianism. A distant cousin by marriage, "Red" Wallace, and his brother had been radical voices in the Bellingham labor movement and distributed left-wing literature from Red's Railroad Avenue secondhand store. But with the advent of war, local workers no longer wanted to hear about class struggle and leftist doctrinal fine points. Their biggest fight—for unionization—had been won, wages were good, and it was time to defeat Hitler and Tojo. At war's end, our leading local political figures became Senator Warren Magnuson and Representative Henry (Scoop) Jackson, both practical New Deal liberals with progressive voting records who also delivered federal contracts and jobs to the home folks.

My generation's parents served in the war and the war effort. We had to take care of ourselves and each other while they were absent. We were what later would be called "latchkey kids." In Bellingham, following our parents' examples, most of us got summer or other part-time jobs in our preteen years. When the June harvest season began, in the early mornings I walked to a downtown parking lot where farmers' trucks would collect us for daily work in Whatcom County berry fields. By the time I was ten I had an after-school paper route, hustled the *Bellingham Herald* on the corner of Holly and Commercial ("*Herald* paaaaper!"), and vended hot dogs and soft drinks at local sports events. All of these things no doubt constituted violations of child labor laws. It was simply what we did to help out in difficult times.

We were largely removed in those days from the outside world. Many families, like my own, had no automobile. Those who did were unable to go more than a few miles from town during the war years because of gasoline rationing. (I first ventured east of Spokane when, as a University of Washington senior, I took the Great Northern Empire Builder to Chicago, and another train to Columbus, Ohio, for a student editors' conference. I took my first airplane flight a year later, in 1955, when I flew from Seattle to New York, where I would attend graduate school; the Northwest Airlines flight took 13½ hours and stopped in Spokane, Billings, Minneapolis, and Detroit.) We saw our first television as high-school students. Wavy black-and-white images, relayed from Seattle, could be seen through department-store display windows along Cornwall Avenue. You had your choice among three channels.

We Depression kids were not the Greatest Generation. But we saw it and tried to emulate it. Our growing-up experience made us a We rather than Me generation. The Korean War, which broke out during our teenage years, was just as unpopular as the later Vietnam War. Yet it never occurred to us to protest the war or to seek asylum from it in Canada. Like it or not, Depression kids reported for duty. The political leaders probably most representative of our generation were 1984 and 1988 Democratic presidential nominees Walter Mondale and Mike Dukakis—honest, hardworking, modest, substantive, serious, and generally unappealing to voters outside their own generation and their party's core constituencies.

Participation in high-school and college class reunions in recent years has been, for me, a dramatic step back to another time and other values. Serving as master of ceremonies at my fifty-fifth high-school class reunion in 2006, I observed that we probably constituted a representative snapshot of our generation. Two-thirds of the class were still living, and a majority of these attended the reunion. Class members spoke mainly of their long marriages and their families and of fond growing-up recollections. None mentioned money or professional status. Perhaps one in six of us had entered college directly from high school; others had gone into military service or to work. Yet a huge percentage of class members had been teachers or employed otherwise in education. Others had worked in medicine, the military, and other serving professions. A majority were involved in community volunteer service of one kind or another. The names of deceased class members were read aloud; they were genuinely missed.

The changes in our hometown of Bellingham, I thought, reflected changes in American society at large. The city's population had increased from a static 30,000 during our growing-up years to 75,000 in 2006, with additional population just outside the city limits. The city had not one high school but three. The payroll jobs in canneries, wood, pulp and paper mills, and a coal mine had been replaced by white-collar and no-collar jobs in higher education, hi-tech, and service industries. The waterfront industrial area was being cleared for green-space and business/residential development. In our graduation year, 1951, the city had one black family, a few Asian families, and one Latino family. The nearby Lummi Indian reservation provided our only other firsthand contact with minorities. By 2006 the city still had a far smaller percentage of minority residents than did Seattle or nearby Vancouver, B.C. But in Bellingham and surrounding Whatcom County, a diverse minority community had formed and been welcomed.

Homeland security had become an immediate issue in our town. Coast Guard and Border Patrol facilities and staff had been strengthened to deal with cross-border movement of terrorist suspects and trafficking in weapons, drugs, and people. Back in our time, both Americans and Canadians had crossed the nearby international border at will.

Our Class of 1951 had, I thought, been clearly marked by our entry point into American life, and remained basically unchanged. There we were, together, still looking out for each other and trying to do the things our role-model parents would have expected of us. We came up in demanding times, stuck together, and came through. Yet we also grew up pre–drug culture, pre–Vietnam and Watergate, pre–political assassinations, pre-cynicism, and with limited options compared to the myriad choices that later generations would face. I suspect most Depression kids would tell you that times today are better but that we were fortunate to come in when we did. Whatever else they did, those years provided us with a sense of duty and responsibility that seems to be missing today.

There was, of course, a flip side to the duty/responsibility values with which we grew up. In the 1950s our society as a whole accepted far too readily policies and actions that should have been questioned. Having passed through both depression and major war, Americans of that period bought homes and automobiles, went to college, started big families, sought jobs with security, and focused on enjoying a consumer-goods-centered "good life" they had missed in the previous two decades. They also, however, continued their World War II habit of obedience to government directives and, as the Cold War came to dominate U.S. foreign policy, were all too willing to accept huge allocations of public resources to national defense and restrictions on their civil liberties.

The University of Washington, then as now, had a reputation as a center of liberal political thinking. But during the McCarthy era several faculty members were accused of Communist affiliations. Most were accused falsely. During my undergraduate years there (1951–55), political dissent was minimal. One day I saw a posted notice of a meeting called to discuss McCarthyism at the home of a favorite history professor, Giovanni Costigan. I attended, expecting to find at least fifty to sixty students (on a campus of 16,000); no more than a dozen were present. I wrote a senior thesis on the Oppenheimer Case (which centered around nuclear scientist J. Robert Oppenheimer's loss of his government security clearance), and another research paper on the so-called Centralia Massacre, a bloody confrontation in 1919 in Centralia, Washington, between American Legionnaires and Industrial Workers of the World members (known as Wobblies). The clash had resulted in deaths, including the lynching from a bridge of a young Wobbly, and jail sentences for others who may or may not have been involved in the incident. I spent time in Centralia reviewing documents and interviewing people who had witnessed the events. But few classmates had interests beyond the campus or their search for a job after graduation. As an editor and columnist for the campus daily, I wrote principally about campus issues.

I left the sometimes isolated and provincial Pacific Northwest in August

1955 to attend the Columbia University Graduate School of Journalism. New York was a revelation. I lived in a $7-a-week room on West 122nd Street near the Columbia campus and saved my money for Broadway shows, jazz clubs, and Dodgers, Yankees, and Giants games. Evenings and weekends my J-School classmate Dick Schaap and I rode a crowded subway one and a half hours each way to Jamaica, Queens, and part-time work in the sports department of the now-defunct *Long Island Press.* Our pay of $8 per night barely covered our subway fare and the cost of a meal, but we considered ourselves well on our way to becoming big-time sports writers. (Dick, as it turned out, was to have a long career as one until his untimely death during routine surgery in 2001.) The J-School assigned its sixty students to daily coverage of New York events, as though we were working for one of the daily newspapers. I was fortunate to draw assignments to interview Governor Adlai Stevenson, then pondering a second run against incumbent Dwight Eisenhower in the 1956 presidential election, and former president Harry Truman, who invited me to join him for a brisk morning walk around midtown Manhattan before buying me breakfast at the Sheraton-Astor coffee shop in Times Square.

During that year in New York I was to meet my future wife, Jean Covacevich, a Kansas girl who had been raised partly in Mexico City and who was studying for her own master's degree at Columbia Teachers College. I also had my first exposure to the American South. When midterm vacation time came, my classmate John Lee (later to be a senior *New York Times* editor) invited me to join him as he drove south to pick up his fiancée, Becca, at her family home in Baltimore and on to his home in Walterboro, South Carolina. As we crossed the 14th Street Bridge connecting Washington, D.C., to Virginia, we were suddenly in another culture. Confederate flags and decals appeared on shops and shop windows along Highway 1 and became more and more commonplace the farther south we drove.

John drove me around Walterboro. It was like a punch to my solar plexus. Public restrooms and drinking fountains were labeled "Colored" and "White." So were waiting areas at the bus and railroad stations. Black neighborhoods were abysmally poor. Shacks, their paint peeling, sat on pilings several feet above the ground. Books, articles, films, and photographs had not prepared me for what I should have expected. John's parents, who were hospitable and generous, must have been pleased to see me depart a few days later on a train to Florida. I filled much of their time with lectures about racism and questions about their presumed acceptance of it. They clearly were on the right side of things but taken aback by my own certitudes. It dawned on me, when I left, that I had spoiled John's and Becca's visit. But immersion in the 1950s South made me almost physically ill. On the way back from Florida I stopped to explore Savannah, the home of J-School classmate Ross Stemer, then drove back north with him to New York. New York, to a transplanted Northwesterner, had seemed an unfamiliar culture, but after the South it seemed like home.

In mid-1956, having returned to Seattle after graduate school, I began what I thought would be a journalistic career by working weekdays for United Press and weekends for the *Seattle Times* before accepting a full-time offer from the *Times* at a big pay increase (from $65 to $85 per week). I expected to remain there until retirement.

As the 1950s came to a close, Eisenhower and a Republican-dominated Congress governed conservatively and cautiously. Domestic reforms were few and incremental. Democratic congressional leaders Sam Rayburn and Lyndon Johnson, both Texans, recognized Eisenhower's war-hero popularity and seldom challenged him directly. (They had, however, intervened with Eisenhower in 1954 to block the proposal of Vice President Richard Nixon and Joint Chiefs Chairman Admiral Arthur Radford to use U.S. nuclear weapons to save French forces at the decisive Indochinese battle of Dien Bien Phu.) They accepted liberal domestic-reform proposals by Senators Paul Douglas, Hubert Humphrey and others, and grudgingly allowed Democratic National Chairman Paul Butler to form an advisory council that issued foreign- and domestic-policy manifestos that were more leftward than those that could be passed in Congress.

The country was, in fact, on the verge of a new decade of tumult and change, and my own life was taking a path that would put me in the middle of it.

2

CAUGHT UP IN THE COLD WAR

Military service was obligatory in those days. You either were drafted or volunteered for reserve duty in one of the armed services. I chose the Army Reserve. After attending weekly meetings for eighteen months, I received a call to six-month active duty in 1957, after I had been at the *Seattle Times* for barely a year. I went through basic training at Ford Ord, California, then was assigned to military intelligence school at Fort Holabird, Maryland, in the industrial outskirts of Baltimore.

I am probably one of the few Americans who can attest to enjoying both Army food and Army training. I welcomed the "take all you want, eat all you take" policies of the enlisted mess halls. At Fort Holabird I found myself placed unexpectedly in charge of a thirty-eight-man group of intelligence-analyst trainees, all privates and all college graduates. The school dispensed with much day-to-day military routine and even left us to manage ourselves, hence my designation on my first day at Holabird as my training group's leader— for what reason I will never know. Our thirteen-week training course was a college-level immersion in all aspects of intelligence, ranging from counterintelligence techniques to photo interpretation to document analysis. In one class we concentrated on Indochina, identifying military installations and targets. We were warned pointedly that our research should not be seen as indicating a U.S. intention to become militarily involved in the area, and were reminded that, as all our work was classified, our Indochina work should never be mentioned outside our training group.

I had intended to return to the *Seattle Times*, and a Seattle-area Reserve unit, after my active-duty service. However, while visiting New York on leave, I interviewed and was hired for a staff position at *Sports Illustrated* magazine. After completing my Holabird stint, I drove to Mexico City to visit Jean, who was living there with her father. She, too, was going to return to New York, to complete her Teachers College graduate work. We married and honeymooned in Mexico. By the time we got back to New York, early in 1958, staff cutbacks at *Sports Illustrated* had eliminated the job for which I had been hired. Jean, in the meantime, had enrolled again as a full-time student at Columbia. I scrambled to find another job and was offered two at the Hearst-owned *New York Journal-American*—one on the news desk and one as understudy to financial editor Leslie Gould. But I went with my head over my heart and accepted a better-paying corporate public-relations job. So ended, at least for a time, my journalistic career.

My military obligation continued, however, so my Army career did not end. I attended once-weekly Reserve meetings and did two-week summer duty with strategic-intelligence detachments in New York and then Boston. My assignments reflected events of the time. On one occasion, I vetted the dossiers of freedom fighters who had fled Hungary after their failed uprising against the occupying Soviets. A surprising percentage of them, I found, had been Nazi-sympathizing members of the pre–World War II Arrow Cross Party. The Russians had taken the opportunity to dump them across the border into the West—just as Cuba's Fidel Castro later would dump political opponents and outright criminals into Florida. Shortly after Castro came to power, I put together background profiles on the principal figures around him. At another time I researched the potential effects of a Soviet nuclear attack on the United States. Only Oregon and northern Maine, I found, would emerge relatively unscathed.

Jean and I moved to Boston in September 1960, when my advertising/public-relations employer dispatched me there to service its Raytheon account and to scout new business in New England. While in Boston, I did volunteer work for Senator John Kennedy's presidential campaign. The first of our four children, Ted, was born there the following May. We had a top-floor apartment at the corner of Pinckney and Brimmer streets, with a terrace overlooking the Charles River. My office was a fifteen-minute walk away on Newbury Street. Life truly was good. Then, in the fall of 1961, a few weeks before my military obligation was scheduled to end, everything changed.

Soviet chairman Nikita Khrushchev, after a meeting in Vienna with the new American president Kennedy, judged him soft and decided to test him. The Soviets erected a wall separating East Berlin from West Berlin. It was an open challenge which could not go unmet. President Kennedy responded, in part, by calling to active duty 150,000 U.S. Reservists. Because my seven-person Reserve unit specialized in Soviet intelligence, we were recalled in October to duty at the Pentagon, where we had trained the previous March, and were assigned to the USSR Branch of Army Intelligence's Eurasian Division. (Our overall boss was the assistant chief of staff for intelligence, Major General William Quinn, better known later as the father of socialite and gossip columnist Sally Quinn, who was to marry *Washington Post* editor Ben Bradlee.) We set up shop in Room 2B-527, in the low-status B-ring of the Pentagon, to update and rewrite on a crash basis the handbook on Soviet forces and tactics. I neither read nor spoke Russian. Our unit consisted of three officers and four enlisted men. As the only one of our detachment with a background in writing and editing, I soon found myself point man in preparing what could be a U.S. manual for World War III.

Had the times not been so dangerous, our Pentagon stint could have provided material for a television situation comedy. Our detachment's commanding officer, Lieutenant Colonel Walter Hertz, a Jewish émigré from pre–World War II Germany, was in civilian life an international economist. He puffed constantly on a pipe and took a wry view of the world. He delighted in characterizing Germans as "willing to follow anyone standing on a soapbox and wearing a Sam Browne belt." An advisor in our unit's office was a Colonel Schulties—his rank in the German Army in World War II—who after the war had been hired as a Soviet expert by the U.S. Army. Over his desk hung a situation map depicting the Wermacht's point of furthest advance toward Moscow. Colonel Schulties wore a monocle, clicked his heels when addressed, and although he wore civilian clothing seemed always to be in full-dress uniform. He and Hertz, surprisingly, got along quite amiably, exchanging jokes and stories.

Across the hallway, U.S. Army attachés from the Soviet Union and Iron Curtain countries checked in for debriefing. Often doubling over in laughter, they told stories of kidnappings, cross-border shootings and violence, and James-Bondian close calls.

A few days after we reported to the Pentagon, each member of our unit was given a red, white, and blue wallet-size identification card. The card instructed that, in the event of nuclear attack, we were to drive our private cars south to Fort Bragg, North Carolina, on highways that would be reserved for military traffic. The card should be shown to any military policeman or civilian law-enforcement officer who tried to stop us. I pictured myself and my wife and baby in our 1957 Pontiac trying to get through blast aftereffects, fallout, and chaos to Fort Bragg—which would likely have been obliterated in any nuclear attack. The warning time for such an attack, on missile launch from the USSR, was one-half hour.

The Army then was organized around the concept of a Pentomic Division set up to fight with tactical nuclear weapons. Such weapons were seen as being much like other weapons, only bigger and more powerful. In Western Europe, it was presumed, the use of such weapons would be necessary to block an invasion by Soviet and Warsaw Pact conventional forces, which were sure to outnumber and outgun their U.S. and NATO counterparts.

There were big problems, of course, with the Western strategy. Tactical nuclear weapons might be able to block a Soviet/Warsaw Pact invasion through the Fulda Gap and into Western Europe. But they also would destroy much of Germany. They also could lead to counter-use of such weapons by the Soviet Union and to a rapid escalation culminating in the exchange of strategic nuclear missiles. Our hypothetical scenarios indicated that if Soviet/Warsaw Pact conventional forces were not countered by tactical nuclear weapons, they likely would reach the English Channel in something like twelve days. (The dilemma, of course, was equally perplexing for the Soviets if the scenarios played out.) Our unit was instructed to stand by for possible transfer to Heidelberg, Germany—in which case, I calculated, we would be dead or overrun in about a week.

As we prepared for the unthinkable, we received regular visits from a tweed-wearing civilian analyst from Secretary of Defense Robert McNamara's office. The secretary, he explained, was especially concerned that American forces had such a large ratio of noncombat troops supporting combat troops as compared with Soviet forces. We explained that the Soviets were a continental power, near homeland sources of support and supply, whereas the United States was thousands of miles and an ocean distant from the actual European battlefield and thus required a huge "tail" for its combat forces. In any case, we suggested, we were too busy preparing for a possible near-term war to spend time considering this longer-term question. After one such vexing discussion, Hertz remarked that he had decided to move our office to the latrine down the corridor. "It is the only place in this building," he said, "where people come knowing their business, conduct it, and promptly leave."

Even under the threat of war, Americans and American soldiers must have their baseball. The crisis had begun shortly before the start of the 1961 World Series. Thus it was not surprising that the television in the Army Intelligence situation room was tuned to the series as it got under way. Brass sat left to right in front of the set, according to rank. As more senior officers entered the room, others would move down a chair to accommodate them.

An enlisted man, I stood well to the rear. Not long after the opening pitch, a white phone rang on the desk of the master sergeant at the situation-room door. All heads turned. "Yes it is," the master sergeant said to the phone. "No they are not. That is all I can tell you, Mr. Anderson." Who was it? "That was Jack Anderson, the columnist," the sergeant explained. "He wanted to know if all the brass was in here watching the World Series while we were nose to nose with the Soviets."

We did complete a successful rewrite of the handbook. But before it was done, the Berlin Crisis had eased and the threat of war had receded. My 1961 recall to military duty seemed a rude disruption when it first happened, but I came away, at the end, with great regard for the professionalism and dedication of the career military with whom I had worked. As a low-ranking enlisted man, I had gone to the desks of Army, Navy, and Air Force officers throughout the Pentagon and had received without exception prompt information and support from them. The career intelligence officers in the USSR Branch were particularly impressive, performing with calm and often gallows humor when beset by demands from elsewhere in the Pentagon. The associations I made there lasted well beyond my unit's release from duty in 1962. For many years thereafter I lectured at the Defense Intelligence School, the Industrial College of the Armed Forces, Army War College, and various military-intelligence seminars, always introduced as a homeboy who had moved on to responsibilities in civilian life. In 1988, twenty-six years after my unit's Berlin Crisis stint, a retired colonel with whom I worked then invited me to speak to his Connecticut civic club, meeting my flight from Washington, D.C., at LaGuardia Airport in New York and driving me to the meeting.

3

A NEW GENERATION TAKES OVER

The generation that had fought World War II was about to take power from the generation that had led the war.

The 1960 presidential contest between John F. Kennedy and Vice President Richard Nixon was closely fought, and represented a point of departure for the country. Adlai Stevenson, the 1952 and 1956 Democratic nominee, had run to the "soft" side of Eisenhower and been defeated decisively both times. Kennedy, by contrast, ran to the hawkish side not only of Senator Hubert Humphrey (Stevenson's liberal heir within the Democratic Party) in the contest for the nomination, but also of Nixon in the general election campaign.

Kennedy narrowly defeated Nixon in nationally televised debates mainly because he projected greater coolness and style than the sweating, glowering Nixon in need of a shave. He threw Nixon off balance in the debates, and in the campaign, with charges that the Eisenhower administration had allowed a dangerous "missile gap" to develop between the United States and the Soviet Union, which he asserted was producing more intercontinental ballistic missiles than the United States. Kennedy charged the administration with being too weak in its posture toward the People's Republic of China and pledged to defend several obscure islands off the Chinese mainland—Quemoy, Matsu, and the Pescadores—from any Chinese aggression. He also charged the administration with suppressing a United States Information Agency poll showing that American prestige was waning around the world.

The missile gap and the USIA poll proved effective political weapons—even though both as a matter of fact did not exist. The hard line toward the PRC was an abrupt departure from the Democratic Party's historically more accommodating position toward our Korean War adversaries. Nixon was placed at tactical disadvantage on issues that previously had worked in the Republicans' favor. The domestic side of Kennedy's campaign agenda proved equally effective. The aging Eisenhower had appeared undisturbed by flat economic growth and employment numbers. Kennedy pledged to "get America moving again" with modern tax, trade, and other economic policies. Eisenhower had little affection for Nixon and did not campaign strongly for him.

The electoral outcome was in doubt until the dawn hours after election night. The pivotal state of Illinois, where downstate votes had given Nixon the lead, suddenly turned as a flood of late Kennedy votes materialized in Chicago. Many analysts believed that Chicago mayor Richard Daley had doctored the returns in Kennedy's favor. (A joke at the time had one Chicago Democratic worker telling another, "Give my regards to your father. I thought he had died ten years ago, but saw that he voted for Kennedy twice yesterday at my polling place.") Nixon, to his credit, did not challenge the Illinois result. He conceded and called for unity.

On taking office, Kennedy found himself tested in the 1961 Berlin Crisis, and then again a few months later in the Cuban Missile Crisis, which followed the aborted CIA-sponsored invasion of Cuba at the Bay of Pigs. The Bay of Pigs venture had been planned during the Eisenhower administration; Kennedy, with some reluctance, agreed to go forward with it. It was a debacle, stopped at the beach by Fidel Castro's Cuban forces. Years later, Kennedy's key White House counselor, Ted Sorensen, would tell me that "we came to the White House thinking we knew everything and soon learned we knew little." Kennedy also found himself with a growing U.S. commitment on his hands in South Vietnam. The 1954 Geneva accords, following the French defeat in Indochina, had called for a free national election to determine the government of a united Vietnam. But the United States and its allies, fearing a victory by North Vietnamese Communist leaders, had moved to partition the country. American military and other advisors were becoming more numerous in the South. The assassination of South Vietnamese president Ngo Dinh Diem, following a White House–sanctioned coup, shook Kennedy. He had expected Diem to be forced from power but not to be executed. The situation began to deteriorate as one ineffectual South Vietnamese leader after another succeeded the tough, authoritarian Diem.

Domestically, Kennedy came under fire from Democratic liberals for his caution on civil-rights legislation and passive posture toward racial tensions that were rising in southern states. But he moved aggressively to implement modern economic policies that would invigorate the domestic economy. The chairman of his Council of Economic Advisors (CEA), Walter Heller, a former University of Minnesota economist, was principal author of the speech defining the new administration's economic posture that Kennedy delivered at Yale University soon after taking office. The administration proposed, and then quickly moved to congressional enactment, personal and business tax cuts, including an investment tax credit, and the historic Trade Expansion Act of 1962, which would commit the country to open international movement of goods and capital.

Presidential advisors and Cabinet officers sometimes are chosen after measured consultation and screening, sometimes ad hoc. The 1960 Kennedy presidential transition team was more careful and professional than most. Yet some of its principal appointees, especially in foreign policy and national security, proved disastrous. Another, Heller, was perhaps JFK's most fortuitous choice (just as economic advisor Robert Rubin was to prove the same for President Clinton thirty years later). As both Heller and Humphrey would tell me later, Heller's appointment as CEA chairman came through anything but a deliberative process. Humphrey had lost the 1960 Democratic presidential nomination to Kennedy, but the two were personal friends. Humphrey worked actively for Kennedy in the general-election campaign. Late in the campaign Kennedy came to Minneapolis to deliver a speech at the University of Minnesota. At a reception prior to the speech, Kennedy met and spoke for a few minutes with Heller, a leading member of the university's economics faculty.

Weeks later, as Kennedy began to form his administration, Humphrey received a phone call from the president-elect: "Hubert," JFK asked, "what was the name of that tall economist you introduced to me at my speech in Minneapolis?" Humphrey told him it was Walter Heller. "Do you think highly of him?" Kennedy asked. "Yes, he is first rate," Humphrey replied. "Do you think he would serve on my Council of Economic Advisors?" Kennedy further asked. Humphrey, taken aback by Kennedy's readiness to appoint someone he'd barely met, said he would call Heller and sound him out.

Heller, when he received Humphrey's call, told him it would be an honor to serve on the Council of Economic Advisors. However, he was about to become the economics department chairman and had a strong obligation to the University of Minnesota. He could not accept a CEA appointment for anything short of the chairmanship. (Heller later told me he was sure his response would take him out of the running for an appointment and make it easy to stay in academia.) Humphrey called Kennedy back: "Walter says he would serve but only as chairman." "That's okay," Kennedy answered, "he can be chairman if he wants. Tell him he's got the job."

Like many others, I had been inspired by Kennedy's campaign against

Nixon, who was the Republican most despised by liberal Democrats. My favorite for the 1960 Democratic nomination had been Humphrey, whose historic 1948 speech at the party's national convention in Philadelphia had galvanized his party behind civil-rights policies previously blocked by Southern Democratic congressional leaders and committee chairs. A civil-rights majority plank, favored by President Truman, straddled the issue and was expected to pass the convention with little difficulty. Humphrey, the young mayor of Minneapolis, took the podium on behalf of an uncompromising pro-civil-rights minority plank. His brief but fiery speech ("Some say we are rushing the issue of civil rights. I say we are 172 years late! ... We must emerge from the shadows of states' rights into the bright sunshine of human rights!") brought convention delegates to a standing, cheering frenzy, and the minority plank to unexpected approval. Southerners stalked out of the convention and formed a Dixiecrat Party with Strom Thurmond as its 1948 presidential candidate. On the left, progressives rallied behind the candidacy of former vice president Henry Wallace. Yet the party's new civil-rights posture energized other Democrats and independent voters and helped Truman win an upset victory over Republican nominee Thomas Dewey. I was not quite fourteen when I heard Humphrey's Philadelphia speech via radio in Bellingham. The noise and excitement—but, more importantly, Humphrey's unalloyed idealism and courage—moved me.

Humphrey was, above all, engaged and passionate. Kennedy was cooler and more calculating. Humphrey, it could be said, was upper-Midwest progressivism incarnate, Kennedy a product of the tough-minded, play-for-keeps Boston political school. Yet either, it seemed to most Democrats, was unquestionably a better prospective president than Nixon

In March 1961, while my Army Reserve unit was training at the Pentagon, I was invited, as a spear-carrying 1960 campaign volunteer, to the White House mess for lunch. I wore the only civilian suit in my Army locker. I sat wide-eyed in the presence of Ted Sorensen, Larry O'Brien, Kenny O'Donnell, and others whose campaign television exposure had made them celebrities. It was St. Patrick's Day, and the mess tables were decorated in green and white. After lunch, while touring the White House, I encountered Kennedy himself in a corridor. He led me into the Oval Office. Over the door was a "No Irish Need Apply" banner, bordered by shamrocks. The president presented me with a green carnation from a silver bowl on his desk. Returning to Boston, after my visit, I gave Jean the carnation, the White House mess place card bearing my name, and an autographed Kennedy photo I had been given. They remain together today in my study, mounted in a frame.

My White House visit, followed by my Pentagon duty, gave me Potomac Fever. I had moved my family from Boston to Washington, D.C., for the duration of my Army tour. I decided to stay. If it didn't work out, I thought, I would not return to Boston but would go back west to Seattle.

Then a chance street-corner meeting with an old high-school friend, Ed Stimpson, took me in an unexpected direction. Stimpson, a protégé of Washington senator Warren Magnuson, was serving as representative in the capital of the 1962 Seattle World's Fair. The European Communities (Common Market, Coal and Steel Community, and Euratom), forerunners of today's European Union, were opening a pavilion at the fair. But European staff, he said, were encountering problems. The EC was looking for an American who knew Seattle to manage the pavilion. Would I be interested? The hiring decision lay with Leonard Tennyson, a former Marshall Plan staff member and NBC correspondent, who served as director of an EC public affairs office in Washington, D.C. The still-forming EC had no diplomatic representation in the United States. George Ball, whose law firm represented EC interests, had been instrumental in establishing a Washington office, staffed by Americans with European experience, which was part of the official Brussels bureaucracy. Its job was to explain EC policies to Americans in government, the media, academia, and the private sector, and to explain American policies to Brussels. After a brief interview, Tennyson hired me for the Seattle job. As I was about to depart for Seattle, however, Tennyson's deputy resigned. Within a few days Walter Hallstein, the Common Market president, would be making an official visit to the capital to meet with President Kennedy, congressional leaders, the media, and others, and to deliver a speech to the National Press Club.

Tennyson asked that I remain in D.C. temporarily to help with the Hallstein visit. Just as I had found myself dealing at the Pentagon with Soviet issues, lacking reading or speaking knowledge of Russian, I now found myself representing the EC with the barest knowledge of its institutions and purposes and without speaking or reading knowledge of French, its official language. The latter made little difference with Hallstein, a German law professor who had been a war prisoner in Mississippi during World War II. Learning what I needed to learn, I drafted background papers for the Hallstein visit, helped draft his Press Club remarks, delivered him to his White

House meeting with President Kennedy, briefed the press afterward in the White House lobby, and generally coordinated his visit arrangements.

A cornerstone of the Kennedy foreign policy was establishment of what was called an "Atlantic Partnership" with the European Communities. Thus Hallstein's visit was predestined for success. Nonetheless, it went well. Hallstein was pleased. I was asked to remain in Washington, D.C., as Tennyson's deputy rather than going to Seattle as originally planned.

As at the Defense Department during my Army duty, I found myself in the company of people exceptionally devoted to their mission. Jean Monnet, the father of the New Europe, had vowed to end through practical means what he saw as civil wars in Europe between Germany and France. He thus proposed to link first the economies and then the politics of Western European countries into common institutions that would make war among them next to impossible. The Coal and Steel Community, European Atomic Energy Community (Euratom), and European Economic Community (Common Market) would form the basis for common policies and cooperation among the six original members: Belgium, France, Germany, Italy, the Netherlands, and Luxembourg (Great Britain initially held back from membership). A European Defense Community was discussed but set aside as premature. A European Parliament, consisting of members of the six countries' national parliaments, would provide a basis for parliamentary control of bureaucratic institutions in Brussels and Luxembourg and later, perhaps, become a body resembling the U.S. Congress.

Monnet, in fact, saw a future federal Europe much like the United States. The organization of European leaders that he established and led to move the idea forward was called the Committee for the United States of Europe. The opposing vision to Monnet's was that of Charles de Gaulle, who as French president would veto British membership in 1963 and take France temporarily out of NATO's military command structure. De Gaulle envisioned a looser European coalition of countries without strong centralized institutions, in which France could continue to play a strong role and pursue its own interests. He particularly opposed British membership in European institutions, seeing "the Anglo-Saxons"—i.e., Great Britain and the United States—as having no place in continental economic and political evolution.

As it happened, I was present in Brussels in January 1963 when de Gaulle cast his brutal veto of Britain's application for EC membership. Seated in the "listening room" separated from the actual negotiating room by glass windows,

I joined other EC staff awaiting de Gaulle's final decision in the matter. French foreign minister Maurice Couve de Mourville rose from the table and read briefly from notes to transmit de Gaulle's message. He then tore the notes into pieces and placed them in an ashtray on the table. As the ministers left the room, I entered it and swept the pieces of Couve's notes, written on Hotel Amigo stationery, into my pocket. Just like my 1961 Kennedy memorabilia, the torn notes and my EC pass to the proceedings are now framed in my study.

The moment was emotional. British negotiator Edward (Ted) Heath had drinks at the bar in a downtown Brussels hotel and then stood atop a table to denounce de Gaulle, cheered on by an admiring British and American press. Sicco Mansholt, the Common Market Commission's Dutch vice president, similarly denounced de Gaulle. Robert Marjolin, the Commission's French vice president and an ardent Europeanist, made embarrassed small talk with Couve, who himself seemed embarrassed by the message he had delivered.

Monnet, characteristically, saw the episode as a temporary detour on the road to European unity. Although not formally affiliated with any of the Community institutions, Monnet turned to our Washington, D.C., outpost for assistance with his visits to the United States. It thus fell to me to make and staff his appointments, help with his speeches, and travel with him as necessary outside Washington, D.C.

Monnet was a visionary but intensely practical. Before World War II he had been a salesman for his family's wine company. His approach in politics remained that of a salesman. When in Washington, D.C., he would renew contact not only with White House and State Department supporters of European integration but also with key members of Congress, foundation and academic figures, and the media. Columnist James Reston of the *New York Times* and *Washington Post* publisher Katharine Graham were close friends of Monnet. Making his rounds, Monnet delivered the same basic sales pitch to all: namely, that a peaceful, united, federal Europe in partnership with the United States was the best guarantor of European and world peace. In a pattern I soon would come to recognize in American politicians as well, Monnet liked to end his working day with a recapitulation of its events. He would invite me to join him at his Westchester apartment suite in Washington, D.C., or in his hotel room on the road, for wine and gossip. Monnet would share his thoughts about everything from American and European national policy to the personality traits of people he encountered on his sales rounds to his observations on cuisine.

Monnet had two fundamental operating principles from which he never wavered. They had served him well as he attempted to break through centuries of national rivalries and grievances in Western Europe.

The first was what I thought of as his Mountaintop Principle. "Suppose," Monnet would say, "that you must climb a mountain never climbed before. You do not blindly hold to the course you planned at the mountain's base. Weather or unforeseen obstacles may force you to stop and reconsider at the end of the first day. Then you try a route of ascent not visible when you began your climb. On reaching the next level, you may again find yourself stymied. So, again, you seek an alternative route—perhaps several alternative routes. You can be entirely flexible about the paths you take. But you must be uncompromising about your objective, which is to successfully reach the mountaintop."

The second, related principle was what I thought of as his Table Principle. "Two or more parties are at a conference table to discuss a difficult question that has proved insoluble over a long period," Monnet would say. "They disagree sharply on many aspects of it. If the parties sit on opposite sides of the table, and proceed from their established positions, they will never come to agreement. However, if the parties sit on the same side of the table—and place the problem on the opposite side—they will see things in an entirely different light and have a chance for success."

These practical salesman's principles have reasserted themselves at critical moments over the past fifty years when the European Union's path to unity seemed blocked. They also were similar to operating principles being employed, perhaps less consciously, in the U.S. Senate and then the presidency, by Lyndon Johnson.

In November 1963 I accompanied Jean Rey, the Common Market Commission's foreign minister, to a Capitol appointment with then–vice president Johnson. There were no other guests in Johnson's reception room. As we waited perhaps five minutes, the telephone did not ring. When we entered his office, it was clear that Johnson was otherwise unoccupied—he seemed grateful for Rey's visit. Their discussion ran well beyond its scheduled time. Rey, a Belgian whose daughter was attending UCLA, commented as we left the Capitol: "Johnson is out of the loop." A few days later Johnson would be president.

November 22, 1963, was Jean's and my sixth wedding anniversary. We planned dinner at home with our sons Ted and Robert (two daughters, Terry and Sue Ellen, would be born by 1967). Rather than going to my EC office on Farragut Square that morning, I was scheduled to lecture at the Defense

Intelligence School, then situated in old World War II–vintage buildings on the Mall. The topic was the triangular relationship involving the United States, Western Europe, and the USSR and its Eastern European satellites. Some fifteen minutes into the lecture, a Navy captain strode into the room, walked to the podium, moved me aside and announced that "President Kennedy, Vice President Johnson, and Texas governor John Connally all have been shot and killed in Dallas. Stand by for further information." He turned on his heel and left the room.

No one spoke or moved. Those in attendance were career officers from all branches of the service and conditioned to perform their duties in all circumstances. After a few minutes had passed and no further information was forthcoming, we simply picked up as if nothing had happened. I completed a shortened version of my presentation and we moved to discussion. Then, from the back of the room, a loudspeaker announced: "This is a correction and update. President Kennedy has been shot and killed. Governor Connally has been wounded. Vice President Johnson is unharmed and has been sworn in as president." At that point we adjourned. The officers left the room without comment among themselves. I began to walk, as if compelled, toward Lafayette Park, opposite the White House. I joined a handful of others there who were standing in silent vigil. I suddenly became aware that hours had passed. I saw that perhaps a thousand people had joined the vigil. It was twilight. The White House portico was lighted, but the windows in the second-floor mansion remained dark. I caught a city bus to our home in northwest Washington. The passengers were as silent as those who had stood in Lafayette Park. Jean and I spent the evening, our boys on our laps, watching television coverage of the day's events.

The next morning I sent a long cable to Brussels assessing the likely policies to be pursued by President Johnson. I also reported to the Europeans, whose own experience made them susceptible to conspiracy theories, that Johnson had nothing to do with Kennedy's assassination. Concerned about the poisonous political climate prevailing in Dallas at the time, Johnson in fact had urged Kennedy not to make the trip. We also received inquiries from embassies of the six EC member countries. Even though the six sent their most skillful diplomats to Washington, we found that they were often unable to understand or interpret American political events. (Later, after I entered U.S. government service, I often discounted cables coming from U.S. embassies abroad because I had seen how difficult it was for even the most knowledgeable and experienced European diplomats to understand our relatively transparent society.)

The impact of President Kennedy's 1963 murder would not be replicated until the September 11, 2001, terrorist attacks on the World Trade Center towers and the Pentagon. Such an event, to most Americans, was simply unthinkable. Political assassinations took place elsewhere, not in the United States. Kennedy and his young wife had, after all, been in the White House less than three years. They were associated with hopeful beginnings, not tragic endings.

The new president Johnson was respected but not loved or admired. He assumed governance smoothly and with broad public support. To signal continuity, he asked the Kennedy Cabinet, including Attorney General Robert Kennedy, and key Kennedy White House staff to remain in their jobs. Being a practical man, he resolved to use the memory of Kennedy to help mobilize public and bipartisan congressional support for unpassed legislation. He and Senate Whip Hubert Humphrey, the principal sponsor and advocate of the Civil Rights Act, successfully recruited Senate minority leader Everett Dirksen's support for 1964 passage of that landmark bill. Relatively uncomfortable with international affairs—and certainly with the inherited involvement in Vietnam—Johnson chose initially to fly by autopilot, continuing generally to accept the counsel of JFK's holdover team, including Secretary of State Dean Rusk, Secretary of Defense Robert McNamara, and National Security Advisor McGeorge Bundy.

There also was a 1964 national election to consider. Johnson's poll ratings were high entering that campaign year. But he knew that his base in the electorate was shallow. He feared in particular that Robert Kennedy might go so far as to challenge him for the Democratic nomination. Robert Kennedy had opposed Johnson's presence on the 1960 Kennedy ticket and had treated him with disdain during his vice presidency. There was open talk in the national Democratic Party, just prior to JFK's death, that for the 1964 campaign President Kennedy intended to replace Johnson as his running mate with North Carolina governor Terry Sanford. There also was the matter of the open vice presidency. Johnson would need to select a 1964 running mate who would bring political strength to him within both the party and country. The most obvious choice would be a Northern or Western liberal who was not Robert Kennedy.

4

HELPING HHH

The next five years would prove to be the most demanding and rewarding of my life. They brought work with Hubert Humphrey through two national campaigns and his vice presidency, and during the Johnson administration's Great Society triumph and Vietnam tragedy.

As 1963 ended, I had never met Humphrey, my boyhood hero and now the Senate Whip and unchallenged leader of liberals in the Congress and the country. I had met Jack Piotrow, his foreign policy assistant, in the course of my congressional rounds on behalf of the European Communities. On one occasion Humphrey had made a Senate speech containing factual errors concerning Europe's Common Agriculture Policy (CAP). I called the errors to Piotrow's attention and, quite promptly, Humphrey made another Senate speech correcting them, though nonetheless pointing to the difficulties the CAP might pose to grain producers in his native Midwest. I was impressed by Humphrey's willingness to correct himself on a matter vital to his home constituents. Senators seldom did that.

Humphrey's 1960 run for the Democratic presidential nomination had been beaten by a better financed, better organized Kennedy campaign. It seemed likely that those money and organizational weaknesses would keep Humphrey from ever reaching the presidency in a rerun. Moreover, barring unforeseen circumstances, Johnson would be heading his party's ticket in 1964 and perhaps 1968. Humphrey's best chance to become president, it seemed to me, was to become Johnson's vice president and, from that political base, to win the presidency itself.

Just before Christmas 1963, I called Violet Williams, Humphrey's secretary, introduced myself, told her I wanted to help Humphrey, and asked for an appointment with him. She suggested I first meet with Bill Connell, Humphrey's administrative assistant and chief political aide. An appointment was set for a few days later. The evening before the appointment I decided it would be best not to come empty-handed to the meeting. I drafted a several-page memo entitled "How Hubert Humphrey Can Become President by First Becoming Vice President." The memo proposed the particulars of a behind-the-scenes political and media campaign around the theme that the Kennedy assassination had underscored the importance of the selection of a vice president fully capable of serving on short notice as president.

I was asked to meet again a few days later with a group including Connell; John Stewart, Humphrey's legislative assistant; Max Kampelman, a former Humphrey legislative assistant who was now his personal attorney; and Herb Waters, Connell's predecessor as administrative assistant. They asked questions about my proposal. Afterward, Connell told me Humphrey also had reviewed it. Would I come on board and implement it? (Later Humphrey would tell me: "It was the plan I had been looking for. It was the obvious way to proceed but no one seemed to have realized it.")

Taking leave from the European Communities job would be difficult. My boss there, Len Tennyson, had taken a sabbatical, and I was acting director of the office. Yet, I thought, I could make a real difference if I could help Humphrey to a place on the 1964 national Democratic ticket. My leave was granted on the condition that I come to the office on a periodic basis until Tennyson could get back from Europe. Early in 1964 I began my work on Humphrey's behalf at a small desk in his Senate Office Building offices, suite 1313. I shared the room with Stewart, an American Political Science Association intern, and a secretary. The run-up to the 1964 Civil Rights Act was under way at that time. Stewart, Humphrey's staff man on the bill, and others were in and out of the office and on the phones constantly. When things got hectic, I would move across the hall to a Senate committee room under Humphrey's control or work out of a vacant office at Kampelman's downtown law firm.

I interrupted my work for Humphrey for a few days to help manage another visit to Washington by Monnet. One of the appointments I made for him was with Humphrey. The two men had never met. I brought Monnet to Humphrey's Senate office at the appointed hour. Humphrey, characteristically, was running late. Finally, I asked Vi Williams, Humphrey's secretary, how late she thought Humphrey would be. "Go see for yourself," she said. "He's in his office." As I entered Humphrey's inner office, I saw that his bathroom door was ajar. He was wearing a sleeveless undershirt and shaving with a straight razor, his face lathered. "I know that Monnet is here," he said, "but I can't see him without shaving and changing my shirt. He is a very important man."

Humphrey and Monnet discussed European-American issues for an hour.

Humphrey raised questions about the Common Agricultural Policy and also expressed skepticism about the concept of a European Multilateral Nuclear Force (MLF), then under discussion in the policy community. The force was seen by advocates of European integration as a means not only of bringing Western European countries into greater defense cooperation, but also as part of a natural evolution of the Atlantic Partnership "twin pillars" concept, which would make a united Western Europe and the United States more truly equal partners. Humphrey, the father of the Nuclear Test Ban Treaty, worried about nuclear-proliferation issues and also questioned whether the MLF might prove to be a more divisive than unifying political issue in both Europe and the United States. (As it turned out, Humphrey's assessment was right, and the project eventually was abandoned.)

Back at Monnet's Westchester suite, I told him that I was taking leave from the EC to help Humphrey gain the Democratic vice presidential nomination. I gave him one of the background papers I had prepared advocating Humphrey's candidacy. Monnet was skeptical. He had found Humphrey personable but had felt far more comfortable with the Kennedys. "You would do more good helping us than helping Humphrey," he said. I told him I was committed to the venture but, if Humphrey's candidacy failed, I certainly would return to my EC job. Monnet grunted.

The Humphrey campaign plan was simple and straightforward. I prepared memoranda giving the "best man" rationale for Humphrey's candidacy. Other memos were prepared and updated, displaying independent polling data that showed Humphrey to be the favorite among Democratic voters and prospective Democratic convention delegates for the vice presidential nomination. Favorable magazine and newspaper articles were reprinted. I selected Humphrey photographs, and wrote brief captions, for a photo book to be distributed at the Atlantic City convention. The United Auto Workers paid for it. Mailings went out to Democratic leaders around the country and to key media. Humphrey already was receiving regular requests for appearances on network news shows. We promoted more. Humphrey himself stayed apart from all of it, although he periodically would stop by my desk to ask, as if casually: "How are things going? Any news?" I knew that he was restraining his natural impulse to plunge into open campaigning. Connell and I drew up a list of Democratic Party leaders and officeholders who felt favorably toward Humphrey, and began calling them to solicit their public endorsements of Humphrey's nomination.

At about this time James Rowe Jr., a former assistant to President Roosevelt, prominent Washington, D.C., attorney, and friend of both Johnson's and Humphrey's, passed along the word: The president welcomed Humphrey's not-so-quiet campaign for the nomination. But he wanted to be kept abreast of all developments on a daily basis. Thus, at the end of each business day, we dispatched an updated looseleaf notebook to Rowe's office. It displayed news stories, endorsements, polling data, and other information concerning our campaign's progress that day. He passed it on to Johnson.

Johnson, it turned out, had granted a similar hunting license to Humphrey's Minnesota colleague, Senator Eugene McCarthy. It was not McCarthy's nature, however, to launch an effort such as ours. In any case, he had not been as active as Humphrey in the national party, and few Democrats around the country were prepared to endorse him. (Jane Freeman, wife of Agriculture Secretary Orville Freeman, who had been Humphrey's assistant in the Minneapolis mayor's office, reported to us, however, that Abigail McCarthy, Senator McCarthy's wife, had told her that McCarthy felt he had assurances that he would be nominated. Lady Bird Johnson, the First Lady, was reported to be a strong McCarthy advocate.) McCarthy's voting record was more conservative than Humphrey's. He also had been friendly toward oil and other business interests in the Senate Finance Committee. He was Catholic. It was conceivable that LBJ might pass over Humphrey, we thought, in favor of another Minnesotan who would give Johnson less competition for the limelight in the White House and would go down more easily with Johnson allies who did not like Humphrey's outspoken advocacy of liberal policies domestically and of dovish policies internationally.

Johnson requested that Humphrey send him a memorandum stating his views on Vietnam. Humphrey did so, asserting that U.S. forces should be kept in an advisory capacity. Their number should be limited. They should not become involved in combat. At the same time, the United States should help the South Vietnamese government with all aspects of economic development, with particular stress on land reform, and U.S. leverage should be used to reduce government corruption and to encourage the building of democratic political institutions. Johnson told Humphrey those views coincided with his own. His public statements confirmed it.

As the Democrats' national convention neared in Atlantic City, allies of Robert Kennedy began telling journalists that a Kennedy candidacy for the vice presidential nomination should not be excluded. Journalist Joseph Kraft, in an *Atlantic Monthly* article, argued that Johnson should designate no vice presidential nominee and leave the matter to be decided on the convention floor by the delegates. Robert Kennedy, he said, might well be the nominee under such circumstances. (Adlai Stevenson had left the nomination open at the 1956 convention, where Senator Estes Kefauver fought off a strong challenge by John F. Kennedy for second place on the ticket.) Robert Kennedy was scheduled to deliver a tribute to his martyred brother at the convention. The emotion generated by the speech could, we thought, lead to a stampede among delegates toward Robert Kennedy and go so far as to override Johnson's wishes about his running mate. Connell and I made calls to party leaders; we began to find some who had received exploratory contact from Kennedy loyalists. Johnson cut off all speculation when, in an almost laughably transparent action, he announced publicly that he was removing from consideration for the vice presidential nomination all members of his Cabinet (including, of course, Attorney General Kennedy).

By the time of the Atlantic City convention we had, through phone calls and personal contact, built a network of Humphrey supporters in each of the state and territorial delegations. We had set up a telephone switchboard in the Humphrey campaign suite upstairs in the Shelburne Hotel. We also had gone so far as to prepare Johnson-Humphrey signs and buttons, to be placed in boxes under chairs on the convention floor, to materialize magically if and when Johnson put Humphrey's name into vice presidential nomination.

Just before leaving for Atlantic City, we launched a last-minute blitz to lend momentum to the effort. In the course of it I was to gain a useful insight into Humphrey's modus operandi. Several major newspapers had endorsed a Humphrey vice presidential candidacy. So had a number of national labor and civil-rights leaders and Democratic officeholders. But there were a few big-name holdouts who could be particularly helpful to us. One was Humphrey's good friend California governor Edmund G. (Pat) Brown, whose public endorsement could put Humphrey over the top. On a Saturday morning, a few days ahead of the Atlantic City convention, I called Eugene Wyman, the Democratic national committeeman from California, to ask that he talk with Brown and ask if he would publicly endorse Humphrey.

"Is this OK with Johnson?" Wyman asked. I assured Wyman that Johnson had authorized Humphrey to seek such support. A few moments later, Wyman called back. Brown would be pleased to make the endorsement but Humphrey should call him directly to seal the deal. He gave me Brown's Hickory-exchange private phone number in Sacramento. Brown was standing by. I called Humphrey, who said, "I'll call him right now and report back."

Two hours passed. I was worried that the endorsement might come too late to make Sunday newspapers. I called Humphrey again. "What happened?" I asked. "Well," Humphrey said, "Pat said he would be pleased to endorse me. But he said *Life* magazine was coming out this week with a picture of him as a vice presidential possibility. He was afraid his endorsement now might kill the *Life* photo and any story. He wanted them for his scrapbook and for his grandkids. So I told him to take his time and endorse whenever he pleased." "But the convention is in a few days," I said. "Later on is no good." "Well," Humphrey said, "Pat just wanted his moment and I couldn't take it away from him." In the years to follow I would witness many instances in which Humphrey's goodheartedness—or, putting it another way, lack of jugular instinct—would cost him dearly politically. But it also was his enduring strength. It simply was not in the man to benefit at others' expense, to use political muscle, or to hurt those who hurt him. He was guileless and at times as vulnerable as a child.

When Bill Connell and I attended Humphrey's funeral service in January 1978, in a church in St. Paul, Minnesota, the entire congregation wept while a black choir sang old spirituals. The streets near the cemetery were jammed with thousands of people who had stood for hours in freezing weather to see their hero home. The cemetery itself was equally jammed. I thought back to Johnson's funeral service in Washington, D.C., five years earlier, at the National City Christian Church. Tears may have been shed at Johnson's Texas burial, but, at the Washington service, there were none. Several hundred persons who had known or worked with Johnson in Congress or in his administration sat respectfully through the eulogy delivered by W. Marvin Watson, his former chief of staff, and then walked out into bright sunshine to renew friendships and swap Johnson stories.

I also have thought often of a phone call Humphrey received early in his vice presidency from Franklin Roosevelt Jr., who had called him a "draft dodger" while campaigning for John F. Kennedy in the hard-fought 1960 West Virginia primary that had sunk Humphrey's presidential chances. Roosevelt had been appointed under secretary of commerce by Kennedy and remained in the job under Johnson. "Hubert," Roosevelt said over the speakerphone in Humphrey's Capitol office, "I need your help. Johnson is going to fire my ass. I have nowhere else to go. Can you save me?" "Frank," Humphrey responded, "I will call Lyndon right now and see what I can do. He worshiped your father. I cannot believe he would want to do this to you." I asked Humphrey: "After what he did to you in West Virginia, why would you want to help Frank Roosevelt?" Humphrey looked at me with surprise. "After all he has done for me," he said, "it's the least I can do for him." I could see he wasn't being sarcastic.

A small Humphrey group traveled to Atlantic City a few days in advance of the 1964 convention. One was Walter (Fritz) Mondale, the Minnesota attorney general who was a Humphrey protégé and who would be appointed to his Senate seat when Humphrey became vice president. He would play an important role in the credentials committee at the convention. I had not met him until a few days previously, when he was introduced to me in Humphrey's Senate office as "a person very important to the senator." He was wearing a tight-fitting green sharkskin suit.

Those of us staffing Humphrey's convention presence were few in number. I shuttled between our headquarters at the Shelburne and a motel down the boardwalk where I would staff Humphrey's appearances as a guest commentator for ABC-TV News (he had signed up for the commentator role before his campaign for the vice presidency had developed).

Shortly after the convention opened, Connell and I were riding with Humphrey as his car became gridlocked in traffic on its way to the convention hall. We heard a familiar voice call out from a nearby motel window: "Hubert!!!!" It was Jim Rowe, the go-between between Johnson and Humphrey. We pulled over. Humphrey and Connell went to Rowe's room. Rowe told them that Johnson was leaning toward Humphrey as his running mate, but first Humphrey would be called upon to resolve a seating dispute involving the Mississippi delegation. The integrated Mississippi Freedom Democrats had been picketing on the boardwalk and were demanding seats in the delegation. The implication: If Humphrey did not resolve the dispute, Johnson would choose someone else.

Back at the hotel, Americans for Democratic Action's Joseph Rauh, United Auto Workers president Walter Reuther, the NAACP's Clarence Mitchell, and other labor and civil-rights leaders gathered to strategize. It was vital to them that Humphrey be on the ticket. They would work with the Freedom Democrats and their supporters to find a solution. Mondale was assigned the task in the credentials committee of getting it done. (Johnson, of course, knew that all of this would happen if liberals thought their favored vice presidential nominee was in danger.) In the end, a few seats were set aside for the integrated Freedom Democrats and the crisis was over.

But Humphrey had not yet finished passing through Johnson's gauntlet. Johnson instructed him to go to a helipad where a helicopter would pick him up and fly him to Washington for a meeting with the president. (As Humphrey departed the hotel, I noted that Eugene McCarthy was in the lobby, holding a press conference announcing that he would request that Johnson remove his name from vice presidential consideration. He felt manipulated. Little did he know, I thought, that Humphrey's deal had not yet been sealed and that he might be withdrawing prematurely.) When Humphrey reached the helipad, he was startled to find there Senator Thomas Dodd of Connecticut, who also had been invited to meet with Johnson.

Humphrey and Dodd rode together in a limousine from National Airport to the White House. Humphrey was kept waiting in the car while Johnson met with Dodd. Finally, he was ushered into the Oval Office. Johnson, as Humphrey later told it, explained to Humphrey that Dodd was not under serious consideration as his running mate. Dodd faced a reelection campaign in Connecticut and Johnson merely wanted to give him some exposure. (It also, I thought, served LBJ's purposes to have it thought that he was considering a Catholic from the Northeast as a running mate.) He did, however, want to have a serious talk with Humphrey before they proceeded further.

Johnson wondered if their personalities fit. It was very important that he and his vice president present a common front to others. He had held his tongue and been loyal to President Kennedy even when he thought mistakes were being made. Humphrey was well known for freely speaking his mind. Johnson wanted him to continue to do that if he became vice president, but never in the presence of others. Could Humphrey accept that discipline? Humphrey said he could.

And so it came to pass that Hubert Humphrey was nominated as Johnson's running mate at the 1964 Democratic National Convention. In later years, I sometimes would be asked to name the high point of Humphrey's vice presidency. Only half jokingly I would answer that "it was the night of his nomination in Atlantic City. Everything went downhill from there."

The convention nominated Johnson, but without emotion. Humphrey's nomination opened floodgates of emotion. The convention delegates, most of whom had stood with Humphrey in party and policy fights since his 1948 civil-rights speech, let loose a roar and marched triumphantly around the floor.

Our banners, signs and buttons, carefully hidden until the actual moment of nomination, suddenly appeared all over the hall. (They would have become real collector's items, I thought at the time, if someone else had been nominated.) As I joined the joyful procession, I passed beneath Johnson's seat in the gallery. He was glowering.

John Stewart wrote a draft of Humphrey's acceptance speech. But the White House provided a final draft that depicted the Republican presidential nominee, Senator Barry Goldwater, as an extremist out of step with mainstream America. Most Americans had rallied around a series of policies and government actions, the White House draft indicated, "but not Senator Goldwater." That was the theme to be pursued throughout the fall campaign: Goldwater was painted as a dangerous kook who would risk nuclear war, destroy Social Security, and keep his promise to saw the eastern seaboard off the continent. Johnson stood above the campaign battle; it was really Humphrey who ran against Goldwater. Representative William Miller, a former Republican national chairman who was Goldwater's running mate, was generally ignored and went home to Buffalo from the campaign trail a week before election day.

Jean and our children had gone to her mother's home in Kansas while I was in Atlantic City. When I arrived back home from the convention, late in the night, I found a telegram stuck in the front-door mail slot of our house on Brandywine Street in the District of Columbia. I opened it. It read: "Bravo. Jean Monnet."

5

THE GREAT SOCIETY

Now, more than forty years after the Johnson-Humphrey campaign, Medicare, Medicaid, the Civil Rights and Voting Rights Acts, federal aid to education, efforts to stop nuclear proliferation, and consumer protections are considered "givens" in our national life. But in the early 1960s they were not.

Advocates of these causes had fought for them throughout the postwar period, but in Congress, a coalition of Southern Democratic committee chairs and conservative Republicans had blocked them. Large portions of the electorate were opposed to them for a variety of reasons. Some saw them as federal impingements on states' rights or local control. Others saw them as expansions of government which, down the road, would bust the federal budget. Nuclear and other arms control proposals were seen during the Cold War as dangerous symptoms of softness. Charges of racism are all too easily and often unfairly made today. But then, millions of Americans held racist core values. Lynchings and race riots had taken place right through the 1940s.

In 1962 President Kennedy had signed the Trade Expansion Act, and in 1963 he had signed Humphrey's Nuclear Test Ban Treaty. Johnson had used Kennedy's murder to generate support for passage of the 1964 Civil Rights Act. But the dam did not break until the Johnson-Humphrey landslide victory over the Goldwater-Miller ticket helped to bring Democrats overwhelming majorities in both the U.S. Senate and House in 1965.

After the 1964 campaign I was invited to join Humphrey's vice presidential staff in a position yet to be defined. Johnson had given Humphrey only a shoestring budget with which to run his office, so a payroll slot also had to be found for me. In the meantime I returned to my job with the European Communities and, as a volunteer, helped coordinate Humphrey's activities relating to the 1965 presidential inauguration. The latter task was a crash course in Human Behavior in the Presence of Power.

Many people at that time were engaged in politics because of their commitment to a public agenda. But more—and far more nowadays—were in politics either because money or power might flow to them from their involvement or because they were just plain intoxicated by their proximity to the main game. The inaugural activities themselves consist of a series of receptions, dinners, entertainment events, and private soirees as well as the official swearing-in ceremony and inaugural parade. To me, all of these things were a distraction from the exciting task of governance that lay ahead. But to thousands of people, from all over the country, they were ends in themselves. Serving as a Humphrey representative to the inaugural committee, I suddenly found myself swamped with hundreds of phone calls, visits, and even offers of cash from men and women who desperately wanted access to inaugural-event invitations and tickets. I found it far more draining than the nominating and general-election campaigns had been. In addition, I found myself being buttonholed by Democrats seeking appointments in an administration that already was largely filled by holdover appointees. I did not know at that point what position I would hold in the vice president's office or what, if any, patronage powers the vice president might have. As the actual inaugural neared, I was driven to bed by fatigue and a fever. But I was summoned back to the maelstrom less than twenty-four hours later.

Several inaugural dinners were held at Washington, D.C., hotels on the eve of Johnson's and Humphrey's swearing in. Jean and I attended one at the Mayflower Hotel. We were seated next to a crew-cut newly elected congressman from Indiana—just as eager and green as I was—and his wife. Lee Hamilton later would in a long career become one of the most respected legislators of our generation, serving as chair of the House Foreign Affairs Committee and the Joint Economic Committee, and receiving frequent mention as a possible secretary of state or Democratic vice presidential candidate.

Later, at one Sheraton-Carlton Hotel reception largely populated by Democratic liberals, I saw inaugural fever at its worst. Most of those attending would never have supported Johnson for the Democratic presidential nomination, and many had been disappointed earlier by Kennedy's selection of him as his running mate. Yet, when Johnson entered the room, I saw all move en masse toward the president, nearly crushing him in the doorway. There they were, reaching out, hoping to be recognized, calling the president's name. It was an embarrassing, grasping display.

During this in-between period, Humphrey asked me to review some of his personal files as he prepared to shift from the Senate to the vice presidency. Among other papers I reviewed was his correspondence with Johnson. The letters between them, though both were national figures at the time, could have been written by idealistic college sophomores. Both men spoke of an unfinished progressive agenda and of the means for achieving it. There was an undertone to the correspondence, however: Johnson clearly was trying to bring Humphrey within his sphere of influence. There were invitations to the LBJ Ranch in Texas and special emphasis on the civil-rights issues that Johnson knew were closest to Humphrey's heart. Humphrey, for his part, offered to work with Johnson to get legislation passed. But he had not accepted the invitations to Johnson's ranch.

I also read memoranda and documents from Humphrey's time as mayor of Minneapolis and leader of the Democrat-Farmer-Labor (DFL) Party in Minnesota. It was fascinating to gain insights on a younger Humphrey, fighting organized crime as a big-city mayor and resisting Communist influence in the postwar DFL. Orville Freeman, his college friend and assistant as mayor, Eugene McCarthy, Representative Don Fraser, and others all were there as young political reformers. There also were notes Humphrey had taken regarding his historic 1948 civil-rights speech in Philadelphia. At the last moment, the notes indicated, Humphrey had lost his nerve regarding the speech. After all, the incumbent president Truman opposed the minority plank Humphrey was supporting. Humphrey, who revered his father, a South Dakota druggist, asked him for advice. His father told him he must go ahead. Humphrey later confided to me, "I finally mustered the courage to walk toward the podium to deliver the speech. My knees literally were shaking. But, as I mounted the podium, Ed Flynn, the Democratic boss of the Bronx, took me by the shoulder and told me he and others were with me. I suddenly felt freed and gave the speech that was in my heart."

A federal payroll slot was found for me. I would be carried on Commerce Secretary John Conner's payroll at a salary of $20,000 per year. (That remained my salary four years later, at the end of Humphrey's vice presidency. It never occurred to me to ask for a raise or to anyone else to suggest that I receive one.) My initial staff role would be to manage an assignment Humphrey had been given by Johnson: to reduce the so-called "travel gap"—the money being spent by Americans traveling overseas as compared to that being spent in the United States by foreigners—which was contributing to an overall U.S. international payments deficit. We formed a Cabinet task force that, on the one hand, would launch a privately funded "Discover America" campaign to encourage Americans to travel within the country, and on the other, would resist Treasury Secretary Henry (Joe) Fowler's attempts to impose restrictions on capital movement. I picked up staff responsibility for trade policy and European affairs, thanks to my prior EC experience. I also became Humphrey's speech coordinator, assigning the texts to vice presidential staff and others, editing them, and writing most of the principal ones myself. These assignments all impinged on the turf of staff members who had been with Humphrey in the Senate. Yet frictions were kept to a minimum. All organizations, including political organizations, reflect the character of the people who run them. Humphrey commanded enormous respect and loyalty among his staff, all flowing from his idealism and large-mindedness. It would have seemed disloyal for any of us to get bogged down in personal or turf disputes.

In the early days of Humphrey's vice presidency, it appeared that he would be at the center of everything. One evening I rode with him in his limousine as it traveled from Capitol Hill to his office in the Executive Office Building (EOB), next to the White House proper. A radio message instructed him to proceed directly to the White House for a meeting on legislation. As we pulled into Executive Avenue, the small street between the White House and the EOB, the vice president stepped quickly from the car and signaled for me to join him. The meeting was being held in the state dining room. I saw immediately that I should not be there—no White House or congressional staff were present, only President Johnson and the Democratic chairs of Senate and House committees. I turned to leave, but Humphrey nodded that I should stay. I sat behind Johnson, out of his view, while Humphrey sat behind the opposite side of the table, facing the president.

This, I thought, was a movie scene. The lights in the dining room were dimmed. LBJ sat astride a backward-facing chair at the center of a long table. The committee chairs, all white, male, and middle-aged, sat respectfully on both sides of the table. Johnson spoke: "Claude!"

Claude Desautels, a member of the Johnson legislative-liaison staff, emerged from behind a curtain at the north end of the room. "Claude," Johnson said, "bring me today's *Washington Star*." Desautels already had it in hand and rushed with it to Johnson's side. Johnson then read aloud a story that reported that his Great Society legislative package was moving more slowly than anticipated (in fact, it was moving expeditiously).

Johnson thereupon asked each chairman to report on the status of legislation in his committee. He sat silently until all had reported. Then, one by one, he responded to the report each had given—in most cases indicating greater knowledge of the situation in each committee than its chairman. Then Johnson's voice suddenly rose. He spoke as if he were a high-school football coach giving a locker-room pep talk to teenagers: "We are going to make history together. We are going to pass Medicare, Medicaid, federal aid to education, the Voting Rights Act, a war on poverty—if we can muster the will to do it. Can you do it? Can you do it for your country and for your president?"

"Yes, Mr. President," they responded in a shout. "Yes!" I watched Representative Hale Boggs of Louisiana, sitting across the table. He had become excited, his face reddened. He rose from his chair to shout, "Yes, Mr. President!" but, as he did, he stumbled backward and both he and his chair crashed to the floor. As Boggs's neighbors rushed to help him, Johnson rose. "Alright, boys," he said, "that is what we will do. Hubert, you take over and handle the details." He strode quickly from the room. "Well, fellas, what can I say?" Humphrey said. "We already know the details. Meeting adjourned." The Great Society was gaining momentum and would be enacted that year.

Humphrey was lobbying hard for the program on the Hill. I had been submitting his speeches for review, prior to delivery, to Bill Moyers at the White House. Moyers seldom had any comments or suggestions. Then, one morning, he called to inform us that the president had instructed him to no longer review the speeches. The president announced the same at a Cabinet meeting. We were trusted to be on our own.

Humphrey felt confident about his relationship with Johnson. A few days after the legislative meeting, I was with Humphrey at a meeting in the White House basement. When it ended, Humphrey suddenly said, "Let's see what Lyndon is doing," and began marching up the steps toward the Oval Office. Johnson's secretary, Juanita Roberts, seemed a bit surprised at the vice president's unscheduled appearance, but suggested cordially that we wait in the Oval Office while the president completed a meeting outside in the rose garden with Senator Frank Church and a group of his constituents.

As we waited in the Oval Office, Humphrey pointed out marks left four years earlier on the floor leading to the rose garden by President Eisenhower's golf shoes. Johnson kept wire-service machines, chattering noisily, in closed boxes in the corner. Humphrey lifted the lid of one to see what was in the news. Then, while Johnson's meeting continued in the rose garden, he began to circle slowly around the room to the president's desk. Finally, he stood behind it. He scanned the papers on the desk. He put his hand on the back of the president's chair as if to pull it backward. My God, I thought, he's going to sit at Johnson's desk in Johnson's chair! I fully expected Johnson to enter the room and see it happening. Then Humphrey withdrew his hand and quickly moved back to the other side of the desk. "We probably shouldn't be in here," he said. At that moment Johnson entered the office with Senator Church in tow.

Johnson had his arm around Church's shoulder. Church turned amiably to Johnson and spoke in the exaggerated, formal way that he often did. "Mr. President," he said, "when it comes to policy in Vietnam, I hope that you intend to use the velvet glove as well as the mailed fist." We, but not Church, could see Johnson flinch and his eyes grow cold. My first thought was that he was about to break Church's neck. "Why Frank," he replied, "you know that has always been my policy and will continue to be so." As Church left the room, I could see that Johnson was mad as hell.

Johnson's reaction to Church, I thought later, foretold how Johnson quite soon would come to regard Humphrey.

In his January State of the Union speech, President Johnson virtually ignored Vietnam. But he called a National Security Council meeting in February to discuss strategy in Vietnam following attacks by Viet Cong guerrillas (not North Vietnamese main forces) on American barracks at Pleiku and a hotel in Qui Nhon where troops were housed. Eight Americans had been killed at Pleiku, twenty-three in Qui Nhon. National Security Advisor McGeorge Bundy, who had been present in Saigon at the time, had cabled Washington, urging reprisals against North Vietnam. (My own reaction, on reading his cables, was to wonder: Why the excitement? Guerrilla attacks are what happen in a guerrilla war. We should spend our energy, I thought, on devising better on-ground security against them.)

Only Under Secretary of State George Ball disagreed with Bundy's proposed escalations. (Senate Majority Leader Mike Mansfield and Foreign Relations Committee Chairman J. William Fulbright had doubts but did not dissent publicly.) Initial bombing strikes had been made against North Vietnam, but now stronger, sustained measures were to be formally considered.

Humphrey had believed Johnson's 1964 campaign assurances that he would not widen the scope of the Vietnamese war. He did not think that the guerrilla attacks provided any reason for a bombing campaign against North Vietnam; in fact, Soviet Premier Alexei Kosygin was visiting North Vietnam at the time and could regard such an escalation as an obvious provocation. The conflict, Humphrey thought, should be contained, and political/economic efforts emphasized to stabilize the situation in South Vietnam.

I was asked to prepare brief talking points to that effect for him prior to the meeting.

Johnson polled those at the table as to whether a second round of retaliatory strikes should be made. Humphrey said he opposed the strikes. Any decision, he said, should at least be deferred until Kosygin departed Hanoi. Johnson, however, ended up ordering new attacks. LBJ had turned a policy corner. He also was furious with Humphrey for having broken their understanding, reached prior to his vice presidential nomination, that he would not dissent in the presence of others. Humphrey, returning to his office from the meeting, was unaware that he had violated any understanding. Johnson had asked a direct question in an official meeting about a situation where American lives and interests were at stake, and he had given a direct and honest answer. Johnson left Humphrey off the list of attendees at an NSC meeting a few days later—even though by statute he was an ex officio member of the National Security Council. Humphrey subsequently submitted to Johnson a memorandum (largely prepared by his former Senate staff member Tom Hughes, then director of the State Department's Bureau of Intelligence and Research) making the argument that an escalation not only would be a foreign-policy mistake but would weaken the administration's political position domestically and endanger Great Society proposals. The president hesitated. But in the end, he not only escalated the conflict but, perhaps heeding Humphrey's warnings of domestic repercussions, launched Operation Rolling Thunder (as the bombing campaign was to be called) without publicly acknowledging the policy change it implied. On March 2, 1965, Rolling Thunder began with more than 120 U.S. and South Vietnamese aircraft attacking North Vietnamese targets.

Out-and-out war with North Vietnam had begun. Humphrey was to be punished and pushed out of national-security issues for more than a year. Johnson thereafter avoided official NSC meetings, and instead lunched regularly with Rusk, McNamara, and Bundy, leaving Humphrey largely in the dark except for information we could glean from daily cables and from meetings we scheduled at our own initiative with members of the administration and outside policy specialists.

Humphrey's exclusion was made embarrassingly clear in late April. Humphrey had long been associated with Latin American policy and was known as legislative sponsor of the Alliance for Progress and of a treaty establishing Latin America as a nuclear-free zone. Yet he was largely excluded from administration discussions regarding disorder in the Dominican Republic. The island nation's pro-American government of Donald Cabral had been overthrown. The previous president, Juan Bosch, who himself had been overthrown in 1963, appeared on the verge of returning to power. Bosch, in fact, was anti-Communist and more democratic than Cabral. U.S. Ambassador W. Tapley Bennett, who misread the situation, foresaw the establishment of a Castro-like regime in the Dominican Republic and cabled for intervention by U.S. Marines.

Early on a Saturday I received a phone call at home from Venezuelan Ambassador Enrique Tejera París, whom I knew socially. He had an urgent message regarding the situation in the Dominican Republic. Could I come to the embassy? I told Humphrey of the call. He knew the ambassador and regarded him highly. He would join me at the embassy after dropping off some laundry in his Chevy Chase, Maryland, neighborhood. The ambassador's message was not a surprise. He informed us that he had been asked by other Latin American ambassadors to warn strongly against any U.S. military intervention in the Dominican Republic. Bosch posed no threat and was pro-American. Moreover, the intervention would have a strong negative effect on opinion throughout the hemisphere and would seem to signal a return to the U.S. gunboat diplomacy of earlier decades. He had been asked to transmit the message to Humphrey because Humphrey was known to be a friend of Latin America and a strong advocate of democratic reform. Other Latin countries were prepared to serve as intermediaries to attempt to restore order in the Dominican Republic.

Humphrey and I returned directly to his Executive Office Building office. No staff or secretaries had arrived yet. I drafted a report on the Venezuelan message; Humphrey reviewed it. I typed a final copy, placed it in a red-tag (urgent) envelope for Johnson's eyes only, and sent it across to the White House. Within a half hour we learned that Johnson had dispatched more than 20,000 troops to the Dominican capital of Santo Domingo while we were at the Venezuelan Embassy.

6

VIETNAM AND LITTLE ELSE

Despite his public and private vows of restraint in Vietnam, Johnson had used an ambiguous encounter in the summer of 1964 between U.S. and North Vietnamese vessels in the Tonkin Gulf to gain passage of a Tonkin Gulf Resolution in the U.S. Senate. The resolution gave Johnson broad authority in conduct of the war. Floor manager for the resolution was Foreign Relations Committee chairman J. William Fulbright, who would later become an opponent of the war. (In a Senate floor speech, Fulbright at one point declared that it was folly to predict American failure in Vietnam merely because France had failed there. "One American is worth ten Frenchmen any time," he declared, "and I do not restrict that to military matters.")

Senator George McGovern of South Dakota, a Humphrey protégé and his next-door neighbor on Coquelin Terrace in suburban Chevy Chase, Maryland, was skeptical. So were Democratic senators Allen Ellender of Louisiana, Frank Lausche of Ohio, Gaylord Nelson of Wisconsin, and several Republicans. On August 7, however, when the resolution came up for a vote, only Wayne Morse of Oregon and Ernest Gruening of Alaska, both Democrats, voted no. The House of Representatives approved it without a single dissenting vote.

The Tonkin Gulf Resolution later would be used to lend legitimacy to whatever escalations Johnson chose to undertake, including the initiation of Operation Rolling Thunder early in 1965.

Humphrey's National Security Council opposition to Rolling Thunder had cost him dearly. He felt fiercely loyal to Johnson, yet by speaking candidly when he thought Johnson sought candor, he found himself placed in purgatory. White House staff, Cabinet members, and media covering the presidency all are highly aware of who is up, who down in a president's estimation, moment to moment. Word spread quickly that Humphrey had lost Johnson's confidence. Balanced, serious White House staff members such as Harry McPherson and Douglass Cater continued to treat the vice president with deference and respect. On the other hand, Marvin Watson, Johnson's chief of staff, treated Humphrey as he thought Johnson wished, doing things such as forcing him to get clearance for use of aircraft or executive-branch resources. Humphrey was well liked by his Secret Service detail, and two senior members disclosed to me that Johnson was tapping the phones in the vice president's Executive Office Building suite. When I passed that information to Humphrey, a look of sadness crossed his face. We agreed that no one else would be told and that Humphrey and the rest of us would continue to speak on our telephones without constraint.

One morning Johnson's assistant Jim Jones called to inform that the person with whom John Rielly of the vice president's staff was planning to have lunch that day was a KGB officer at the Soviet Embassy. "Do whatever you want," Jim said. "We just wanted you to know." I passed Jones's message to Rielly, suggesting he proceed as he wished. "I didn't know he was KGB," Rielly said, and cancelled the lunch. Jones could only have known of the lunch through taps on either our or the Soviet Embassy's phones, or both.

Smelling Humphrey's blood in the water, Johnson assistants Joseph Califano, McGeorge Bundy, and Walt Rostow were particularly patronizing toward him. Califano persuaded Johnson to strip Humphrey of some his administration civil-rights responsibilities and transfer them to him. One morning, while I was standing at Humphrey's desk, Califano phoned to instruct him to report to his (Califano's) office within a half hour. I asked Violet Williams to call Califano back, telling him that the vice president would have time to see him in his vice presidential office later that afternoon. Humphrey was a generous and forgiving person who seldom spoke ill of anyone, yet he made no secret of his belief that Califano was a power-hungry self-seeker operating well beyond his mandate. He felt the same about Bundy and Rostow, Johnson's national security advisors. Both, he felt, played on Johnson's feelings of intellectual insecurity—they were Ivy Leaguers whereas Johnson had attended a Texas state teachers college—to give him bad advice on Vietnam and reinforce their own positions.

Late in 1965, Bundy dropped by the vice president's EOB office for an early-evening chat. As he rose to leave, he asked Humphrey, "Do you think we can see things through in Vietnam and still meet our domestic and other obligations?" Humphrey was wary of Bundy's motive in asking the question. "What do you think, Mac?" he responded. "I think the United States of America can do whatever it wants to do," Bundy said. "So do I," Humphrey responded.

"Except when it can't," I said to Humphrey as Bundy exited the room. Humphrey nodded, touched his finger to his lips, and looked toward the door that had closed behind Bundy.

Johnson would force Bundy's resignation in 1966, but Rostow stayed on to the end of his administration. Rostow sent regular notes to Humphrey expressing his admiration and friendship, but to others he derided him as weak and unreliable on Vietnam.

Johnson received copies of Humphrey's daily schedule. The vice president was scheduled to meet one afternoon with Cleveland industrialist Cyrus Eaton, an old Humphrey friend who had just returned from meetings in Moscow with Kosygin. We had read in cable traffic our Moscow Embassy's reports on the Eaton visit. There was nothing remarkable in it. Eaton was known to oppose the Vietnam War; he and Kosygin had exchanged ideas about it. Humphrey not only wanted to hear from Eaton personally, but regarded it as useful to maintain communication with war critics. Early that morning, Humphrey buzzed me on the intercom to come to his office. "Walt Rostow just phoned me," he said, "suggesting that I not meet with Cyrus Eaton today. I told him you would talk with him and discuss his reasoning." Humphrey's face reflected disgust.

I walked from the EOB to Rostow's West Wing basement office. Rostow spoke as though he were disclosing something of great gravity: "You probably saw the cable traffic on Eaton's visit to Moscow. Let me show you back-channel [CIA] cables, which tell a fuller story." He placed a sheaf of cables on the coffee table between us. I read them. There was no significant difference between them and the State Department cables Humphrey and I already had seen.

"I see nothing here which should cause the vice president to cancel his visit with Eaton," I told Rostow. "It's in the president's interest that Humphrey keep lines open to critics. Beyond that, the cancellation itself could become an issue." I took the five-minute walk back to our EOB offices to report on my conversation with Rostow. Before I could speak, Humphrey waved his hand. "Don't bother," he said, "Johnson just this minute called and gave me a direct order to cancel the Eaton meeting."

Humphrey responded to his frustrations by intensifying his advocacy of Great Society programs and accepting out-of-capital speaking invitations. His morale lifted outside Washington. Ordinary citizens and Democrats responded to him warmly. He drew particular strength from visits to Job Corps training centers, Title I programs for disadvantaged school kids, and private programs such as the Reverend Leon Sullivan's Opportunities Industrialization Centers. He gave speeches and media interviews on behalf of the Johnson domestic program. He also began to speak out for the Johnson Vietnam policy.

Working with Humphrey on his speeches, I got a full sense of his frustration. The Vietnam drafts I brought him all were carefully phrased. I knew his reservations and wanted to keep him an honest man. He would not want overenthusiastic defenses of Vietnam policy to be thrown back in his face later.

Humphrey's staff and friends became split. Bill Connell and Max Kampelman, in particular, urged Humphrey to support the president unreservedly. John Rielly, the vice president's general foreign policy staff assistant, and Tom Hughes at the State Department wanted to nudge him the other way. As one major foreign-policy speech loomed, I found myself in an outspoken confrontation, in Humphrey's presence, with Connell and Kampelman. Finally, Humphrey ordered me to "toughen up the speech." When I resisted, Humphrey moved within an inch of my face and began to recite arguments on behalf of our role in Vietnam. I refused to back up. I answered his arguments. I knew Humphrey was not really angry but was testing my counterarguments. To let us both off the hook, I told him I would return the next morning with a new version of the speech. Late that evening, when I returned home, Kampelman called me: "You're pressing Humphrey too hard," he said, "and he resents it. He has enough pressure on him. Don't add to it." I felt no personal anger toward either Kampelman or Connell, as we increasingly pulled Humphrey in opposite directions on Vietnam. They had been loyal friends and staff members of Humphrey's long before I had; they were devoted to his well-being and what they saw as his best interests, just as I was. There were tensions, but we remained friends and still are.

The next morning, with Connell and Kampelman absent, I brought a fresh draft of the speech to Humphrey. "I don't want to see it," he said. "Go back to the original draft. Keep giving me what you think I should say." Humphrey's final speech texts always came from my typewriter—and were released accordingly to the media—so I was determined not to let him pass a point of no return on Vietnam. Yet, especially in extemporaneous remarks and in interviews, he began to approach that point.

One morning Humphrey called me into his office and asked that I hire a speechwriter "who really believes in the war" to prepare his Vietnam drafts. He would, of course, continue to expect me to edit them and do the final versions. I interviewed several candidates, including one who was then writing speeches for McNamara and another with more dovish credentials from the

State Department. But none seemed to be Humphrey's kind of person. I reported that I could not find the right candidate, although I had made an honest effort. Moreover, I said, I thought he would be making a terrible mistake if he became a cheerleader for a war he did not fully support. He let the matter rest.

Humphrey was genuinely torn, in any case, on the substance of the policy. He had not wanted the war escalated or the U.S. role in it expanded. But he also was a staunch anti-totalitarian. He had fought and defeated strong Communist influence in the postwar Democrat-Farmer-Labor Party in Minnesota. He was not a Cold Warrior, and in fact was often criticized as being wishful or unrealistic with his proposals for nuclear-arms control and reduced tensions with the Soviet Union. Yet he did not doubt the fundamental necessity of confronting unequivocally the Soviet probes and pressures against the West. At that point he did not question the necessity of a continuing U.S. involvement in Vietnam—what he questioned were the means and degree of involvement. (A few others, including myself, already considered the U.S. presence in Vietnam to be a fundamental strategic mistake. No vital American interests were at stake there, we thought, and therefore we should be moving steadily toward responsible disengagement.)

Johnson suddenly offered Humphrey a chance to escape his involuntary confinement within the administration. In mid-1966 the vice president was asked on short notice to fly to the Pacific and Asia to mobilize support in the wake of the Honolulu Conference at which Johnson had met with South Vietnamese leaders. The traveling party included Connell and Rielly, National Security Council staff member Jim Thomson, and, for part of the time, Averell Harriman, U.S. ambassador-at-large for Southeast Asian affairs; I did not accompany Humphrey on the trip. Jack Valenti of Johnson's staff also was on board. Anxious to regain Johnson's favor, Humphrey made extravagant public statements on behalf of his Vietnam policy and, in an after-hours conversation, shocked Thomson in particular with a tirade about the threat of Communist expansion in Southeast Asia. After having visited the war zone in Vietnam, Humphrey was photographed at his next Asian stop waving his hat and smiling, campaign style. The photo appeared on the front pages of many U.S. newspapers. The image was jarring. I sent an immediate cable to him suggesting that he tone down his rhetoric and adopt a more serious external demeanor.

During the course of the trip, the National Security Council staff member who ran the cable room brought me by hand all cables filed from our embassies along the route. He also gave me copies of confidential cables, from

Valenti to Johnson, reporting on Humphrey's day-to-day statements and activities. These clearly were not intended for our eyes. But the NSC staffer, who was African American, admired Humphrey and thus made the "mistake" of including Valenti's daily spy reports with the other cables.

Humphrey returned to the capital having been restored at least partially to the president's graces. But he had seriously damaged his standing among Democrats, columnists, academics, and other opinion leaders with doubts about the war. Rielly and I arranged a private dinner at the Fairfax Hotel at which Humphrey would have a chance to talk about Vietnam policy with a dozen independent outside scholars familiar with Southeast Asia. George Carroll, a CIA officer attached to the vice president's office, also attended. Rielly and I had hoped the session might lead Humphrey to temper his increasingly strident views on the issue. But rather than seeking the knowledgeable input of his guests, Humphrey began the session by asking the scholars how he might sharpen his public arguments on behalf of the war. One then asked: "But why should the United States be fighting Hanoi?" Before Humphrey could answer, Carroll, an ardent anti-Communist, shouted: "Because they are damn Reds!" He pounded the table with his fist. Rielly and I tried to steer conversation in more productive directions, but the atmosphere had been poisoned. Afterward I walked with Humphrey to his limousine. "How do you think it went?" he asked. "It was a disaster," I told him. "You wasted everyone's time and demonstrated you weren't interested in learning anything. Our guests arrived expecting a substantive discussion; you disillusioned them all." Humphrey took the criticism but did not respond.

He began to be jeered at public appearances by liberals who had been his core political supporters. Americans for Democratic Action, of which Humphrey had been a cofounder, was a bastion of antiwar opinion. The labor movement still supported Johnson on Vietnam, but individual union locals and members, particularly within the United Auto Workers, began to express dissent. The African-American constituency was the only one that remained unshaken in its support for Humphrey. Humphrey, who could not conceal his emotions, was wounded as old loyalists fell away. One evening, riding home in his limousine, Humphrey read a James Reston column in the *New York Times* that was particularly scathing regarding his support for the war. Tears started to run down his cheeks. "Don't worry about it," I said, "it's not personal; it's about the policy." "No," Humphrey said, "it is about me. And Scotty Reston is a friend who matters to me."

As the months passed, my vice presidential staff duties kept expanding. Humphrey habitually overscheduled himself, and his days often were a chaotic rush from office appointments to executive-branch meetings to speeches. Both he and the staff were being spread too thin. I was asked to take responsibility for his overall scheduling, and thus priorities, on top of my other work, which still included coordination of his speech preparation. I also served as director of additional Cabinet task forces that Humphrey chaired and as coordinator of his communications activities. I was working seven days a week, seldom less than twelve hours daily. Then an embarrassing incident expanded my role further.

Humphrey had accepted a speaking engagement in Buffalo. When he arrived in his vice presidential Lear jet, a few hours ahead of the speech, he discovered that it was a black-tie event. He was wearing only a dark business suit. Humphrey was, after all, vice president of the United States, and his audience would not have been insulted had he addressed them in a business suit. He might even have made a joke of it and told them they were over-dressed. But, wanting to do the right thing, Humphrey instructed the staff member accompanying him to "get me a black tie right away so I can be properly dressed." The staffer solved the problem by sending the jet back to Washington to pick up Humphrey's tuxedo. The episode got into the press, and Humphrey was made to look foolish. His staff and friends were outraged and embarrassed on his behalf.

Thus Humphrey asked me to take on an additional role: I was to continue my present duties but, when he traveled out of the city or the country, I was to accompany him and ensure that everything proceeded professionally. I was a glutton for work, but could see immediately that this was one job too many. Thus I relinquished the time-consuming scheduling responsibility with some relief.

He made one further request of me: "Listen," Humphrey said, "I know I often respond to things emotionally. I need you to be rational and objective. When you see me make a dumb mistake, I want you to correct it immediately. Don't consult anyone else. Tell me about it later. And if someone needs a decision, and you know my thinking, give them an answer. I must clear away everything but the biggest decisions from my life." Later, in a staff meeting, he said that "I am the boss but Ted is my boss." Of course he did not mean that literally, but merely to signal to others the role he had asked me to play.

We proceeded accordingly for the rest of Humphrey's vice presidency.

Of course I did not "correct" him on matters of fundamental policy; I took great care not to abuse or exceed the mandate he had given me. By that time we had become sufficiently close that, with a raised eyebrow or glance across a room, he could signal his intentions and reactions to me. I could respond with my own nonverbal signals—a shrug, skeptical expression, or nod. He could begin a thought, I could end it, and vice versa. In advance of all but major speeches, we would exchange shorthand comments about subject matter and theme, and I would place the texts in his hands just before delivery. On all matters but Vietnam, in any event, we thought alike. I vowed to myself not to let him down.

In April and May 1967, Johnson dispatched Humphrey to Western Europe, not only to mobilize support for his Vietnam policy but also to enlist European leaders' help in any behind-the-scenes efforts that could bring North Vietnam to the negotiating table on a realistic basis. He also was to generate support for the nuclear nonproliferation and international monetary reform initiatives being undertaken by the administration. Prior to leaving the capital for Western Europe, I worked with the State Department and United States Information Agency to prepare exhaustive notebooks documenting all Johnson peace initiatives toward North Vietnam. We gave these to French president Charles de Gaulle, German chancellor Willy Brandt, British prime minister Harold Wilson, and heads of other European governments. They remained skeptical that Johnson genuinely sought a negotiated settlement in Vietnam.

In 1965 I had accompanied Humphrey to the Paris Air Show. During his visit he had met privately with de Gaulle, who had worn a simple French army uniform without any medals. De Gaulle at that time had offered to work behind the scenes to achieve a negotiated peace with Hanoi, but Johnson had not accepted his offer. During the 1967 visit, Humphrey was to be de Gaulle's guest at a formal dinner at the Elysée Palace. U.S.-French tensions were high at the time, not only regarding Vietnam but also regarding the sharply differing American and Gaullist visions about future U.S.-European relations. I drafted a dinner toast for Humphrey that honored France's past contributions to American freedom and celebrated prior U.S.-French collaboration, but which dealt straightforwardly with the fact that there were present differences. Humphrey, on reviewing it, directed me to prepare instead a new text that lauded in great detail not only French contributions to Western civilization but also de Gaulle's lifelong patriotism and willingness to stand against majority opinion on behalf of principle. When Humphrey delivered the revised toast that evening, it

This Hooverville (as such shantytowns during the Great Depression were called, after President Hoover) sprang up south of downtown Seattle in the early 1930s. (Pemco Webster and Stevens collection, Museum of History and Industry, Seattle)

Striking mill workers and National Guardsmen clash in Tacoma, Washington. The author's father joined Bellingham, Washington, mill workers in similar confrontations. (Seattle *Post-Intelligencer* collection, Museum of History and Industry, Seattle)

(Facing page, top) Franklin Delano Roosevelt campaigns for president in downtown Seattle, 1932. (Seattle *Post-Intelligencer* collection, Museum of History and Industry, Seattle)

(Facing page, bottom) Minneapolis mayor Hubert Humphrey delivers his historic speech on behalf of his civil-rights plank at the 1948 Democratic National Convention in Philadelphia. (Humphrey Institute, University of Minnesota, Minneapolis)

The author and his parents, Ted and June Van Dyk, at the time of his graduation from the University of Washington, 1955. (Author's collection)

Potomac Fever contracted. A White House mess matchbook and place card, and the photograph and green carnation presented to author by President Kennedy in the Oval Office during the same visit, St. Patrick's Day, 1961. (Author's collection)

Having been recalled to active military duty as a strategic intelligence analyst during the Berlin Crisis, the author sits at his Pentagon desk, 1961. Note the Central European situation map in the background. (Author's collection)

(Facing page, top) President Kennedy meets with Jean Monnet, father of the European Union, in 1962, during the period of the Atlantic Partnership between the United States and the European Communities. (Corbis)

(Facing page, bottom) Hundreds of thousands of civil-rights marchers move through Washington, D.C., to the Lincoln Memorial in 1963. The historic march helped to build national support for passage of the 1964 Civil Rights Act, which was sponsored by Senator Humphrey and signed by President Johnson. (Corbis)

Uneasy riders. President Johnson and Hubert Humphrey stage a photo op at LBJ Ranch, following Humphrey's nomination as Johnson's 1964 running mate. (Humphrey Institute, University of Minnesota, Minneapolis)

Hubert Humphrey congratulates new South Vietnamese president Thieu and vice president Ky at their inaugural in Saigon, November 1967. A significant meeting between Humphrey and Thieu followed. U.S. Ambassador Ellsworth Bunker stands on the far left, and the author can be seen in the background just to the right of him. (Author's collection)

To Ted Van Dyk with appreciation — Lyndon Johnson

The author and President Johnson, following the loyalty meeting LBJ called with White House staff in December 1967. (Author's collection)

(Facing page, top) Eugene McCarthy, Hubert Humphrey, and delegation chairman Jess Unruh at the caucus of the California delegation during the 1968 Democratic National Convention in Chicago. (Corbis)

(Facing page, bottom) Campaign manager Larry O'Brien, Hubert Humphrey, and the author review the author's draft for Humphrey's pivotal September 30, 1968, national broadcast from Salt Lake City declaring an independent position on Vietnam. (Author's collection)

Former Georgia governor Jimmy Carter and Senator Walter Mondale campaign together following their nomination at the 1976 Democratic National Convention. (Corbis)

(Facing page, top) Student-faculty mixer. Students and junior faculty exchange blows during violent student protests at Columbia University in 1968. (Corbis)

(Facing page, bottom) The long shot. Senator George McGovern campaigns for the Democratic presidential nomination, 1971. (Corbis)

Vice President Mondale swears the author in to the Carter administration in the Roosevelt Room at the White House, 1977. The author's wife, Jean, holds the Bible, while their children, Terry, Ted, Sue Ellen, and Robert (left to right), look on. Standing to the far left is Assistant Secretary of State Joseph Duffey. (Author's collection)

The author and Senator Ted Kennedy participate in a discussion of health-care policy at the National Press Club, 1981. (Author's collection)

Senator Paul Tsongas talks with *Washington Post* columnist David Broder (on the far left) and other journalists during his presidential nominating campaign, 1992. (Corbis)

became clear that his instincts were better than mine. As de Gaulle listened, tears formed in his eyes. Later, in private, he renewed his offer to work behind the scenes toward a Vietnam settlement.

Harold Wilson and Willy Brandt were old friends of Humphrey's from international social-democratic meetings of the prior decade. I accompanied Humphrey to a weekend at Wilson's country home at Chequers; the prime minister's foreign- policy aide, David Owen, later to be foreign secretary, also was present. The next day, at 10 Downing Street, Wilson hosted a luncheon in Humphrey's honor. Afterward, Wilson took Humphrey aside and told him he wanted to have a one-on-one talk. Humphrey requested that U.S. Ambassador David Bruce and I accompany him—I presumed because Humphrey was concerned that his own side of the discussion could later be misrepresented. Wilson uncomfortably accepted our presence. He then spoke directly: "Hubert, I must break with Johnson on the war. My party is against the war. British domestic opinion is against the war. I not only must break; I must speak out forcefully against U.S. policy." Humphrey was dismayed. He earlier had requested Wilson's help in exploring all avenues to a negotiated peace. He could imagine Johnson's reaction if Wilson, following Humphrey's visit, were to denounce U.S. policy. "Harold," he said, "do not do this. You don't know Lyndon Johnson. He will make you pay a higher price than you imagine. Do not cross Johnson. I am making a personal appeal to you." As it turned out, his plea was successful. Wilson did not make the outright break he had threatened.

During the London visit we sat in the gallery of Parliament and enjoyed the give-and-take of the question period in which government ministers and members of Parliament exchanged quick-witted barbs. Humphrey loved it. He nudged me as debate became particularly entertaining, and chuckled as telling verbal blows landed. It was the best preparation he could have had for his session scheduled immediately afterward with Labour MPs.

Humphrey's performance was the best I saw in his four years of the vice presidency. He was in his element with parliamentarians whose overall context he understood and, for the most part, shared. Just as in the question period he had just witnessed, the MPs peppered Humphrey with one provocative question after another regarding U.S. policy in Vietnam. He did not meet them with the simplistic arguments that had in the previous year too greatly characterized his domestic defense of the war. Speaking without notes, he made more sophisticated arguments from the perspective of a social progressive confronted with the sometimes uncomfortable duty of confronting totalitarianism of the left. He acknowledged U.S. mistakes in conduct of the war, but pointed to the risks that an abrupt withdrawal would generate elsewhere in the world. He also enumerated Johnson diplomatic initiatives of recent months and said he welcomed British assistance in undertaking new ones. His impact on his audience, I thought, was approximating the one he had made at the 1948 Democratic convention where he had, by the force of his oratory, changed his party's historical position on civil rights. At the end, the Labourites were cheering and came to the podium to rally around their American cousin.

Media had not been allowed in the meeting. However, a U.S. embassy officer and I had taken careful notes, identifying the questioners one by one, and writing down Humphrey's responses verbatim. We read these aloud to the small group of American media covering Humphrey's European mission. Several Labour MPs in separate interviews praised the vice president's performance. The next morning's *New York Times*, on page one, column eight, carried a full account of the meeting and characterized it as a diplomatic triumph. Humphrey might not have turned European opinion, I thought, but he had moved to more intellectually supportable discussion of the war. The overwhelmingly favorable media coverage, elsewhere as in London, showed Johnson that Humphrey had not lost his political fastball. Finally, and most importantly, it helped Humphrey regain his self-esteem, which had been damaged over the previous two years.

On our flight home we drafted a private report to Johnson summarizing reactions from European leaders on all issues covered, including Vietnam. It urged Johnson to have no illusions about the prospect of their support for anything but a negotiated peace and American withdrawal in the shortest time frame possible.

Anxious that there be no more Buffalo-tuxedo incidents on the European mission, I had made certain that Humphrey had ample time to review his briefing books, and had accompanied him to all meetings. I took the notes at the meetings and sent cables to Washington immediately thereafter. I did regular media briefings on board Air Force Two and on the ground. Our report to Johnson was delivered to him within an hour of Humphrey's return via helicopter to the White House South Lawn, where a delighted Johnson met Humphrey in a staged welcome home. I took great satisfaction that the trip had gone by the book and that Humphrey had performed superbly.

Yet, afterward, it became clear that it would be impossible to keep any

Humphrey activity fully troublefree. I had accompanied him to all his European meetings except for a meeting at the Vatican with the Pope. It was expected to be mainly ceremonial, and the vice president was accompanied by another aide who was Catholic. Ten days after our return to Washington, Humphrey materialized at my desk and emptied a briefcase on it. "Here are some leftover odds and ends from Europe," he said. "I've been carrying them around. Why don't you go through them?" Amid the items I found a Vatican envelope addressed to President Johnson. I opened it. It contained a letter, signed by the Pope, offering thoughts about a Vietnam peace settlement and his good offices in reaching it.

Johnson, I thought, would vent if he learned that Humphrey had for ten days misplaced a letter to him from the Pope. On the other hand, I thought, how was he to know that Humphrey had received and misplaced it? I placed the letter back in its original Vatican envelope, sealed it, marked it for priority handling, and dropped it into the White House mail system. We heard nothing about it and thus presumed that Johnson believed it had come to him through normal diplomatic mail.

Later in 1967, Humphrey undertook a three-week mission to ten African countries, carrying along several Democratic campaign contributors designated by Johnson, including Edgar Bronfman of Seagram's and his wife, Anne, Maurice Tempelsman, who had mineral interests in Africa, and Dwayne Andreas, chairman of Archer Daniels Midland and already a major Humphrey supporter and contributor. We were accompanied on the mission by a number of American journalists. I objected to the presence of the donors, but Humphrey did not want to raise the issue with Johnson. In order to soften the reporters' predictable suspicion about their involvement, we gave each donor a substantive research assignment: they were asked to submit written reports regarding various aspects of the African countries' policies, and they pursued independent daily schedules apart from the vice president's official meetings. At the end of the mission we submitted these reports as an annex to Humphrey's written report to the president. On the whole, their work was valuable.

During the mission we experienced one of the strangest incidents to mark Humphrey's vice presidency. Kenya had just emerged from a long period of anticolonial violence. The degree of Jomo Kenyatta's involvement with Mau Mau terrorists before becoming president of Kenya had been a subject of much speculation. President Kenyatta was to host an official luncheon in Nairobi for Humphrey, who was popular in Africa as an anticolonialist and domestic civil-rights advocate. At the luncheon I sat next to the economics minister, Tom Mboya, who often appeared on U.S. television interview shows; we were seated directly across from Kenyatta and Humphrey. I asked Mboya about his own political ambitions in Kenya. He laughed. "I have no future in Kenya," he said. "I belong to the wrong tribe. I have reached my limits here." Watching Kenyatta, I could see his beaming pride at serving as the vice president's host. He looked distinguished in a dark suit with a red rose in his left lapel.

A waiter bent over Kenyatta's shoulder to serve the soup course. As he did, soup spilled from the serving tureen onto Kenyatta's lapel and over the rose. Kenyatta stiffened. His eyes widened. He rose from his chair, pinned the waiter against the wall behind, and began smashing his fist into his face. Blood spurted from the waiter's face as he stood helplessly and took the blows. It was clear that Kenyatta did not mean to stop. The waiter fell back against the wall and sagged beneath Kenyatta's continuing blows. When Humphrey turned and saw what was happening, he looked almost physically ill with distress. The Kenyan vice president, Daniel Arap Moi, rushed from the end of the table, placed himself between Kenyatta and the waiter, and pulled the waiter to at least temporary safety out of the dining room.

Kenyatta reseated himself, wiping his suit with a napkin. Moi returned to his own chair. The rest of us, including Humphrey, were stunned and finished luncheon in robotic fashion. Afterward, we faced a practical problem. One of the other guests at the luncheon, serving as "pool" representative for the traveling American press, had been Anthony Astrachan, a foreign correspondent for the *Washington Post*. Three years earlier, Astrachan had done advance work in Humphrey's vice presidential campaign. Humphrey's press secretary, Norm Sherman, spoke with Astrachan, appealing to him to keep the matter private lest a diplomatic incident be precipitated. He did so but, before the African trip was over, other reporters somehow learned what had happened, as did the *Post*. It caused Astrachan trouble both with his newspaper and with his colleagues. Yet the matter remained private and never came to public view. A short time later, Mboya was killed in a Nairobi automobile accident. He had been correct in saying he had no future in Kenya.

Humphrey also was dispatched that year to South Korea to attend the presidential inauguration of Park Chung Hee. A far more important and pivotal mission took place in November 1967. Humphrey was assigned the task of representing the United States at the inaugurations in Saigon of South Vietnamese president Nguyen Van Thieu and vice president Nguyen Cao

Ky. As I planned the trip, I arranged that time be set aside for meetings with South Vietnamese dissidents and intellectuals, for inspection of economic-development projects in the countryside, and of course for meetings with American troops and their commanders.

We stopped en route to Saigon in Honolulu, where we had requested a briefing on the military situation as seen by CINCPAC (the Commander in Chief, Pacific). Yet the briefing, when it took place, consisted solely of film demonstrating supposed pinpoint bombing of North Vietnamese targets, accompanied by verbal arguments for its continuance. I was about to ask that we receive the comprehensive briefing we had requested, but Humphrey, reading my mind, grabbed my arm beneath the table to restrain me. He asked a few polite questions of his own and we quickly departed the briefing session.

We were joined on the final leg of the flight by Marine Colonel Herb Beckington, who had been Humphrey's vice presidential military aide for two years but who then was assigned as a civil affairs officer in the I Corps area in northern South Vietnam. During his months in Vietnam, Beckington had sent me a series of handwritten letters that generally painted a more pessimistic picture than what was in the official cables and reports. I had them typed and passed to Humphrey, who trusted Beckington.

Flying into Saigon, the vice president asked Beckington to give him a candid briefing. Beckington described pervasive South Vietnamese government corruption, popular support for the Vietcong, and the dubiousness of General William Westmoreland's "search and destroy" strategy, which was killing large numbers of Americans and Vietnamese while doing little to change the situation on the ground. An alternative "clear and hold" strategy, favored by many in Washington and in South Vietnam, would have concentrated on control of coastal and other population centers rather than sending American units to seek engagement with the enemy in the countryside. Villagers and their possessions were being evacuated from their homes in often remote areas and resettled in refugee camps. Even if American units won their battles with the Vietcong and North Vietnamese units, they could not occupy the territory, which quickly reverted to enemy control. There was nothing in Beckington's briefing that Humphrey had not read and heard often from other sources. Yet it had a strong effect on the vice president, who released pent-up feelings as our plane neared Saigon. "I'll be damned if I will be part of sending more American kids to die for these corrupt bastards!" Humphrey said, rising from his seat. "We've got to do something about this."

We spent time in I Corps as well as in other areas of operation. In one heartbreaking episode, Humphrey entered a Quonset hut outside a hospital, where our most grievously wounded troops were receiving intensive care. He spoke with each man and held his hand. Most, it was clear, would not make it. I walked through the general hospital wards, where eighteen- and nineteen-year-olds were missing limbs and seated in wheelchairs. Overwhelmed with depression, I left the wards and walked outside into the sunshine. I became aware of the presence of others. Perhaps fifty ambulatory GIs, some on crutches, stood in a circle around me, obviously looking for some news they could grasp. I had nothing I could tell them, certainly no pep talk. Humphrey was exiting the Quonset hut. As I walked over to meet him, I saw that he was grim and focused.

Things came to a head when Humphrey met with Ky and then with Thieu at the presidential palace in Saigon following their inaugurations. U.S. ambassador Ellsworth Bunker and I accompanied him. Humphrey connected easily with Ky, a former combat pilot, who told him he willingly would give his life for Vietnam but that his duties as vice president gave him little real power. Humphrey told him he was in a comparable position in the United States. Humphrey's meeting with Thieu took place in the president's ceremonial office. We Americans sat in chairs around a low coffee table while Thieu sat alone on a sofa. He wore a white linen suit and impassively smoked a Gauloise cigarette. The pack sat on the coffee table alongside an ashtray. After an exchange of pleasantries, Humphrey got quickly to business. He spoke more bluntly than Johnson would have wished.

It would be important, Humphrey said, for the South Vietnamese government to follow through on the pledges of reform contained in President Thieu's inaugural speech (which had been written by U.S. embassy staff). More importantly, he said, South Vietnam should soon take on greater responsibility for conduct of the war. "Mr. President," Humphrey said, "I must tell you that American public opinion and congressional opinion will not support American involvement at the level now existing. Your new government must not rely on us to sustain your economy or to do the bulk of the fighting." Thieu puffed his cigarette and responded as if he had not heard what Humphrey had said. "We have appreciated your help," he said, "but we also know that you must maintain your current levels of support for several years, and perhaps even increase them for a time."

Humphrey was taken aback. "Perhaps you did not understand me, Mr.

President," he said. "It will be impossible for us to sustain current levels of support." "Yes, yes," Thieu said, waving the hand holding his cigarette. Then he rose from the table, escorted us from his office, and that was it.

As we walked down the palace's front steps, Humphrey asked Bunker: "Was I too tough on him? I don't think he gets it." Bunker cleared his throat. "No," he said, "he needs to hear these things." At that moment a Vietcong mortar round struck an Australian embassy car not 100 yards from us.

We stopped in Malaysia and Indonesia before returning to Washington. On the day of our return, Humphrey submitted a report to Johnson that painted a cold picture of the situation on the ground and recommended a gradual phaseout of the U.S. involvement in Vietnam. It stressed the need for economic and social reforms in South Vietnam, the need for the Thieu-Ky government to establish positive relations with the new parliament, and the need for the United States to pare back both its military and its economic presences. It warned of "chaos and decomposition" if the new South Vietnamese government did not build a solid base of popular support. A day or two later Johnson asked Humphrey to give a verbal briefing to the Cabinet and invited congressional leaders. Before Humphrey could speak, Johnson passed him a handwritten note: "Hubert, keep it upbeat, keep it short, then sit down." He complied.

A short time after his return, Humphrey addressed the Grocery Manufacturers of America in New York. The speech made a careful assessment of the trade-offs implicit in the Vietnam involvement. On balance, it said, the risks of withdrawal appeared greater than the risks associated with maintaining the commitment. But it was far from a cheerleading speech. Audience response was sober and restrained. A few days later, a laudatory letter regarding the speech was received from an old Republican adversary of Humphrey's. It was the most responsible and careful discussion of the issue he had read, Richard Nixon said.

7

1968

Both public and internal pressures were driving Johnson toward a reexamination of Vietnam policy. The events we associate with 1968 really began in the middle of 1967.

Johnson received word that the federal budget deficit would be $28 billion, about twice that predicted only six months earlier. Johnson could not continue to wage war and also maintain the Great Society without seeking a tax increase. Humphrey and Arthur Okun, chairman of the president's Council of Economic Advisors, agreed in a luncheon discussion that Johnson simply could not escalate further in Vietnam and hope to hide the costs from voters and taxpayers.

After equivocating, Johnson went to the Congress in August to request a temporary personal and corporate tax surcharge of 10 percent. He also announced a plan to increase U.S. troop levels in Vietnam by 45,000, to 525,000. Representative Wilbur Mills, chairman of the House Ways and Means Committee, and Senator Russell Long, chairman of the Senate Finance Committee, both had doubts about a tax increase. Republican senators John Sherman Cooper and Clifford Case were angry about the plans for military escalation. So, in particular, was Democratic senator George McGovern, who described it as "a turning point." Representative Tip O'Neill of Massachusetts, a key House Democrat who later would be Speaker, declared the war unwinnable and asked for a U.S. withdrawal.

Johnson began grasping for a way out. He asked Robert McNamara and the Joint Chiefs of Staff to bring fresh military pressure on Hanoi, and at the same time explored both formal and informal means to get peace negotiations going. In late August he signaled to Hanoi that he was willing to stop aerial and naval bombardment of North Vietnam if Hanoi would talk in good faith. He temporarily suspended bombing in a ten-mile radius around Hanoi. But he got no response.

Late in November the Senate approved without dissent a resolution drafted by the majority leader, Mike Mansfield, to bring the Vietnam conflict to the

United Nations Security Council. Johnson nominally had supported the resolution. But he had no intention of asking the UN to intervene.

During this same period, Johnson told McNamara, Earle Wheeler (chairman of the Joint Chiefs), and General William Westmoreland that they should strike immediately whatever bombing targets they thought worthwhile, because it was clear U.S. opinion had turned against the bombing campaign. (The directive really was superfluous, given that everything on the target list in North Vietnam already had been hit twice over without reducing the flow of manpower and material into South Vietnam. Wider bombings and a naval blockade would have made a difference. But Johnson refused to allow them, fearing Soviet reaction.) At the end of the month Johnson informed McNamara—who he thought was becoming frayed and unstable—that he was to become president of the World Bank. He would be replaced as defense secretary by Washington, D.C., attorney Clark Clifford, a former aide to President Truman who had been a periodic counselor of Johnson's. Clifford was not a man compelled by idealism or moved by illusion. He had a strong sense of personal self-interest. He had no tie to previous policy and would shun association with failed ventures.

Late in 1967 I received a call from Jim Jones, the president's assistant, asking that I come immediately to the basement of the White House West Wing. I found myself in a group of perhaps thirty Johnson staff—only the half-dozen most senior were absent. President Johnson told us he had assembled us to thank us for our hard work. He then slid quickly into a story about how, as a young congressional staff member new to Washington, D.C., he had become seriously ill and lay in a Doctors Hospital room. He awoke in a feverish haze, he said, to see a sleeping man seated next to his bed, a cigarette smoldering in his hand. That man at his bedside, he said, was none other than the great representative Sam Rayburn of Texas, who was there because of his loyalty to Johnson's father. It was loyalty, Johnson said, that separated exceptional from ordinary people. It was loyalty that was called for in the difficult times of the moment. Disloyalty, on the other hand, was deplorable and easily recognized. (I thought of Johnson's velvet-glove, mailed-fist discussion two and a half years before in the Oval Office with Senator Church.) Then, all amiability, Johnson invited each of us to have an individual photograph taken with him. I received mine with a personal inscription a few days later. I suspected there was a reason I had been invited. My views and activities on Vietnam policy were well known, and someone probably had thought I needed a loyalty lecture to hold me, and perhaps Humphrey, in line. Nonetheless, I was pleased to receive the signed photograph and Johnson's appreciation.

Here I must digress to say that Johnson could at times be ferocious. Yet at no time in his presidency did I have any contact with him or with most of his closest staff that was not positive and professional. I resented the patronizing way in which Joseph Califano, McGeorge Bundy, and Walt Rostow sometimes treated the vice president and tried to avoid unnecessary contact with them. I was left out of some meetings at which Vietnam was the subject matter. But no one ever attempted to pressure or silence me.

As 1967 ended, polls indicated that about two-thirds of the American people were dissatisfied with Johnson's conduct of the war.

As Johnson's fortunes waned, so did Humphrey's. The vice presidency, which had seemed his best and perhaps only route to the presidency, now entrapped him and limited his political latitude. He was constrained on domestic policy as well. Following urban riots, he had said, in off-the-cuff remarks, that if his children were living in the conditions besetting many slum dwellers, he would lead a revolution himself. At a national mayors' conference in New Orleans he called for "a Marshall Plan for the cities." Johnson had chastised him both for seeming to condone violence and for promising a new federal program when the budget was in deficit.

Clifford, on becoming defense secretary, instituted a comprehensive A-to-Z review of Vietnam policy. We shared with him Humphrey's November report to Johnson. But he did not consult Humphrey. As press leaks made Clifford's review public, Clifford was made to appear the central figure in the reexamination. In the meantime, opposition to LBJ's Vietnam policy was building within the Democratic Party.

During this time, Allard Lowenstein, a former student intern in Humphrey's Senate office, was trying to recruit a challenger to President Johnson in the early Democratic presidential primaries. Senator Robert Kennedy had always held Johnson in not-so-private contempt, but when Lowenstein approached him, he declined—at least for that moment. In December 1967, Senator Eugene McCarthy took the plunge. As he did, I thought back to his petulant withdrawal three and a half years earlier from consideration as Johnson's vice presidential nominee, and wondered how much his candidacy might be based on a desire to pay back Johnson for that perceived slight. His candidacy immediately attracted college-age volunteers who began to flood into New Hampshire in anticipation of that state's presidential primary. McCarthy's campaign gained momentum after the North Vietnamese Tet offensive of January 30–31, which resulted in North Vietnamese military defeats but shocked Americans with its force and magnitude.

Johnson's and Humphrey's friend Jim Rowe and Postmaster General Larry O'Brien were scheduled to serve as heads of Johnson's 1968 reelection campaign. O'Brien already had drafted a campaign plan. (Johnson passed the original copy of the memo for comment to Humphrey, who in turn passed it to me to draft his response. While doing so, I managed to spill a full mug of coffee on O'Brien's original, drenching it thoroughly.) I knew that O'Brien, who had been a key campaign and legislative advisor to President Kennedy, would serve Johnson loyally. As O'Brien told me one evening, "Lyndon Johnson appointed me to the Cabinet. The Kennedys never did. I wouldn't abandon him for Robert Kennedy or anyone else." Some close to Johnson distrusted O'Brien, however. Rowe believed that Johnson was being dilatory in implementing O'Brien's plan, and that White House staff chief Marvin Watson and John Criswell, a Democratic National Committee official, were bypassing both O'Brien and himself in making campaign plans. He sent a letter to Johnson resigning his campaign position. He withdrew it only after being reassured by the president that he and O'Brien would be heeded.

I had come to regard Rowe as a mentor and often confided in him. Early in 1968, as McCarthy's candidacy gained momentum in New Hampshire, I told him, "I believe in Humphrey and will stick with him through all of this. But if I were new to politics or just out of college, I must tell you that my instincts would put me in New Hampshire working for McCarthy." "Me too," Rowe said.

The New Hampshire primary was held March 12. Only McCarthy's name was on the Democratic ballot. Johnson's was not and had to be written in. Johnson took 49.5 percent of the vote, McCarthy 42.4 percent. Yet McCarthy's showing had been a surprise—if Johnson was serious about reelection, he would have to win decisively the next primary, April 2 in Wisconsin.

On March 16, the situation became more complicated as Robert Kennedy changed his mind and announced his own candidacy for the Democratic nomination. McCarthy and his supporters were bitter, charging Kennedy with dividing peace forces and pursuing his own candidacy only after McCarthy had paved the way. (Friends of mine on Robert Kennedy's staff would tell me later that he had decided to challenge Johnson before the New Hampshire primary but thought it impractical to enter there at the last minute).

The president dispatched O'Brien to Wisconsin to make a quick situation analysis. In his report, which Johnson shared with Humphrey, O'Brien said that he had been unable to find enthusiasm for Johnson even in Milwaukee union halls, where support for Vietnam still was relatively strong. He had called meetings of LBJ supporters; only a handful had turned up. There was strong peace sentiment in Wisconsin. The Kennedy family was popular there, and McCarthy was from next-door Minnesota. If Johnson expected to carry the primary, he would have to throw people and resources into the breach right away. Johnson then decided that former governor Terry Sanford of North Carolina, a Southern progressive who had supported John F. Kennedy for president in 1960, should replace O'Brien as a campaign leader. On March 31 Watson and Rowe met with Sanford in the White House to discuss the upcoming campaign.

That same morning, Humphrey was preparing to depart for Mexico and the signing of the Treaty of Tlatelolco, which he had sponsored and which effectively barred nuclear proliferation in the Western Hemisphere. I normally would have gone to Humphrey's apartment in southwest Washington—he had moved from the former family home in Chevy Chase—armed him with his briefing papers, and then ridden with him to either National Airport or Andrews Air Force Base for the flight. On March 31, however, I was to meet him at the airport. Humphrey's wife, Muriel, would be joining him for the flight to Mexico City. My wife, Jean, who spoke Spanish, was to serve as Mrs. Humphrey's interpreter during the visit. (Jean's father, a Mexican citizen, had been invited to attend that evening's dinner at the U.S. ambassador's residence in honor of Mexican president Díaz Ordaz.) As Jean and I headed to the airport, a radio message crackled in our Secret Service car advising that President Johnson had just arrived at the Humphreys' apartment. This was completely unexpected. What was going on?

As we boarded the Air Force jet, I asked Muriel Humphrey why the president had come to their apartment. "Ask Hubert," she said. "He refuses to tell me. They talked privately in the bedroom." Humphrey, who normally confided everything, told me he would discuss the matter with me later. That evening in Mexico, following dinner, Humphrey unexpectedly asked President Díaz Ordaz if he would mind joining him in the ambassador's study to listen to a radio speech by President Johnson; Díaz Ordaz gracefully agreed.

I was surprised and thought it bad form that Humphrey would shift the focus from the Mexican president and U.S.–Mexican relations to a speech back in Washington by Johnson.

The speech was about Vietnam. As the conclusion neared, Humphrey moved close to the radio speaker. Then we heard Johnson announce that he would not seek reelection to the presidency. President Díaz Ordaz raised his eyebrows and said nothing. Muriel Humphrey was annoyed: "Hubert," she said, "why didn't you tell me? How could you?" Humphrey then explained that he had not known definitively what Johnson would say. Johnson had shown him two alternative endings to his speech—one renouncing his candidacy for reelection, a second announcing his intention to run—and had told him he was undecided as to which one he would deliver. He had instructed Humphrey to tune in and learn his decision. In the meantime, he was to say nothing about the matter to anyone, including Muriel.

Pounding began on the study door. A number of American reporters had accompanied us to Mexico City. They, too, had listened to Johnson's broadcast. But the transmission on their radio had been bad. Some had understood Johnson to say he was stepping down from the presidency immediately, making Humphrey president. Norm Sherman explained to them that this was not the case. Moreover, in answer to their next question, Humphrey had made no decision as to whether he would be become a 1968 presidential candidate himself.

Humphrey instructed that he wished to neither receive nor return any phone calls from the United States, a flood of which already had begun coming to the U.S. embassy switchboard. Above all, he did not wish to discuss his own possible candidacy with anyone. Bill Connell, the vice president's longtime administrative assistant, called me from Washington. Bill said that, no matter what the vice president's wishes, he intended to call Democratic, labor, and other leaders around the United States to request that they not commit to McCarthy's or Kennedy's candidacies until Humphrey's plans became firm. Even if he began calling immediately, he said, it would be difficult to hold some of them in place. He intended to leave an implication that Humphrey would run. I told Bill that I would not tell Humphrey, at least that night, that he was proceeding accordingly. Humphrey did return one phone call. It was from Margaret Truman Daniel, former president Truman's daughter, urging him to immediately declare his candidacy. He told her he had made no decision.

The political situation within the Democratic Party was Shakespearean. Its cast included an incumbent president, Johnson, who had been elected by a landslide four years earlier and then successfully enacted historic domestic legislation, only to be driven from office by his conduct of an unpopular war. Another character, Robert Kennedy, was the younger brother of the martyred president who had preceded the incumbent. He and Johnson disliked and distrusted each other. A third character, Eugene McCarthy, was a somewhat quixotic professorial type who viewed the other two with scorn. A fourth main character, Humphrey, had been leader of his party's liberal wing and, therefore, its likely standard-bearer on the war issue—except that he had forfeited the position by serving as Johnson's vice president. Humphrey, alone among the four, neither hated nor was hated by any of the other three.

Humphrey returned from Mexico City to a chaos of calls, meetings, press speculation, and pressure. Among other things, if he intended to seek the nomination—and enter presidential primary contests—he would have to meet filing deadlines in a number of states. Polling data showed Humphrey winning the nomination handily in a three-way matchup against Kennedy and McCarthy. But national polling data meant nothing. It was state-by-state polling data that mattered. In most states, Humphrey was the preferred candidate but no certain winner, depending on the dynamic of the three-way race as it evolved week by week.

O'Brien, following Johnson's withdrawal, quickly shifted to Robert Kennedy's campaign. Other Democrats began aligning themselves. Then, three days after Johnson's March 31 withdrawal, a surprise took place in Wisconsin. Johnson's and McCarthy's names both were on the presidential primary ballot. But, since Johnson had renounced a candidacy, McCarthy was expected to build on his New Hampshire momentum and gain a decisive victory. Kennedy had not yet gotten rolling, and Humphrey still was out of the game. McCarthy won with 56 percent of the vote. His defeat in New Hampshire had been narrow but had provided momentum. His victory in Wisconsin had been smaller than expected—expectations had worked against him. Then, on April 4, Martin Luther King was assassinated in Memphis. The nation was thrown into shock.

Johnson formally designated April 7 a national day of mourning. Humphrey flew in his Lear jet to a Long Island event to deliver a tribute to Reverend King. Humphrey, John Stewart (his legislative assistant and principal aide on the 1964 Civil Rights Act), Phil Zeidman (the Small Business Administration's general counsel, who had written the draft of the day's speech), and I had soft drinks in our hands as the plane began its return approach at twilight to National Airport. Sitting at the right windows of the plane, Stewart and I simultaneously shouted: "Look, over there!" Huge plumes of smoke were rising from the downtown area and from 14th Street. Flames could be seen. After the plane landed, we were hustled quickly into Humphrey's limousine, which sped back to the White House. All the way along the route, across Memorial Bridge, past the Lincoln Memorial, on curbs of streets leading to the White House back entrance, soldiers stood a few feet apart with fixed bayonets. No other citizens were in sight. When we entered the Executive Office Building we found that White House and vice presidential staff were being driven home in staff cars: the city was under curfew. Police, troops, and firefighters were struggling to restore order in neighborhoods beset by looting, fire, and violence. I phoned my family to make sure they were safe. Late that night I drove home, alone, up Massachusetts Avenue into our American University Park neighborhood. Mine was the only car on the road.

A few days later Humphrey was in Memphis to deliver a speech. While he spoke, Bill Welsh of the vice president's staff and I met privately with Jesse Epps and other leaders of the garbage workers' strike, which Martin Luther King had traveled to Memphis to support. They had not trusted local law enforcement, or even the Federal Bureau of Investigation, to hear what they had to say. They had good reason to believe, they said, that the Memphis Police Department had played an active role in the murder. They had names and specific information. After his speech, we told Humphrey about the garbage workers' allegations. He was not surprised. I was flying onward with Humphrey from Memphis, but Welsh said he would return to Washington and inform Attorney General Ramsey Clark promptly. (While writing this book, I checked with Welsh, long retired, to see what had happened in his meeting with Clark. Welsh, unfortunately, had forgotten the whole episode, including the Memphis meeting with the garbage workers, and could shed no light on it. I feel certain he contacted Clark as he said he would.)

Humphrey continued to temporize about a presidential candidacy. Iowa governor Harold Hughes and Vermont governor Phil Hoff both urged him to resign the vice presidency and thus free himself completely from his association with Johnson and the war policy. Others, including Bill Connell, thought it unwise to compete with McCarthy and Kennedy for peace votes.

A shift on the war also was likely to alienate Johnson, who, after all, still possessed the power of the incumbency.

Humphrey, who had spent much of his life pursuing the presidency, was strangely flat and detached as primary filing dates passed and a candidacy became more difficult. Finally, it was too late to file for any primaries, and if Humphrey were to run he would have to do it in states where caucuses and conventions chose national-convention delegates.

As days passed, Humphrey consulted supporters in person and by phone. After a meeting in mid-April with a half-dozen staff and friends in his office, Humphrey remained noncommittal. Afterward I commented to Max Kampelman that Humphrey's indecision amounted to a decision. "This is not easy for Humphrey," Kampelman said. "Maybe he shouldn't run. He has been hurt before when he ran for president. He'll let us know—or not."

At the end of every working day, no matter how late, Humphrey made it a practice to eat cheese and crackers and have a highball with whomever was still in his office at that hour. More often than not during that early-1968 period, his secretaries, Vi Williams and Marsha Sheppard, and I were the ones who ended his day with him. One late-April evening, Humphrey invited me to sit a while afterward. "I've got to make a decision about a presidential candidacy," he said. "It can't wait. Tell me what you think."

"It seems clear cut to me," I said. "You've wanted to be president for a long time. This probably is the best chance you will have. You have a certain vision of the country. The presidency is the best place to achieve it."

"At one time I would have said that too," Humphrey said. "And what you say about the presidency is true. But I have an intuitive feeling that bad things are going to keep happening. I feel them lying just ahead. I don't know what they are. But, if I run, I feel I'll be engulfed by them." Soon thereafter, Humphrey declared his candidacy in a beautifully fashioned statement drafted by Labor Secretary Willard Wirtz, a former speechwriter for Adlai Stevenson.

Humphrey's immediate task was to name his nominating-campaign leadership. O'Brien would have been a logical choice, but he had signed on with Robert Kennedy. Instead Humphrey named two cochairs. They were his friends and protégés, senators Walter Mondale of Minnesota and Fred Harris of Oklahoma. Both were young and liberal. Mondale was a longtime Humphrey loyalist; Harris had become close to Humphrey during the latter's years as vice president, and he shared Humphrey's optimistic, buoyant nature. Neither Mondale nor Harris could be labeled by critics as yes men for Johnson or the Vietnam war. But in naming them as operational heads of his campaign, Humphrey was breaking a prime rule of electoral politics: Never appoint a campaign manager who holds or seeks elective office. No matter how dedicated to the candidate, an active politician always will be torn between the candidate's interests and his or her own.

Humphrey had lost a month's time to McCarthy and Kennedy while he pondered a candidacy. He was not on primary ballots. He lacked money. It was imperative that his campaign proceed with energy and a sense of momentum. Mondale and Harris, however, were sitting senators who had to spend much of their time in their Hill offices. They began assembling a campaign organization deliberately. Humphrey—as well as Connell and I—quickly became impatient. Harris in particular objected to what he saw as Connell's refusal to defer to his and Mondale's roles as cochairs. I found myself in the role of middleman, fending off Mondale's and Harris's complaints. I explained that Connell was proceeding aggressively, in part, because they were moving slowly. Humphrey would not tell them how he felt, but I was telling them on his behalf.

The two senators saw politics as being essentially the pursuit of a candidate's public agenda, as did Humphrey. I generally shared that view. The candidate should stand up for ideas in which he believed. People and organizations would support or not support him accordingly. In an intraparty contest, however, one or more candidates may share many of the same ideas. In this instance, Humphrey, McCarthy, and Kennedy all were from the same branch of the Democratic family, although they differed by degree on the central issue of the war. Thus other factors had to come into play.

Connell believed, as he always had, that Humphrey's base of support in a nominating contest against McCarthy and Kennedy had to start with Southern and border-state Democrats, who were unlikely to support the other two, and with longstanding Humphrey supporters in organized labor and the civil-rights communities. Robert Kennedy would find support in the latter two communities, but McCarthy would find little. Mondale's and Harris's instincts and politics, however, led them to emphasize more greatly the competition for antiwar and liberal-activist support. Coincidentally, such an emphasis also served their own personal political interests. Humphrey later balanced their leadership by appointing Terry Sanford as chairman of a national citizens' committee that would work outside the formal nominating process to mobilize support among business, labor, academic, agriculture, and other constituencies. It would have its own communications and advertising budgets.

I accepted Connell's premise that Southern and border-state Democrats would be vital to Humphrey's nomination. Those delegates, along with minority and mainstream labor delegates, conceivably could outweigh the combined forces of McCarthy and Kennedy at the Chicago convention. But we could not hope to win the general election from that base. Richard Nixon or George Wallace would carry most Southern and border states. A winning Democratic electoral map would have to be essentially the same one that had brought JFK the presidency in 1960—states north of the Mason-Dixon Line, Pacific Coast states, and Texas. Those states could not be won without antiwar Democratic and independent votes.

A *Newsweek* magazine article during this period portrayed Humphrey's vice presidential staff as divided into two feuding factions. One, led by Connell, was said to support the Vietnam War and loyalty to Johnson. Another, supposedly led by me, was said to be more liberal and dovish. The article mischaracterized the situation: although there were disagreements on the staff, they were of degree. We were not in angry conflict. "I am a liberal, too," Connell once told me. "I want to end the war too." That was true.

I responded to Harris's and Mondale's cases of the slows by initiating the formation of a campaign issues and research operation and the appointment of a number of policy task forces that would develop independent Humphrey positions on international and domestic issues. The most important of these, of course, was to be the one on Vietnam. A number of people were part of the effort, including David Ginsburg, who had been staff director of the Kerner Commission (on domestic disorder); New Deal economist Bob Nathan; Zbigniew Brzezinski, whom I had recruited for the campaign from the State Department policy planning staff; and Harvard professor Samuel Huntington. John Rielly and Tom Hughes also participated actively. Humphrey asked me to monitor the work closely to ensure that it not only reflected his current views but took into account his dual role as presidential candidate and sitting vice president. He wanted to stake out an independent position, but at the same time not be perceived either by war critics or by the president as manipulating the war issue.

A few days after Humphrey's declaration of candidacy, I received a phone call from George Christian, the president's press secretary. "I am going to read you a statement which we intend to issue later today," Christian said. He then read aloud a text announcing that from that day forward Humphrey no longer would meet with the National Security Council or Cabinet. Nor would he participate in administration policy discussions relating to Vietnam or other foreign-policy issues. This reflected his new status as a presidential candidate. "Wait a minute, George," I said. "The vice president was elected by the American people. He serves in his job by statute. What if something were to happen to the president? Would it be appropriate that the vice president had been uninformed and was out of the loop? Did you know that Democrats have been in here urging Humphrey to resign the office and to break with Johnson? He has refused to do so because he feels he has a duty to serve as vice president. I don't think the statement is appropriate." After a moment Christian responded cheerfully: "Oh, if you don't want it, of course we won't do it."

No statement was issued, but over time the policy effectively was implemented. The range and number of cables reaching us dwindled. Humphrey was in fact not invited to attend executive-branch meetings he normally as vice president would have attended. After Humphrey's nomination that August in Chicago as Democratic presidential candidate, Johnson would keep him even further at arm's length by insisting that Republican nominee Richard Nixon and third-party candidate George Wallace join Humphrey on conference calls in which Johnson briefed them simultaneously on developments in Vietnam policy. We gathered information independently from friendly State Department and Central Intelligence Agency sources willing to share it. On one occasion, I flew overnight from the campaign to Washington to meet at his home with Bill Bundy, assistant secretary of state for Asian affairs, and examine cables LBJ had withheld.

McCarthy and Kennedy, competing in Democratic primaries, were gaining the lion's share of media attention in the nominating race. However, Humphrey's overall poll ratings were holding up. State caucuses and conventions remained far more numerous then than primaries. While McCarthy and Kennedy were dividing delegates elected in primaries, Humphrey was winning the non-primary states decisively. Robert Kennedy had initially surged ahead of McCarthy in the competition for primary-elected delegates, but McCarthy had broken his momentum with a May victory in the Oregon primary. Humphrey's overall delegate lead was substantial Then, on June 5, the country was to receive yet another shock.

The California Democratic primary, the last and biggest in the presidential nominating process, was to be held on that date. Humphrey on that day was campaigning in several states and time zones. Finally, that evening, we were riding in a car from the Colorado Springs airport to overnight at the Air Force Academy, where Humphrey was to deliver the commencement speech the following morning. The dashboard lights provided sharp relief to the darkness in and outside the car. "What are you thinking about tonight's California primary?" I asked Humphrey, presuming he would answer that he wanted a McCarthy victory to slow the stronger contender, Kennedy. "I want Bobby Kennedy to win as decisively as possible," Humphrey said. "I want it to be so one-sided that McCarthy will be driven from the race entirely." "Bobby Kennedy and I understand each other," he went on. "We've talked privately on a couple occasions you don't know about. If I am nominated, he'll campaign for me without reservation. If something should happen so that he's nominated, I'll campaign for him. But, if McCarthy stays in the game, he'll damage both of us. I know Gene and I have affection for him. But he's a spoiler. I want him gone tonight."

We arrived at the vice president's guest cottage on the Academy grounds. Humphrey asked for a highball and turned on the television set to watch the California returns. I went to bed. What seemed a split second later, David Gartner, Humphrey's personal assistant, shook me awake. "Humphrey says to get up," he said. "Robert Kennedy has been shot!"

Almost immediately Humphrey received phone calls from Pierre Salinger and Steven Smith, who were with Kennedy at the Ambassador Hotel in Los Angeles. Kennedy was gravely wounded, they reported, but still alive. Could Humphrey arrange immediate military air transportation to Los Angeles for a Boston neurosurgeon who might be able to save him? Humphrey contacted Air Force brass who were present at the Academy for the next morning's speech. He gave them the doctor's name and phone number and said the doctor was standing by for instructions. Yes, they said, they would provide the transportation immediately. Five minutes later, however, Humphrey received another phone call. The White House had refused to approve Humphrey's request for the aircraft. It would not be available.

I neither made nor received the calls regarding the aircraft; Humphrey and Gartner were the only persons involved. I witnessed their ends of the conversation, however. Humphrey rose and went briefly to his bedroom after receiving the news about the cancelled aircraft. Observing his body language, I could see that he was humiliated and ashamed. The Kennedy family arranged the neurosurgeon's flight on their own. After examining Kennedy, he reported the situation hopeless.

Humphrey, understandably, was as dispirited as he had been after Martin Luther King's assassination. Moreover, we had no idea whether Kennedy's killing might be part of a larger scheme in which Humphrey, McCarthy, and perhaps others might also be targets. Early the next morning I informed Air Force Secretary Harold Brown that the vice president would be unable to deliver the commencement speech and would return immediately to Washington. Brown and several Air Force generals came to Humphrey's cottage door to appeal the decision. We left quickly and sat in silence during the flight back to Washington. The period between Robert Kennedy's murder and the August 27 Democratic convention in Chicago was painful for the country, for the Democratic Party, and for the principal actors in the drama. Humphrey had no heart for further campaigning, and for the most part remained in Washington. A few days after Kennedy's death, McCarthy called on Humphrey in his Executive Office Building office. Immediately after the meeting, Humphrey summoned me and told me what had happened. McCarthy, he said, had told him that he wanted a graceful exit route from the campaign but needed Humphrey's help to accomplish it. His supporters, he said, would denounce him if he withdrew his candidacy without gaining concessions on the Vietnam issue that motivated them. Could Humphrey make one or two symbolic concessions on Vietnam which he (McCarthy) could use to justify his withdrawal? They had come to no agreement, Humphrey said, and he found it difficult to see how they could. I told Humphrey it was an offer he should not lightly refuse. If McCarthy were to formally withdraw from the nominating race and endorse Humphrey, it would be worth some concessions on Humphrey's part. After all, there were several places where he could move toward McCarthy— perhaps even informing Johnson beforehand that he was doing it to bring Democrats together behind ongoing Johnson peace initiatives. Humphrey thought I was being wishful in that regard and that Johnson would be hostile toward any perceived concession to McCarthy. Shortly after the meeting, McCarthy left on vacation until the eve of the Democratic convention.

In later years I found typed notes of the McCarthy meeting, dictated by Humphrey during the same period, which painted a different picture of the discussion than what he had told me. His written version made it appear that McCarthy had delivered what amounted to ultimatums, which Humphrey felt compelled to reject. My instinct is that the verbal report Humphrey gave me, just after McCarthy had departed, more closely reflected reality than the version he later dictated. Humphrey was straightforward. His differing versions of the meeting remain puzzling to me. (McCarthy, preparing his own files, asked in 2004 for my own recollections of the encounter, which I related to him as above.)

At the time of Robert Kennedy's death, Humphrey had almost enough delegate strength to clinch the nomination. Kennedy's supporters had conceded as much to us. Senator Ted Kennedy and key Kennedy operatives had gone to the vital Pennsylvania caucuses, just before the California primary, and seen Humphrey forces, led by Mondale and Harris, win a decisive victory. Yet, with Kennedy's death, the myth began to spread that he, not Humphrey, had been on the verge of nomination when Sirhan Sirhan raised his pistol in the Ambassador Hotel. McCarthy had suspended his campaign. Humphrey, going into the Chicago convention, was in the uncomfortable position of having no real opposition for the nomination but facing unfocused anger from antiwar forces.

It also was clear, in the weeks prior to the convention, that organized attempts would be made to provoke violence on the streets of Chicago with the aim of radicalizing opposition to the Vietnam War and to Humphrey's nomination. I read regular FBI and Secret Service reports citing names of the organizers, their sources of funding, and their plans for Chicago. Quite obviously, government informers had infiltrated the groups.

It remained a high priority for Humphrey to issue an independent Vietnam statement prior to the convention. Informal meetings were taking place in which we passed the word to former Kennedy and McCarthy supporters that Humphrey was prepared to embrace a Democratic platform that made a strong statement for peace—just so long as it did not contain provisions for a unilateral U.S. withdrawal or imposition of a coalition government on Saigon. But the platform process, we knew, could be unpredictable. We would do best by issuing a definitive Humphrey position well in advance of Chicago.

Our Vietnam policy task force had been meeting regularly since May. It had prepared several working versions of a policy paper, which I carried with me in my briefcase. Humphrey gave his general blessing to the exercise. In the meantime, he was encouraged by what he regarded as Johnson's good-faith efforts to reach a negotiated settlement with Hanoi. Peace in Vietnam would, of course, remove the issue from the campaign year and allow Humphrey to run from a position of strength against his old adversary, Richard Nixon, in the general election. In March and April, General Creighton Abrams, the commander of our forces in Vietnam, had ordered record numbers of search-and-destroy missions, resulting in high American casualties.

These had heightened domestic dissent. Then, in July, in the in-between period leading to the Democratic convention, Johnson ordered renewed B-52 bombing along North Vietnamese infiltration routes north of the demilitarized zone between North and South Vietnam. The volume of bombs dropped was double that of the year before. This, too, inflamed antiwar activists. But the increased military pressure on Hanoi, we felt, was intended to strengthen the hand of U.S. negotiators at the Paris peace talks that had begun in May. Perhaps Johnson could bring peace quickly. That is what he had said he wanted to do when he withdrew his own presidential candidacy on March 31.

Our campaign Vietnam task force completed a final draft in June of what it considered a worthy independent statement for Humphrey. It was in many ways a restatement of the message Humphrey had carried months before to South Vietnamese president Thieu at his inaugural and in his report afterward to Johnson. It proposed a reduction in American forces and overall presence in Vietnam. It suggested reciprocal steps by both sides that could reduce the level of conflict. It suggested that, if North Vietnam showed good faith, bombing of North Vietnam might be suspended. It did not propose a unilateral U.S. withdrawal from the country or the imposition of a new regime on Saigon. It was, however, an unmistakably more accommodating posture on the war than that of Johnson. And it would be seen as such by any objective analyst. Humphrey asked me to edit it. Then he edited it. Mondale and Harris saw it. Finally, at the task force's urging, Humphrey agreed that he would present the document to Johnson and express his intention to issue it promptly. He would explain that he continued to support Johnson's efforts toward peace, but that, as a presidential candidate in his own right, he had an obligation to tell the party and country what he would do about Vietnam if elected.

Humphrey requested a late-afternoon appointment with Johnson. I promised task force members that I would inform them of the result. They should stand by for a possible meeting the next morning to discuss text changes that might be indicated. Humphrey put the report in a brown envelope, walked across Executive Avenue to the White House West Wing, and entered the basement entrance. I expected the meeting to last an hour or so. But twilight soon turned to darkness. Hours passed. Our vice presidential offices emptied. I sat alone awaiting Humphrey's return. Finally, he came back. He went directly to his bathroom, left the door open, and began furiously washing his hands. (It was his habit, when stressed, to engage in energetic cleaning and hand-washing. Once, at his Chevy Chase home, I had seen him remove canned goods from a shelf and dust both the cans and the shelf for more than an hour. It was a holdover, old friends said, from his duties cleaning the family's South Dakota drugstore shelves and fixtures.) "What happened?" I asked him. "Lyndon and Lady Bird had friends with them in the mansion and we never got a chance to discuss the Vietnam statement," Humphrey said. "I'll try again later."

"You mean you were there for hours and never discussed the matter?" I said. Humphrey was a poor liar. "No," he said, "I'll tell you what happened. Johnson said he was doing his best to negotiate a peace. He thought my paper would complicate and confuse the negotiations. In fact, he told me that it would endanger American troops like his son-in-law [Marine Captain Chuck Robb] and cost lives. I would have their blood on my hands. He would denounce me publicly for playing politics with peace." "Did you believe him?" I asked. "I had to believe him," Humphrey said. Then he paused. "You know," he said, "I've eaten so much of Johnson's shit in this job that I've grown to like the taste of it." "Don't worry," he said, "I will try later."

It was not a report I could pass along to the Vietnam task force members. I immediately called two I knew to be habitual leakers to the media. I passed along Humphrey's story that Johnson was in the presence of others and that the needed discussion had not taken place. Sure enough, the *New York Times* carried an item the next morning attributing to unnamed sources the report that Humphrey was preparing an independent statement on Vietnam but had not yet discussed it with Johnson.

The Paris peace negotiations were not progressing as we had hoped. North Vietnamese forces went on the offensive in South Vietnam. President Johnson reciprocated. Thus, moving toward the August 27 Democratic convention, the chances of a peaceful settlement seemed to be diminishing.

A week before the convention, Tom Finney, a senior McCarthy campaign advisor, called me to ask: "Is McCarthy going to be Humphrey's running mate?" "Highly unlikely," I told him. "Then the two of them should meet as soon as possible," Finney said. Humphrey was at his apartment in southwest Washington. We arranged that McCarthy would meet him there immediately.

Humphrey related afterward that McCarthy, who had returned from his vacation, told him, as he had in their earlier discussion after Robert Kennedy's death, that his supporters would not understand an immediate McCarthy endorsement of Humphrey either before or during the Chicago convention.

However, after a very brief period, McCarthy would make an endorsement and do whatever he could to aid Humphrey's campaign.

In the meantime, off to the side, we were working with McCarthy and Kennedy supporters to draft a Democratic platform plank on Vietnam behind which the party could unify. Ted Sorensen, an ex–John F. Kennedy aide, was participating constructively in the drafting. Richard Goodwin, representing McCarthy, was being more difficult. Goodwin, also a former JFK aide, had stayed as a speechwriter in the Johnson White House but had later been fired by Johnson. He had enlisted with the McCarthy campaign prior to the New Hampshire primary, shifted to Robert Kennedy's campaign after his entry into the race, and then returned to McCarthy after Kennedy's assassination. Although McCarthy seemed willing to be accommodating on the plank, Goodwin did not. On the other side of the issue, Secretary of State Dean Rusk and NSC advisor Walt Rostow were being kept abreast of the drafting process. (Though Rusk was a full-blown Vietnam hawk, his State Department executive secretary, Ben Read, was a strong supporter of Humphrey's and helped us within the administration as much as he could.)

Just before the convention, Humphrey flew to the LBJ Ranch to meet with Johnson. This was the only time over a two-year period when I did not accompany Humphrey on a trip or to a vital meeting. Instead, he was accompanied by Bill Connell, a Texan himself, who was well regarded by Texans in the White House. Bill had not lived in Texas for years, but in the presence of the Johnson staff he reverted to a Texas drawl. We often laughed together about it.

Before their departure, I gave Humphrey the final, updated draft of our Vietnam task force statement. We discussed the fact that negotiations for a peace plank might or might not bear fruit prior to Chicago. The best course for Humphrey would be to issue his own preemptive statement prior to the convention, thus letting him define the terms of reference on the issue. He said he would raise the matter again with Johnson.

I joined Humphrey and Connell on the vice president's aircraft in the Midwest after the LBJ Ranch meeting. Neither would tell me what had transpired. Humphrey was tight-lipped and pretended to be busy reviewing papers. The omens were not auspicious as we arrived in Chicago for the convention itself. Combat in Vietnam had intensified. Organized demonstrators were gathered in Grant Park and elsewhere in Chicago. As he often did when he felt nervous and insecure, Humphrey had asked at least a dozen friends and supporters to submit proposed drafts of an acceptance speech.

Humphrey was met at the airport by Chicago mayor Richard Daley. Humphrey, at heart a populist reformer, was always uncomfortable around machine politicians like Daley. The mayor had also met us on an earlier visit to Chicago, a few weeks before. Before leaving the plane, Humphrey had asked: "What on earth should I say to Mayor Daley?" "Why don't you let him speak first?" I said. "I suspect he may have an agenda." Indeed he did. The vice president was in charge of the administration's summer-jobs program, intended to help big cities keep young people constructively occupied and out of trouble. Within sixty seconds, Daley asked Humphrey: "Mr. Vice President, how much money can Chicago expect for the summer jobs program?" Humphrey responded: "How much do you need, Mr. Mayor?" I pulled out my notebook and took down the details of Daley's request.

As we arrived at the Conrad Hilton Hotel on Michigan Avenue, we found Chicago police much in evidence. Knowing of the danger of organized violence, Daley had requested that federal troops be sent to Chicago. When he could not get a definite commitment, he had denounced Attorney General Ramsey Clark and declared that Chicago police would act as necessary to maintain order. We also found in evidence several representatives of the Johnson White House, including Marvin Watson and Under Secretary of Agriculture Charles Murphy, who had been sent by Johnson to monitor and, if necessary, become involved in the platform process. Johnson had renounced his candidacy for reelection, and yet his representatives were telling reporters that he might change his mind and run after all. Senator Ted Kennedy had assured Humphrey that he would support his candidacy. Nonetheless, Kennedy representatives in Chicago were telling media that he might be open to a draft supported by, among others, Mayor Daley (later, Kennedy would tell me he had little idea of the things being said and done in Chicago in his name).

The Johnson representatives were determined to control the convention, even though Johnson's vice president was its putative nominee. Watson told Humphrey officiously that Johnson expected him to toe the line on Vietnam policy. Johnson then called Humphrey to reinforce the message. Johnson also intervened directly in the platform process. We had worked out with peace advocates a Vietnam plank to which neither Rusk nor Rostow had objected. Johnson, however, objected. His allies controlled the platform committee and would block it. McGovern, serving as standard-bearer for former Robert Kennedy supporters, and McCarthy then drew up their own peace plank, which, predictably, was rejected by a two-to-one margin in the LBJ-controlled platform committee. The convention as a whole rejected the minority plank by a 60–40 margin. The majority plank, which was adopted, was Johnson's. But the media treated it as if it were Humphrey's. We were paying the price for not having previously declared our own position.

Looking backward, the convention seems a surrealistic blur. In the streets, several thousands of demonstrators confronted and fought with Chicago police. Some carried Vietcong flags and were there to provoke violence. A majority were McCarthy supporters and other young peace activists caught in the melee. Police indiscriminately arrested all. The smell of tear gas reached to Humphrey's headquarters in a suite on the thirty-second floor. So did profane chants denouncing Johnson and Humphrey. I went to the lobby, intending to witness events from street level. I took one step beyond the transom overhanging the sidewalk and was seized by a policeman. I broke his grasp. Ashtrays and glasses were being thrown from upper floors on both police and demonstrators below. Shards of glass flew up all around. Police nightsticks were flailing. I saw one bystander, a woman, thrown headfirst into a stairwell outside the hotel, by a man not in uniform. I quickly retreated to the lobby, which was filled with wafting tear gas we had only caught whiffs of upstairs. Back in the thirty-second-floor suite, Norm Sherman told me that some of the glassware being thrown into the street was coming from McCarthy's suites a few floors below. A number of McCarthy workers and volunteers had been badly beaten in the streets and were being treated and bandaged there. Sherman and I went to the McCarthy floor and spoke with some of the injured volunteers.

On the convention floor, delegates were outraged at the street violence. Some of them, and media too, alleged that Mayor Daley's police were forcing Humphrey's nomination and Humphrey's Vietnam plank down the throats of the convention. Humphrey was unsure whether Daley even supported his nomination. And the platform plank was Johnson's rather than his own. Senator Abe Ribicoff, an old Humphrey friend, placed in presidential nomination another old friend, McGovern, stating that "with George McGovern we wouldn't have Gestapo tactics on the streets of Chicago." On the convention floor, one speaker after another was rising to denounce Johnson, Humphrey, and the war. Daley, Texas governor John Connally, an LBJ stalwart, and others were denouncing the demonstrators and peace advocates. No one was making Humphrey's case.

I rushed from the Hilton to the convention hall. I urged Mondale, Harris, and other high-profile Humphrey supporters onto the floor to make Humphrey's case, then urged them back again. I grabbed some by their jackets and literally pushed them toward floor cameras. Chaos reigned in the streets and in the hall. Voters watching on national television could only conclude that Democrats and chaos were indistinguishable.

When I returned to the hotel, Bill Welsh asked me to meet with Deputy Attorney General Warren Christopher, who was observing events on behalf of Attorney General Clark. Christopher would later become a friend with whom I would work closely. Christopher declared that the Chicago police were completely out of control. He used the words "police riot." He urged that Humphrey immediately and publicly denounce the actions of Mayor Daley and his police. I told him Humphrey had no authority in the matter. Daley commanded the police force. Had Christopher considered asking his boss, Ramsey Clark, or their boss, President Johnson, to make a statement on the matter? They had federal authority. The vice president was in a terrible in-between position in which he held no power and in which anything he said would be misunderstood or meaningless.

Connell was doing his best to hold Southern, border-state, and labor delegates in line. Governor Buford Ellington of Tennessee, a courtly supporter of Humphrey's nomination, approached me with a request that he and other Southern governors be allowed to meet with Humphrey either before or just after his prospective nomination. I watched impatiently in the suite as Humphrey friends and advisors sat around a table writing and rewriting an acceptance-speech draft I knew would never be delivered. Willard Wirtz, Bill Moyers, Jack Valenti, Bob Nathan, and others had submitted their own suggested drafts. Various components were being accepted and rejected by the ad hoc group led by Wirtz. As the evening wore on, the convention finally began its roll-call vote. Humphrey, despite all, was nominated.

Two hours earlier the speech-drafting group had given me its final draft. It read like the committee product it was. I edited it, had it typed, and gave it to Humphrey. Then, barely an hour before his departure to the hall to accept the nomination, I heard what I expected. Humphrey shouted for me to come immediately to his bedroom. He handed me the draft, asked me to rewrite it from scratch, and asked that I return it to him as soon as possible. It was too late to start from scratch. I edited and rewrote the committee product, but in the end the speech remained less coherent and strong than it should have been. It did reflect Humphrey's instinct toward forgiveness and reconciliation ("Neither vindication nor repudiation will bring peace [in Vietnam] or be worthy of our country"). He asked that the text of St. Francis of Assisi's prayer be included in the speech. I thought it inappropriate and dissuaded him. Rather than riding with him to the convention hall, I stayed behind in the Hilton to watch the speech as the American people would. My friend John Stewart and I settled back in easy chairs in front of the television in the now-empty suite and poured ourselves drinks. As speeches were made on Humphrey's behalf, both CBS and NBC chose not to televise them, but instead showed footage of street rioting from the previous day, leaving a false impression that Humphrey was being nominated inside the hall while protestors were being beaten outside. Finally Humphrey took the podium.

The atmosphere in the hall, as in the country, was subdued. It was time for a sober examination by the candidate and his party of what lay ahead. However, after every other line of the speech, a band near the podium would blare noisily as if at a pep rally. Stewart and I gritted our teeth. I ran to the nearest Signal Corps phone and asked to be connected to the conductor at the podium. "Stop the damn music!" I shouted. "Keep quiet until the speech is over." "Who is this?" he said. I said the first thing that came into my head: "This is the man who will lift your Musicians Union card." The music stopped. Then Stewart and I were surprised again. We had heard Humphrey relent and agree to remove St. Francis's prayer from the speech. But there he was, reciting it. En route to the hall, we found out, Humphrey had asked Gartner to call the Chicago Public Library, take down the text of the prayer, and insert it in the speech.

When Humphrey returned to the Hilton, we proceeded with the Southern governors' meeting. The governors sat in a semicircle around the room. Connell and I joined Humphrey, as did Larry O'Brien, who would replace Mondale and Harris in running the general-election campaign. Ellington thanked the vice president for agreeing to the meeting, then quickly turned things over to Governor Connally, who was to be spokesman. "Mr. Vice President," he said, "our delegations all supported your nomination, even though you have not always been a popular figure in our states. We believe we made the difference for you. We also believe we can make the difference for you in the general election. To do this, we believe you will need a running mate from our part of the country." Humphrey asked the other governors their views on a running mate. They echoed Connally's. Most recommended Connally as the running mate; no other names were mentioned. O'Brien, who had just come on board, said he thought the running mate should be "someone who knows working people and can build a bridge between union members and peace voters, someone from an industrial state or perhaps from New England, perhaps someone who is Catholic and understands ethnic politics. He need not necessarily hold elective office." Whereupon O'Brien rose and exited the room, saying he did not want his presence to inhibit discussion. Humphrey looked over at me. O'Brien, we both thought, was suggesting himself.

Then Humphrey spoke: "I am thinking of a running mate you will like— Senator Ed Muskie of Maine." Dead silence. Muskie, the governors were thinking, comes from a small state with few electoral votes and is completely unknown in our region. Connally spoke again: "I would offer another suggestion, if you are going in that direction instead of the one we recommend. It is Cyrus Vance, our Vietnam peace negotiator in Paris. I served with Cy in the Defense Department and he is a fine public servant, although he has not held elective office." Humphrey quickly rose, thanked the governors for their support, and left the room. Connell remained behind to stroke the disappointed governors. As we walked back toward Humphrey's suite, the vice president said: "Cy Vance. Where did that come from? And Connally would be the last man I would trust as my running mate. Didn't he know that? And what about O'Brien? What next?" (Several years later I would tell Vance the story of Connally recommending him as Humphrey's running mate. He was astounded; it was the first he had heard of it.)

Back in the suite, a small group of friends and supporters had gathered to celebrate Humphrey's nomination. But it was not the joyful occasion one might have expected. The strife and disorder had saddened all of us. Voices were hushed. Arthur Krim, a film producer and longtime friend of Johnson, the Kennedys, and Humphrey, introduced to me his guest, a young crew-cut actor, whom he said had supported Robert Kennedy and would like to support Humphrey. It was Warren Beatty, who would become a good friend and collaborator in future political causes. I was told that visitors were asking for me down the corridor. They were Fred Dutton and Charles Guggenheim, who had been strong Robert Kennedy supporters and now offered to help however they could and to enlist others. But McCarthy had not been heard from. Nor had many other Democrats whose support would be vital in the fall campaign. We had no illusions that evening about the uphill task Humphrey faced in the general election. The Democratic Party was divided. The late-August convention, the latest ever held by a major party, left us with little time to organize and raise money. Division over Vietnam was, if anything, worse than it had been before the convention. We also knew that moderate and independent voters must have been offended and repelled by the general turbulence surrounding the convention. Humphrey had the nomination he always had sought. But the presidency seemed light years away.

Humphrey's next task was to choose his running mate. He had told the Southern governors he was thinking of Muskie. But, contrary to the impression he left with them, his decision had not been made. Had Humphrey gained the nomination from his old liberal base in the party, it might have made sense for him to select a Southern running mate, as John F. Kennedy had selected Johnson. We knew that Humphrey, most of all, would want someone he regarded as fully qualified for the office and with whom he could be comfortable as president. He certainly would not want a Vietnam hawk. His ideal running mate would be one who could help unify the party and also appeal to independent voters. With former Alabama governor George Wallace in the race as a third-party candidate, Humphrey also needed to consider running mates who could blunt Wallace's populist appeal. There was no single person who filled all those bills.

A number of people had campaigned for the job. Connally had been quickly rejected. Senator Fred Harris, who had cochaired Humphrey's nominating campaign, badly wanted to be his running mate. Governor Richard Hughes of New Jersey also had lobbied for the job and had gone so far as to prepare a printed brochure, which he gave to us. An intermediary had suggested that New York governor Nelson Rockefeller, a friend of Humphrey's, might entertain a crossover from his own Republican Party to join Humphrey's ticket. Sargent Shriver, then serving as U.S. ambassador to France, had sent a handwritten letter to Humphrey asking to be considered, and suggesting that his wife, Eunice Kennedy Shriver, would be prepared to help with campaign financing. Humphrey had broached the job with Senator Ted Kennedy, who said he could not entertain a candidacy in 1968 but would support Humphrey. The two had been friends ever since Kennedy, then a University of Virginia Law School student, had prevailed on Senator Humphrey to visit Charlottesville and address a law forum. Humphrey and Muskie had been friends in the Senate, although not close friends. During the course of the nominating campaign they had met several times, and Humphrey had been impressed with Muskie's presence and common sense. Like Shriver, Muskie was Catholic.

Humphrey retired to an anteroom for a rubdown. Connell, Kampelman, and I stood while he lay face down on the massage table. Humphrey asked each of us our personal preference for the job. Connell suggested that Harris might be a good fit. He had gotten crosswise with Harris on occasion during the nominating campaign, so I was surprised by his recommendation. Kampelman suggested Shriver, who later would join his law firm. I favored Muskie, mainly because I thought his calm persona would be a good balance to Humphrey's hotter style. We knew that Humphrey liked and respected all three men and that all had substantive views similar to his. But he gave us no indication of his thoughts and went to bed.

At seven the next morning I entered Humphrey's bedroom as I always did, to start him on his day and discuss its agenda. I expected to find him still asleep. He was a notorious night owl. Instead, Humphrey was sitting upright in bed, wide awake. He immediately began speaking as if continuing the conversation of the night before. "Had any more ideas about the vice presidential candidate?" he asked. "Do you still like Muskie?" "Yes I do," I said, "but you also might want to consider Gene McCarthy. Traditionally, the vice presidential candidate has been the runner-up for the presidential nomination. You also need someone to help unify the party. You both are from Minnesota, but McCarthy could change his official residence to New York; we've researched it." Humphrey quickly dismissed the notion. "McCarthy is out of the question," he said. "The job is too important for that." "Frankly," he said, "I've leaned to Muskie for quite some time. Let's get him up here and I'll make him the offer."

I dialed Muskie's room in the Hilton. I kept getting a busy signal. I feared that any moment someone else would enter the room and try to persuade Humphrey to reopen the issue. I walked through the suite toward the elevators. I would simply go to Muskie's room. In the hallway I encountered Bill Welsh, who had served as Senator Phil Hart's administrative assistant before joining Humphrey's staff. He had worked with Muskie and admired him. He asked if Humphrey had made a decision on his running mate. I told him it was Muskie and that, in fact, I was heading to his room. Welsh joined me. As we approached the elevators, we found a large number of reporters standing by. As we boarded an elevator, they all jumped on behind us. As the doors closed, Welsh and I stepped back into the foyer. The elevator took the reporters downward without us. We took a freight elevator down. When we knocked on Muskie's door, he answered. He was putting cuff links into his shirt. When he saw us standing there, he dropped the cuff links. His aides and staff, Don Nichol, George Mitchell, and Nordy Hoffman, let out a cheer and shook our hands. We could be there for only one reason. In the background, Jane Muskie was on the phone. "Before we seal the deal," Muskie said, "I want to have a good private talk with Hubert." We accompanied him to Humphrey's suite.

Since Welsh and I had left, several of the vice president's friends and supporters had indeed gone into his room and urged him to reopen his running-mate decision. I gave Muskie some coffee and the morning newspapers and told him Humphrey would be with him shortly. I then returned to Humphrey's room. He signaled that I should leave and not be a part of the meeting. Then, a half hour later, Humphrey emerged, welcomed Muskie warmly, and took him aside for a private discussion. A short while later they reemerged, arms around each other's shoulders, smiling broadly. The Humphrey-Muskie partnership would have some rocky moments, but it proved to be quite effective.

8

A NEAR MISS

The Humphrey-Muskie campaign spent the first part of September 1968 pulling the Democratic Party together. On the campaign trail, almost as much time was spent in private meetings with party leaders as in public outreach. An Associated Press story, written from Houston, stated that "Vice President Humphrey spent an active day here in rooms and suites at the Rice Hotel."

Humphrey got a badly needed emotional lift during this period from a national black ministers' meeting convened at Cobo Hall in Detroit, arranged by staff member Ofield Dukes. All Protestant denominations were represented. Wherever we went, the Vietnam issue was a presence. Not on this day at Cobo, however. One speaker after another pledged to work intensely until election day on Humphrey's behalf. Humphrey said he would work twenty-four hours a day in the presidency for the social-justice agenda so close to his heart. At the end, everyone gathered on the stage with joined arms, swaying together and singing, "Like a tree that stands in the water, we shall not be moved!" As we left Cobo in Humphrey's car, he said: "If I win the election, I'll never forget this day. I'll be the best president black Americans ever had." Both of us were still wiping our eyes. The 1965 Voting Rights Act had empowered black voters, and they turned out in record numbers in November 1968, almost all for Humphrey.

It became clear, however, that unity would be impossible until Humphrey gave the party's peace wing reason to return to the fold. George McGovern and most former Robert Kennedy supporters had rallied immediately to Humphrey. But in the wake of the Chicago chaos, Eugene McCarthy and many of his supporters held back their support. In the meantime, we were surprised by the strength being shown by George Wallace's third-party campaign, not only in the South but also among traditionally Democratic blue-collar voters in northern industrial states. Wallace's "law-and-order" platform had unspoken subthemes of racism.

Nixon, nominated by Republicans earlier in August in Miami to be their candidate, was critical of the Johnson administration's conduct of the war, but failed to offer specifics of his own. He later was quoted as saying he had "a secret plan to end the war." He never used those words directly but that, indeed, made up the substance of his Vietnam position. He may well have been thinking of General Dwight Eisenhower's 1952 campaign pledge that "I will go to Korea" to end the unpopular war there.

Humphrey, as he campaigned, gradually began edging toward the independent stance he originally had planned to take prior to the Chicago convention. Standing behind podiums bearing the vice presidential seal, he took to declaring: "Put the presidential seal in front of me and I will make peace!" The line always drew immediate applause. O'Brien made a practical case for adopting a new and definitive Humphrey statement on Vietnam. In a general campaign staff meeting he said, "We cannot hope to win this election without carrying both New York and California. We cannot carry New York and California without the peace vote."

O'Brien called me on the campaign plane to ask if I thought Humphrey would deliver the independent statement both of us previously had wanted him to make. I told him that I thought he had no option but to do it. Among other things, peace hecklers and, to a lesser degree, Wallace hecklers were disrupting most of his campaign appearances. Media were focusing on the disruptions and not on a series of international and domestic policy proposals that he was offering in speeches and white papers. The Vietnam issue had to be dealt with decisively.

The campaign at that point was nearly broke. At mid-September, cash on hand totaled about $200,000. O'Brien and I discussed the possibility of using it to buy half-hour blocks of national television time to deliver speeches on Vietnam and law and order. The statements would be delivered from television studios. No other campaign activity would be scheduled on those dates, thus forcing media to focus on the statements. If the Vietnam speech were scheduled, I said, Humphrey would recognize that it had to be one that once and for all defined his own position. O'Brien proceeded. Half-hour time slots were purchased for September 30 and early October. The Vietnam statement would come first, the law-and-order statement second.

We told Humphrey that the television time had been purchased. He asked, as I knew he would, that several Vietnam drafts be solicited. Bill Moyers prepared a draft. Willard Wirtz sent in ideas. George Ball, who had resigned as United Nations ambassador to join the campaign, began preparing a statement as well. I collected them as the September 30 broadcast date neared.

On September 28, in Seattle, Humphrey endured the worst heckling he had received over the course of the campaign. Even reporters traveling with us were upset by its ferocity. In the meantime, O'Brien, Harris, Connell, and others were arriving in Seattle, as they knew Humphrey would be reviewing his definitive Vietnam text the following day. September 29 was a Sunday. A cruise on Elliott Bay had been chartered for Humphrey friends and staff, and a late-afternoon meeting was scheduled to discuss the speech at Humphrey's suite in the Olympic Hotel.

Early that morning, at his shaving mirror, Humphrey was cool and focused. He seemed to me to be exactly the same as he had been the previous November after exiting the Quonset hut in Vietnam where he had held the hands of the dying GIs. Humphrey asked if I had collected the various drafts. I told him I had them with me. The most useful was Ball's, which made a good policy case but not the political case required in a pivotal national television broadcast. Ball's draft argued that Europe was vitally important to American security but Vietnam was not. It urged a reorientation of foreign policy priorities accordingly. "I don't want to see any of them," Humphrey said. "You know what I can and should say. Do your own draft right now. Bring it back to me while everyone is out on the boat. I don't want a lot of hawk-dove debate taking place around me. I want to sign off on this before this afternoon's meeting."

I returned to our Olympic Hotel staff office. I drew on the task-force document that Johnson had dissuaded Humphrey from issuing prior to the Chicago convention, on phrases and language Humphrey had been using at campaign stops, and, finally, on ideas and concepts I knew he embraced but had not yet fully and independently expressed over the previous year. I dictated a text to Humphrey's sole traveling secretary, Marsha Sheppard, who typed a reading copy for the vice president's review. The text stated that Humphrey wanted to examine the future rather than dwell on the past, and to meet his obligation to the American people to tell them exactly what he would do about Vietnam if elected president. It outlined proposals for mutual military de-escalation both by North Vietnam and by the United States and its South Vietnamese allies. It called for a cease-fire. It also called for an unconditional cessation of American bombing of North Vietnam. Finally, a closing section of the speech dealt with clear differences between Humphrey and Nixon on domestic policy and challenged Nixon to a series of nationally televised debates.

Humphrey reviewed the speech and was satisfied with it. He asked that copies be made for discussion at the afternoon meeting. At the meeting, participants were surprised to find that the process had already moved so far. Minor changes were agreed upon, but none that altered the basic message of the text. Later that evening, as we arrived in Salt Lake City, where the speech was to be televised the following day, an updated version of the draft was distributed to a reconvened group, now joined by former Democratic national chairman John Bailey and Bill Welsh of the vice president's staff. Welsh brought a message from the capital that Averell Harriman and Cyrus Vance, the U.S. peace negotiators in Paris, had requested that any proposal for a bombing cessation should make it contingent on North Vietnamese behavior. The bombing issue, though less significant than many others, had been given symbolic importance in domestic political debate. O'Brien, Harris, and I argued that my original language, making the bombing halt unconditional, should remain unchanged. But in the end we yielded to Harriman's and Vance's request, which had been passed by an emissary to Ball back in Washington. The new bombing language was added to the text. By then it was after midnight. I took the final marked-up draft with me to my room. Within the next hour, there were two separate knocks on my door. It was Harris, then O'Brien, making sure that I had the text in my safekeeping and that no one had further meddled with it. Ball arrived in Salt Lake City during the night. As the final speech copy, to be delivered from the studio and released to the press, was about to be reproduced and distributed the next morning, Welsh brought me several short proposed additions by Ball. They were entirely in the spirit of the final draft and I worked them in.

Ball briefed reporters in a hotel conference room. We faxed copies of the speech to key Democratic senators and House members. Harris began calling them, one by one, to ask them to make public statements of support. I joined Humphrey at the television studio to find that Edgar Berman, the vice president's physician, who fancied himself a political strategist, had made a text change on the teleprompter regarding the bombing halt. I noticed it only when Humphrey began delivering the speech. Fortunately, the text change went unnoticed by the media, and reporting proceeded on the basis of the speech we had distributed. As the broadcast began, I received a phone call at the studio from former U.N. ambassador Arthur Goldberg, nominal chairman of our New York campaign, who had been vacationing at his Virginia farm. Why had he not been given the speech for his approval? he asked. I told him we had solicited his and other views on the content of the speech a few days earlier but had not heard back from him. Humphrey himself was the only person whose final approval was sought. Goldberg said that, in that light, he felt compelled to withdraw from the campaign. I asked him to read the text before making any such decision. He never followed through on his threat.

Senator Ted Kennedy made an immediate public statement praising the speech. Other party leaders followed suit. At my suggestion, we ran television commercials with telephone numbers to be called if viewers wanted to make financial contributions to the campaign. We received $300,000 in small contributions almost immediately. I felt after the broadcast that the speech had helped Humphrey, but not dramatically. I was wrong. Our next campaign stop, October 1 in Nashville, Tennessee, drew a large crowd. The only hecklers were those from the Wallace campaign. As we moved back north, we found that this was not to be an isolated instance. From the time of Humphrey's Salt Lake City speech until election day, he received no major heckling on Vietnam. It was as if someone had turned off a switch.

There is a point in any political campaign when you know whether you are winning or losing. Crowds grow or diminish, become enthusiastic or remain merely attentive. Money flows to the campaign or stops. From September 30 onward, Humphrey was a man liberated. He became again the happy, idealistic progressive who had once led his party's liberal wing. His off-the-cuff speeches became crisp. He answered media questions concisely and with confidence. Most of all, he began to draw strength from ordinary people at campaign events, on motorcade routes, and at hotel entrances shouting encouragement and reaching out to him.

In September, in Brooklyn, New York, Humphrey had ridden in a convertible in a night parade. He and all of us in the car were drenched with urine thrown from apartment windows along the parade route. A month later we drove through the same streets as people, ten abreast, shouted his name and held Humphrey-Muskie-Peace signs above them. The campaign had taken wing.

As Humphrey began to close in on Nixon, the Republican candidate resorted to one of the dirty tricks for which he was famous. Madame Anna Chennault, the widow of former World War II General Claire Chennault, was a cochair of his campaign. Nixon had instructed Bui Diem, the South Vietnamese ambassador in Washington, to maintain private communication with Madame Chennault on matters relating to Vietnam. In mid-October she approached the South Vietnamese with a request that they attempt to stall negotiations then developing in Paris between the North Vietnamese and Harriman and Vance. They would get a better deal under a President Nixon, she told them, than under a President Humphrey. Nixon, she said, would not halt bombing of North Vietnam, as Humphrey proposed, and generally would stick by the Thieu government. On October 25, Nixon gave a speech in which he accused President Johnson of attempting to accelerate diplomatic activity in order to help Humphrey's presidential campaign. Johnson, who had been equivocal about supporting Humphrey, was infuriated by the Nixon charge and launched a tough political attack on Nixon two days later.

We became aware during this period of the contacts between Chennault and the South Vietnamese—a friend in the Johnson White House learned of them through intercepts and informed us. Johnson's and Humphrey's friend Jim Rowe was traveling on our campaign plane at the time. He was the law partner of Tommy Corcoran, a fellow New Deal figure who served as the attorney and good friend of Madame Chennault. I asked Rowe to return to Washington immediately and to inform Corcoran that we knew of Chennault's overtures to the South Vietnamese, which were in violation of the Logan Act prohibiting the intervention of private citizens in official negotiations. He also was to pass a direct message to the South Vietnamese ambassador that we knew of the communications between Nixon and the Thieu government, and that if Humphrey were elected president he would take them into account. Moreover, the South Vietnamese should not delay the developing Vietnamese peace talks but should join the United States and North Vietnam at the conference table. Rowe said he would call back with a report when his mission was accomplished.

Just before this sequence of events, Humphrey had attempted to see Johnson briefly one Saturday morning during the vice president's last pre-election visit to Washington, D.C. Peace discussions had stalled, and he wanted the president's personal assessment of the situation. I called Jim Jones, then LBJ's chief of staff, from New York the day before to request the meeting. Johnson initially turned down the request. When I persisted, Jones said LBJ would see Humphrey promptly at noon in the Oval Office. Humphrey must be prompt, however, because Johnson was leaving immediately thereafter for a weekend at Camp David. Humphrey had a campaign rally that morning in Prince Georges County, Maryland. Rather than going directly to the White House, he stopped en route at his apartment to change his shirt. At 12:01 PM I received a call from Jones: "Humphrey is late. The meeting is cancelled." From my window I could see the vice president alighting from his limousine at the West Wing basement entrance. "He is thirty seconds away, Jim," I said. "Please ask the president not to cancel the meeting." When Humphrey arrived at the Oval Office door, however, Jones blocked his way and indicated that the president would be unable to see him. Humphrey turned and walked back to his EOB office. "I told Jim I was trying to run for president and was a couple minutes late," he said. "I said I'd had enough of this stuff and the president could just cram it. I could see Johnson through the door and I know he heard me. I hope he did."

On the Sunday before election day, Humphrey spoke to a capacity crowd at the Houston Astrodome. It was to be the final rally of the campaign. I had prepared a text for Humphrey that expressed unalloyed idealism about the country and his plans for it. Win or lose, I wanted him to end his campaign with a message embodying his belief that "voters should vote their hopes, not their fears."

President Johnson joined him on the podium. Governor Connally, however, was absent. As the rally got underway, Hal Lauth, a Humphrey advance man, brought me an Associated Press dispatch saying that Connally later that day would endorse Nixon. Bob Strauss, a Texas fundraiser close to Connally, stood nearby. I showed him the wire story. He took it and jogged the 100 yards from the podium in the center of the Astrodome to the stands, where, I presumed, he wanted to make a phone call I would not overhear. A few minutes later he returned to say that Connally had assured him he would not endorse Nixon. Strauss could give no reason why Connally was absent from the Astrodome rally.

A White House phone rang at the base of the podium. I moved over to pick it up. Johnson sat immediately above it. As I took the call, he watched me. So far as I could tell he was thinking that "these people are acting like they own the place while I am still president." Johnson had no way of knowing I was talking to his old friend Jim Rowe.

"I have some bad news," Rowe said. "I've talked with everyone involved and it is clear that the South Vietnamese are going to sit tight and wait for Nixon. They are not coming to the peace table." Remembering the unpleasant Humphrey-Thieu meeting of a year before in Saigon, I was not surprised. Thieu was in fact correct to believe that he would get a better deal with Nixon than with Humphrey.

The reception of Humphrey's speech energized him. He boarded his campaign plane, bound for Los Angeles, telling jokes and bantering with the campaign press corps. As the presidential race had narrowed and neared its end, the press not only occupied seats on our campaign plane, they filled three additional jets.

After takeoff I brought Humphrey the message from Rowe that the South Vietnamese government was waiting for Nixon and would boycott peace talks. Knowing Madame Chennault's long-standing ties to Chiang Kai-shek and Chinese Nationalist hardliners, I remarked that "the old China Lobby is still alive and well and fouling our politics." That set Humphrey off. "The China Lobby is not going to decide this election," he declared. "I want you to issue a statement on arrival in Los Angeles stating that, if the South Vietnamese do not come to the peace table, I would as president withdraw support from the government of South Vietnam."

I knew that Humphrey's reaction was emotional and that he really did not intend to make such an abrupt policy turn. Moreover, many would see it as a desperation political tactic. Instead, I issued a statement indicating that, if the South Vietnamese refused to come to the conference table, Humphrey as president would send American negotiators there without them. That in itself was a strong statement, made without regard to the U.S. policy stance of the moment. Humphrey thanked me the next morning for tempering his original statement.

Latter-day historians and journalists have questioned why we did not at the time publicly reveal the secret Nixon-Thieu scheme to bulldoze peace talks. Theodore White, in his book *The Making of the President: 1968*, praised Humphrey for his forbearance and sense of responsibility in not using the issue publicly. There were indeed high-minded reasons we did not reveal the Nixon chicanery publicly, but there also were practical political reasons. Polling data had shown Humphrey pulling even with Nixon. We arrived in Los Angeles to find that a Harris Poll had Humphrey running three points ahead nationally. Making a bombshell charge, on election eve, could have made Humphrey seem desperate—especially since Nixon could have been expected to brand it a lie. Also, how were we to explain the source of the information? We hardly could disclose it as a national-security intercept which we then were using in a political campaign. President Johnson more properly and credibly could have exposed and denounced publicly the Nixon backdoor diplomacy. But after discussing that option with advisors, he did not.

The twenty-four hours in Los Angeles were exhilarating, and consumed every remaining ounce of Humphrey's energy. The vice president campaigned in downtown streets to huge crowds. The traveling press corps, which had begun the campaign distinctly cool to Humphrey, jumped out of press buses and began racing alongside Humphrey's motorcade. Some held Humphrey-Muskie signs aloft. *New York Times* correspondent R. W. (John) Apple held the right fender of Humphrey's limousine as he ran. We feared for his safety. Black and Latino supporters in particular surged toward the motorcade. One young black man came to the window of Humphrey's car as it was temporarily stalled in downtown traffic. Our Secret Service detail flinched. Humphrey rolled down the window. The two grasped hands. "I believe in you, Mr. Humphrey," the man said. "You are the only man I can trust." Humphrey responded: "You are right, brother, I will never let you down. Help me get my chance and I will be sure you get yours." It was corny stuff but entirely authentic and moving.

We fought through a big crowd of cheering supporters as we returned in early afternoon to the Century Plaza Hotel. Humphrey and Muskie, who had flown to Los Angeles separately, were scheduled to participate in a national telethon that evening. The telethon would include participation of both a studio audience and callers—in contrast to a carefully staged and canned Nixon broadcast. Humphrey fell into bed for a nap. In our Century Plaza staff room, Norm Sherman told me he had found a day-old message from Gene McCarthy. If McCarthy came to Los Angeles, could he appear on the telethon to endorse Humphrey? By then it was too late, but Norm called McCarthy with instructions about placing a phone call to the telethon. We would be sure the call was given featured treatment.

Bob Squier was producer of the telethon. He had been an employee of Minnesota Public Radio when I had hired him for Humphrey's 1964 vice presidential campaign as a media advance man. His concept of the telethon was to make it an open, unencumbered dialogue between Humphrey and Muskie and ordinary citizens. Senator Ted Kennedy had taped a segment to be included in the telethon. We made room for McCarthy's telephone call. The show was not quite as spontaneous as it appeared. Questions from the studio audience and callers were authentic. They were typed on note cards to be read on the air. Off camera, however, Squier gave me the cards to review. I selected the ones which touched on the issues we most wanted raised.

Humphrey and Muskie ended up performing beautifully on the national broadcast, and afterward the campaign was inundated with positive phone calls and financial contributions. Behind the scenes, however, it had been quite a struggle to bring it off. The broadcast format was not easy, and time was required to brief both Humphrey and Muskie beforehand. Moreover, they needed to arrive at the studio with sufficient time to rest, have their makeup applied, and do a brief walk-through. Muskie, when he learned of the early arrival time at the studio, was displeased. He followed me to my room at the Century Plaza. He told me he had not wanted to make a scene in Humphrey's presence but had never required more than five minutes to prepare for any television show. I asked him to humor us. At the appointed time, he indeed arrived at Humphrey's suite, ready to go.

Humphrey, however, could not be wakened from his nap. Mrs. Humphrey had joined him in Los Angeles, and I did not want to walk into their bedroom as I would have done if Humphrey were alone. I knocked several times and called through the door. Mrs. Humphrey answered; she said she would wake the vice president. Ten minutes later, I knocked again. Mrs. Humphrey called me in. She had not been able to wake her husband. I pulled him to his feet, opened wide all drapes and windows, and got him moving while telling him exactly the minutes remaining until we must leave Century City for Burbank. Muskie, meantime, sat outside, saying nothing and smoldering. Finally we departed the Century Plaza, a full hour behind schedule. Humphrey and Muskie sat side by side in the back seat. From the front, I told them time had run out for preparation and gave them a verbal briefing on the telethon format, along with the usual reminder cards concerning key issues and talking points to be stressed. The limousine arrived at the Burbank studio a bare ten minutes ahead of air time—as it turned out, five minutes sooner than Muskie had said was necessary. The candidates strode directly from their car onto the set. Squier had begun to believe the show would have to start without them.

The next day, election day, found us in Minnesota. There is a grandeur about the actual exercise of democracy. The vice president and Muriel Humphrey cast votes at their rural polling place near Waverly, Minnesota. So did others, mainly farmers and shopkeepers, all wearing plain clothing. The country had passed through a year of war, assassinations, and civil unrest. Yet, in Waverly as in Los Angeles and New York City, decisions about the future would be made by individuals peacefully expressing their will. It was a beautiful, blue-sky fall day.

In the early afternoon Humphrey phoned me at our election-night headquarters at the Leamington Hotel in Minneapolis and asked me to join him at his home on Lake Waverly. When we had traveled to Minnesota over the past two years, Humphrey had always invited me to join him and his family in Waverly, but I usually demurred. He needed private time away from business and staff. I, too, needed private time to phone my family in Washington, D.C., to sleep late in the morning, and to be away from Humphrey. I would stay at the Leamington and drive as necessary to Waverly for work sessions. Others who have worked in such jobs, whether in the private or public sectors, recognize how important it becomes to get personal time.

On this day I found Mrs. Humphrey and their children in their home and yard, as any other family might be on a semi-holiday. Humphrey was watching early election reports on a small black-and-white television set near the kitchen. As I entered the back door nearby and saw him watching the reports, a look crossed his face as if I had caught him in some guilty pleasure. A voice inside me told me to make careful note of every detail of this day. A vase of flowers sat on a checkered tablecloth on the kitchen table. I focused on a photograph on the wall that showed Humphrey, Gene McCarthy, and myself, wearing topcoats and hats, in the front row of Metropolitan Stadium in Minneapolis at the opening of the 1965 Twins-Dodgers World Series. No tensions, protests, or strife, just three years before. Only goodwill and baseball. Bright fall leaves remained on some trees in the yard; many had fallen. Lake Waverly was still and empty of boaters. The only sound came from the TV set. Time seemed suspended. As it turned out, I would never again visit the Humphreys' Waverly home.

I knew how difficult the day would be for Humphrey. At a certain point in the campaign, he held little hope for his candidacy and was campaigning because he must. Over the previous month, however, momentum had moved in his direction. When I had told him two days earlier of the Harris Poll, showing Humphrey leading Nixon by three percentage points, he had pretended not to hear. He did not want to raise his hopes and risk having them broken.

Before leaving the hotel for Waverly, I had checked for mail and messages. There was a letter from Jim Rowe. The campaign had a formal transition process, vetting potential nominees for appointment in January, should we win the election. But in addition Humphrey had asked Rowe to send me a letter outlining his own views about Cabinet and other appointments, as well as immediate postelection steps which he would recommend to generate national unity. When I opened Rowe's letter, however, I found only a single handwritten sheet. He was not sending anything longer, the note said, because he had gone through the electoral map a number of ways and could find no way that Humphrey could win the election. He was not coming to Minneapolis for election night, he said, because he did not have the heart for it.

I did not tell Humphrey of Rowe's note. I hung around the Waverly house until the Humphreys returned in mid-evening to the Leamington to join campaign supporters. Minnesota had loved Humphrey in good times and bad, and a large crowd jammed the Leamington's downstairs ballroom. Upstairs, campaign staff took phone reports, state by state, from key precincts. They ran ahead of the information which network news broadcasts were able to obtain. I shuttled between the Humphreys' personal suite and the staff area, collecting updated information. As the evening wore on, it became clear that the election would be determined in New Jersey and Ohio, where Nixon and Humphrey were running head to head and where Wallace voters were more numerous than expected. (I remembered, in particular, a day campaigning in northern New Jersey and visiting the campaign headquarters of Democratic representative Pete Rodino. Posters of Rodino and Wallace, but none of Humphrey, covered the walls.) Illinois, expected to be close, was going for Nixon. Daley and upstate Democratic leaders had written off the Humphrey-Muskie ticket in September. Democratic billboards in Chicago carried the names of state and local candidates but not those of Humphrey and Muskie.

A week earlier, Bill Welsh had come from Washington to give me a document prepared by campaign analysts and attorneys. It suggested that neither Humphrey nor Nixon might win outright on election night. Humphrey might need to bargain with Wallace in order to win an Electoral College victory. Humphrey had wasted few words on Wallace during the campaign. He viewed him with distaste and believed he had traded on racial fears to sustain his third-party candidacy. Humphrey had not been asked what he would do if Wallace held the balance of power in deciding the election. I had told reporters on several occasions that he would not compromise with George Wallace in any circumstance. Welsh urged me to withhold further such statements and to caution Humphrey against them as well. I acknowledged the information but thought it highly unlikely that Humphrey would want to negotiate with Wallace, whereas I was sure that Nixon would.

The Humphreys sat watching the television set in their suite. Then, after midnight, Larry O'Brien called Humphrey. Urban precincts in New Jersey and Ohio were not generating the usual Democratic margins. The election was lost. Humphrey rose from the sofa, hitched his trousers, and said, "The American people will learn they just elected a papier-mâché president."

Mrs. Humphrey and I exchanged glances. "Are you thinking the same thing I am?" she asked. I was. We both were thinking of Humphrey's habitual lateness for appointments and plane flights. When he no longer was vice president, the world would not wait for him. Humphrey asked me to prepare a concession statement. I already had a draft in my left suit pocket. It read:

> I have today sent the following telegram to Mr. Nixon.
>
> "According to unofficial returns, you are the winner in this election. Please know that you will have my support in unifying and leading the nation. I am confident that, if constructive leaders of both our parties join together now, we shall be able to go on with the business of building the better America we all seek—in a spirit of peace and harmony."
>
> Senator Muskie and I wish to thank the people who supported our nomination and election. I wish especially to thank my family and campaign staff. I intend to continue my dedication to public service and to the building of a responsive and vital Democratic Party. I shall continue my personal commitment to the causes of human rights and of peace.
>
> If I have helped in this campaign to move those causes forward, I feel rewarded. I have done my best. I have lost. Mr. Nixon has won.

Humphrey then added a final paragraph:

> The democratic process has worked its will. Now let us get on with the urgent task of uniting our country.

He began to write more, but thought better of it and crossed it out with heavy ballpoint markings.

The Humphreys went to the downstairs ballroom, where the vice president delivered the statement, adding personal thanks to Mondale, Harris, and others on the podium. A man to whom tears came easily, he took this moment in an unruffled manner. The Minnesotans in the ballroom cheered the Humphreys long and loudly, bathing them in affection. As I joined them in the elevator back to their suite, I found to my surprise that I was the one crying.

I awoke early the next morning feeling empty. The Humphreys had returned to Waverly. I felt desperately lonely for my wife and four children in Washington, and I joined media and staff on a charter flight back to Washington National Airport. Within thirty seconds of taking my seat, I fell asleep. I next awoke at the door of our home on Brandywine Street in Washington. Bill Connell's wife, Phyllis, had taken me, sleepwalking, from the plane, put me in a staff car, and brought me home.

At home over the next few days I examined my feelings about what had happened. My first wonderment was that I had performed under pressure, seven days a week, up to twenty hours a day, over a period of months—really, two years—and was neither ill nor exhausted. I had managed to overcome, as if it did not matter, a shattered right wrist suffered during a campaign-picnic game of touch football before the Democratic convention. It had forced me to wear an awkward cast for twelve weeks and to do everything, including writing, left-handed. (Humphrey, on learning of my injury, called to express sympathy but then quickly asked if I had broken my right wrist or my left. I told him not to worry; I would do the work regardless.) I was sorely disappointed that Humphrey had lost. He had lost narrowly, but the margin made no difference to me. One vote or one million, the outcome was the same. I also felt what I had to admit was a feeling of relief. The Cabinet and principal players in the Johnson administration had served since President Kennedy's inauguration in 1961. They were wonderful, dedicated people, but most had run out of gas. Nonetheless, they would have provided the cornerstone of a Humphrey administration to take office in 1969. I also had dreaded the transition process, which would have taken place over the next two months. A good-hearted Humphrey had given dozens of people good reason to believe they would be appointed to key Cabinet and other positions. It would have fallen to me and one or two others to tell most of these loyal Humphrey supporters that they were not getting the big jobs they thought were coming.

I also felt less regret at Nixon's victory than I thought I would. I had grown up despising Nixon for his campaigns against Jerry Voorhees and Helen Gahagan Douglas in California and for his McCarthyism as a member of Congress. He seemed to me an insecure, paranoid person who had subsumed all else to his political career. He appeared prepared to use any means to justify his political ends. Humphrey, by contrast, was driven by his commitment to a public agenda. Yet, I thought, Nixon's very pragmatism would lead him to liquidate our involvement in Vietnam just as quickly as we would have done it. We had intended, if Humphrey had won, to transform his Salt Lake

City statement into immediate policy. Vietnam was not Nixon's war, I thought. He would want to begin his term by removing it as a distraction.

I also thought the Humphrey campaign had suffered so many self-inflicted wounds that we could not have expected to make the contest close. The greatest of these, I thought, had been Humphrey's reluctance over a long period to establish his own independent position on Vietnam. It was undeniably a difficult thing to do for a vice president serving a demanding president such as Johnson. Yet, I thought, the circumstance was extraordinary, and Humphrey's greater duty was to the American people. I did feel, though, that I had done everything I could to encourage his independence. In mid-November, however, at lunch with Martin Agronsky, a CBS television correspondent who revered Humphrey and who also was an avid Vietnam dove, I was brought up short on that count. "I blame you for Humphrey's loss," he said. "If you had tried just a bit harder, you could have turned him sooner on Vietnam." I expressed disbelief. "Yes you could have," he said. "We [in the media traveling with Humphrey] could see him turning, but you didn't press him hard enough at the decisive moment."

I do not know whether Agronsky was correct in his judgment. I did, however, regret one decision the campaign should have made but did not. Terry Sanford, chair of the Humphrey national citizens' committee, saw more clearly than anyone else the threat that George Wallace posed to Humphrey's electoral chances. In early October, after Nixon had definitively refused to debate Humphrey, Sanford proposed that Humphrey challenge Wallace to debate. He gave me a memo, which I shared with Humphrey, suggesting that Wallace was drawing traditional Democratic voters away from the Humphrey-Muskie ticket, and that some could be pulled back if Humphrey confronted and defeated Wallace in open debate. He proposed that Humphrey challenge Wallace to a series of televised debates in both northern and southern states. If Wallace agreed to debate, Humphrey surely would expose him in the course of debate as a racist posing as a populist. If he did not agree, he would be paired with Nixon as afraid to debate. At that juncture, however, Humphrey was entirely focused on bringing peace voters back to his candidacy and on drawing distinctions between himself and Nixon. Sanford's proposal that Humphrey challenge Wallace seemed a distraction. Yet, as it turned out, Sanford had been entirely correct in pointing to Wallace voters—later to be characterized as Reagan Democrats—as the pivotal voting bloc in the campaign. We should have acted on his proposal.

I did not, as many around Humphrey did, feel resentment toward either Johnson or McCarthy. Johnson, I thought, had in one historic legislative session achieved his ambition of completing and perfecting his hero Franklin Roosevelt's New Deal. In signing the 1964 Civil Rights and 1965 Voting Rights Acts, he had known that he likely was ceding the Democratic Party's formerly solid South to Republican control for at least several decades. He had been trapped in Vietnam in part by relying on President Kennedy's holdover advisors and by his fear that he would appear weaker than JFK on national-security policy if he withdrew. Whenever in Johnson's presence, I had seen in his eyes something that said "Help me."

It was true that LBJ bullied the vulnerable in his White House and Cabinet and respected only those who stood up to him. And, as president, he had to be held accountable for U.S. escalations and other mistakes in Vietnam. Yet I could not hate him, and continued to hold him in respect. I had also come to know and admire most of the Johnson White House staff. One of my prized keepsakes is a letter I received from Johnson, then in exile in Texas, in September 1970, expressing his sympathy on my mother's death, which mutual friends had told him about. His mother, too, had died of cancer, the letter said. I wrote back that, after two years of Nixon, the country missed him more than he knew.

McCarthy, whatever his initial motives, had stepped forward to undertake a peace candidacy in the New Hampshire Democratic primary when others would not. He had remained true to himself. In my view, he would have withdrawn from the race in Humphrey's favor at any time after Robert Kennedy's assassination, had Humphrey given him reason to do so. After the debacle of the Chicago Democratic convention, McCarthy had been driven miles away. Nonetheless, by election day, he had come home to Humphrey and tried to help him win. In challenging Vietnam policy and a sitting president of his own party he had shown courage and independence. In subsequent years, after his retirement to western Virginia, McCarthy sometimes would come to Washington for lunch. He would show me articles he had written for a rural newspaper and always expressed affection for Humphrey. McCarthy told me he felt he had been "excommunicated" by the Democratic Party. He pretended not to care, but clearly did.

I felt respect and affection, too, for the Humphrey staff. I had worked with most of them since 1964. The Humphrey staff was motivated, as was Humphrey, by substantive issues. Like our boss, we gave the work everything we had, all the time. We shared the same storm-tossed lifeboat. There was not a single staff member I would not count on in a moment of need.

Kennedy and McCarthy supporters were also animated by a positive agenda and, in subsequent years, many would become close friends and collaborators in various causes. Since 1968 I have attended Johnson, Humphrey, Kennedy, and McCarthy reunions and felt at home at all of them. Some in each camp felt animosity toward those in others; I saw us all as being part of the same family, divided temporarily but sharing larger, lasting values.

During the postelection period I also came to consider what might have happened had Humphrey not joined Johnson's 1964 ticket. It seemed then that his vice presidency would present his only chance to ascend to the presidency. I did not for a moment regret suggesting and implementing a strategy that helped him become vice president. It was pursued at a time before the Vietnam War had expanded as it did. We had no reason to believe, in the summer of 1964, that Johnson would pursue an escalation of the American role there, which he had pledged to resist. If Vietnam had become in 1964 what it was in 1965, I would never have proposed a Humphrey vice presidential candidacy.

Knowing his temperament and instincts, it seemed certain to me that, had Humphrey remained Senate Whip, he would have joined his colleagues in their Vietnam dissent. If Lowenstein, his former intern, had then approached Humphrey to run in the New Hampshire primary in 1968, it seemed likely to me that Humphrey would have done it—presenting a straight-up Johnson-Humphrey contest for the Democratic presidential nomination.

In the closing days of Humphrey's vice presidency, after I already had begun a new job, I wrote him a long letter expressing the hope that he could put the bad experiences of the office behind him and once again be his own man. He wrote back that he already was beginning to feel liberated. Regrettably, I was to find a few years later, he was never to become fully able to do that.

*   *   *

There are two matters associated with the 1968 campaign that I will describe here as I saw them and knew of them. They came to public view long after the campaign had ended.

During the early part of Humphrey's vice presidency, I responded to an invitation by an old University of Washington classmate, Graham Molitor, who at that time was working as a political and policy researcher for Nelson Rockefeller, to visit the Rockefeller offices in the U.S. Rubber Building in Rockefeller Center when I was in New York. Molitor was concentrating on domestic policy research but also had assembled several filing cabinets' worth of files on Richard Nixon, and he showed some of these to me. They constituted what is normally known as "negative research." During that visit I was introduced to Henry Kissinger, who was following foreign-policy issues for Rockefeller and who, I was told, also maintained exhaustive Nixon files. It was no secret that Rockefeller held Nixon in contempt. He later would oppose him for the 1968 Republican presidential nomination.

After Rockefeller's defeat for the nomination by Nixon, I recalled my visit to the U.S. Rubber Building and the existence of the Nixon files. I asked Zbigniew Brzezinski—whom I had recruited from the State Department Policy Planning staff for the Humphrey campaign research staff, and who knew Kissinger—if he would ask Kissinger to share his Nixon files. Kissinger said he would do so. The matter of the files was widely discussed in the Humphrey research operation, and their arrival was awaited eagerly. However, just before Brzezinski was scheduled to pick up the files, he received a call from Kissinger's secretary informing him that the transfer would not be possible because Kissinger had just become a Nixon advisor. I thought nothing further of the matter until the closing days of the campaign, when it appeared possible that Humphrey might in fact win the election. I spent a Saturday afternoon in Washington, D.C., sifting through some of Humphrey's personal mail. It was the same day Humphrey had tried to see Johnson regarding the progress of Vietnam negotiations and been turned away at the Oval Office door. I was surprised to find among the letters one from Kissinger expressing his admiration for Humphrey and his willingness to serve in a Humphrey administration.

In 1977, while serving in the Carter administration, I attended a ceremony in the Capitol at which Humphrey was presented an award. Kissinger, who was participating in the ceremony, praised Humphrey for his statesmanship. Humphrey, to my amazement, remarked that, had he been elected in 1968, he might have chosen Kissinger as his secretary of state. Brzezinski, then serving as Carter's national security advisor, was also at the ceremony and winked at me when we both heard this remark. Both of us thought the notion absurd. Never in 1968 had I heard Humphrey mention Kissinger, much less indicate he saw him as a potential secretary of state. I had presumed that

U.N. Ambassador George Ball would receive that appointment. It was a notion, I was sure, that must have come to Humphrey several years later, after his return to the U.S. Senate. I could not imagine the two having any basis for a president–secretary of state relationship.

So the matter rested until 1980, when Seymour Hersh, who was writing a book about Kissinger, called me to ask about these events. He already had the essential details from some other source. I confirmed the story, as above, and Hersh included it in his book.

At the time of the book's release, I was in Germany. In the middle of the night I was awakened in my hotel room by a phone call from Dwayne Andreas, the chairman of Archer Daniels Midland Company, who had ties to many people in both the Democratic and Republican parties. I had known him since 1964, when he was an active Minnesota financial supporter of Humphrey's, and he had been a donor to the Center for National Policy, which I then headed. Not surprisingly, he also had ties to Kissinger, who at this point was a private citizen. He was calling at Kissinger's request, he said, to ask that I join him (Andreas) and Humphrey's old friend Max Kampelman in issuing a public statement denying all aspects of the 1968 episodes as related in Hersh's book. They had been reported in the *New York Times*, and Kissinger feared that they were seriously damaging his reputation. Andreas read the *Times* account to me over the phone. I told him that he, Kampelman, or anyone else would be ill advised to issue a denial on Kissinger's behalf. The account, in fact, was correct. Moreover, a number of people in the Humphrey research operation had known about Kissinger's offer of the Nixon files. I also had mentioned Kissinger's job-seeking letter to Humphrey to several colleagues at the time. I suggested that he advise Kissinger to take a brief offshore vacation. The matter would pass and be forgotten.

An hour later Andreas called again. Kissinger was highly agitated, he said, and needed our denial badly. I would not make any denial, I told him. Given that neither he nor Kampelman had any basis for knowing the facts of the matter, I said, I would advise them not to do so either. I again suggested he advise Kissinger to disappear for awhile.

Some thirty-six hours later, when I landed back in the United States at Kennedy Airport, I found television camera crews awaiting me outside U.S. Customs. They sought comment on the story, which had been kept alive by Kissinger's heated assertions that Hersh's account consisted of "slimy lies." I ducked the crews. On reading newspapers the next day, I saw that Kampelman had in fact issued a statement on Kissinger's behalf. The line of the day, however, was from Norm Sherman, Humphrey's vice presidential press secretary, who said that so far as he knew, the Hersh account of Kissinger's actions did not amount to slimy lies but to "slimy truths."

Nelson Rockefeller was a main character in another matter that came to partial light after the campaign. Prior to the 1968 Democratic convention, Endicott (Chub) Peabody, a former Massachusetts governor who was supporting Humphrey's nomination, approached me on the campaign airplane. He had talked informally with Nelson Rockefeller, he said, and had found that he was an enthusiastic friend of Humphrey's. That was something we already knew. Beyond that, Peabody said, he believed Rockefeller would be willing to serve on Humphrey's ticket.

Humphrey, I knew, should be kept at a remove from any such discussion. We already had our hands full trying to bring the Democratic Party together. It could be harmful if, prior to the Chicago convention, it was thought Humphrey was reaching out to a Republican, albeit a moderate Republican, as a running mate. I told Peabody to proceed informally but that, if anyone asked, we would have to deny being directly involved in the matter. Afterward, I told Humphrey about the discussion. He doubted Rockefeller would want to be number two on a Democratic Party national ticket but he asked that I follow the matter and keep him posted.

Peabody reported later that Rockefeller remained interested but seemed more noncommittal than he had in their first discussion. I told Peabody to let the matter rest. Like Humphrey, I felt that the whole thing, if pursued, was likely to end in a blind alley after expenditure of too much time and energy.

That fall, Humphrey and Richard Nixon addressed the annual Al Smith Dinner in New York, a forum traditionally addressed by both major-party candidates. After the black-tie dinner, private receptions were held for friends of both candidates; Dwayne Andreas hosted one for Humphrey. Charles Engelhard, the minerals billionaire (thought to the model for the Goldfinger character in James Bond movies), and his wife, Sophie, were there. Both were major Democratic contributors. Also present, surprisingly, were former New York governor Tom Dewey and Nelson Rockefeller and his wife Happy—people not usually on the guest lists at parties honoring Democratic presidential candidates, especially when the Republican candidate was being feted just down the hall.

Happy Rockefeller walked directly over to me. "Are you the vice president's assistant?" she asked. I told her I was. "How is the campaign going?" she inquired. I told her things were looking better. "How are you fixed for money?" I told her we needed it.

"Nelson and I think Nixon is a real shit," she said. "I'll talk to Nelson and see if we can't get you some real money." Whereupon she walked over to Humphrey, who was seated on a sofa. She sat next to him and pointed to me, obviously relating our conversation. I could see Humphrey nodding his head to confirm what I had told her. Then she crossed the room and joined her husband. Later, as the Rockefellers left the party, she waved to me and pointed to her purse. The following week the campaign began making television buys it had previously been unable to make. I asked Bob Short, the campaign treasurer, where the money was coming from. "You know where it is coming from," he said. I presume that the Rockefellers were, in fact, the source of the money, which in those days could be contributed in unlimited amounts and without today's reporting requirements. Our television advertising spending probably equaled Nixon's during the last two weeks of the campaign.

Months after the election, Chub Peabody told the media that Humphrey and Rockefeller had been quite close to forming a ticket prior to the Chicago convention. That exaggerated report took on life of its own and has been repeated in other accounts of 1968. The Rockefellers' probable financial support for Humphrey, however, has never before been reported. If Richard Nixon were alive to hear of it, it no doubt would confirm his worst suspicions of the treachery surrounding him.

9

IN TRANSITION

Had we known what would happen during the Nixon presidency, I am certain that Johnson, Humphrey, McCarthy, the Kennedys, and all Democrats involved in the 1968 election would have made whatever extra effort was necessary to win the presidency for Humphrey.

Nixon had campaigned with a "bring us together" slogan. Yet his "Southern Strategy" was based on a crude political calculation that disaffected white Southerners would form a new political base for the Republican Party. Few believed he would continue the American involvement in Vietnam. Yet more casualties were incurred there after his election than during the Kennedy and Johnson presidencies combined. The Voting Rights Act, Medicare, Medicaid, federal aid to education, and other Great Society–era initiatives had become embedded in national life and could not have been reversed, any more than Social Security and other New Deal initiatives could have been reversed after President Franklin Roosevelt's tenure. Nixon's continuance of the Vietnam commitment, and the Watergate scandal which eventually brought him down, were to prove his most damaging legacies. They contributed to a general public cynicism about politics that has not been overcome to this day.

Humphrey, by contrast, would have liquidated American involvement in the war. Nixon's opposite in temperament, Humphrey would have been incapable of launching the paranoid series of covert operations that became known as Watergate—or of lying about them. His style of governance would have been open and inclusive. Humphrey simply was incapable of playing Americans off against each other on the basis of race, religion, ethnicity, or regional differences.

Nixon's domestic initiatives did provide a point of departure from the Great Society. He undertook environmental legislation that the Johnson Administration had not. His "new federalism" concept of domestic governance was to devolve power to state and local levels while maintaining the federal government as a central tax collector. Thus his concept of "revenue sharing," in which the federal government was to collect taxes and then distribute them to lower levels of government with few strings attached.

He made one big policy change, which at the time seemed incremental. That was Nixon's sponsorship of affirmative action, in which quotas and set-asides were to be reserved for minorities in hiring and contracting, school admissions, and other parts of American life. It began with the so-called Philadelphia Plan, administered by Labor Secretary George Shultz, in which unions and employers in the notoriously discriminatory construction industry agreed to guarantee minority involvement. The concept then spread generally. Until then, the traditional Democratic and liberal approach had been to first eradicate legal barriers to equality through such measures as the Civil Rights and Voting Rights Acts, and then improve the skills of minorities through education, job training, and other programs that would help them have a more equal chance at the economic and social starting lines. Such programs were income rather than race based. Title I of the Elementary and Secondary Education Act and Head Start were perfect examples. Children from poor families were provided with extra education assistance to enable them to catch up to their peers. The Job Corps was another, in which poor kids were given practical skills training to prepare them for work. Most, though not all, of such children were from minority families.

President Kennedy had once used the words "affirmative action" in a memo. But it was never contemplated, before Nixon, that any Great Society, anti-poverty, or civil-rights initiative would be explicitly race-based or attempt to guarantee not just opportunity but also an outcome. The cornerstone 1964 Civil Rights Act, after all, prohibited discrimination either in favor of or against any person on the basis of race, gender, religion, or ethnicity. Yet today, transformed from affirmative action to "diversity," this Nixon-era reorientation has created de facto quotas and guaranteed school admission, employment, job promotion, and public contracting outcomes in many parts of American private and public life. Where such policies are denounced, it is often, ironically, on the basis that they are vestiges of the 1960s Kennedy and Johnson eras.

In the early 1970s, when this reorientation took place, congressional liberals who had championed civil rights almost universally questioned it. But, in deference to minority leaders who liked the idea, most stood silent. At an Americans for Democratic Action conference, I argued on behalf of affirmative action as a temporary means to compensate for past discrimination. But Humphrey, among others, thought the concept would be abused and, in the future, would provide a pretext for reactionaries to turn back the civil-rights clock. In 1972 George McGovern proposed to campaign advisors that he outrightly oppose a related device—busing for purposes of school desegregation—but was dissuaded because it was thought his opposition would be misunderstood among black leaders who then supported it.

The Democratic Party's future course was determined in part by a decision, made during the period between Humphrey's electoral defeat and Nixon's presidential inauguration, to which Humphrey attributed little importance at the time. In his spare moments during this period, Humphrey was contemplating his choice as Democratic National Committee chairman during his party's upcoming period out of the White House. Up until 1968, but not since, losing presidential candidates became "titular leaders" of their parties for the ensuing four years, made statements on behalf of the party, and also appointed the party chairman. For example, Adlai Stevenson, after his defeats in 1952 and 1956, had appointed Paul Butler as national chairman.

Butler provided witty partisanship to the party and also presided over the Democratic Advisory Council, which issued statements on both foreign and domestic policy that went well beyond those that congressional leaders Sam Rayburn and Lyndon Johnson were prepared to make. Many of these ideas later became congressional initiatives or were incorporated into Kennedy and Johnson White House proposals.

Humphrey was undecided between two options as party chairman: Fred Harris, who had cochaired his presidential nominating campaign and whom he had passed over for the vice presidential nomination; and Terry Sanford, the progressive former governor of North Carolina, who had chaired his campaign's national citizens' committee. Humphrey spoke briefly with both men before his departure for Oslo, Norway, where he had been dispatched by President Johnson as his representative at the funeral of former United Nations Secretary General Trygvie Lie. We were accompanied on the trip by Margaret Truman Daniel, President Truman's daughter, and her son. She entertained us all with outspoken opinions on many subjects; she definitely was her father's daughter. While we were in Oslo, Angier Biddle Duke, then the U.S. ambassador to Denmark, called to urge us to make a stop in Copenhagen on the way back to Washington. His secretary in the embassy was Angie Novello, who had been Senator Robert Kennedy's secretary. They kept their promise to put on a party that would make us feel we had won, not lost, the November election.

After the party, at our Copenhagen hotel, Humphrey received a beseeching call from Fred Harris. He badly wanted the DNC chairmanship, and pled his case for more than an hour. Humphrey made no commitment. But I knew he had affection for Harris and admired his ambition and energy. Humphrey's soft heart, I thought, would cause him to give Harris the job over Sanford, whose temperament restrained him from active campaigning. He eventually did. Harris formed a Policy Council analogous to the Butler-era Advisory Council. Humphrey was the council's chair. Its staff director was my friend and former Humphrey-staff colleague John Stewart, who also served as the DNC's director of research and communications. I also served on the council, as did many others who had been involved in the party over the previous decade. But it was heavily weighted toward party activists who had been Robert Kennedy or Eugene McCarthy supporters in 1968 (and who both Humphrey and Harris wanted to draw actively into party affairs). It was underweighted with Southern and border-state moderates. Similarly, Harris himself, still a sitting senator from Oklahoma, cast his personal lot mainly with the same more liberal constituency. Sanford, not then holding public office, most likely would have cast a wider net. Harris, probably unconsciously, was narrowing the party base; Sanford would have broadened it. As it turned out, Harris eventually was to lose his Senate seat because of Oklahomans' perception that he had more interest in Gloria Steinem and New York limousine liberals than he did in the home folks. As the 1972 electoral cycle approached, the party had increasingly become the instrument of its most active and liberal constituencies—defined mainly by their 1968 opposition to the war in Vietnam. My own orientations were the same. Commissions put together to reform the party's nominating procedures and rules were also weighted in the same direction. The party indeed had new energy. But it was gradually losing support south of the Mason-Dixon and in traditional labor unions; there was no Henry Wallace emerging to split the party from the left, but the way was being paved for an appeal from a George Wallace on the right.

As Humphrey's vice presidential term ended, I had to make decisions about my own next move. I did not realize it at the time, but my marketability was probably at an all-time high. Humphrey's vice presidency and the 1968 campaign period had brought me a lot of personal exposure. A number of offers came from business, academia, the media, and elsewhere. I took them too much for granted, having been accustomed to being at the center of things in national government and politics. Connell proposed that he and I establish a small consulting practice that would also provide staff support to Humphrey during his out-of-office period. Humphrey said he would welcome this, but I felt a strong need to be on my own after living Humphrey's life and schedule for nearly five years. I told Humphrey of some of my options and sought his advice. He, in turn, suggested that I talk to former Health, Education, and Welfare secretary John Gardner, who was then forming Common Cause. "John is a wise man" he said. "You should see what he says." Gardner's office, in contrast to Humphrey's, was an island of calm. He gave me good advice: "You've been involved intensely for several years," he said. "You have a young family. Do something with less pressure and play with your kids."

I was geared too high to take his advice. Finally, I went to see Humphrey again and described my options to him. One was the vice presidency of Columbia University, where help was needed to restore the campus after a period of disruptions by the Students for a Democratic Society and a host of protest activities. Andrew Cordier, a former senior United Nations official and dean of Columbia's School of International Affairs, had replaced Grayson Kirk as Columbia's president. But the university administration continued to be run mostly by Kirk's appointees. Cordier needed someone from the outside, with political skills if possible, to help him change the culture in a hurry. After hearing me describe the various offers I was considering, Humphrey said: "Your choice is obvious. You belong where the action is. Go to Columbia."

I did, even before Humphrey's vice presidential term had ended. I accepted the Columbia job on the understanding that I would serve just a year or two, helping restore things to normal. Cordier was himself a transition figure, expected to use his diplomatic skills to quiet the situation and then to turn the reins over to a younger, long-term successor. My family stayed in Washington, D.C. I took a room in faculty housing on campus, where I could quickly be found if after-hours disturbances developed. I flew back to Washington Friday evenings and returned to Morningside Heights late Sunday nights.

Columbia had undergone riots, building occupations, and general chaos in 1968. The unrest had not reached the intensity of the turmoil of the 1968 Chicago Democratic convention and the ensuing presidential campaign, but, like other universities, Columbia was accustomed to being a slower-paced island of scholarship and not an arena for guerrilla theater and arrests. A famous photograph of students occupying President Kirk's office, one smoking a cigar with his feet on the president's desk, summed things up. I arrived to find most faculty and administrators prepared to blame the university's difficulty wholly on "outside agitators" and unwilling to acknowledge any need for internal change. They were partly, but not wholly, correct. Antiestablishment tumult was rising worldwide. In the United States, it had coalesced around the Vietnam War issue. Because students formed the core of the antiwar movement, the most liberal campuses, such as Columbia and the University of California at Berkeley, became focal points for political action. They were not the reason for the tumult, but they became its venues.

Cordier was generous in letting me define the parameters of my job and make new hires to supplement existing staff. Among those I brought on board were Martin Gleason, a former assistant to Senator Paul Douglas; Kirby Jones, a former member of Robert Kennedy's campaign staff; and Fred Neilsen, a respected New York community organizer. Carl Hovde, the dean of Columbia College, agreed to my theft from his own staff of Dan Carlinsky, a talented writer and editor. My office was directly above Cordier's, on the second floor of Low Library, the university's main administration building. I was to be responsible for the university's relations with government, the media, and various external constituencies. But my main job, Cordier made clear, was to help him tame the campus.

The campus Students for a Democratic Society (SDS) chapter may have been notorious, but it hardly was a behemoth capable of challenging a major university. Some 250 students on campus generally fell within the SDS orbit. But of these, perhaps only fifteen or twenty were committed to the group's core ideological beliefs. Most of the others simply had vague progressive leanings or liked to consider themselves radical. In my first week on campus I attended a campus colloquium among faculty members and SDS members. The faculty members, traditional liberals and social democrats, made linear presentations. The SDSers stunned them by not responding in kind— instead, their spokespersons hurled angry slogans and accusations. SDS supporters in the audience booed and shouted down the professors when they attempted to speak. One faculty member, trying to respond to the chanted slogans, blurted into the microphone: "I used to know the answers to all that; but it has been so long I've forgotten them." The fact was, the SDS playbook was straight from the playbook of the 1968 Chicago Democratic convention agitators, and had its origins in Hard Left and fascist tactics of the 1930s and before. Its intellectual content was at bumper-sticker level.

President Kirk had responded to the SDSers exactly as they hoped he would. Television and newspaper images of demonstrations, sit-ins, building occupations, arrests, and police batons gave the demonstrators what they wanted. Cordier initiated a number of shrewd moves to counter the damage. He agreed to open Low Library to public meetings and forums—including those sponsored by all campus groups except SDS. We encouraged a liberal reform group, Students for a Restructured University, that papered the campus with handbills questioning university policies and gave students a non-radical alternative for protest. Cordier hosted a series of breakfasts and luncheons at his residence for a crosssection of neighborhood and campus critics of the university. Some of the guests were stoned, and the Cordier dining room reeked of marijuana during their presence, but Cordier treated their comments with seriousness. University trustees, including financier Ben Buttenweiser, *New York Times* publisher Arthur (Punch) Sulzberger, and federal judge Frederick Van Pelt Bryan, held meetings with editors of the *Columbia Spectator*, the campus newspaper, and with other undergraduates. Dan Carlinsky began putting out an independent campus newspaper that kept students updated on a large number of curriculum and governance reform efforts being launched by the administration.

SDSers had attempted to recruit black students at Columbia into their protests, but were notably unsuccessful. Their efforts were doomed because the objectives of the two groups were fundamentally opposite. SDS and other agitators attacked the fundamental values underlying American society and the university. Black students, by contrast, wanted to rise within that society and saw the university as their way to do this. Cordier and several deans developed a black-studies program and met with black student leaders on a regular basis, drawing them farther from possible association with radical groups. The SDS political base on campus was shrinking perceptibly.

There were still some demonstrations and a few building occupations—attempts at recapturing the 1968 glory days—but we did not call New York City police to the scene. Instead, campus police managed the situation. We were careful to avoid creating martyrs. After buildings eventually were cleared, we admitted media, cameras, and students to see the gratuitous and pointless damage done to the buildings by the occupiers.

We handled the radicals with time-honored political tactics—dividing their forces, isolating them, removing their targets of opportunity. But the campus community as a whole was not always easy to manage. A few weeks after my arrival, I received an invitation to be guest of honor at a faculty club luncheon to be attended by what I was told would be a welcoming group of some twenty-five senior faculty. When I arrived, I found the faculty members had something else in mind. I was subjected to two nonstop hours of complaints about the inconveniences the student disorders had caused them, threats of their departure for other universities, and attacks on Cordier and myself for "legitimizing" student complaints by undertaking campus reforms. Notably absent from the group were Columbia faculty friends I had known during my Humphrey days, including Zbigniew Brzezinski, Russian scholar Marshall Shulman, and law professor Richard Gardner.

It was a prime example of university professors at their worst. I had dealt with many leading academic figures during my time with the European Communities and with Humphrey. In those contexts, I had not formed a high regard for them as policymakers or administrators, but their input as outside counselors and experts had been invaluable. On their own turf, however, I found that their self-absorption and pettiness could be extreme, tending to validate the dictum that faculty politics are so intense because the stakes are so small.

I had come to know and respect David Truman, Columbia's provost and a man who had seemed destined to become the university's president—until he found himself a fall guy for the Kirk regime's 1968 troubles. He had devoted his life to the institution. However, in the early spring of 1969 he was preparing to depart for Mount Holyoke College, where he had accepted the presidency. There had been no notable farewell occasion for Truman among administrators or faculty. In his final hours on campus I found him alone in his office at the lunch hour. I invited him to the faculty club, where we sat a few feet away from a table of a dozen of the campus's most prominent professors. As we were having dessert, a spokesman for the group walked over. "David," he said, "I want you to know how much we will miss you and how badly we all feel about what happened to you." Truman responded: "Too late now, you bastards. Where were you when I needed you?"

The academic class is what it is. It would be a mistake to believe that advanced degrees correlate with common sense or talent outside a particular field. Yet we desperately need what academe can be at its best: that is, a collection of independent scholars who can provide knowledge and critical analysis to the society at large. Columbia Faculty Senate meetings, if witnessed by SDS, would have given the radicals ample ammunition for their broadsides. But they were and are mainly irrelevant. It is the individual scholars, and their work, that matter at any academic institution. Trustees, administrators, and students are transient. The faculty *are* the university.

By late spring 1969, the campus had returned nearly to normal. How normal became clear to me one evening as I was leaving Low Library for dinner. A few days earlier I had received by messenger, in a brown wrapper, a book produced by students that rated professors and courses on campus. I had found it uproarious. But there was no indication of the sender. As I walked down the Low steps, I noticed that an SDS meeting was breaking up at a nearby building. As it did, several figures came rushing toward me in the dusk. "I'm too tired tonight for one more ideological go-around with these guys," I thought. But that was not their purpose, it turned out. "Ted," they said, "did you get our faculty rating book? What did you think of it? We thought you would like it." The revolution, I thought, was over.

I was being worn down by the weekly commute to and from Washington, D.C. I needed to be with my family full time, but I did not want to bring them to Morningside Heights. I found a house in Rye, New York, that seemed right for us. But before moving on it, I decided to try a trial commute. It involved driving from the house in Rye to the station, boarding a train to Grand Central, taking a subway shuttle to Times Square, and then taking the IRT subway line uptown to 116th Street. I did it once. As the school year neared its end, I told Cordier I had decided to return to the capital. I had done the job I had come to do. "Uncle Andy," as we called him, rose from his chair and pointed outside his window to the green campus and the students crossing it. Across the way stood the splendid library building. "Just look at that," he said. "Can you imagine that I, from a small town in Indiana, am president of this place? What a wonderful chance to do good things. But we are not done yet." Had Columbia and my family been in the same place, I would have stayed, I told him. But I was never going to make a career as an academic administrator. I needed to go home. A few days later I donned cap and gown for the Columbia commencement. Cordier, a strong bear of a man, gave me a glass of wine and huge hug in his office. Over the summer, I made my resignation known.

As I packed my office, I listened to a broadcast on the campus radio station. "Vice President Van Dyk has resigned," a youthful-sounding announcer said. "He will be remembered as the 'Shane' of Columbia University. He rode into town, made it safe for normal life, and rode out again." Not bad, I thought.

I was on the Columbia campus again in summer 2005, for a Graduate School of Journalism program. As I walked into Low Library, I saw that preparations were being made in the rotunda for a formal dinner. The stairway to my old office had been blocked by security. If you stepped in the right place in the entry hall, I found, you could still create an echo. I introduced myself to the staff person supervising the event preparations. She said I was remembered. I doubted it. As I departed via the front steps, I saw the campus to be just as green and resplendent as the day Andy Cordier had pointed to it in 1969. I stopped at the West End bar on Broadway for a sandwich and a beer, then descended the steps into the subway station to go back downtown. If I had been here at another time in my life, I thought, I would have stayed a while.

Back in Washington in the fall of 1969, I founded a consulting firm which would provide income for my family and also a base from which I could remain involved in national politics and causes. My clients were drawn mainly from groups and organizations with which I had worked in the Johnson-Humphrey administration. They came over time to include United Airlines, Eli Lilly & Co., the Hertz Corporation, J. Walter Thompson Co., Midwestern and Southern dairy cooperatives, the governments of Greece and Pakistan, the American Gas Association, the Washington Senators baseball team, and various pro-bono ventures. I joined the board and executive committee of Americans for Democratic Action, which I continued to admire for its fierce defense of liberal principles, served on the Democratic National Committee's policy council, and cofounded with several 1968 Kennedy and McCarthy campaign leaders an organization we called Referendum '70. It endorsed and raised money for anti–Vietnam War candidates running in Democratic primary contests. I helped recruit three young political organizers to run it. Each later made his own mark in national life. Ken Bode would serve as staff director of the party's reforming McGovern Commission and then become a distinguished educator and television political journalist. Verne Newton would serve in national political campaigns and in the Carter administration, write several nonfiction books, and become director of the Roosevelt Library in Hyde Park, New York. Paul Offner would become a Wisconsin state legislator and then, in Washington, D.C., a national authority on poverty and welfare reform.

The Vietnam War's continuance seemed to me an outrage. Nixon clearly had bought into the same "domino theory" that had sucked presidents Kennedy and Johnson ever deeper into Vietnam. He frequently stated his belief that if Indochina fell to communism, the rest of Southeast Asia would follow. He pursued diplomatic overtures to Hanoi, which was not forthcoming in its responses. As members of his administration later reported, he also felt indebted to South Vietnamese president Thieu for having helped him win the 1968 presidential election.

In March 1969, Nixon had ordered the bombing of targets in Cambodia known to be sanctuaries for North Vietnamese troops mounting operations in South Vietnam. Congressional leaders became concerned that Nixon's escalations would make American disengagement more, rather than less, difficult. Senator George McGovern delivered a scathingly critical speech on the Senate floor, and then, in May, traveled to Paris to meet in person with North Vietnamese and National Liberation Front negotiators. He distrusted what Nixon and his national security advisor, Henry Kissinger, were telling the country and Congress, and wanted to get a firsthand sense of our adversaries' objectives.

Nixon took a practical step that same month to subdue domestic dissent on Vietnam. He proposed changes in the Selective Service system that would make most American males over nineteen exempt from the draft. A new lottery system, moreover, would give draft-eligible nineteen-year-olds clear notice of their chances of being drafted. Campus protest subsided substantially. College students who had been opposing the war on policy or moral grounds suddenly felt less impelled once their own hides were no longer at risk.

In September, North Vietnamese leader Ho Chi Minh died. A few weeks earlier, he had sent Nixon a letter calling for the withdrawal of U.S. troops from Vietnam, leaving South and North Vietnamese to sort things out for themselves. Kissinger, on the other hand, proposed a dramatic escalation of violence against Hanoi to force serious peace talks on bases more acceptable to the United States. But Nixon held back. Congressional criticism of the war was increasing. New York Republican Senator Jacob Javits called for substantial U.S. troop withdrawals. Nixon then announced the planned withdrawal of 60,000 American troops by the Christmas season. The announcement was timed to precede national peace rallies scheduled for October 15. The rallies nonetheless attracted broad support in every region but the South. Vice President Spiro Agnew was dispatched to make public statements characterizing the protestors as, among other things, "an effete corps of impudent snobs." Then, after news of the My Lai massacre surfaced in mid-November, Nixon announced further U.S. troop withdrawals to take place in the spring of 1970.

Early in 1970 the covert U.S. troop involvement in Laos became known, although Nixon flatly denied it as late as March. On April 30, taking a huge political gamble, Nixon announced to the nation that he had ordered an out-right U.S. invasion of Cambodia to strike North Vietnamese forces there. It soon became clear that some North Vietnamese forces and weapons had been destroyed in the invasion, but nothing had happened to fundamentally dis-rupt North Vietnamese operations in South Vietnam.

The pattern continued: Nixon announcements of peace initiatives; incre-mental U.S. troop withdrawals; increasing applications of force on North Viet-nam to bring Hanoi to terms. What Nixon was missing, of course, was that Ho Chi Minh's letter of August 1969 did not represent Hanoi's negotiating position. It represented Hanoi's nonnegotiable bottom line: the 1954 Geneva Accords—broken by the United States and its allies—had provided that Viet-nam should be one country as determined by citizens of both North and South. Nixon, like Johnson before him, had become entrapped in day-to-day tactical decisions about conducting the war in Vietnam and managing polit-ical opposition in the United States. He simply could not disengage himself and take a necessary strategic decision in the American interest.

I had already concluded, several years before, that our involvement in Vietnam was the result of a mistaken lesson drawn from World War II by our national leaders. Had we faced down Hitler and Imperial Japan at an early stage, the thinking went, we could have averted the bloody tragedy of World War II. We had successfully faced down the Soviet Union in Europe after World War II by forming the North Atlantic Treaty Organization and by challenging Soviet expansionist impulses elsewhere, and thus had averted World War III. We had done it again in the Korean War. Similarly, the rea-soning went, we had to use American power assertively in Southeast Asia at an early stage, lest a red tide from China through Indochina engulf the entire region later on.

The situation in Indochina, of course, had little to do with the spread of communist ideology or the projection of Soviet or Chinese power. It had to do with the historic struggle of a country to establish its independence and autonomy and to expel not only colonial but Chinese influences. American interests would have been best served, following France's retreat from Indo-china, by simple adherence to the Geneva Accords, letting the people of the country determine its fate in a national election. Successive American pres-idents and foreign-policy establishmentarians could not grasp the concept, although it now is generally accepted.

While serving Humphrey in the Johnson White House, I could try to do something by working, through the vice president, within the administration and the national political process. Now, on the outside, I found myself becoming as agitated as outsiders in my own Democratic Party must have felt in 1967–68 about the Vietnam issue. This led me to join in founding the Referendum '70 group. I also began actively helping Democrats in the Congress who continued to challenge the war.

It was during this period that I found myself involved in part two of a conflict with the Central Intelligence Agency which had begun several years earlier, during Humphrey's vice presidency.

In 1965 Sam Brown and Jim Johnson, at that time president and vice president of the National Student Association (NSA), met with Humphrey and me to report on their recent inspection trip to South Vietnam. They invited Humphrey to visit NSA headquarters in Washington. He did. It was apparent that the place had been painted and cleaned up within the previous twenty-four hours. A few months later, Phil Sherburne, the new National Student Association president, asked for an appointment with Humphrey to discuss what he said was a private and sensitive matter. The matter, it turned out, was the NSA's financial support and control by the Central Intelligence Agency. Not only Brown and Johnson, he said, but NSA officers since the Cold War period had been working with the CIA to further international objectives set forth by the agency. Most National Student Association staff did not know of the arrangement; only a few top officers did. Humphrey was surprised. So was I. We thought such an arrangement wholly inappropriate. Sherburne asked if Humphrey would help secure alternative funding for the NSA so that it could become independent of CIA influence. Humphrey asked me to take on the project, but to do so carefully and without President Johnson's knowledge. Thus letters were sent by the vice president to several corporate leaders with whom he had a close relationship, asking them to meet with Sherburne and consider funding help for the NSA. Charles Schultze, then director of the Bureau of the Budget, told me that he knew the CIA was subsidizing various organizations but was unaware of the specific NSA involvement. Sherburne checked back with news that he had run into blind alleys everywhere in soliciting private funds.

Several months later I received a phone call from Sherburne, whose NSA presidential term by then had expired. He wanted us to know that *Ramparts* magazine would soon publish an article laying out full information about the CIA-NSA relationship. Humphrey's and my roles might be made public.

Within moments of Sherburne's call, Humphrey buzzed me on the intercom and asked me to come to his office. Sitting there was Cord Meyer, the CIA official responsible for liaison with the National Student Association and other private organizations. He was seething with anger. Wiretaps obviously had been placed on Sherburne's telephone. Meyer knew about our roles in helping him, about his efforts to secure independent funding, and about the *Ramparts* article. I suspected that Meyer had intervened with the potential private donors to scare them away from Sherburne.

"Do you know," Meyer asked, "that Phil Sherburne is seriously disturbed and under psychiatric care? He is not someone you should ever have dealt with." "What is more," he said, "you have no business interfering with CIA activity." I responded by telling Meyer that I doubted Sherburne was disturbed. Even if he was, it was irrelevant to the question of the CIA-NSA relationship, which was wholly inappropriate. "No one elected you," I told Meyer. "You are sitting in the office of the vice president, who was elected by the American people. Who are you to be delivering a lecture here on the appropriateness of the vice president's or my actions?" Humphrey said nothing. I rose and returned to my own office down the hall. I have no idea what he subsequently told Meyer; I suspect he simply rose to signal that the meeting was over.

The *Ramparts* article did appear, in 1966. It made no mention, however, either of Humphrey or of me. It did mention that Sherburne had met with Doug Cater, an LBJ assistant who would have been sympathetic to his message. When the matter became public, the CIA-NSA relationship ended. Neither Humphrey nor I heard a word on the matter from President Johnson or anyone on his staff.

The second part of my conflict with the CIA began in 1970, after I had joined with others to found Referendum '70 and had become active on a daily basis in the antiwar movement. My secretary, Glenda Temple, reported to me that she had met and dated several times someone who subsequently told her he worked for the CIA. He had asked her to spy on me, to keep phone logs, and to give him photocopies of my correspondence. She refused and ended the relationship. I then called two friends whom I knew to be former CIA officers. I told them what had happened, and of my earlier brush with Cord Meyer, and asked them to deliver a message directly to their ex-colleagues at the CIA: Cease and desist or I would go directly to media and Democrats in Congress and cause the agency pain. My friends both responded that the CIA had no domestic role—certainly no surveillance role—and that I must be mistaken. I told them I was not mistaken and to pass along the message. I then filed Freedom of Information requests for CIA documents in which my name might appear. Over an eighteen-month period, I kept trying without getting any response. Eventually I did receive via regular mail a handful of documents, but with all substantive information blacked out "because of national security requirements." The only thing readable was a section listing some of my known associates, including mainly Democratic officeholders, Democratic National Chairman Larry O'Brien, and some of my consulting clients.

News reports surfaced later that the CIA had indeed been conducting illegal domestic activities, including surveillance of U.S. citizens. As far as I could tell, the agency left me alone after my message to my two ex-CIA friends. Had I had any other indication of surveillance, or any inkling that this was a general practice, I would have taken the issue public. Looking back, I now regret that I did not do so immediately.

I had not seen much of my old boss Humphrey since leaving his staff. I contributed some general input to his 1970 Minnesota campaign to reenter the Senate, and I dropped by his Senate office periodically after his return to the capital. But the old, close relationship had waned. In 1971, I joined him at his apartment in southwest Washington for a drink and gossip. When our conversation turned to Vietnam, I was shocked to find that he had completely erased from his memory many of the pivotal events surrounding his involvement in the issue. He had forgotten the showdown meetings with Johnson prior to the Democratic convention in Chicago. He had blanked out the details of platform negotiations at the convention itself. Finally, he asked: "Why do you think we lost in 1968?" I told him I thought we had lost, most of all, because voters had not gotten an early and clear picture of where he stood on the Vietnam War. "For a long time you seemed weak and equivocal when voters wanted someone who was strong and unequivocal," I said. "Voters needed to know if you were with the antiwar forces or if you intended to just plain stick with Johnson." "You're right," he said, "I've thought about it often. I should have stuck with Johnson."

I felt at that moment, though I did not tell him, as though I had just learned that a loved one had been hurt in a serious accident. Was Humphrey still that greatly in Johnson's thrall? It was more complicated than that. I had little doubt that, if elected president, Humphrey would have ended the Vietnam War as he had pledged in his campaign. He was the same man I had served and revered for his idealism. But clearly he had been so scarred by 1968 that three years later he was still trying to find his way back. I drove home feeling bone-deep sadness for the pain being borne by this truly good man.

Senator George McGovern had emerged as perhaps the strongest single spokesman opposing Nixon's continuation of the Vietnam War. He was cosponsor, with Oregon Republican Senator Mark Hatfield, of the McGovern-Hatfield Resolution, which had become the principal legislative vehicle of war critics. The resolution would have stopped all funds for the war after December 1970, and required withdrawal of all U.S. troops by mid-1971 unless Congress first declared war. McGovern's and Humphrey's instincts were almost exactly the same. Humphrey had sponsored McGovern's appointment as Food for Peace director in the Kennedy White House. Despite their differences on the war, McGovern had been the first Democrat to stand by Humphrey after his 1968 nomination in Chicago. Both had progressive South Dakota roots, and they had been next-door neighbors in suburban Maryland, their children's handprints imprinted in the sidewalk between their homes. They also shared a deep loyalty to the Democratic Party as an institution. McGovern, in fact, had begun his career as a party organizer, working door to door in South Dakota.

When McGovern was scouting for a new staff assistant, early in 1971, I referred to him Gordon Weil, who had worked with me a decade earlier at the European Communities' Washington office. I contributed speech and policy ideas to McGovern, as I did to other antiwar Democrats. In mid-1971 he formally declared his candidacy for the Democratic presidential nomination. Initial public-opinion polling gave him almost no chance against other possible Democratic contenders. Nonetheless, I thought his commitment to the antiwar cause, combined with his commitment to the Democratic Party as an institution, formed the basis for a candidacy that could result in his nomination or, at a minimum, move the Democratic Party strongly and unequivocally toward his position on the war. I felt prior loyalty to Humphrey and friendship for Senator Ed Muskie, whom I had favored as Humphrey's 1968 running mate. But I felt that Humphrey had been damaged by the war issue and should not attempt another presidential candidacy. Muskie had performed well during the 1968 general-election campaign, but behind the scenes he had often displayed bouts of temperament that I thought ill suited him to a presidential candidacy. Even Humphrey's unlimited tolerance had been strained at times by them. (On one occasion in October 1968, Muskie had called Humphrey at 2 AM in Philadelphia, after a hard day's campaigning, to urge cancellation of an upcoming campaign rally in Chicago. When Humphrey proved too sleepy to comprehend Muskie's message, Muskie ordered me awakened to transmit advice from *Saturday Review* publisher Norman Cousins that the campaign should bypass Chicago until election day, lest memories of the divisive convention alienate peace voters. Humphrey's predictable reaction the next morning: "Does Ed think we can win the election by writing off Illinois? Does he think we can win Illinois by ignoring Chicago?")

I went to Humphrey's office to tell him that I thought he should not undertake his own candidacy for the 1972 presidential nomination. I also told him that I had decided to help his old friend McGovern. He said he had made no decision about his own candidacy, wished McGovern well, and was not surprised at my decision to support a candidate I thought most committed to ending the Vietnam War. I could see, though, that I had hurt him. He paused a moment, then passed me a particularly tough-on-Nixon Herblock cartoon from that morning's *Washington Post*. We laughed over it. Then Humphrey said: "Help George. End the war."

10

CRUSADE AND CATASTROPHE

Gary Hart, who in 1968 had been a campaign organizer in Colorado for Robert Kennedy, was serving as director of George McGovern's presidential nominating campaign. His campaign experience, however, had been almost wholly at the local level. McGovern and his wife, Eleanor, had affection for Hart and appreciated his early commitment to the McGovern presidential candidacy. But both were concerned that his marriage was being strained by his absence from Colorado and that he lacked experience in national politics. After I offered McGovern my volunteer services, he asked that, as a first task, I meet with Hart and assess what was going on at the campaign headquarters. McGovern wanted me to help build a full campaign structure. He hoped Hart would concentrate on national organizing. Frank Mankiewicz, Robert Kennedy's 1968 campaign press secretary, would come aboard in a few days and would serve as principal campaign spokesman. I told McGovern I wanted to receive no financial compensation. I would continue to conduct my consulting business in downtown Washington in the mornings and would spend afternoons and evenings at the campaign headquarters on Capitol Hill. Hart and Mankiewicz, I knew, would be working for modest campaign-staff salaries.

I arrived the next morning at the McGovern headquarters, situated in low-rent quarters on 1st Street N.E., to begin my situation analysis. Hart kept me waiting forty-five minutes in the tiny reception room. I had not known or met him before. He greeted me with the same enthusiasm with which he might have greeted news of a diagnosis of Hansen's disease.

I found good news and bad news. Two excellent campaign coordinators, Joe Grandmaison and Gene Pokorny, were on the scene in the key primary states of New Hampshire and Wisconsin. The bare-bones headquarters organization was fortunately anchored by Rick Stearns, a former Rhodes Scholar and McCarthy volunteer who kept watch on state-by-state activities. No priorities had been set among primary and caucus states. No broad fundraising organization was in place. No policy research or media efforts had been organized. No formal scheduling or advance operation existed. The campaign was largely existential, mainly focused around McGovern's out-of-town trips and speeches and networking among 1968 peace activists. His Senate office continued to function as his central base of operations, with Gordon Weil, legislative assistant John Holum, and others providing him excellent staff support.

If you believe that national candidacies spring spontaneously into being, you are mistaken. Winning campaigns typically are the result of careful planning; losing campaigns most often are improvisational and harum-scarum. Candidates usually seek the presidency only after having spent many years of their lives thinking about it.

Just as a successful commercial product must have a comparative advantage over competitors, so must a successful national candidacy. Humphrey, in seeking the 1964 vice presidential nomination, had had the advantage of seeming the party leader best prepared to succeed to the presidency on short notice, should that be required. McGovern, in 1971, had the advantage of being the candidate for the presidential nomination most identified with opposition to the Vietnam War. Other Democrats, in varying degree, opposed the war. But, if you were a Democrat committed to ending the war, McGovern was your man. Because antiwar Democrats then were the most intense participants in the party nominating process, they were a potentially potent base from which to launch a candidacy. There also were a number of independent antiwar groups that could collaborate with the campaign. One was Vietnam Veterans against the War, cofounded by a former Navy Swift Boat commander, John Kerry. Kerry, wearing combat fatigues, was a familiar figure around campaign headquarters. To ensure that he got first claim on this key constituency, McGovern had taken the unprecedented step of declaring his candidacy in the middle of the year preceding the national election.

There is a sound rule in politics: nail down your base and keep it nailed. McGovern, as his campaign proceeded, never strayed from his base on the central issue of Vietnam. But many of his core supporters, it would turn out, had agendas beyond the war which he would never be able to satisfy. That would become apparent only later, after his nomination, during the party platform process.

McGovern's antiwar base also would serve him well in fundraising. Direct-mail appeals, coordinated by Morris Dees (head of the Southern Poverty Law Center) and Jeff Smith of McGovern's staff, already had begun when I arrived on the scene. We added regional fundraising chairs to be responsible for more traditional, big-contribution efforts in various regions of the country. We also would seek big contributions from individuals principally motivated by the antiwar cause.

Scheduling and advance operations might, to an outsider, seem to be minor nuts-and-bolts matters, but they make a big difference in building support for a candidate. A candidate is badly served by responding ad hoc to various speaking invitations, which may not be in the right places to the right groups. Thus I instituted a scheduling and advance operation, and hired Steve Robbins to run it. It placed McGovern on a systematic basis in the particular states and media markets that were most important in the nominating process. The same system is being used today: presidential candidates spend much of their time in early-primary and early-caucus states, and very little in states that come later in the process—except for places where serious political money can be raised.

An ideal schedule will have the candidate in at least two and, if possible, three media markets daily. That will allow for local television coverage in each market, a newspaper editorial-board or interview session, and a public event which will generate enthusiasm among party activists, union members, and others important in the nominating process. Private time must be spent with donors and key leaders. Televised events should begin as early as possible in the day, so that they can be replayed several times over the course of the day. For that reason, travel to the next city on the candidate's schedule should always be done at the end of each campaign day; television coverage can thus start first thing the next day in a new market. Events held after prime-time local news broadcasts are, in any case, lost to media coverage. Better to be moving onward to the next stop at that hour. I had instituted for the first time in 1964, in Humphrey's vice presidential campaign, the concept of a separate media advance. I recruited a half-dozen media professionals to work solely with broadcast and print media in the same way that general advance work was traditionally done with political and community leaders. One was Bob Squier, who produced the 1968 Humphrey-Muskie election-eve telethon and later went on to provide professional campaign counsel to numerous Democratic candidates at all levels. These advance coordinators also made sure that media traveling with the candidate were serviced professionally during the stop. I hired similar media advance staff for the McGovern effort.

A skillful advance person, once assigned a city, will touch all important political and organizational bases before the candidate's arrival. If a public event is scheduled, a room will be secured that is slightly smaller than the expected crowd, thus creating the impression of an overflow. The advance person will work with local organizations to build the crowd, busing it from elsewhere if necessary. He or she will prepare note cards, to be handed to the candidate before arrival, that list all the people (and their identification) he will encounter at each event. Personal data will be listed so that the candidate can mention a daughter, spouse, or someone else close to the supporters being courted, and give special, specific recognition to key people. Woe unto the advance person who forgets to list and identify the individuals seated on a podium or at a head table at an event. The candidate should recognize each by name in the opening remarks. The worst offenses are to omit someone important, to misspell his or her name, or to lead the candidate into a mispronunciation of the name. The able advance person will also provide the candidate with information about any embarrassments, indictments, scandals, or other negative matters that may be associated with anyone the candidate will encounter.

Small matters to the candidate may loom quite large to local leaders. Thus an effective advance person will be sure that the right people ride with the candidate from the airport, have a private moment with him, or are seated near him or her at a public event. I have seen angry scenes of local elected officials and key supporters fighting with each other over who would sit in the front and back seats in the candidate's limousine or in a follow-up car. No one who considers himself important wants to be seen in a second-tier position. The advance person should have all the pecking orders correct.

If general and media advance work has been done successfully, the candidate will seem to glide gracefully from one place to another, never missing a cue, always saying the right thing, emanating power and competence. On the other hand, bad advance work can make the candidate appear a klutz.

I also made sure that McGovern had background papers before each out-of-town event, which gave brief summaries of the nature of the community: the unemployment rate, ethnic breakdown, per-capita income, principal industries, and recent political and social history. When both Mankiewicz and I had arrived officially on the scene, we convened planning sessions at which Stearns and his staff gave us up-to-date information on the situations in the various states. Hart brought into the process Pat Caddell, a young pollster who later conducted opinion surveys for several other Democratic campaigns. After these sessions we were able to decide which states should receive the greatest time, money, and organizational effort. It was no surprise that we had little support or potential in states south of the Mason-Dixon line. We would have to concentrate on the Northeast, upper Midwest, and West Coast, with obvious priority going to the earliest nominating contests. If we did not do well in an early primary, the game would be over quickly.

I retained a young group of advertising and design people to produce bumper stickers, posters, and campaign buttons right away. Charles Guggenheim, the filmmaker, would produce campaign television commercials as actual state-by-state contests began.

McGovern had well-developed and well-publicized views on Vietnam, agricultural policy, and a few other issues. He had already issued an alternative defense budget proposing sharp cutbacks in overall U.S. defense spending. But in many other policy areas he lacked fully developed views. I enlisted Jamie Galbraith, a young economist (and son of John Kenneth Galbraith) working in the headquarters, to join me in putting together a "McGovern on the Issues" booklet, which would set forth more developed positions for the candidate on major foreign and domestic issues. We began by listing, for each policy area, the legislation McGovern had either sponsored or cosponsored. We then compiled all his public statements and grouped them into the same categories. Where his record was thin, we drafted suggested policy positions for him. I suggested only one major change to a prior McGovern position. I thought that the proposed dollar, manpower, and weapons-system cuts in his defense budget would seem excessive even to many antiwar voters. They certainly would seem so to everyone else. But, in reviewing our "McGovern on the Issues" draft, McGovern made only one revision: he insisted on leaving his big defense cuts intact in every detail.

Hart, Mankiewicz, and I interviewed and hired several aggressive young organizers for the field organization, including an Oxford pal of Stearns's, Bill Clinton, whom we sent to Texas. I recall that at his interview Clinton was wearing highly polished cordovan shoes and his best suit. When asked when he could start, he said, "How about right now?"

Mankiewicz filled an enormous gap by establishing regular contact with New York and Washington, D.C., columnists and political journalists, who mainly were sympathetic to McGovern's candidacy but who had lacked a campaign contact point.

A Humphrey or Kennedy campaign, drawing support from labor and other organized groups, could be a mixture of top-down and bottom-up organization. But the McGovern campaign, essentially an insurgency, had no option but to be bottom-up. We simply were not going to get the endorsements, money, and support from elected officials or organized groups that establishment candidates could secure. In 1971, most such support was already flowing to Muskie. We made contact with established groups and leaders—after all, we would need them later if McGovern won the nomination—but had no illusions regarding their endorsement in the nomination race.

It became clear in the fall of 1971 that Hart was unhappy with what he saw as his diminished role. Before Mankiewicz's and my arrival, he had been accustomed to being the sole campaign spokesman and presiding much as he wished over the campaign's small headquarters and field staff. He clearly was uncomfortable that Mankiewicz and I made decisions, without much discussion, about matters that were second nature to us but that he was encountering for the first time. Hart preferred to do things by committee. Even though he was responsible for field organization, he wanted Mankiewicz and me to interview each job candidate. We would have preferred that he just move ahead with those people he wanted to hire.

Things came to a head when Gene Pokorny, our Wisconsin coordinator, came to town to seek approval for his budget and to talk strategy in his state. He brought with him the layout and prospective copy for a campaign newspaper he proposed to issue regularly in Wisconsin. Hart and I sat down with him to review his plans. I told him that the newspaper was a good idea but noticed that some of the copy attributed to McGovern positions that he did not hold. A misstatement, I told him, could be exploited by the opposition. He should go forward with his newspaper but give us a quick look at copy before publication, to be sure it accurately reflected McGovern's views. The campaign had to tell the same story in all states.

I thought nothing more of the discussion until, a few days later, McGovern told me that Hart had brought Pokorny to his Senate office. Both, he said, had demanded that Hart be given full control over campaign activity, or field organizers would resign. My request for review of Pokorny's publication was unreasonable, both had said, and demonstrated the need to keep all decision making with Hart. Joe Grandmaison in New Hampshire, McGovern said, felt the same way. (Later Grandmaison would tell me that Hart had cooked up the whole tempest. "Pokorny and I would never have resigned," he said. "It was Hart's thing.")

The campaign structure which he had asked me to construct was largely in place, McGovern said, and he thought it perhaps best to let Hart have the authority he sought to run it. He was going to ask Mankiewicz to restrict himself increasingly to media contact. He wanted me to stay actively involved in his campaign, however. Would I begin traveling with him, as I had traveled with Humphrey, and become his full-time counselor and advisor?

I told him that I would be pleased to travel with him periodically but that, as I was still operating my consulting business, I could not do it full-time. I would sit in on planning sessions, troubleshoot in key states, draft periodic statements, and do whatever had high priority as his nominating campaign proceeded. McGovern announced to headquarters staff the following day that Hart again would be in charge, Mankiewicz would be a comanager but largely concentrate on media, and I would become a senior advisor and troubleshooter. Mankiewicz and I both absented ourselves from the staff meeting.

I was disappointed that Hart had acted as he had. Hart, it seemed to me, had put his ego ahead of his candidate's interests. I also worried that the campaign would slide back toward the unfocused pattern that I had found on my arrival. I went back to spending more time at my downtown business office and continued my involvement as I had told McGovern I would. Later, when McGovern ran into snarls in both the both primary and general-election campaigns, I came to regret that I had not agreed to travel with him full time as he had asked.

Especially after McGovern neared the presidential nomination, there was more than enough work and public exposure for everyone in his campaign. Hart, I thought, came to realize that. I never discussed his earlier conduct with him; I simply resolved to watch carefully what he said and did.

As the year wore on, McGovern's chances for the nomination seemed slim. As 1972 dawned, he drew only 4 percent support as the preferred candidate of Democratic voters in a national poll. Ed Muskie, Alabama governor George Wallace—then running as a Democratic rather than third-party candidate—and others were far ahead of him. Moreover, the McGovern campaign treasury was all but empty. Morris Dees and Jeff Smith had kept grassroots contributions coming to the campaign, but without immediate infusions of money, McGovern might not be able to reach even the first, important New Hampshire primary. Liberal Democratic contributors were invited to a last-ditch Sunday meeting at McGovern's Washington, D.C., home. The night before, and earlier that day, Mankiewicz had met with Max Palevsky, a California high-tech executive and major donor, and implored him to make a large contribution to keep the campaign alive. He finally came through with $100,000. (Later, after McGovern's presidential nomination, Palevsky demanded as the price for his further support that he be named campaign policy director, a position I was to fill. McGovern turned him down and Palevsky withdrew.) Palevsky's contribution, and the commitments of others attending the meeting, almost certainly kept us from closing down as 1972 began.

We were down, but there was no quit in the candidate or those immediately surrounding him. He and others of us at the showdown fundraising meeting gave upbeat, optimistic presentations on the campaign's strategy to gain the nomination and win the election. Our basic thesis, which held up through the nominating season, was that candidates with intense, loyal bases of support—such as McGovern's base in the peace movement—could make stronger showings in primary contests than candidates with broad but thin bases of support, such as the favored Ed Muskie. Then, once past the primaries, we would be able to mobilize a unified Democratic Party against a vulnerable President Nixon.

Soon after this meeting I accompanied McGovern to New Hampshire for his official filing of candidacy. A corporal's guard of media treated the event sneeringly. They questioned why McGovern, a prairie populist, would even bother to challenge Muskie in a New England state next door to his native Maine. I had drafted a brief declaration of candidacy for McGovern and had prepared note cards for use in interviews that day. One card, which he liked and used, stated that "Ed Muskie's pending victory in New Hampshire is the easiest to predict since George Romney's in 1968." (Michigan governor Romney, after saying he had been "brainwashed" by military briefers in Vietnam, had quickly fallen out of the front-runner position in the Republican nominating race that year.) Privately I asked Grandmaison for a district-by-district assessment of our potential vote. It did appear that, without some Muskie glitch on the order of Romney's, we were unlikely to be competitive. McGovern, animated as always by the peace cause, maintained absolute faith in his candidacy. Over drinks that night in McGovern's room at the University of New Hampshire, we tried to top each other with jokes about famous underdogs who had won unexpected victories.

The next important primary, after New Hampshire, would be in Florida. Rick Brown was the campaign's on-site director, working out of a headquarters in a former paint store in Coral Gables. I flew to Florida, bought time for local television commercials (with campaign checks which, it later turned out, bounced), raised money, visited local coordinators around the state, gave media interviews, and represented McGovern in negotiations with the other Democratic campaigns over ground rules for a prospective candidate debate. Our campaign's limited objective was to outpoll New York City mayor John Lindsay, who was the principal competitor for our slice of the electorate in the nominating contest. If we fared badly in New Hampshire, as was possible, and finished behind Lindsay in Florida, we clearly were done.

It was balmy in South Florida on the eve of the New Hampshire primary. I stood outside our paint-store headquarters with young volunteers, watching a television set mounted near the entrance. Suddenly, in a snowy scene, something strange was happening with Muskie. He was denouncing Manchester newspaper publisher William Loeb for what he considered attacks on his wife, Jane Muskie, and appeared to be crying, simultaneously wiping tears and snowflakes from his cheeks. Muskie's tears—if, in fact, they truly were tears—had a devastating effect on his campaign. He won the primary, just as Lyndon Johnson had won it four years earlier, but his margin proved far thinner than anyone anticipated. McGovern unexpectedly ran a strong second, only nine points behind.

Just before leaving for Florida I had received a heartfelt letter from Humphrey. He had decided to enter the race, beginning with the Florida primary. He wanted me to reassume the role I had filled for him in 1968. I wrote back that I could not abandon McGovern. If McGovern fared badly and was forced to withdraw, then I would help Humphrey. I felt a heart tug toward Humphrey, but I had made a commitment to McGovern six months before and would keep it.

Muskie, still the front-runner for the nomination, mounted a dreadful Florida media campaign showing north-woods scenes intended to illustrate his record as an environmentalist. Humphrey counted on black, labor, Jewish, and traditional New Deal voters in the state. Senator Henry (Scoop) Jackson competed for the same votes and appealed to hawkish voters in the party. Wallace could count on conservative panhandle voters. Lindsay's campaign seemed based on the hope that transplanted New Yorkers in South Florida would see him as president. A televised debate was scheduled under auspices of the state Democratic Party. Fortunately for the McGovern campaign, all candidates but McGovern and Lindsay dropped out of the debate—thus giving McGovern a clear shot at defeating Lindsay in the contest that mattered to us. Lindsay's staff person at the debate was Sandy Berger, whom I later would hire as a McGovern campaign speechwriter and researcher. As it turned out, McGovern won the debate decisively. At one point Lindsay stated that McGovern's home state of South Dakota had a higher crime rate than New York's. "Yes," McGovern responded, "South Dakota is a truly evil place." "I knew I had him before the debate even began," McGovern said afterward. "His hands were shaking so badly under the table that he dropped all his note cards on the floor." We survived Florida, finishing slightly ahead of Lindsay; both candidates drew single-digit percentages. Lindsay was out of the race.

The next important contest was in Illinois. But we had made no effort there and simply left the field to Muskie. The Muskie campaign won a huge delegate victory over McGovern's, but because we had not contested there the media treated the whole matter as a nonevent. We had done our best to condition media expectations by pointing to Wisconsin, where Muskie, Humphrey, and McGovern all would be on the ballot, as the decisive contest.

By that time the McGovern campaign had become beneficiary of a syndrome that normally develops as a campaign evolves. Media covering the campaign—mostly liberal and mostly antiwar—had become captivated by the McGovern campaign's story line. Just like Eugene McCarthy in 1968, McGovern had come from nowhere in New Hampshire to a strong second-place showing. Moreover, Muskie, the establishmentarian favorite for the nomination, not only had gotten a fright in New Hampshire but had made only a middling showing in Florida. If McGovern's managers said Illinois did not count—even though it was a huge, delegate-rich state—then why not go along with them and define Wisconsin, as they did, as the campaign's most important contest? That would feed the story line of Muskie, the establishment favorite, falling and McGovern, the underdog peace champion, rising.

We had no option but to define Wisconsin as decisive. We had not won in either New Hampshire or Florida. Wisconsin, with a strong peace movement and a superb organization built over many months by Pokorny, was our best and only chance to make a breakout. Which is what happened. Muskie ran respectably but split the traditional Democratic vote with Humphrey. We publicly announced Muskie's candidacy as being on the ropes, although he at that point had amassed far more delegates than McGovern. Media bought into it. I flew from Wisconsin, the morning after our victory there, to Pennsylvania with Joel Swerdlow, a field organizer who would help me set up a campaign there. The McGovern campaign had little support in Pennsylvania and

$2,500 in its bank account. The Massachusetts primary, to be held on the same day, had to have first priority. Massachusetts had perhaps the strongest anti-war sentiment in the country, and a strong McGovern organization on the ground. (As it turned out, it would be the only state carried by McGovern in the general election.) Swerdlow and I made a sweep of television stations in Pittsburgh, Harrisburg, and Philadelphia, giving upbeat interviews. Humphrey had enjoyed strong support over many years in Pennsylvania and was expected to win there. But we pursued the theme that this would be the state where Muskie was driven from contention and the field cleared for a Humphrey-McGovern showdown in the final primary contests. We generated as much free media coverage as possible and raised a few thousand dollars for a token paid-media campaign. We concentrated on turning out peace voters, and counted on national media coverage from Massachusetts to spill over into the Pennsylvania primary. McGovern personally spent only a day and a half in the state, hitting Philadelphia and its suburbs for a series of short rallies.

We held one fundraising event at the home of a longtime leftist and peace activist. As it ended, and television cameras recorded McGovern's departure from the downtown Philadelphia townhouse, two men in their sixties approached McGovern, shouting, "George, remember us? We were all Henry Wallace delegates together at the 1948 Progressive Party convention." McGovern shook their hands, said nothing, and entered his car. "Truth is," McGovern said as the car moved away, "I remembered them quite well. I was a Henry Wallace delegate in 1948, but no one knows it today. It's an issue I just don't need." Whereupon a member of his Secret Service detail leaned over from the front seat and added: "Yes, and our background check indicates your host tonight was a Communist Party member in the 1930s."

Our base of support in the Quaker State proved to include more than just former Communist/Progressive Party members. On election night we drew a huge Pennsylvania vote—prompted mainly, I thought, by the national momentum generated in Wisconsin and Massachusetts—and ended up with thirty-eight convention delegates. McGovern called from Boston, incredulous. I told him I thought he had just won the nomination.

Coming down the final stretch, the contest did end up as a McGovern-Humphrey showdown. Some in the McGovern campaign made scathing remarks about Humphrey as the California primary loomed. I concentrated instead on positive efforts on behalf of McGovern, and took on the management of the New Jersey primary, to be held the same day as California's.

The California primary exposed weaknesses in McGovern's candidacy. He was committed to ending the Vietnam War. He knew agricultural issues well. But he was not as well grounded as I had thought he would be in economic and domestic policy issues. Even before the primary season he had picked up a proposal, borrowed from Yale economist James Tobin, for a negative income tax. He did not really understand the proposal, but he espoused it, and began illustrating it by explaining that, for instance, a taxpayer under the proposal "might receive a federal payment of, say, $1,000" if in the right income bracket. Critics began calling it "McGovern's $1,000 plan." I and others had warned him of the proposal's potential for political damage. But he received no tough questioning from other primary candidates or the media and tended to treat the matter lightly. Then, in a California debate with Humphrey, he was challenged to put a price tag on the proposal and could not.

At our Wilshire Boulevard motel, after the debate, I found Terry McGovern, the candidate's daughter, in tears in an elevator. "Did Dad get to talk with Uncle Hubert after the debate?" she asked. "I feel so badly that they are confronting each other." I told her that I felt badly too, and that they had not gotten a chance to talk. As I entered McGovern's sitting room, I found a note left by Dick Daugherty, his campaign press secretary. It said that McGovern had won the debate easily and that he would win the primary just as easily. I quickly wrote another note stating that the "$1,000 plan" issue was a killer, and that before the second scheduled debate it was imperative that authoritative estimates be made of its prospective effects on the federal budget. I put it on McGovern's bedroom dresser, then headed out to catch my flight to Newark, New Jersey, where I was to preside at a press conference the next morning announcing McGovern's endorsement by Newark mayor Ken Gibson. As I was leaving, Gordon Weil told me that a Brookings Institution economist present in Los Angeles would get to work immediately on developing the numbers associated with the negative-income-tax scheme.

In New Jersey, I watched the second McGovern-Humphrey televised debate. McGovern cited a figure for his plan's budgetary impact but nothing more. I telephoned Weil. Where had the number come from? "We were en route to the studio in McGovern's limousine," he said. "He took your memo from his pocket and wrote a number on it." "Where did he get the number?" I asked, "from the Brookings analyst?" "No," Weil said, "he looked out the car window and just pulled it out of the air."

McGovern's momentum was sufficiently strong that he won the California primary, and thus the nomination. But the Nixon campaign would exploit the $1,000 issue as Democratic opponents had not. It would be used to paint McGovern as an economic innocent prepared to give federal checks to every man, woman, and child in the country. McGovern, it was quite true, did not pay attention to the fine print of his negative-income-tax proposal or to many other areas of domestic policy. It was frustrating, but I came in time to understand his mindset. Sitting one weekend in his kitchen, he explained: "I am running for president to end the Vietnam War. If I win the presidency, we will get the best people we can to form a government and to develop a comprehensive policy agenda." For McGovern the war was the thing, sometimes the only thing, and he found it difficult to focus on anything else. During the general-election campaign, when I served as McGovern's director of issues and research, I oversaw the issuance of a number of white papers to establish McGovern's credibility on non–Vietnam War issues. But, by then, the picture had been drawn and it was too late to change it.

The $1,000 plan damaged McGovern before the Democratic Party's Miami Beach nominating convention. Other developments would damage him before and at the convention—foremost among them his selection of a vice presidential running mate.

Preparing for the convention, I took on two responsibilities. The first, and by far most important, was to represent McGovern on the Democratic platform committee. The second assignment, which I received mainly because I was one of the few people in the campaign with contacts in other parts of the Democratic Party, was to represent him on the arrangements committee.

In the platform committee, our organizational vulnerability became apparent. McGovern convention delegates, unlike those of other Democratic candidates, came to the process with an insurgency mindset. For many of them the Democratic nomination, more than the presidency itself, was the main prize. Many also were there as much as representatives of single-issue or single-interest groups as they were as individuals. Our McGovern platform staff not only had the task of finding majority support for key McGovern planks, but also of fighting off efforts on behalf of minority planks by our own delegates. Fortney (Pete) Stark, a northern California banker and congressional candidate, attempted a coup in which he and a handful of other McGovern delegates would supplant me and our official staff, perceived as too moderate, in leading the McGovern caucus. We put down the putsch promptly, and Stark apologized. "I am sure you guys wanted to punch me out," he said. I told him that was exactly how we felt.

Fred Harris, another McGovern delegate, had a proposal to do away with all tax deductions, including the politically popular home-mortgage and medical-expense deductions. Women's groups, welfare-rights proponents, agriculture interests, small-business organizations, and other subgroups were all pushing hard for their own planks. It was easy for them to bring their issues to the general convention floor, because party rules provided that only 10 percent of platform committee members were needed to bring a plank forward for a full-convention debate and vote.

The McGovern platform committee staff was highly professional. It included Gordon Weil, Harvard Law professor Abram Chayes, former Connecticut Senate candidate Joe Duffey, Steve Schlesinger, Verne Newton, and former Muskie campaign staffer Richard Leone, among others. I had also recruited New York representative Bella Abzug, California representative Phil Burton, and other liberal McGovern platform committee members to serve as "whips" among their fellow delegates. According to national terms of reference, Abzug and Burton were on the leftward fringe; among our delegates, however, they were pragmatic centrists.

The platform committee process, held in Washington, D.C., before the convention, proved manageable, even though our platform staff often had to depend on Humphrey, Muskie, Wallace, and other delegate votes to override dissident McGovern delegates who wanted, especially on social issues, more strident planks than the general electorate would tolerate. Richard Neustadt, a Harvard professor who was chairing the process, was unprepared for the combat in which he found himself immersed. He voluntarily stepped aside on the second day in favor of McGovern delegate and Newark mayor Ken Gibson, a tough guy from a tough town.

The committee product did, in the end, contain several sections spelling out excessive demands of various key political constituencies at the expense of the country at large. We resisted and modified them as best we could, but it was indisputable that the draft taken to Miami Beach would, if subjected to close examination, present a number of easy political targets for the Nixon campaign in the fall. Richard Leone of our platform staff watched committee members argue at the Washington meeting for special "rights" for their own particular groups, and remarked: "Shouldn't we do something for the nobility? Their rights have eroded in recent years." Frank Mankiewicz, watching the process from the back of the ballroom, made a frequently quoted observation, paraphrasing a 1930s popular song title, that "every little meaning has a movement all its own."

While our platform team was resisting such special provisions in downtown Washington, McGovern was being subjected at his home to in-person and telephone demands from key supporters. On the phone, I urged him to hold firm; he, in turn, urged me to make as many concessions as I could without giving away the store.

At the end of the process, I rallied the Humphrey, Muskie, Jackson, and Wallace platform representatives to raise their arms aloft with Gibson and me for the benefit of television cameras. We together declared the platform draft a success and the party unified. I knew, though, that the display of unity owed more to the mutual goodwill of the platform professionals than to genuine consensus among the factions represented.

At Miami Beach, we attempted to manage the platform process not only with the team that had operated in Washington, but also with a tighter whip system. We had at least one key whip planted in each of the fifty state delegations. I briefed all McGovern organizers on the majority and minority planks, and gave Rick Stearns, running floor operations from a trailer outside the convention hall, a detailed memorandum explaining which planks had to pass unchanged, which could be amended, and which could be a "free" uninstructed vote for delegates. He was in communication with the delegations by phone and walkie-talkie. Our platform team shuttled back and forth among delegations to explain and sell our positions. I negotiated on the convention floor with officeholders and other political leaders who wanted podium time or wanted to deal on one plank or another. In short, we did everything by the political organizational book.

What we had not foreseen, however, was that delegates who had felt thwarted at the 1968 Chicago convention were determined to have catharsis on the 1972 Miami Beach convention floor—no matter what the effect on the fortunes of McGovern, their nominee.

The middle-American national audience watching the Miami Beach convention on television saw a scene that seemed in its own way as chaotic as the Chicago convention four years before. The 1972 event appeared more Woodstock than party convention. Social issues, usually kept out of first-line political dialogue, were being debated avidly. Minority planks, taking advantage of an easy procedural path to the convention, seemed to consume a major share of the party's evening business. The McGovern convention was, to no one's surprise, a peace convention. But it also was turning out to be the "acid, amnesty, and abortion" convention later derided by Republicans, the national media, and a "Democrats for Nixon" national group that organized quickly thereafter.

The convention floor was noisy, and proceedings were confused. Fred Harris's plank removing all tax deductions had more strength than he knew. As a vote approached on his proposal, I passed a note under the podium to Representative Yvonne Braithwaite Burke, who was presiding. "This plank must lose," it said, "it is political poison." When Burke called for a voice vote it was apparent that the "ayes" supporting Harris had a slight edge over the "nays" opposing him. Burke did not skip a beat as she brought down the gavel and announced the plank defeated. No one, apparently including Harris, noticed, and the dance went on.

Alaska senator Mike Gravel made a speech nominating himself for vice president. Soapy Owens, a United Auto Workers leader and Iowa delegate, told me that Eugene McCarthy, who was somewhere in the rear of the hall, had asked him to ask me to arrange for him to address the convention that evening. "What does McCarthy want to say?" I asked. Owens said he would check. A moment later he returned: "McCarthy won't say," he said, "he just wants to speak." Iowa senator Harold Hughes, a 1968 McCarthy supporter, overheard the exchange and began telling McCarthy jokes.

Sponsors of minority planks would not withdraw them in the interests of time—even though they were clearly doomed to defeat. McGovern's nomination still had to formally take place, and his acceptance speech was yet to be delivered. Finally, McGovern made his "Come Home" speech, but too late for most viewers except those in the Pacific Time Zone to watch. It was misbilled by many in the media as a call for American isolationism. Far from it: the speech was a call for withdrawal from Vietnam, but also a call for return to traditional American values in domestic society. What voters understandably had missed during the nominating campaign was that McGovern's opposition to the Vietnam War did not necessarily mean that he supported free-spending, big-government policies at home. On domestic policy, in fact, his instincts leaned less toward big government approaches than, for instance, those of Johnson or Humphrey.

Prior to the next convention, in 1976, I proposed, and the party adopted, a change in platform rules to require that a minority plank receive 25 percent rather than 10 percent of committee votes in order to be debated on the convention floor. But that change did little good in 1972. The platform—and the "acid, amnesty, and abortion" label attached to McGovern delegates and the party—hurt us in the fall election. But at least as much damage was to come from events surrounding McGovern's selection of a running mate.

Throughout the period leading up to the Miami Beach convention, McGovern clung to a belief that Senator Ted Kennedy would agree to serve on his ticket. When I raised the running-mate issue with him on an airplane flight two weeks before the convention, McGovern said: "I know that Ted Kennedy, when it comes down to it, will serve on my ticket. I don't need alternatives." Kennedy had told others he was not interested in the nomination. McGovern, I thought, must have some secret knowledge not shared by the rest of us. So it came to pass that, on the evening of his own nomination, McGovern was definitively informed by Kennedy that he was unavailable.

Gary Hart called an early-morning meeting the next day of the twenty to twenty-five core campaign staffers, to discuss alternatives. Many names were suggested. Various persons were assigned to check out backgrounds of a final half-dozen to be presented to McGovern. The last on the short list was Missouri senator Tom Eagleton, a Catholic border-state politician with strong organized-labor support; Gordon Weil was given this background-check assignment. He reported later in the day that Eagleton once was thought to have a drinking problem but otherwise checked out. Weil's report seemed unimportant, in any case, since Boston mayor Kevin White's name had been forwarded to McGovern by then as the group's recommendation. McGovern phoned White, asking him to stand by for final confirmation of his selection. White's name was passed to Stearns in the campaign situation room, and he placed it on the official papers to be submitted to the convention. Then a bizarre series of events changed everything.

Economist John Kenneth Galbraith, a McGovern delegate from Massachusetts, phoned McGovern to report that his Massachusetts delegation would walk out of the convention if White, a Muskie supporter, was placed on the ticket. Later we found out that Senator Kennedy, though not willing to serve himself, had bridled at the thought of White—whom he regarded as a Massachusetts second banana—on his party's national ticket, and had put Galbraith up to his call to McGovern. McGovern yielded to the threat.

With McGovern in his suite were his wife, Eleanor, his secretary Pat Donovan, Hart, Mankiewicz, Weil, Daugherty, former Kennedy advisors

Pierre Salinger and Fred Dutton, and myself. In a few hours McGovern would be required to offer his vice presidential nominee to the convention.

Earlier that day, Mankiewicz had leaked to the media the names of possible running mates, some of whom were not on the list of finalists. They mainly had been mentioned to stimulate support among the constituencies they represented. Several had called to inquire about their status. Thus I had joined Representative Wilbur Mills, chair of the House Ways and Means Committee, and several of his friends at a luncheon. I sought his advice about economic proposals and tax policy. I also tried to avoid raising their hopes unnecessarily. Bill Dodd of the United Auto Workers, a staunch McGovern supporter, phoned to report that UAW president Leonard Woodcock was entertaining in his suite a number of senior union officers who took the possibility of Woodcock's nomination seriously. We arranged that I would call Woodcock's suite, that Dodd would answer, and that we would conduct a discussion in which Dodd would answer my questions about Woodcock's positions on various public issues. "Leonard knows he is not going to be chosen," Dodd said, "but he has to save face with his officers."

After ending his phone discussion with Galbraith, McGovern strode toward his bedroom. "I'm going to ask my friend Gaylord Nelson to join me," he said. "I know I can trust him." None of us spoke. We all knew that Nelson, a senator from Wisconsin, was too much an upper-Midwest carbon copy of McGovern, and would add no strength to the ticket. Moments later McGovern reemerged to report that "Gaylord cannot do it. But he strongly recommends Tom Eagleton." He turned to Pat Donovan: "Get Tom Eagleton on the phone."

I was standing next to McGovern as he waited for Donovan to complete the call. I had once taken McGovern and Eagleton, together, to a Chicago convention of one of my consulting clients. "Ted, you know Tom Eagleton," he said. "Would he be a good choice?" Before I could answer, Eagleton was on the line. "Tom," McGovern said, "I need a running mate. Will you do it?"

As matters unfolded, Eagleton was found not to have had a prior drinking problem but to have undergone shock therapy for depression. When this came to light, McGovern at first "supported Tom Eagleton 1,000 percent," but later abruptly dropped him from the ticket. Before then, however, an unfortunate failure of communication short-circuited a chance the two men might have had, right after the convention, to discuss and come to terms with the shock-therapy issue.

Following the Miami Beach convention, Hart and Mankiewicz took a

Caribbean vacation. Both of them, it turned out, had found out by then of Eagleton's medical history. McGovern also knew, but I did not. A few days after the convention Eagleton was scheduled to appear on the CBS Sunday interview show, "Face the Nation." I went to his Bethesda home the day before to brief him on the policy positions McGovern had taken, and to suggest questions that might be raised on the broadcast—and our recommended answers. Afterward, Eagleton said: "George and I have not talked since I was nominated. I would really like to have a good discussion with him before we both start campaigning." Eagleton was scheduled to leave for Hawaii two days later. McGovern also would be hitting the road. I called McGovern and passed along Eagleton's request. He said he would call and meet with him.

The morning of the broadcast, I received a call from Hart and Mankiewicz asking that I observe Eagleton's performance closely. How had he reacted to his briefing the day before? I told them he had been quite professional and that, further, he would be seeing McGovern, presumably later that Sunday. Eagleton did well on the broadcast, although I did note that he appeared to sweat unduly throughout. Moments after it ended, I received another phone call from Mankiewicz; I gave him a report. I then heard from Eagleton—he had not been contacted by McGovern. I was perplexed. I called McGovern again. He said he had been tied up. He suggested that, rather than him meeting with Eagleton later that day, I should travel with Eagleton to his Hawaii campaigning, advise him, and see how he performed. I told McGovern that I did not think that was a good idea. Traveling media would think I was some sort of watchdog on Eagleton's plane. Moreover, I had confidence that Eagleton would do well. His principal assistant, moreover, was Doug Bennet, who had worked closely with me in Humphrey's vice presidential office. I had complete confidence in Bennet's competence; he was well briefed. McGovern said he would go with my judgment. I surmised later that McGovern, knowing of the emerging problem, had not wanted to meet with Eagleton because he was not decided on how to deal with it. Had I known of the shock-therapy issue, I would at a minimum have acceded to McGovern's request that I remain with Eagleton for a few days. I also would have argued against dumping Eagleton.

I had no input into McGovern's eventual and unprecedented decision to drop his running mate. McGovern then had to launch a new running-mate search, which unfolded as ragged and attenuated. At one point an agreement was reached with Ed Muskie that he would serve as vice presidential candidate in 1972 as he had in 1968. But Hart and Mankiewicz reported they could not agree with Muskie's managers on logistical and other nuts-and-bolts arrangements, and the deal fell through. Fortunately, media did not learn of this episode. By the time Sargent Shriver, a loyal good soldier, finally agreed to serve, McGovern's credibility had been severely damaged, and the campaign made all but unwinnable.

McGovern and our campaign staff, animated as most still were by the Vietnam issue, fought just as hard against uphill 1972 odds as our Humphrey crew had fought in 1968. I had great confidence in my policy and speechwriting staff. Bob Shrum, who had been with the Muskie campaign, quickly became McGovern's favorite speechwriter; early in the campaign he began traveling on the campaign plane, rooming with McGovern's Senate assistant, John Holum, himself a first-rate writer. At headquarters, Sarah Ehrman of McGovern's Senate staff helped anchor our research efforts. Milt Gwirtzman, a former Kennedy speechwriter, helped coordinate the efforts of Sandy Berger, Steve Schlesinger, John Bartlow Martin, and other speechwriters. I wrote occasional major speeches myself. Ben Heineman Jr. coordinated domestic-policy research efforts. Walt Slocombe worked on national security issues. Lisle Carter and Jerry Donovan coordinated several policy task forces. Lenny Ross, a brilliant former Quiz Kid and later tragic suicide, wrote witty economic policy analyses in record time. Verne Newton coordinated the efforts of Democrats on Capitol Hill. I also watched over the efforts of a national citizens' committee, run by my friend Joe Duffey, and a special group concerned with outreach to ethnic and Catholic voters, which included Ken Schlossberg, Gerry Cassidy, and the theologian Michael Novak.

Hart for some reason convened no campaign-staff meetings. I established, however, an 8 AM daily policy/communications meeting. My old Humphrey colleague John Stewart also attended. He was part of a staff group, housed on the top floor and led by former Democratic National Chairman Larry O'Brien, that was intended to broaden the campaign's outreach to more traditional constituencies.

After the convention, McGovern faced the same party-mending tasks that Humphrey had faced after the Chicago convention four years earlier. O'Brien had come on board to help with that. Most of the party's leading elected officials had not, in fact, been delegates to the Miami Beach convention. Most had signed on early with Muskie's candidacy and thus been left on the outside. Many had not even bothered to go to Miami Beach. Thus, shortly after Labor Day O'Brien convened a meeting of senior Democratic senators and house members at his suite in the Sheraton-Park Hotel in Washington, D.C. Its purpose was group therapy. Those assembled made one complaint after another about McGovern or his campaign. Representative Tip O'Neill inadvertently summed up the feelings of most of those in attendance: "McGovern was not supposed to be nominated. Ed Muskie was supposed to be nominated. We were not even members of our own state delegations to the convention."

Washington Senator Warren Magnuson had sat silently through the meeting in a large, brown upholstered chair, his cane beside him. Finally, he could tolerate no more of his colleagues' whining. "What is going on here?" he growled. "This is ridiculous. The Republican nominee for president is Richard Nixon. It's that fucking Nixon. What more do we need to know?" No one had an answer to that question and the session quickly broke up. The next morning Magnuson's assistant, Norm Dicks, appeared in my office at campaign headquarters. He would be pleased to take responsibility for helping mobilize Senate offices on McGovern's behalf. We thereafter held regular weekly meetings at the Capitol that were attended by staff of all Democratic senators. Once we had our campaign systems in order, I was pleased with the quality of our efforts. But, as in 1968, they were overshadowed by the fundamental weakness of the campaign against a Nixon candidacy that should have been more vulnerable than it was.

Earlier in 1972 a puzzling burglary had taken place at Democratic National Committee offices in the Watergate office complex in Washington, D.C. Before long it became apparent that Nixon's Committee to Reelect the President and the White House itself might have been involved in the break-in. Howard Hunt, a former CIA agent, had been tied to the break-in and subsequent cover-up. He had disappeared from public view; I enlisted former CIA colleagues to find him, but none could. Moreover, mysterious phone calls smearing then-Democratic front-runner Muskie had surfaced during the New Hampshire primary. Muskie, as he told me later, thought the McGovern campaign was behind them. But they were part of a Nixon effort. Strangely unyouthful demonstrators materialized suddenly to jam the lobby at the McGovern Miami Beach campaign hotel during the Democratic convention, and received ample television coverage. It wasn't clear what they were demonstrating about, but they helped create an aura of confusion around the campaign. McGovern was frustrated in particular by the damage the negative-income-tax and Eagleton issues had done to his campaign, while Nixon remained undamaged by the Watergate incident, which seemed directly tied to his staff, and the continuance of the Vietnam War. Bob Shrum's language in his speeches for McGovern was strident. McGovern's off-the-cuff rhetoric was even more strident, and the more strident he became, the more he unsettled a middle-minded electorate.

I urged Mankiewicz, Weil, and Holum, traveling on the campaign plane, to temper McGovern's rhetoric. Mankiewicz, suffering from back trouble, came off the campaign for a week, and I replaced him on the plane. McGovern would restrain his rhetoric at one campaign stop, then break loose again at the next. As we reached Minneapolis, where McGovern was to address a huge outdoor rally at the University of Minnesota, he asked me to listen to a tape from a Boston radio station in which a caller, saying he was a Vietnam combat veteran, described in brutal terms the carnage he had witnessed there. It was dramatic but over the top. Moreover, who knew if the radio caller was authentic or someone who was disturbed? I gave the tape to Weil, who put it in his briefcase.

Suddenly, in the midst of the rally, McGovern signaled to Weil to play the tape aloud to the crowd. He did. The reaction among the thousands of students was stunned silence. McGovern then went on with his speech, which drew polite but not strong applause. As staff and traveling media walked to their buses afterward, *Boston Globe* columnist Bob Healy remarked: "What is going on? I doubt that guy on the tape ever left Fort Devens." What was going on was that McGovern, trailing badly in the campaign, was trying desperately, by any means at hand, to make the American people share his moral outrage at the continuing war.

The last month of the campaign was a slow wind-down to defeat. Peace advocates kept the campaign financed with thousands of small contributions, which arrived each day in dozens of mail sacks. We sent all but a handful of headquarters staffers into the field—the political equivalent of giving rifles to Army cooks and clerks and sending them to the front lines.

McGovern thought the campaign needed new and independent input. He asked Washington, D.C., attorney and former defense secretary Clark Clifford to chair a weekly meeting of a private advisory group. He asked me to serve as secretary of the group, to make weekly situation reports at its meetings, and to fax minutes of the meetings overnight to him on the campaign trail. The group's existence was to be kept secret from Hart, Mankiewicz, and other members of his campaign staff. Its members, besides Clifford, included Senator William Fulbright, former interior secretary Stuart Udall, UAW executive Bill Dodd, and a former chairman of the Council of Economic Advisors, Art Okun. Clifford insisted on keeping tight control of the sessions, which were held in his law offices. On one occasion Paul Warnke, his law partner and a senior McGovern campaign defense advisor, entered Clifford's office as the meeting was underway. I beckoned him in; Clifford asked him to leave.

The advisory group's advice was not extraordinary. The campaign's situation was clear: only some disastrous external event—the full flowering of the Watergate scandal or a horrendous setback in Vietnam—was likely to change the fundamental political situation. The group did, however, make input on several developing problems that arose in the campaign's final weeks.

One involved a Nixon dirty trick of the first order. I received a call from the Democratic mayor of Terre Haute, Indiana. A man flashing a Senate investigator's badge, he said, had appeared at the city records bureau and demanded to see a birth certificate listing George S. McGovern as the father of a child born out of wedlock. He had left with a copy of the certificate. What should he do, the mayor asked? I told him to do nothing unless asked about the matter. If asked, he should tell the truth about it.

I informed Hart, Mankiewicz, and Weil of the call. Owen Donley, McGovern's former Senate administrative assistant, Weil, and I became an ad hoc group monitoring the matter. McGovern readily acknowledged that, as a teenage Army Air Force trainee during World War II, he had fathered a child in Terre Haute. His wife, Eleanor, did not know of it. Then, that evening, the headquarters switchboard operator told me he had received a call as follows: "We know about McGovern's illegitimate child. The story will be in the St. Louis *Globe Democrat* tomorrow morning."

There was nothing for McGovern to do but inform Eleanor of the matter and to prepare for the news story. He also called the mother of the child in Portland, Oregon, to inform her of the upcoming story. The mother, in turn, informed her daughter, who had not known she was McGovern's daughter. The story, however, did not appear in the next morning's *Globe Democrat* (which, coincidentally, had been the former workplace of Nixon speechwriter Pat Buchanan). I arranged for our St. Louis headquarters to post a staff member at the *Globe Democrat* at midnight daily to review the next morning's edition and to let us know immediately if and when the story appeared. It never did. It was, however, effective psychological warfare. The McGoverns, over the final month of the campaign, began each day uncertain whether the disclosure would be made. Although it was not used in the campaign, after the election the Nixon White House found a way to use it anyway. White House chief of staff Bob Haldeman, testifying in early 1973 before a congressional committee, made the matter public—saying that its nondisclosure during the campaign season provided proof that the Nixon campaign had been high-minded and ethical.

When I brought the matter to the Clifford advisory committee, the reaction was interesting. All members but Clifford felt that the course we had taken was the correct one—that is, to not raise the matter ourselves but, if it became public, to simply tell the truth about it. Clifford, crossing his hands in the shape of a steeple, said: "That would be the wrong way to handle this matter. I have found that in such instances there is no option but to lie completely from the beginning. There is no politically satisfactory truthful answer. Therefore we must give an untruthful answer. I handled several such matters in this manner for President Kennedy and I can assure you they ended satisfactorily in each instance." As it turned out, we did not have to deal with the matter publicly before election day. I doubted, however, that McGovern would have been likely to follow Clifford's counsel—although I transmitted it to him promptly after the meeting.

Perhaps the deepest cut for McGovern came in late October, when Nixon's national security advisor, Henry Kissinger, falsely announced that "peace was at hand" in Vietnam. We undertook a quick but broad telephone survey to get a sense of voter reaction to the Kissinger claim. The survey found, disappointingly, that most voters were inclined to take Kissinger's statement at face value. But their overwhelming reaction had been about another matter entirely. It was the first time Kissinger had appeared on national television to make a lengthy broadcast statement. Voters' primary reaction, as expressed by one person interviewed, was that "we did not know Kissinger had such a heavy foreign accent. We thought he was a native-born American."

Survey data also told us that McGovern was losing votes among labor-union members and traditional Democrats—largely as a function of the campaign's counterculture associations. Hart asked me to prepare scripts and television commercials by Humphrey and Ted Kennedy appealing for Democratic voters to return to their party. Milt Gwirtzman and I accompanied Charles Guggenheim, who produced the campaign's commercials, to Humphrey's office and Kennedy's home to film the commercials. Both scripts ended: "Come home to the Democratic Party now." We ran the Humphrey/Kennedy appeals during the campaign's final week.

The Sunday before election day I went to McGovern's Washington, D.C., home to prepare him for one last national interview show. He and Eleanor had flown back from California campaigning the night before. McGovern was still in pajamas. His running mate, Sargent Shriver, called to wish him luck, but McGovern did not have the heart on an early Sunday morning to cope with Shriver's upbeat cheerfulness. I told Sarge that McGovern was in the shower and I would pass on his good wishes. Later, en route to the television station, McGovern sat silently reading his briefing materials, and then remarked: "It was that fucking $1,000 and that fucking Eagleton." Yes, I thought, and it also was the Nixon White House, which had arrogantly pursued a mistaken war and gotten away with it, and in the campaign had said and done as it pleased without being held properly accountable.

That evening I received a phone call from Rick Stearns. He had gone to California to do what he could as things wound down. "I've got good news and bad news for you," he said. "First, the good news: we've received a major endorsement. Now, the bad news: it was by the Manson Family." It was true.

The next morning I was quoted in a *New York Times* front-page story as admitting that "it would be an uphill climb" to an electoral victory. That was an understatement. One of the campaign's major financial contributors took violent exception to my remarks as being defeatist, and demanded that I be publicly relieved of my duties. Hart dismissed his criticisms, but also told him that I had been fairly quoted. Hart had heard me say it himself, but he also had heard me say, often, that if we played the full nine innings hard, anything could happen.

We did play the full nine innings. Despite our apparent looming defeat, McGovern, a week before, had asked me to enlist Clark Clifford and Ted Sorensen to act as cochairs of his presidential transition. We set up a meeting for the day after the election at McGovern's home. In the meantime, Hart, not knowing of McGovern's and my actions, independently asked Harry McPherson, a former counsel to Lyndon Johnson, to fill the same role.

On election day I cast my vote as polls opened near our home in Potomac, Maryland, then drove to our campaign headquarters, which had moved from Capitol Hill to a downtown office building at 1907 K Street, for the general election. McGovern himself was in South Dakota. Most headquarters staff had long since been sent to the field. I went to my fifth-floor office to find that most of my policy staff already had packed up. I sat at my desk for a moment. Just after Labor Day someone in our policy group—I always suspected Heineman or Berger—had suspended a huge inflatable biplane model over my desk, in honor, I thought, of the McGovern alternative defense budget of which I was known to be skeptical. I had left it there. Someone else had affixed "Democrats for Nixon" bumper stickers to my office wall as a constant reminder, to all staff who entered, that the campaign's first task was to reclaim Democrats who had strayed from their party. In that pre-computer age, an outer office had throughout the campaign clattered non-stop with the noise of a dozen typewriters producing speech drafts, policy papers, and daily research sheets critiquing Nixon policies. The room now was silent. No phones rang.

I walked from floor to floor through the building. My old friends Larry O'Brien, Stan Greigg, John Stewart, and Joe Mohbat—the "regular Demo-crat" crew on the top floor—welcomed me. I was one of only two or three McGovern campaign staff who ever entered their premises. The next floor down contained the mail room, where dozens of mail sacks had been received daily, filled with small contributions from mostly antiwar supporters. The cam-paign now was over, but I found the room still filled with bags of unopened mail containing money. They continued to come for weeks after. On lower floors I chatted with Rick Stearns, Eli Segal, Harold Himmelman, Joel Swerd-low, and other senior campaign staff whom I particularly admired. Stearns, back from California and sitting alone in his office, simply said, "See you next time." I saw for the first time a posted notice that authorized only a handful of staff to be present in the building that evening—no others were to be admit-ted. That accounted for the place's relative emptiness.

Early returns brought us no false hope. We knew by the dinner hour that Nixon would win by a landslide. Gary Hart was in his office with Henry Kimmelman and Miles Rubin, who had spearheaded big-money fundrais-ing. Kimmelman spoke of chartering a last-minute jet to go to McGovern's side in South Dakota. Hart had brightened when I came in, probably because he knew I could be counted on for dark humor in dark times. Kim-melman and Rubin were not gallows-humor guys, so Hart and I waited until they left to exchange some jokes at our own expense. I knew that Hart would be returning to Colorado to launch his own campaigns for public office. I mainly wanted to see my family and read a novel or two.

Mankiewicz later would unsuccessfully seek a congressional seat in sub-urban Maryland. In the course of his campaign it was discovered that, despite being a McGovern campaign leader, he had not voted in 1972. "As it turned out," he said, "we lost by more than one vote." McGovern himself would subsequently lose his U.S. Senate seat and retire in Washington, D.C. I was to see him there periodically. He would not become the salon celebrity or lecture-circuit millionaire that some losing candidates become. He remained the serious and idealistic person I had first known when he was Humphrey's next-door neighbor. When I wrote some essay of interest to him, he unfailingly would send me a complimentary note. Twenty-four years later, when my beloved wife Jean died, he was among the first to call and express sympathy. He had done the same, early in the 1972 campaign year, when my father had died of a fall. He would share with me his beautifully written manuscript celebrating the life of his daughter Terry, who had died tragically of alcoholism around the time of Jean's death. We met at lunches and rekindled a friendship.

Nixon won reelection with nearly 61 percent of the vote nationwide. The McGovern campaign carried only Massachusetts—hence the "Massachusetts Knew" bumper stickers that cropped up after Nixon's ignominious departure from office. McGovern had been labeled during the campaign as both mushy and an extremist. He was in fact neither. His courage as a World War II bomber pilot, early opponent of the Vietnam War, and long-shot candidate for the presidency was unquestioned. He was an intelligent man who, if elected president, would have governed wisely and humanely. Like Humphrey four years earlier, he had conducted himself honorably in his campaign.

McGovern's former staff and volunteers in fifty states would, down the road, hold high public offices and be active forces in their communities. Nixon, by contrast, would be disgraced and driven from the presidency. In my book, the winner in the 1972 campaign was McGovern, the loser Nixon.

11

STRANGE PRESIDENTS, NIXON AND CARTER

To those of us active in national politics during the 1960s and 1970s, it seemed incredible that Richard Nixon had rebounded from a presidential-election loss, a humiliating California gubernatorial-election loss, Watergate, and Vietnam to be twice elected president. Yet, if Albert Camus' remark that "character is fate" ever was to have relevance, it certainly came to apply to Nixon, whose feelings of inferiority and paranoia led him to an internal vision in which he was surrounded by enemies who had to be destroyed before they could destroy him.

Nixon made his political mark with charges of disloyalty approaching treason against real and imagined political adversaries in his California campaigns and in the Congress. He clearly violated the Logan Act, which prohibits private citizens from conducting national diplomacy, in his 1968 scheming with South Vietnamese president Thieu to block Vietnam War peace negotiations so that both he and Thieu might benefit politically. The 1972 break-in at the Democratic national headquarters in the Watergate office complex led him into cover-ups and lies which in the end brought down his presidency. Many theories have been advanced regarding the purpose of the break-in. To those knowledgeable about activities at either party's national headquarters, the break-in seemed absurd. No major secrets—certainly no secrets justifying the risk of the presidency itself—exist in party headquarters. Real power and planning in any presidential campaign rest not at party headquarters but in the organizations of the candidates themselves.

My own theory about the Watergate break-in is that Nixon feared that Democratic Chair Larry O'Brien might have files there regarding a relationship between Nixon's brother, Donald Nixon, and government officials and private individuals in the Dominican Republic, or regarding Nixon's own relationship with the Howard Hughes organization. O'Brien himself had such relationships. Whether or not O'Brien had any such files, however, they never came to light in the 1972 campaign, and were never mentioned by any Nixon associate as the purpose of the break-in. Otherwise there was no apparent justifying reason for so large a risk.

After Nixon's 1972 reelection, it became known that he had authorized surveillance of political and Vietnam War critics, and also break-ins at their homes and offices. The existence of a Nixon "enemies list" became public. A front-page story in the *Washington Star* revealed that Frank Mankiewicz and I had been singled out for special Internal Revenue Service scrutiny of our tax returns. (It probably was the best IRS insurance I could have secured; in the years since, I have never received a tax audit.) During 1974 congressional investigations into campaign "dirty tricks," Gary Hart, Mankiewicz, and I were subpoenaed by Republican committee staff for questioning about alleged McGovern-campaign tricks rivaling those of the Nixon campaign's. I also was asked about alleged 1968 Humphrey-Muskie campaign espionage and sabotage directed toward the Nixon campaign. It gave me an opportunity to read into the record the fact that there had been none. In 1968, Humphrey staffer Eiler Ravenholt had followed the Nixon campaign with a tape recorder to record any damaging public statements that might be delivered by vice presidential candidate Spiro Agnew. In 1972, the McGovern campaign had discussed but discarded the option of dispatching a similar researcher to record Nixon and Agnew statements. Richard Tuck, a renowned Democratic trickster, had during Nixon's California and presidential campaigns planted good-humored signs and bumper stickers ridiculing Nixon at his various campaign stops. That was it. At the end of my deposition, I remarked that Nixon apparently lived in an imagined universe populated only by dishonorable people. To my surprise, the Republican congressional staff members nodded agreement and laughed.

During the same period, United Airlines received an inquiry from a federal agency about an allegation from an anonymous source that, while helping the McGovern campaign, I had arranged for United, one of my consulting clients, to provide charter aircraft to the campaign at below-market rates. This would have amounted to an illegal political campaign contribution by the airline. Eddie Carlson, the United Airlines CEO, was a Republican who also had close ties to Democratic Senator Warren Magnuson, a fellow Seattleite. I had done no more than refer campaign staff to United executives who dealt with charters. They had leased planes to the campaign at market rates.

Treasury Secretary John Connally was at this time being charged with having accepted a bribe from Midwest dairy cooperatives to fix federal milk-price supports at artificially high levels. I found myself, along with several other Democrats, being investigated for undertaking illegal activities to further the same cooperatives' legislative objectives. An Associated Press reporter told me he had been informed by "a reliable Republican source" that I was receiving fees from the cooperatives that were being "laundered" into campaign money for prominent Democratic candidates. I told him it was untrue. I and other co-op consultants were also on the receiving end of a lawsuit brought by dairy-cooperative members in Texas alleging that their general funds had been misused for political purposes. The IRS questioned me on the issue as part of a tax investigation of the dairy groups, and I appeared before both a federal grand jury and Watergate committee staff to answer questions about co-op activities. Media coverage routinely listed my name along with those of Connally, Nixon attorney Herb Kalmbach, and several Democrats as having consulting relationships with dairy groups. It was news to me that some had any such relationship.

I had given co-op officers straightforward political and policy advice and solicited support on their behalf from Democratic senators and members of Congress. I had arranged for prominent Democratic officeholders—including Senators Humphrey, Muskie, McGovern, Eagleton, Hughes, Harris, Mondale, Nelson, William Proxmire, and Adlai Stevenson—to speak to their conferences and meetings. I had done nothing illegal, although some others, it turned out, had. To protect myself, I retained Clifford, Warnke, McIlwaine and Finney, the law firm not only of Clark Clifford but also of my good friends Paul Warnke and Tom Finney. Finney, then Warnke, took responsibility for following my various legal travails.

By late 1974, the whole series of events had run its course. I emerged unharmed. But the proceedings had taken huge chunks of my time, distracted me from the consulting practice I had reestablished after the 1972 campaign, and, I feared, cost me enormous legal fees and expenses from the Clifford, Warnke firm, which had gone so far as to dispatch one of its attorneys to Texas to quash the lawsuit against me there. I had received no invoices from the firm along the way, and anticipated a whopper at the end. I called Warnke to request a final, comprehensive invoice. To my surprise, there would be none. "Clark, Tom, and I talked it over," Warnke explained. "We agreed that what happened to you could have happened to any of us. We consider it to have been pro-bono work." Later I would receive occasional requests to advise or help Clifford, Warnke clients. Needless to say, I always responded readily.

One such assignment had legal ramifications of its own. The Clifford, Warnke firm represented Sonatrach, the Algerian energy monopoly. Clifford, I had been told, took royalties rather than fees from Sonatrach as compensation. Cherif Guellal, Sonatrach's man in Washington, D.C., also served as Algeria's unofficial ambassador in the United States because the country did not at that time have official diplomatic representation. He was socially prominent in the capital, where his frequent companion was a former Miss America.

Early one weekend morning I received a phone call from Guellal, who said that both Clifford and Warnke were out of town and had advised him to call me about an emergency situation. Sonatrach had just decided to cancel an enormous contract with a Texas-based engineering company for lack of performance. The company was over budget and behind schedule in developing major facilities in Algeria. I met with Guellal and examined documents regarding the contract; Guellal cabled for more, which promptly arrived from Algiers. I then prepared a white paper stating the facts and background as provided by Sonatrach. A formal Sonatrach announcement, using the white paper as backup, was issued to general and business media both in Algiers and in the United States. I arranged for the Algerian energy minister to fly to Washington, D.C., for a briefing of economic and energy media and to meet with interested U.S. government officials. Months later, however, I found myself subpoenaed to testify in a lawsuit being brought by the Texas contractor. The suit alleged that Sonatrach, the Clifford, Warnke firm, and I had, over a continuing period, conspired in a plan to cause the contractor to lose its business and damage its reputation. I testified that, far from being part of some long-hatched plan, I had begun and ended my role in a two-week period. The suit, in any event, got nowhere.

Early in 1975 I found myself sharing an airplane flight from Washington, D.C., to Indianapolis with Clark Clifford. He suggested that an experienced former nonelected government official should be considered for the 1976 Democratic presidential nomination. He had himself in mind. I told him I thought he would do better to continue in an advisory role.

All the investigative distractions I encountered in 1973–74 could partly be blamed on the Nixon White House's continuing offensives against its perceived enemies. But the dairy-cooperative investigations, and subsequent prosecutions of several co-op officers and consultants, had provided a good lesson to me. I had regarded my dairy clients as being mainly unsophisticated country people trying, often clumsily, to do their best for their members. I had no idea that they or their agents were violating the law. I vowed that, thereafter, I would not again be placed in a vulnerable position by my own ignorance. I still had a consulting relationship with two Southern dairy groups

not involved in the scandals, but when I learned that one also retained a prominent Nixon advisor, I dropped the associations. I had learned that, even after
many years in the capital, including several in the White House, I was still
less savvy than I thought.

After McGovern's loss I had reopened my consulting business. During
the 1972 general-election campaign, I had ceased working as a volunteer for
McGovern but had shut down my business and drawn a nominal staff salary,
wanting to avoid even the appearance that my clients (such as United Airlines) were in any way subsidizing the campaign. It took six months to rebuild
my practice. My offices also became a sort of refugee shelter for out-of-office
Democrats. Frank Mankiewicz and Bob Lifton, a McGovern contributor from
New York, joined me in founding a seminar company, the National Executive Conference of Washington. It was run by Kirby Jones, the former Robert
Kennedy staff member I had hired at Columbia. He had moved to Washington to work with me in my consulting firm, and then had served as deputy
press secretary of the McGovern campaign. Mankiewicz also was writing a
book. Chris Camp Turpin, a former staff member for President Kennedy,
was my office manager. My old Humphrey colleagues John Stewart and Norm
Sherman also were in the suite, pursuing their own independent work, as was
Alan Baron, who had served as executive director of the Democratic National
Committee during the McGovern-Shriver general campaign. He was producing a private political newsletter mainly directed toward the labor community. I sold my consulting business to a client, the J. Walter Thompson
Company, and ran the capital office of its public-affairs subsidiary. After a
year, however, I tired of the paperwork and bureaucracy involved and bought
my company back. Mankiewicz and Jones traveled to Cuba to do a docu-
mentary film, which included a long interview with Fidel Castro, of which
I served as coproducer. I contributed essays to magazines and the editorial
pages of national newspapers. After the 1968 and 1972 campaign ordeals, it
felt good to take a break from presidential politics, even though my office
often served as an informal gathering place for aspiring candidates, political
journalists, and presidential-campaign alumni.

In the meantime, Nixon's presidency, weakened by the Watergate scandal, had ground to its end. In May 1974, the Senate rejected his request to
raise the spending cap on military aid to South Vietnam. Nixon had run into
the same guns-or-domestic-spending dilemma that had hobbled Lyndon
Johnson's last presidential years. The Congress, with tacit Pentagon approval,

sharply reduced budgeted 1975 military aid to South Vietnam. Early in August, communist troops, violating the ceasefire agreement then in place, seized a strategic position near Danang. A day later, on August 9, Nixon resigned.

The area between Danang and Saigon was under siege. A newly inaugurated president Gerald Ford spoke of continued defense of South Vietnam. But he accepted the reduced congressional appropriation. In September he took steps toward national healing. He pardoned Nixon, which probably cost him the 1976 presidential election. Then he offered amnesty for 50,000 draft evaders or resisters. The pardon enraged liberal Democrats; the amnesty angered conservative Republicans. The moves had been large-minded and statesmanlike but were not fully recognized as such until after Ford had left the White House.

After its 1968 and 1972 defeats, the national Democratic Party was hardly a beehive of energy. Texas fundraiser and attorney Bob Strauss had become Democratic national chairman. He was an old-style, spoils-system type who regarded public issues and ideology as being beside the point in serious politics. He set about trying to rebuild the party's finances—and, coincidentally, to generate business for his law firm—and shied away from the kind of policy combat with Republicans that was second nature to earlier chairs Fred Harris and Larry O'Brien. An obscure one-term Georgia governor, Jimmy Carter, volunteered to make the rounds of the fifty states on behalf of the DNC, working with his fellow governors and stirring up grassroots participation. When in Washington, D.C., he made periodic drop-in calls on Democrats unknown to him. On a couple of occasions he killed time between appointments sitting in a vacant office between Mankiewicz's and mine. Carter had a flat personality; we did not know what, if anything, to make of him. He also had an obvious chip on his shoulder regarding liberal-lineage national Democrats. Vicki Bagley, a capital real-estate agent and party hostess, seemed to be his principal sponsor in Washington. At that time she was married to Smith Bagley, a liberal tobacco heir, who told me that Vicki sometimes would link his name to Carter's, and that Carter had used his plantation in Georgia, but that "Carter would not know me if he saw me today." On one occasion, I found my name listed without my authorization as one of a half-dozen sponsors of an event for Carter hosted by Vicki Bagley.

After the McGovern defeat, a number of young, issue-oriented Democrats, who mainly had supported Muskie's 1972 candidacy for the nomination, had founded an organization called the Democratic Forum. It held conferences, commissioned papers and published a magazine, the *Democratic Review*, dealing with both party affairs and public issues. Michael Barnes, Jessica Tuchman Mathews, Cathy Douglas, Cathy Bushkin, and Keith Haller were particularly active in establishing the group. Anne Wexler and Joe Duffey, who had supported McCarthy in 1968 and Muskie and McGovern in 1972, and I were enlisted as older-generation mentors to the group. The forum planned a major Democratic issues conference, to be held in Louisville, Kentucky, in late 1975. I agreed to prepare one of two papers—a domestic-policy piece—that would provide a basis for discussion at the conference and later be published in the *Democratic Review*. To everyone's surprise, the Louisville conference attracted hundreds of Democrats from around the country and a large number of national political reporters. Senators and members of Congress, labor-union presidents, and state and local Democratic leaders registered and attended. Seemingly out of nowhere, committed and reenergized Democrats had emerged, eager to talk about issues and the renewal of their party.

The thesis of my lengthy paper was that Democrats had strayed from their adherence to a unifying, broadly based domestic agenda—such as the "Let's Get America Moving Again" John F. Kennedy agenda of 1960—to a more diffuse agenda flowing from single-issue and single-interest groups that provided votes and money to individual Democratic candidates. Depending on one's outlook, the party could be seen as a captive of labor unions, of the "acid, amnesty, and abortion" counterculture, or of the many constituencies that benefited from government spending associated with federal programs. It was no longer a "horizontal" party, representing the interests of the whole country, but a "vertical" party, reflecting the interests of powerful but narrow constituencies.

Unsurprisingly, many of the single-issue and single-interest groups protested their characterization. Yet, behind the scenes at and after the conference, response to the paper was hugely favorable. Michigan senator Phil Hart, a committed labor-endorsed liberal, pulled me aside in Louisville to say that "if anyone asks me, I will have to denounce your paper. But, between us, I agree with everything it says." A number of Democrats around the country requested copies of the paper. One of them was Jimmy Carter.

On October 1, 1975, *Washington Post* columnist David Broder devoted his column to my policy paper. I remember the date well because it was the last *Washington Post* to be published before a strike of the paper's pressmen interrupted its production for a time. As it turned out, I was to spend most of my waking hours at the *Post* for many of the following weeks, helping management resume the paper's publication, maintain support among its other unions (most notably, the Newspaper Guild), and end the strike by hiring replacements for the striking pressmen.

I had been retained by the *Post* to assist the paper if and when a pressmen's strike might materialize. The union's negotiating posture had been hard. It was clear that a new contract would be difficult to achieve, so contingency plans had been made.

I researched comparable pay and benefit scales in both the Washington, D.C., and other big-city markets; compensation for *Post* pressmen ranked near the top. I also researched comparable data for the *Post*'s other unions and editorial employees. In all cases they ranked high as compared with their counterparts within the city and at newspapers around the country. The information was helpful in ongoing labor negotiations. It also was to be included in a white paper to be issued to other media and to *Post* employees in the event that a strike materialized. I drafted a comprehensive document setting forth issues involving the pressmen, but also explaining the newspaper's general attitude toward its employees and its commitment to continue publication if and when a strike might arise. Late on the evening of September 30, I received a call at my home in Potomac from Mark Meagher, then the *Post*'s general manager. Could I come immediately to its 15th Street offices? Pressmen had damaged their presses, physically attacked a foreman, and walked off the job. The foreman was in a third-floor restroom, wiping blood from his face and clothing, when I arrived.

Early the next morning we issued the already-prepared white paper setting forth the *Post*'s position. We also began informing media and *Post* employees on a daily basis of the course of events. Each morning a written memo was posted outside the newsroom to update editorial staff. The key to success, from management's viewpoint, was to keep Guild members on the job and producing the paper. If they also walked out, the strike could become extremely costly and difficult. The pressmen, for their part, were slow to explain their own position, which remained uncertain. They held rallies at a church near the *Post*'s offices but essentially lacked a positive agenda. Fliers were distributed depicting the *Post* as a 1930s-style sweatshop employer. But they were short on facts. A picket line was formed around the building. Bricks were thrown through windows of lower-floor offices. Jules Witcover, a political reporter, was followed into his work-time parking garage and beaten by strikers. A majority of Guild members, as well as members of other unions at the *Post*, became alienated from the strikers, who seemed to believe that they were waging a Depression-era battle against an unpopular industrial employer.

Katharine (Kay) Graham, the *Post*'s publisher, was conflicted by the strike. On the one hand, she and most of her key staff were generally sympathetic to the labor movement. On the other, she resented the pressmen's sabotage of their presses and the violence against a supervisor. She telephoned Arthur Goldberg, an old friend and advisor, who told her that "labor violence is as American as apple pie." I had told her much the same, earlier that day, and urged her not to be emotionally swayed by the violence. She, her son Donald Graham, Mark Meagher, and the newspaper's production, legal, and communications staffs pulled together remarkably to keep the paper publishing after Joseph Albritton, publisher of the rival *Washington Star*, had refused to let the *Post* use *Star* facilities. Senior staff took on the humblest of tasks to keep the paper running. Kay Graham and her friend Meg Greenfield, the editorial-page editor, spent evenings putting copies of the *Post* into mailing wrappers for out-of-town subscribers. When she recognized a familiar name on a mailing label, Kay Graham would pen a personal note on the wrapper.

This went on, around the clock, for a number of weeks. Meanwhile, inside the labor negotiations themselves, *Post* vice president Larry Wallace was making negligible progress. The *Post* had made tangible proposals; the pressmen continued to follow a strategy of hard-line public and conference-table resistance.

Finally, Kay Graham and Meagher went to the newsroom to deliver a comprehensive report to staff. They recited the number and content of proposals that had been made by the *Post*. When, after this list, they reported that the pressmen had not yet made a counterproposal, there were audible gasps throughout the room. They then announced that replacement workers would be hired. A full-page statement was published in the next morning's *Post* explaining the situation and spelling out the actions to be taken by management. Both Guild and other union members remained on the job. The pressmen had defeated themselves.

During the late stages of the strike, Edward Bennett Williams, the *Post*'s outside attorney, proposed to Katharine Graham that suits be brought against the pressmen for both compensatory and punitive damages. The latter, if awarded, would have the practical effect of crippling the national union. I advised against seeking punitive damages, believing that the *Post* would only discredit itself with Guild and other union members. It was winning its dispute with the pressmen—why attempt to destroy them?

Williams expanded on his proposal in a meeting with Kay Graham and Meagher, which I was unable to attend because of an uncancellable meeting elsewhere. After they told him they were rejecting his recommendation, Williams sent me an angry letter by messenger denouncing me for giving them bad advice and interfering with "his lawsuit." I responded with a letter, copied to the Grahams and Meagher, indicating that what was at issue was not "his lawsuit" but the *Washington Post*'s overall posture toward its unions, the national labor movement, and the Washington, D.C., community. Any lawsuit, in any case, would be the *Post*'s and not his. Kay Graham, on receiving my response, advised me to brush off Williams's tantrum. "He shouts at me all the time," she said. "He can't help it." I received a written apology from Williams the following day.

There were clear parallels between the dynamics in the *Post* conflict and the conflict on the Columbia University campus several years earlier. In each case an active, hard-line internal group had attempted to confront and defeat the generally liberal institution in which it existed. In each instance the institution had taken positive steps which resulted in the isolation and eventual defeat of an adversary that had overestimated its strength outside its own ranks. The *Post*, like Columbia, quickly regained its balance; the paper's circulation and advertising revenue bounced back. The *Star*, not long after, closed down. The *Washington Post* continues today to enjoy positive relations with its several unions. Under Donald Graham, its present publisher, it stands as one of the country's three most influential daily newspapers.

I later would counsel other newspapers on labor-relations issues and, from time to time, would undertake other consulting assignments for the *Post*. But the 1975 assignment was by far the most important. I came away from it with great respect for the Grahams' diligence, integrity, and commitment to the newspaper's employees. In almost constant contact with them over a several-month period, I found them to be always large-minded, honorable, and fiercely devoted to the independence and excellence of the *Post*. More than twenty years later, my wife Jean died after a long struggle with bone cancer. I discovered months afterward that Don Graham had made an extremely generous contribution to her memorial fund at the school where she had taught. My children and I were moved and grateful.

My other consulting clients of the period also presented stimulating assignments. The airline industry was then in the middle of debate about possible deregulation. The president of United Airlines, Eddie Carlson, first opposed and then came to support the concept. I worked with his executives and with Stephen Breyer and others on Senator Ted Kennedy's Judiciary Committee staff to help develop a workable formula for deregulation. I learned a great deal about the pharmaceutical industry from my Eli Lilly & Co. client and took satisfaction in helping Lilly develop an internal issue-management system in which it could examine and reach positions on such issues as national health insurance. One client, the new democratic government of Greece, faced difficulty in dealing with Secretary of State Henry Kissinger, who tilted strongly toward Turkey in the region. At one juncture Kissinger abruptly cut off U.S. security assistance to Greece; I prevailed on the Democratic-majority Congress to restore it in an amount equal to that extended to Turkey. I took particular satisfaction in helping Julian Bond and Yancey Martin, a comrade from the McGovern campaign, raise corporate and labor-union support for their Southern Elections Fund, which aided black local-level candidates in Southern states.

I could not find it within myself to commit to any of the several candidates seeking the 1976 Democratic presidential nomination. I enjoyed running my business, writing, and spending time with my family. We took vacations we had missed before—including extended trips to Portugal, Disney World, Hilton Head and the South, and a San Francisco–to–San Diego drive with many stops en route.

In the 1976 Democratic nominating race, Jimmy Carter, the only remaining moderate in an otherwise liberal field, was portraying himself as "not a politician" but a former Naval officer and peanut farmer. He billed himself as "a nuclear scientist," which he was not. He had served as an engineer in Admiral Hyman Rickover's nuclear submarine program. He had been a hawk in the Vietnam War debate and heretofore absent from national Democratic Party activities. The party's big names and "great mentioners"—those who mentioned people as promising candidates—tended to take him lightly As he campaigned, Carter seldom spoke of substantive policy except to describe the U.S. tax system as "a disgrace to the human race" (he offered no alternate plan). Instead, he emphasized his general lack of prior involvement in politics other than his brief tenure as Georgia governor. He pledged never to lie, if elected president, and declared the American people to be better than their leaders. Recognizing that citizens were disillusioned by events during the Johnson and Nixon administrations, which had been led by lifelong professional politicians, Carter painted his political inexperience as a virtue. As the Democratic primaries proceeded, it became clear that Carter might emerge as the nominee. Liberal support was scattered among several candidates. Both voters and the media clearly liked the story line of a simple peanut farmer and patriot from south Georgia emerging as a "Mr. Smith Goes to Washington" reformer untouched by the cynicism of the capital's establishmentarians. Following strong showings in successive primary contests, Carter never expressed in his election-night statements any economic-, foreign-, or domestic-policy views. He simply would recite the upcoming primary calendar and ask voters to join in his undefined crusade to change things in Washington, D.C.

Carter knew almost no one in Washington. Frank Mankiewicz and I had met him briefly. The Bagleys and another husband-and-wife team, Peter Bourne and Mary King, were Carter's most visible supporters in the capital. Stuart Eizenstat, an Atlanta attorney serving as Carter's principal policy advisor, had previously managed so-called "negative research" in the 1968 Humphrey campaign. He was diligent and intelligent. Al Stern, a Wayne State University professor and periodic Humphrey advisor, was assisting Eizenstat in Atlanta. Both were friends of mine. My McGovern campaign colleague Milt Gwirtzman was occasionally lending a hand to Carter on issues research, working with Eizenstat and Steve Stark, a young graduate student who traveled with Carter. Eizenstat told me that Carter was "a good guy." Another person who worked with Carter told me that he was "petty and vindictive."

I felt a flash of sympathy for Carter when I saw him attempt to speak to a weekend meeting of Americans for Democratic Action (ADA) national-convention attendees during the Democratic nominating season. Other candidates had spoken the previous evening. Carter had no support within the group. As he mounted a chair and began his speech, longtime ADA leader Joe Rauh shouted at him and attempted to drown out his remarks: "Who let you speak?" Rauh shouted. "Why didn't you come last night when everyone else did?" Carter went ahead with brief remarks, stepped down from the chair, and left the hotel ballroom quickly, to minimal applause. His head was down as he walked alone to the hotel entrance.

As Carter's nomination appeared more likely, George and Liz Stevens, who had actively supported Robert Kennedy, McGovern, and various liberal causes, invited a small group to their Georgetown home for dinner and discussion with Carter. The group included Joe Duffey and Anne Wexler, Jim

Flug, a member of Senator Ted Kennedy's staff, Dick Holbrooke, whom I had known since he had served on LBJ's National Security Council staff, Mankiewicz, and myself. Over dessert, Carter asked each of us, one by one, for our public and active support. Holbrooke made an immediate and full commitment. "Jimmy, I will do whatever it takes to help you to the presidency," he said. At the other end of the scale, I was most reticent. Carter might be the party's likely nominee, I thought, but he really had not given us any idea of who he was or what he stood for. Carter seemed annoyed when all of us did not follow Holbrooke's example, and left before we had finished coffee. Afterward, George and Liz Stevens appealed for us to support Carter on the basis, as George put it, that "Carter is going to be the nominee and we should get on board at an early stage." Flug expressed views much like my own: "I would be surprised if many in this group would get on board without knowing more than we do about Carter." In a *Washington Post* interview a few days later, Carter mentioned the dinner meeting and described the guests as fatigued, burned-out cases from past campaigns.

In 1976 my wife, Jean, was suffering from medical problems unrelated to the multiple myeloma that would kill her twenty years later. She was scheduled to enter the National Institutes of Health hospital for surgery in June. Some ten days beforehand, I was in San Francisco for a United Airlines conference. Jean, back home in Potomac, received an unexpected phone call from Carter. He and Rosalyn, he said, knew of her upcoming surgery and were praying for its success. As Jean had never met the Carters, she was somewhat surprised. When I returned from San Francisco, she told me she felt her privacy had been violated by Carter's knowledge of her pending surgery. I told her he no doubt had learned of it from a third party, perhaps Eizenstat, although I had no recollection of mentioning it to him. In any case the Carters were prayerful people and their concern no doubt was genuine.

Midway through the nominating process, a number of Democrats began appealing to Senator Humphrey to announce his candidacy. There was a strong feeling among liberals, in particular, that a mistake was being made and that Carter's candidacy had to be stopped. Humphrey's Senate colleague and protégé Walter Mondale, former Johnson advisor Harry McPherson, and others were urging him on. News reports said that Humphrey would make an announcement about a candidacy the following morning. I was disquieted. Humphrey had never been a spoiler. His entry, if he made it, would be too late to win the nomination for himself. I had not seen Humphrey for months, but I called him at his Washington apartment. Humphrey told me he shared the doubts about Carter felt by many in the party. "I wish I knew him better," Humphrey said, "and that I could feel comfortable with the idea of him in the presidency." I told him we all had doubts about Carter, but that I thought Humphrey would be needlessly diminished by a last-minute candidacy and that, if Carter were stopped, some compromise third candidate would end up with the nomination in any event. He told me he intended to sleep on it.

Well after midnight I was wakened by a call at home. "This is Jack Carter, Jimmy Carter's son," a polite Southern voice said. "My father has been trying to reach Senator Humphrey by phone for quite some time," he said, "but the phone keeps ringing busy. What is his correct number?" I told him Humphrey's home number was 202–554–3302, and speculated that he might have taken it off the hook. "We'll keep trying," Jack Carter said.

The next morning, Humphrey announced that he would forgo a candidacy. Out of curiosity, I called Violet Williams, Humphrey's secretary, to ask if he had spoken with Jimmy Carter before making his announcement. No, she said, they never spoke. Later that day, I was surprised by Carter's public reaction to Humphrey's decision. The standard, party-unifying response would have been for Carter to praise Humphrey and to express hope that he would receive his support. Instead, Carter stated that he regretted Humphrey's decision because he had looked forward to contesting and defeating him. (Later, after he became president, Carter came to respect and work with Humphrey. Mondale, who had urged Humphrey to contest Carter, became Carter's vice president and, as an experienced capital insider, a valuable advisor to him.)

After Carter had clinched the Democratic presidential nomination but before the party's national convention in New York, I finally agreed to help with the campaign. Eizenstat was representing Carter on the platform committee. He asked me to review the platform planks, help develop Carter's own positions, and help him negotiate with other candidates' representatives in the drafting committee. Behind the scenes, I edited and signed off on the final drafts of platform planks to be sure they were substantively and politically acceptable.

At the New York convention, I was given a draft of Carter's prospective nomination-acceptance speech and asked to make suggestions. I made several small ones, and noted that only successful Democratic presidential candidates were listed in the prepared text and other candidates, including Al Smith, Adlai Stevenson, Robert Kennedy, Humphrey, and McGovern—all with constituencies in the hall and in the country—had been left out. I suggested their inclusion. A few days later, in *New York* magazine, an anonymous Carter advisor was quoted as saying that former Kennedy advisor Ted Sorensen and I had presumed to suggest changes in Carter's text and that "they obviously thought they were smarter than Jimmy." It was a strange comment to make, I thought, about suggestions that the campaign had solicited—not unlike Carter's putdown of Humphrey a few hours after having tried desperately to reach him by telephone.

Carter had narrowed his list of vice presidential running mates to a half dozen; Mondale, Muskie, Frank Church, and Adlai Stevenson were thought to be front-runners. Eizenstat asked me to prepare a memorandum summing up the pluses and minuses of the possible vice presidential candidates. At that moment, he said, Church appeared to be Carter's favorite. I admired Church, but he was from a small state, Idaho, which Democrats would not carry in any case, and his Protestant religiosity was too much like Carter's. My memo, which Eizenstat passed to Carter, urged a liberal northern or northeastern running mate who would complement rather than mirror Carter's strengths.

As chance would have it, I was sitting in Stevenson's suite at the Waldorf Astoria in New York when he received the official call from Carter telling him he had not been chosen. It took all of five seconds and consisted entirely of Carter informing Stevenson that he "had chosen somebody else." Stevenson thanked him and then turned to friends in the room: "That was a close call. Imagine if I had been chosen and had to work for the guy." A more courteous call, I thought, would have gone a long way—Stevenson and Illinois would be important to Carter in the coming election.

After Carter's nomination, Eizenstat and Stern arranged that John Stewart and I would meet at the Statler Hilton Hotel in Washington, D.C., with Jody Powell, Carter's campaign press secretary, and Barry Jagoda, another aide, to discuss strategy in prospective televised debates with President Ford. We discussed format and content, and I followed up with a memo as requested. A few days later Eizenstat called from Atlanta to ask if I and others would pull together briefing books with which Carter could prepare for the debates, which had now been scheduled. I also met at the Palm Restaurant in Washington with Jack Watson, an Atlanta attorney who was coordinating Carter's transition activities—that is, staffing and planning for the presidency, should Carter win the election—and afterward faxed him a lengthy memorandum he had requested on people and procedures. I never heard again from Watson. Eizenstat told me that Watson had submitted a memo under his name to Carter regarding transition procedures. As he described it, it sounded like mine. When I told Eizenstat I had not heard back from Watson, although I had called him to make further suggestions, Eizenstat expressed surprise: "Jimmy thinks Jack is working with you just as closely as I am."

Our debate-book team consisted of John Stewart and Bob Hunter, old friends from Humphrey days, and myself. Eizenstat and Stern had worked closely with Stewart and Hunter in the 1968 Humphrey research operation. Hunter by 1976 was serving as Senator Ted Kennedy's foreign-policy staff advisor. We were accompanied to Atlanta by Mankiewicz, who would confer with Powell and Pat Caddell, the Carter pollster who had served the 1972 McGovern campaign. A sizeable policy and research staff already had been assembled in Atlanta that included Dick Holbrooke working on foreign policy and Jerry Jasinowski handling economic policy. I parceled out assignments. The format for the briefing books was straightforward. First, they stated the nature of the problems facing the country in each major policy area. Then they summarized the policies currently being applied by the incumbent Republican administration. Then they presented alternative Carter-Mondale proposals. Where there were no such proposals—which was the case in most instances—we drafted them or appropriated positions endorsed in the party platform. For each policy area, the books would include detailed rebuttals to statements we expected the Ford campaign to make. We also researched our own candidate and assessed weak points that Ford might exploit in the debates. Carter's greatest weak point was that he had few established views. He had, after all, never been involved in national issues and had only one brief term as governor. On foreign and national-security policy he could be described as generally a strong-on-defense Scoop Jackson Democrat (Carter had supported Jackson's 1972 presidential candidacy). On domestic policy, Carter was generally an unformed and undefined populist. It became clear to me why he had avoided talking policy during the nominating period.

Moreover, in researching his political background, we found that the man who promised never to lie to the people had resorted to a dubious stratagem in order to become Georgia's governor. Carter had been the more conservative underdog in a Democratic primary race against former governor Carl Sanders, who was respected nationally as a progressive. The Carter campaign had addressed this by financing a third candidacy, by a black candidate named

King—no kin to the Martin Luther King Jr. family of Atlanta—who took enough liberal and minority votes from Sanders to win the primary for Carter. Fortunately for the Carter campaign, the Ford campaign never learned about or used this information.

As the debates loomed, I set deadlines for final draft submissions from each Carter staff member so that the pieces could be reviewed and, if necessary, rewritten prior to being placed in one of three black loose-leaf binders to be provided to Carter several days ahead of the first debate. The staff work was uneven. Perhaps 50 percent of the submissions had to be substantially rewritten. I wrote general theme material to cover each policy area. David Rubenstein, a young attorney assisting Eizenstat, clearly was the substantive star of the group. When the books were done, we gave copies to Mondale, whom Carter had selected as his running mate, as well as to Eizenstat for submission to Carter. We expected that Carter, having reviewed the books, would then want to meet with us to discuss issues and engage in mock debate. But he preferred to study in seclusion or in the company of only his campaign manager, Hamilton Jordan, and pollster Pat Caddell. Even Eizenstat did not meet with him personally.

I found Carter's campaign headquarters, in the Fairmont Hotel office complex, to be a disconcerting place. Eizenstat and his policy staff operated efficiently—both his staff and Watson's transition staff were populated mainly with Washington, D.C., types with experience in their areas. But the political operation was as quiet as a corporate office. Powell, the press secretary, was open and amiable. But Jordan was often a shadow presence. Just like Gary Hart in the 1972 McGovern campaign, he disappeared for long periods, during which no one in the headquarters appeared to know his whereabouts. Most campaign headquarters are characterized by ringing phones and constant in-and-out traffic. This one was not. Hodding Carter and Patricia Derian, friends from Mississippi Freedom Party days, were working at the headquarters. I joined them for dinner one night and remarked that I found Governor Carter, and the atmosphere around him, to be somewhat strange. The next morning, as I passed Derian in a hallway, she said, looking directly ahead: "You're right. It is strange." I also chatted briefly about it with Ted Sorensen, who had endorsed Carter in New York and was visiting Atlanta. He said he had a similar reaction, but that "since Carter is likely to be president, we have no option but to help him as much as we can."

Since Carter preferred to prepare for his first debate in seclusion, I returned to Washington, D.C., to watch it on television. Eizenstat, Stern, Jasinowski, and others called afterward to discuss it. We all considered Carter's performance to be C-minus at best. He was flat, smiled in the wrong places, did not jump on Ford mistakes, and seemed generally out of his element. Eizenstat asked if I could return to Atlanta with Stewart and Hunter but, this time, leave Mankiewicz behind. He apparently had said or done something which offended someone.

We returned and updated the briefing books. We also watched the Mondale vice presidential debate with Senator Bob Dole. Mondale had been nervous beforehand. But midway through the debate, Dole suddenly began to implode. He referred to "Democrat wars," and then seemed to question whether President Franklin Roosevelt had been right to bring the United States into World War II against Germany and Japan. He clearly was harboring bitterness about his own World War II wound. His views were jarringly isolationist, circa 1940. What could he be thinking in attacking FDR, the century's most popular president? Mondale relaxed, performed well, and clearly was the winner of the matchup.

As the second Carter-Ford debate neared, Eizenstat informed us that Carter again intended to prepare in seclusion and without being exposed to the pressure of difficult questioning or crossfire. The books were complete. I awoke in my Fairmont Hotel room on a Saturday morning, saw no reason to remain in Atlanta, and flew home to spend the weekend with my family. No sooner had I arrived home than I received a phone call from Eizenstat urging me to return. "If Carter learns that you left, he simply will have nothing whatever to do anymore with the people in Washington he needs badly." I spent Sunday with my family, but did return on Monday morning.

Ford, like his running mate Dole had been, proved his own worst enemy in the second debate. No doubt responding to briefings by Secretary of State Kissinger, he challenged the notion that the Soviet Union fully controlled the countries of Eastern Europe. (The so-called Sonnenfeldt Doctrine, which was U.S. policy at the time, appeared to cede Eastern Europe to the USSR's sphere of influence.) Ford of course knew exactly what the relationship was between the Soviet Union and its Warsaw Pact satellites. Someone obviously had told him that he should not publicly acknowledge this domination, lest he alienate American voters of Eastern European descent. But, from his debate formulation, the average viewer might have concluded that he was ignorant of so fundamental a reality. Ford's blunder gave Carter an edge in the debate. It also helped Carter surmount his principal obstacle in establishing his credibility as a prospective president by presenting Ford, an incumbent, as someone who might not be up to the job himself.

I returned to Atlanta briefly before a final Carter-Ford debate. Eizenstat had insisted on being included in Carter's personal preparation for the second debate, and Carter had relented. But Carter remained unprepared for the inclusion of "outsiders" such as Stewart, Hunter, and myself in face-to-face dialogue. I simply reviewed the final, updated versions of the books, made minor changes, and returned home.

In the campaign's final days, Ford pulled gradually within hailing distance of the lead that Carter and Mondale had established following the Dole and Ford gaffes on foreign policy and the earlier Ford pardon of Nixon. I did not have the heart to fly to Atlanta for election-night activities, which presumably would celebrate a Democratic victory. I watched the returns at home with my family. A friend in the campaign called from Atlanta late that evening: "Well, I guess we won—or Ford lost. Jimmy will notice you weren't here." I thought to myself that I had cared a great deal about the presidential election outcomes in 1960, 1964, 1968, and 1972, but this time I found myself still doubting whether the Democratic Party had nominated a qualified candidate. Many of us had pitched in to help our party's nominee, but I had yet to find anyone, outside a small cadre, who felt any real commitment to Carter. It had seemed a campaign, quite literally, without a core.

Shortly after the election, facing service in the vice presidency, Fritz Mondale asked Stewart, John Rielly, Norm Sherman, and me to join him at the Capitol to discuss our experience in the office with Humphrey. His staff members Dick Moe, Jim Johnson, Mike Berman, and Al Eisele sat in. I prepared a discussion memo in advance of the meeting. Everyone recognized, going in, that Mondale's relationship to Carter would be entirely different from Humphrey's to Johnson. Humphrey arrived in the vice presidency to serve a president who had spent many years as Senate leader, vice president, and then president. Mondale, by contrast, would serve a new president not only inexperienced in national policy and politics, but who knew few of the figures he would be dealing with in the capital.

We pointed out, however, that any vice president would do best to avoid line responsibilities for policy areas or operating programs. It was far better to remain, aside from the president himself, the only person in government with no bureaucratic or turf axe to grind. We also warned Mondale to beware ambitious White House staff members who might try to grab power or influence from the vice president. Stewart and I related Humphrey's unpleasant experiences with Califano of the LBJ staff. (Little did we know that Mondale, who lived near Califano in northwestern Washington, already had agreed to push Carter to appoint him as defense secretary.) Mondale, it turned out, quickly earned Carter's trust and would become his invaluable advisor.

The Carter transition operation should have worked well. Lists of prospective appointees, I was told, had been assembled ahead of time. Yet, after Carter's election, only members of Eizenstat's and Watson's staffs quickly found sub-Cabinet or staff jobs in federal departments and agencies. Holbrooke, for instance, who had served as Eizenstat's foreign-policy staff person, became assistant secretary of state for Asian affairs. Anthony Lake, who had filled the same role for Watson, became director of policy planning in the Department of State. Both, as it happened, already knew incoming secretary of state Cyrus Vance well. Carter's management style was to select his top appointees, then let them select their own teams. He had a major problem, however. He had no personal acquaintance with most of the persons he would consider for Cabinet positions. The entire enterprise became a sweepstakes in which ambitious seekers mobilized endorsements, phone calls, and letters on their own behalf from leaders in Congress, organized labor, business, and other constituencies. Then, when appointed, they staffed their departments and agencies with their own associates rather than with independent figures or people who had supported Carter's nomination or election.

Carter refused to appoint Califano defense secretary. But he did appoint him secretary of health, education, and welfare as a consolation prize. Califano brought his own team to the department. Representative Brock Adams, on being appointed transportation secretary, filled his deputy and assistant secretary positions, which normally would be given to senior figures in their own right, with members of his own congressional staff. Carter assured friction on the foreign-policy front by appointing Vance as secretary of state and Zbignew Brzezinski as his national security advisor. Their worldviews differed greatly. Carter also did not know, before their appointment, that Vance and Brzezinski differed sharply in temperament: Vance proceeded in a gentlemanly, by-the-book way; Brzezinski, who had physical proximity to Carter in the White House and ready access to his in-box, was a more aggressive, do-what-it-takes proponent of his own views. Carter admired Brzezinski's high intelligence, energy, and conceptualizing abilities. But the new president was sufficiently inexperienced that he did not recognize the need to carefully seek and consider the views of all of his national-security team before signing off formally on proposals by any one of them.

Thus the Carter administration took shape with an outsider president, insider vice president, a small cadre of Carter loyalists in the White House, and departments and agencies run and staffed by people the president did not know and who did not know him. It began without any coherent policy framework or upward or downward loyalty. It was to end, four years later, in exactly the same condition.

Several people had told me that Carter regarded me highly and that I should expect to be offered a central role in the new administration. Hamilton Jordan called to ask that I write letters endorsing several prospective appointees I knew well. After I had heard nothing for several weeks about my own role, I called Eizenstat. He told me that possible appointees, no matter who they were, were now being asked to campaign for their jobs with endorsement letters and other recommendations. He did know that I had been approved by an ambassadorial-review panel for an ambassadorship, if I wanted one. Newark mayor Ken Gibson had proposed that I be named secretary of housing and urban development. (At another time, I would have been pleased to serve as an ambassador. But at this point Jean and I had four school-age children we wanted to raise in a normal American setting. And there were people better qualified than I to be HUD secretary.) Adams, having been nominated as transportation secretary, and knowing of my longtime United Airlines association, suggested I serve as head of the Federal Aviation Administration. He also told me that "the Carter people really think highly of you. I suppose you can have any job you want." But by that time, most of the senior administration jobs had already been campaigned for and filled.

I would not campaign for an appointment. My friends Stewart and Hunter also refused to campaign, although Hunter eventually joined the National Security Council staff. Mankiewicz, too, heard nothing during the transition period. When Fidel Castro sent a message through Mankiewicz, to be passed directly to Carter, Frank met briefly with the president-elect to transmit it. Carter did not speak to him on receiving the message, but simply walked off.

Ted Sorensen, an active early Carter supporter in New York, was nominated to be CIA director. Several senators, however, threatened to raise critical questions at his confirmation hearings. Sorensen called on Carter to ask that he stick with his nomination; he felt confident of confirmation. Carter told him that, were he not distracted by many pressing issues, he would do so. However, because of these pressures, he preferred that Sorensen withdraw. "For instance," Carter told him, "I have the inaugural program to review." Sorensen thought Carter meant he had to review general arrangements and prepare his inaugural speech. But then he caught sight of the page proofs of the official inaugural program on Carter's desk—the president-elect was personally proofreading the souvenir program. Sorensen withdrew.

Friends in the capital told me how fortunate I was. I was one of the few people in the city who knew Carter and those close to him. My consulting business would thrive, and in a short time I would be wealthy. That was not why I was in Washington, however. I preferred useful public service to making money. I had no great confidence in Carter, but was prepared to do all I could to help him govern successfully.

Then, when I had set aside any thought of Carter administration service, I received an offer of an appointment from an unexpected source. Jack Gilligan, the former governor of Ohio, had been an active antiwar Democrat and a friend. Secretary of State Vance was seeking someone to run the Agency for International Development (AID), and the Reverend Theodore Hesburgh, president of Notre Dame University, had recommended Gilligan, a Notre Dame alumnus whom he knew was devoted to issues of social justice. Gilligan accepted the appointment and then invited me to join him at AID in whatever position seemed appropriate. First, though, the entire agency had to be staffed and a transition process instituted. The State Department transition and staffing had moved forward, but nothing would be done about AID, which was part of State, until an administrator was named. Thus Gilligan, Jack Sullivan, a former staff member of the House Foreign Affairs Committee, and I set about forming a team and setting an agenda on a crash basis. As we set up our transition offices, we received résumés from Carter campaign supporters who had been frozen out when applying to other government departments and agencies. We thus hired people who elsewhere had been rejected because they were known supporters of the president.

Normally, a new administration completely clears out policy appointees of the previous one and puts in place its own. Gilligan, however, was inexperienced in foreign-assistance issues and wanted, in light of our late start, to keep some holdover and career appointees. Most specifically, he was pre-

pared to name as deputy administrator a holdover from the Ford administration who was actively disliked by congressional Democrats involved in foreign assistance. I found myself in the strange position of calling Senators Ted
Kennedy, Paul Sarbanes, and others to get them to withdraw their opposition to his nomination. Gilligan also kept on board several other holdover
appointees. Jack Sullivan became assistant administrator for Asian affairs,
and Gilligan invited me to invent a position that suited my interests. I thus
became assistant administrator for intragovernmental and international
affairs, the number-three position at AID, responsible for relations with other
U.S. government agencies, foreign aid donors, international financial institutions, and long-term policy planning. The job carried with it an additional
assignment: to run a White House committee, the Development Coordination Committee, which coordinated the development-assistance-related
efforts of all U.S. government departments and agencies.

Quite soon President Carter directed that the Development Coordination Committee should undertake a comprehensive review of all such U.S.
policies. I convened the interagency committee and got started on it.

Vice President Mondale gave me a strong send-off by insisting that he
swear me in at a White House ceremony. Afterward, he hosted my family
and friends for coffee in the Roosevelt Room (the former Fish Room). My
friend Joe Duffey, who had been appointed assistant secretary of state for
cultural affairs, brought a Bible to be used in the swearing-in ceremony. Displayed in the Roosevelt Room was the same portrait of Franklin Roosevelt
that had hung behind Hubert Humphrey's Executive Office Building desk
during his vice presidency. My family was presented with a tape of Mondale's remarks and my response—Mondale said that I was trusted by those
in power because of my integrity; I promised to serve in such a way as to
make my friends and family proud. I meant it.

Soon I found myself taking on occasional assignments for Secretary of State
Vance. I had been part of the U.S. delegation to his first overseas assignment,
a conference in Paris of mostly oil-producing and developing countries. En route
to Paris, Vance reviewed the speech prepared for him and asked that I write
another. The original draft amounted for the most part to a stark rejection of
the proposals being made by the emerging countries, which were asking for "a
new international economic order." I wrote a new speech that repositioned the
United States as sympathetic to their concerns, if not yet prepared to agree with
all their proposals. (Put another way, the new draft utilized Monnet's old dic-

tum that problems should be put on one side of the table, to be addressed by the affected parties seated together on the other side.) The next day. at a lunch of the delegation at the U.S. embassy, Vance announced that he would be using my draft rather than the one prepared by State, Treasury, and National Security Council officials at the table. Their reaction was sullen. The speech, however, was well received as the new administration's first major foreign-policy statement. Soon thereafter I drafted a Vance statement for a meeting of the Organization for Economic Cooperation and Development, also held in Paris and at which I also was part of the U.S. government delegation. Thereafter I was asked periodically to do quick reviews, rewrites, or edits of Vance speeches and congressional testimony, in addition to my regular AID duties. I also served on the U.S. delegation to Panama Canal Treaty talks and as AID's representative to the administration's new Human Rights Task Force. I dug into the work and enjoyed it greatly. Before long, however, Gilligan and I had a disagreement that went further than either of us really intended.

My conduct of the government-wide foreign-assistance study had alarmed some of the career AID people, including the holdover appointees Gilligan had kept in policy positions. I saw the study as a way to channel U.S. policy in practical directions it had lacked. State Department officers generally looked down on foreign-assistance programs as vehicles for impractical Peace Corps types and do-gooders who often did not understand practical country-to-country diplomacy. There was some truth to the characterization. AID personnel, for their part, often saw themselves as stalwart heroes defending the Third World downtrodden from the compromises that effete, cookie-pushing diplomats were all too willing to make with their corrupt rulers. There was some truth there, too.

I saw, moreover, that President Carter had only the barest understanding of international-development issues. Put simplistically, he tended to see the process as one in which prosperous churchgoers need only fill their collection plates more fully so that the deserving poor might benefit. I wanted to develop a U.S. policy that combined diplomacy and development. At the heart of such a strategy was "conditionality" for countries receiving aid—that is, our own and multilateral aid should be extended only to those countries willing to change their internal policies so that the aid would be well used. Too much aid was going directly from U.S. taxpayers to Swiss bank accounts controlled by Third World despots. As many analysts put it, the poor and middle-class in the rich world were being taxed to benefit the rich in the poor world.

Most members of our executive-branch task force welcomed such a shift. I hoped that, among other things, it would bring new respect to AID within agencies that heretofore had regarded it as a quasi–United Way operation. We also were moving to a reorganization proposal that would have placed a White House coordinator, rather than AID, in overall charge of foreign-assistance programs.

The holdover appointees at AID reached a state of high anxiety. Gilligan urged me to give them a greater voice in the study committee. I told him I could not do that and still run an objective exercise. It was a dispute between friends that got out of hand. I told Gilligan that we worked for the president and, though Gilligan ran AID, it was the president and not AID we were serving with the study. I resigned. After my resignation, the study committee moved ahead and made the same recommendations I had hoped it would.

President Carter had asked each presidential appointee to sign a pledge that he or she would serve the full four years of his term, thus providing continuity that sometimes had been lacking in previous administrations. When my resignation was received, Hamilton Jordan called. "I have in my hand," he said, "a letter signed by you pledging to serve for four full years. Now you have resigned after a few months." "Yes," I said, "I pledged to serve for four years, but I did not pledge to serve in the same job."

I had intended to leave AID quietly and perhaps serve elsewhere in the administration. The last thing I intended, on resigning, was to embarrass or hurt Gilligan. I knew that his AID appointment was more important to him than mine was to me. I thought the work important but, from the beginning, was more committed to overall principles of public policy than to AID per se. Gilligan should be able to run the place as he wished, I thought, without me pulling in another direction. A *New York Times* story soon complicated things. It brought news of my resignation, contained highly favorable comments about my work from officials at the White House and the State Department, and made Gilligan look bad. I learned later that the piece had been instigated by officials at State. (A year later Gilligan himself was gone, fired by Vance and replaced by my old associate Doug Bennet, who had been serving as assistant secretary of state for congressional relations.) Had Gilligan and I been able to do things over, I have little doubt that both of us would have pulled back from our conflict. I regret now that I left so abruptly and, even more, that Gilligan may have been damaged as a result.

Vance invited me to stay at State—there might be a resignation down the road in a policy position that I could fill. I moved into an office in Tony Lake's policy planning shop, writing speeches for Vance and occasionally for Deputy Secretary Warren Christopher, and in the meantime looking into other opportunities in the administration. Hamilton Jordan and his deputy, Landon Butler, suggested I could have any open position that I thought suitable. They asked White House personnel staff to review with me the list of available appointments. But there was a fundamental problem: I was the first appointee to have resigned; someone else had to resign or be fired to create an opening. There was a vacancy on the Commodities Futures Trading Commission that Barbara McKenzie, a former McGovern campaigner working at the commission, urged me to fill. But, after looking into it, I concluded that I was totally unsuited to the job. Peter Tarnoff, Vance's chief of staff, had conversations with a senior State appointee in which he suggested she might be happier returning to private life. But she failed to take the cue, and Vance was reluctant to fire her. Thus I continued to tread water in the policy planning office. Lake offered to create a permanent position for me there if I wished. My friend Frank Mankiewicz, then president of National Public Radio, suggested I join him there. I had no desire at that point to reestablish my Washington, D.C., consulting firm. In the end, I found myself returning home to the Northwest.

Bill Ruckelshaus had been deputy attorney general in the Nixon administration and had gained fame when Nixon fired him and his boss, Attorney General Elliott Richardson, during the Watergate scandals. He had then opened a law practice in the capital with, among others, my Democratic friends Albert Beveridge and Harold Himmelman. Quite soon we were working together on behalf of two clients, the government of Greece and Eli Lilly & Co., which was based in Ruckelshaus's home state of Indiana. Subsequently, Ruckelshaus had taken a job as senior vice president and general counsel of Weyerhaeuser, a forest-products company headquartered between Seattle and Tacoma, not far from where Ruckelshaus had done military service at Fort Lewis and fallen in love with the Northwest. When the *New York Times* carried news of my resignation from AID, Ruckelshaus had contacted me immediately. He knew I was from the Northwest and loved it as much as he did. He urged me to join him as a Weyerhaeuser vice president and return home. I visited the company headquarters, met George Weyerhaeuser, its president, and contemplated the 3,000-mile move. My wife, Jean, said she would go along with whatever gave me satisfaction. My oldest son, Ted, then in his junior year in high school, said he was willing to move, but urged me to make an immediate decision so that he could make the most of a new place. Thus, in January 1978 my family and I headed to the Northwest. I maintained a consultancy with the State Department's policy planning office, as well as my security clearances, so that I could remain available for periodic writing and other assignments. We moved into a new home on Mercer Island, across Lake Washington from Seattle, and I settled into a corporate routine I had not expected.

Weyerhaeuser was good to me. George Weyerhaeuser was particularly supportive and became a friend. I found myself comfortable with the company's policies, and with the leeway I had to pursue community and other activities as I wished. I became active in the state's Democratic Party and in volunteer groups serving low-income residents. I continued to write regular commentary for local and other publications. My four children became committed outdoor people—Ted and Bob climbed all major peaks in the Cascade Range and worried us with difficult rock climbs. Jean, at first skeptical, came to love the area as well. Then national politics beckoned again.

The Carter administration, beset by high gas prices, record-high interest rates, and a failed rescue mission of U.S. hostages held in our embassy in Tehran, Iran, was imploding just as surely as Nixon's had imploded in the previous presidential term. Polling data showed Carter to be an almost certain loser in the 1980 presidential election. Carter's 1976 personnel decisions had come back to plague him. He had fired several Cabinet secretaries, including Califano and Adams. Vance had resigned in protest when the Tehran rescue mission was undertaken without his agreement. Carter, inexperienced entering the presidency, had been a classic in-box executive—that is, he would deal with issues ad hoc as they came to his in-box, rather than setting clear priorities and sticking with them. Moreover, he had subcontracted Cabinet governance to strangers who proceeded more or less on their own. Morale in the White House itself was low. During a visit from Seattle, I ran into Carter's principal speechwriter in the West Wing lobby. How had I related to Vice President Humphrey and the presidential candidates for whom I had written, he asked? He was frustrated by his inability to work effectively with Carter. On questioning him, I learned that he seldom saw Carter. When a speech was to be written, he would receive a brief memo to that effect. He would then submit a draft, which Carter reviewed and marked up. He then would submit a revised draft. And so on. There was never any face-to-face discussion, much less give-and-take about ideas. That accounted, I knew, for the fact that Carter's speeches always were sterile and contained no firsthand anecdotes or human stories. They had been written by someone with whom he had no interaction. I was reminded of Carter's refusal, during the 1976 campaign, to discuss personally the debate materials we had prepared for him. Another staff member told me that Carter had instituted a White House rule that staff encountering him in corridors were not to make eye contact with him. He did not want his time wasted with smiles or head nods.

Early in 1979 I was asked by the Carter White House to convene a luncheon meeting of Washington State Democratic leaders and campaign contributors to hear a presentation by Carter's prospective 1980 campaign finance chair. After the meeting he asked me to suggest state campaign and finance chairs. When I declined to serve personally in either post, he appeared shocked. By late 1979 I concluded not only that Carter was a likely 1980 loser, but that, one way or another, the Democratic Party had to find another presidential candidate. It would be best, I thought, if Carter disavowed a second term and left the field clear for other candidates for the nomination. Mondale, for instance, could be a viable candidate if Carter gave him leeway to establish an independent position. Failing that, Carter needed to be challenged within the party. Otherwise we were headed for defeat in 1980.

I and others thus called on Senator Ted Kennedy and urged him to consider running for the Democratic presidential nomination. He knew I had helped Carter in 1976 and served briefly in his administration. "What would a campaign against Carter be like?" Kennedy asked me. "It would be nasty but easy," I responded. I knew how soft Carter's support was in the party, and for that matter in his own administration, and presumed that an aggressive Kennedy campaign would drive him from the field, albeit after some harsh confrontations in early primaries.

I could see that Kennedy was reluctant. It went against his instincts to run against an incumbent Democrat. Yet he also saw Carter as an almost certain general-election loser and felt a responsibility to his party. I told him that, if he decided to run, I would help.

Shortly thereafter Kennedy did announce his candidacy. In Washington State, I joined with his friend, mountaineer Jim Whitaker, in forming a "Kennedy for President" campaign organization. I then received a call asking if I would prepare briefing books for Kennedy as I had prepared them for Carter. It was presumed that Kennedy-Carter campaign debates would be held. Even if they were not, the briefing books would be helpful in Kennedy's campaign. I agreed, and took a one-month leave from Weyerhaeuser.

The 1980 Kennedy nominating campaign had the same feel about it as the 1964, 1968, and 1972 Humphrey and McGovern campaigns. People worked intense seven-day weeks. There was a feeling of energy inside Kennedy's campaign headquarters in a former auto dealership in downtown Washington. I knew that, a few blocks away, Carter staff were just going through the motions.

In my office in a conference room adjoining Kennedy's personal Senate office, I worked principally with Larry Horowitz, of his health subcommittee staff, in preparing the briefing books. Peter Edelman, the campaign's policy director, and Kennedy's various Senate staff members all bore down hard to produce the requested research materials. It was a highly competent and motivated group. But it soon became clear to me that Kennedy himself was still ambivalent about the candidacy he already had declared. In what would become an infamous interview with CBS television correspondent Roger Mudd, Kennedy was asked why he was mounting a challenge against Carter. He had no credible answer. I also found that he was reluctant to review his briefing books or to absorb the material within them. It was particularly important that he do so, I thought, because in the primaries he would face not only Carter but Californian Jerry Brown, who offered another kind of insurgency to Democratic and other voters. Unburdened by congressional votes or incumbency in the presidency, Brown could far more easily than Kennedy position himself as an agent of change—as Carter had positioned himself four years earlier. In the briefing books I included positions and statements likely to be heard from Brown. They were far more compelling than those that either Carter or Kennedy could be expected to make. Paul Kirk, Kennedy's former Senate aide, had taken a lead role in his campaign organization. He asked me to make a presentation to a dozen key outside Kennedy advisors regarding the campaign messages to be expected from Carter, Kennedy, and Brown. They all agreed that Brown's outsider message was the most effective.

Just before Christmas of 1979, the briefing books complete, I returned to Seattle to pick up my family for a long-planned vacation in Hawaii. While we were there, Carter made a formal, public refusal to debate Kennedy before or during the primary-election contests. We cancelled a debate preparation session at Kennedy's home that had been scheduled for just after New Year's. I did return briefly to Washington, D.C., to sit in on a couple of Kennedy campaign meetings. I also met with Kennedy to express my disappointment that he had not studied the briefing books his staff had prepared. I told him I intended to return to Seattle and would do what I could in his Washington State campaign. He responded earnestly, said he would bear down on his briefing-book homework, and thanked me for my help. I rode with him on the subway between his Senate office and the Capitol Building. As he disembarked at the Capitol, it came to me that this really was his element and, whether conscious of it or not, he preferred to remain there.

I did not mention to him, although I could have, that I had been dismayed by the way the political side of his campaign appeared to be stumbling and factionalized. That was not what one expected of a Kennedy campaign organization. Steve Smith, his brother-in-law, was serving as campaign manager but seemed completely out of his element. Paul Kirk was highly professional but not fully in charge. (Many months afterward, I stopped by Smith's Park Avenue offices in New York to discuss an unrelated matter. He quickly told me that he felt he had let Kennedy down. "I had no idea what I was doing," he said. "I should have told Teddy that right away and gone back to New York.")

Soon after my return to Seattle, Western-state Democratic platform hearings were held there. California Kennedy supporters Maxine Waters and Dolores Huerta overnighted at our Mercer Island home. I delivered a tough statement on Kennedy's behalf, critiquing Carter policies and reading Kennedy campaign statements into the record. Other Western-state Kennedy speakers followed suit. Carter presentations were desultory. We dominated the day, although Carter, in the East, was piling up a lead in convention delegates.

Kennedy did badly in early campaigning, but he eventually warmed to his task and, coming into the summer New York convention, made strong showings in later primary contests. On the podium after Carter had secured the nomination, he took distance from the president and his body language bristled. I and others had thought he could defeat Carter and strengthen the Democratic Party for the 1980 general-election contest with Ronald Reagan; instead, he had lost to Carter and at the same time made Reagan's victory more certain. Afterward, as we talked politics in his Senate office, he chided me. "You said a campaign against Carter would be nasty but easy," he said. "I was only half right," I responded.

As it turned out, Kennedy's defeat had a liberating effect on him. Having sought the party's presidential nomination and been defeated, he no longer labored under expectations that he should be a presidential nominee and president. Since that time, he has been a truly outstanding senator—a far more serious and effective legislator than either John or Robert Kennedy had been as senators—and likely will be ranked historically near the top. He also has found time for his family that he would never have been able to have as a national candidate or officeholder. I often thought that I and others did him a disservice by urging him toward a 1980 candidacy he otherwise likely would have forgone. He has no doubt had a far happier and more productive life than he would have had he been pushed toward future presidential candidacies.

Back in Washington State, dedicated Kennedy supporters had stuck with his 1980 candidacy even after it was apparent that Carter would be renominated. At the party's state caucuses, after Carter already had enough delegates nationally for renomination, our Kennedy forces stood fast until the end, and even attracted several uncommitted delegates to our cause. A Carter delegate, a state teachers-union official, walked over smiling as the final delegate tally was taken. "Hey," he said, "you guys took all this seriously. We went for Carter because he promised a Department of Education and our union endorsed him. The Kennedy people cared." Yes, I thought, and that was a problem within our party that would make Reagan our president that fall. Few Democrats really cared whether Carter won or lost.

Several congressional Democrats in the Pacific time zone faced tight races. Among them were Washington's Senator Warren Magnuson and Oregon's Representative Al Ullman, a senior and influential member of the Ways and Means Committee. The presidential outcome became clear on election night before voters in the mountain and Pacific time zones had finished casting ballots. Carter conceded publicly to Ronald Reagan early in the evening without giving other Democratic candidates a thought. At many western polling places, voter participation dropped off sharply after Carter's concession. No one can be sure how many Democratic votes were lost that night. Magnuson and Ullman, in any case, lost their seats.

Jimmy Carter has been a productive ex-president. His work for Habitat for Humanity in particular has served as a positive example for Americans that they, personally, can make a difference. He has undertaken diplomatic missions for several presidents (although, in each instance, administration policymakers have seen Carter as an unguided missile who might take positions or make concessions that would cause later trouble). His Carter Center in Atlanta has done useful work. He has won a Nobel Prize. If he somehow could have been an ex-president, without first serving four years as president, the country would have been well served.

Carter, so far as I ever was able to discern, had generally good Sunday-school values and intentions, but no coherent political philosophy. His candidacy mainly was about himself. We should beware of future presidential candidates billing their inexperience as their principal virtue.

12

THE COUNTERREVOLUTION PROCEEDS

We often as not elect presidents who appear to be the opposites—in temperament, personality, approach to public policy—of immediate predecessors considered unsuccessful by the electorate.

Franklin Roosevelt, in 1932, made economic-policy proposals even more conservative than President Herbert Hoover's, as a nation looked for leadership to climb out of a Great Depression. Yet his determined, optimistic disposition, contrasting with Hoover's comparatively flat, bureaucratic approach, gave voters undefined hope that positive change would take place. Only later did Roosevelt, through trial and error, develop his New Deal approach to governance. In the end it took World War II to pull the country out of its economic doldrums.

Similarly, a former war-hero general, Dwight Eisenhower, succeeded a president, Harry Truman, associated with an unpopular (Korean) war he seemed unable to end. Eisenhower, moreover, had a "command presence" not possessed by the populist Truman, and certainly not by Eisenhower's 1952 opponent, Illinois governor Adlai Stevenson. His vague pledge to "go to Korea" was enough in the 1952 presidential campaign to help him win decisively.

By 1960, voters were restive about a stagnant domestic economy and what increasingly was perceived as a lazy, caretaker Republican administration. Eisenhower's vice president, Richard Nixon, lacked Eisenhower's popularity and was given only token endorsement, in any case, by his boss. John F. Kennedy, pledging to "get America moving again," won a razor-thin and controversial victory over Nixon. Kennedy's comparative vigor—pronounced "vigah" by the candidate in a broad Boston accent—gave the impression, as Roosevelt's had in 1932, that more energetic times lay ahead. Kennedy, in taking a harder-line position than Nixon on international affairs, neutralized Republicans' traditional political advantage on defense and foreign policy issues and made the candidates' personal styles a decisive factor.

Nixon's narrow 1968 victory over Humphrey was facilitated in part by his pledge—comparable to Eisenhower's 1952 pledge to "go to Korea"—that he had a firm if undisclosed plan to end the Vietnam War. Polling data also had indicated that the American people thought the Johnson-Humphrey years had brought too much welfare-state government to the country. Nixon, in contrast, offered more traditional less-government-is-best Republican approaches, and also, via shorthand messages, implied that Democrats' active advocacy of racial minorities would be blunted.

Carter's 1976 message that he was "not a politician" but merely a patriotic peanut farmer resonated among voters disenchanted with what they saw as the constant political maneuverings of professional politicians Johnson and Nixon, and then further disillusioned by President Ford's pardon of Nixon. But by 1980, they were prepared for someone and something as far from Carter as they could find. They associated the Carter years with energy shortages, long lines at gasoline stations, high inflation and interest rates, the failed Iran hostage rescue mission, and Carter's talk of a "national malaise" in which he blamed citizens, rather than himself, for the country's failure to act on a public agenda largely centered on limits. Reagan's sunny growth-uber-alles optimism provided exactly the contrast they were looking for. Reagan proposed to strengthen defense, cut taxes, generate prosperity, reduce big government, and, not least, make the country feel good about itself again. As his hero, Franklin Roosevelt, had been the anti-Hoover, Reagan was the anti-Carter.

Democrats had taken Reagan too lightly as a candidate and leader. They discounted his largely successful tenure as governor of California and tended to see him as nothing more than an aphorism-spouting, if personally charming, movie actor who would be overcome by serious national governance. They also had forgotten that, as a onetime liberal and Screen Actors Guild president, he knew the context of voters outside the Republican base.

Reagan soon proved to be a highly skillful national politician and leader. His 1980 campaign rhetoric—while often directed against 1960s Great Society programs—generally lauded the New Deal initiatives of Roosevelt, although this went largely unnoticed by the media. He took care, too, to treat gently the universal, Roosevelt-style programs while taking aim at more narrowly directed federal programs. He ridiculed so-called "welfare queens" for refusing to work while living off the public dole, but drew into his orbit senior citizens benefiting from Social Security.

Reagan's greatest substantive blunder, early in his term, came when he struck a deal with House Speaker Tip O'Neill, a fellow genial Irishman, whereby Reagan would get his requested tax cuts but would not make major spending cuts in Democrat-favored programs. The result: federal budget deficits that quickly were to reach historic peacetime levels. Yet the deficits, while posing danger to the national future, during Reagan's eight presidential years helped keep the economy growing.

In early 1981, Democrats found themselves confused and demoralized by Reagan's unexpectedly one-sided victory. We had, after all, come to view ourselves as the permanent majority party—controlling Congress and since 1965 effectively dominating the national policy agenda. We might lose the White House, as we had to Nixon in 1968 and 1972, but that would happen only under special circumstances.

Several members of the former Democratic Forum met informally at the end of 1980 to discuss next steps. They asked me, in Seattle, to write a short paper outlining the need for a new Democratic agenda—along the lines of the paper I had written in 1975 prior to Carter's election—in the face of a Republican presidency. Michael Barnes, by then a U.S. representative from Maryland, entered it in the Congressional Record. I came to Washington, D.C., just before Reagan's inauguration and met with several former forum members and other Democrats. There was a consensus that the party needed a rallying point for rethinking. We put together a list of Democrats from various wings of the party—Carter administration appointees, Kennedy supporters, alumni of the Johnson-Humphrey administration, advocates of future presidential candidacies by Walter Mondale and Gary Hart, labor and consumer-group leaders and environmentalists—who should be involved in such an exercise. I agreed to chair an ad hoc meeting of such a group immediately after the inauguration. The meeting went much like the 1975 Democratic-issues convention in Louisville. We expected perhaps thirty or forty people to attend the Saturday-morning gathering in a House committee room; several hundred showed up. Attendees endorsed the notion that a new, independent but unmistakably Democratic think tank should be formed to develop alternative policies with which to counter the new Reagan proposals.

A working group—initially including, notably, Kennedy supporters Peter Edelman and Adam Yarmolinsky, former Mondale aide Richard Moe, Carter aide Stuart Eizenstat, Cathy Douglas, several labor-union officials, Eleanor Holmes Norton, Michael Barnes, former Johnson counsel Harry McPherson, and a shifting cast of others—set about recruiting prospective members of the think tank's board and advisory board. I asked Terry Sanford, who was then president of Duke University, to serve as chairman, and former secretary of state Cyrus Vance to serve as vice chair. Both immediately agreed. Howard Samuels, a former New York gubernatorial candidate, agreed to serve as finance chair. Other board members were to include former Carter treasury secretary Mike Blumenthal, former agriculture secretary Bob Bergland, former education secretary Shirley Hufstedler, economist Walter Heller, Goldman Sachs executive Robert Rubin, California venture capitalist Don Gevirtz, actor Warren Beatty, Edelman, Yarmolinsky, Moe, McPherson, Douglas, Norton, industrialist Sidney Harman, former Carter White House aide Jane Harman, Carter counsel Lloyd Cutler, Vernon Jordan, Maxine Waters, Smith Bagley, former deputy secretary of state Warren Christopher, Seattle mayor Charles Royer, consumerist Carol Foreman, Communications Workers president Glenn Watts, United Auto Workers president Doug Fraser, Chicago philanthropist Peter Kovler, and Democratic treasurer Charles Curry. We enlisted Democratic governors, big-city mayors, business and labor leaders, and academics to serve as members of a National Advisory Board. Arkansas governor Bill Clinton and his wife, Hillary Rodham, quickly signed up.

We purposely did not invite sitting senators or members of Congress to sit on our board or advisory board—with the sole exception of Barnes, who had helped launch the venture. To avoid factionalism, we also did not invite prospective presidential candidates to become board members. I and others made the rounds to explain our rationale in not inviting them. (Kennedy, on reviewing the initial board and advisory board lists, jokingly asked, "Why have you included Sarge Shriver on the advisory board?" I explained that we did not consider his brother-in-law to be an active presidential candidate any longer.) I agreed to serve as president and chief executive officer of the new Center for Democratic Policy (which soon changed its name to Center for National Policy, so as to avoid the impression that its purpose was partisanship rather than independent policy development). Somewhat to my family's distress, I agreed to pull up stakes and return, after three years in Seattle, to the now-Reagan-dominated capital.

Around this time, Chuck Manatt, a Californian, was elected Democratic National Committee chairman. Pamela Harriman, wife of Averell Harriman, founded Democrats for the 80s, a political action committee devoted to raising money for Democratic candidates. Both Manatt and Pamela Harriman suggested that the Center for National Policy merge with their operations. I was prepared to go ahead with a merger, because joining either group would have provided the center with the solid financial base it lacked. We had no endowment, and thus had to raise operating funds as we went. But both Sanford and Vance felt it best that we stand apart from the two purely political entities and maintain the center's tax-exempt status.

We faced a problem, however. Corporate and foundation donors shied away from the center because it was perceived, correctly, to be associated with the Democratic Party, even though it was an independent, nonprofit institution. We did not want to be underwritten entirely by any single faction or group. Labor unions gave generously, but we limited the number of union presidents on the board. We did not seek money from donors who wanted us to peddle a certain ideological viewpoint or policy. We had to depend too greatly on moderate contributions from individuals who tended to see the money as being in the same category as political contributions. A large proportion of the annual budget came from our annual Public Service Awards dinner, for which donors purchased sponsorships, tables, and tickets just as they would for a national political dinner. We also sponsored small quasi-political events, attended by Democratic officeholders and celebrities, which raised moderate amounts of money.

The next four years were personally rewarding for me. The Center for National Policy published a wide range of foreign-, domestic-, and economic-policy monographs which were well received in the media and policy communities. We formed broad-based task forces to examine, among other things, U.S. industrial renewal and agricultural policy. No author or participant was paid a penny for his or her involvement. Senate leader Bob Byrd and House Speaker O'Neill convened regular, fully attended seminars at which our papers' authors made presentations and answered questions. Conferences were held at major cities around the country. Ted Kennedy, Walter Mondale, Gary Hart, Massachusetts governor Mike Dukakis, and other party leaders helped us raise money and appeared at our events. I cannot recall our ever being turned down, between the center's founding early in 1981 and the end of 1984, for cooperation or involvement by any major Democrat of any ideological persuasion.

We kept the staff small. Maureen Steinbruner served as research director. Our communications director was Al Eisele, Mondale's vice presidential press secretary and a longtime capital journalist. Keith Haller, from the old Democratic Forum group, initially served as executive vice president, concentrating on organization and conferences; Elizabeth Frawley, a former member of Ted Kennedy's staff, subsequently took on broad conference and congressional-liaison responsibilities. One of our first student interns, during the center's initial year of 1981, was John F. Kennedy Jr., then a Brown University junior. My friend Maurice Tempelsman, who had been a part of the official delegation on vice president Humphrey's 1967 mission to Africa, had taken special interest in John since forming a relationship with his mother, Jacqueline Kennedy. I interviewed John for the internship at a luncheon in Tempelsman's office in New York. His sister had taken an internship in their uncle Ted Kennedy's Senate office, but, as I learned later, their mother and other family members had thought it better that John learn about Washington, D.C., at a remove from the political process itself.

John lived with his aunt and uncle, Sarge and Eunice Shriver, and his Shriver cousins on Foxhall Road, and commuted daily to the center's offices near DuPont Circle. He was earnest, personable, and devoted to his work. He came to learn that he was a celebrity when he did advance work for, and then accompanied me on, a fundraising swing to Southern California. Subjected to sometimes embarrassing fawning by Hollywood types, John maintained his poise and sense of humor. Several fawners suggested that he remain in Southern California, after our week-long trip, to continue fundraising on his own. "My mother doesn't think it would be a good idea for me to keep hanging around Hollywood," he told me the day before our scheduled return to the capital. "Don't worry," I told him, "I wouldn't leave you among these sharks for a moment."

Film-industry powerhouse Lew Wasserman had served as a founding member of the center's board, although he limited his activity to an annual contribution. Warren Beatty, who had served conscientiously and without seeking limelight in the Robert Kennedy and McGovern campaigns, continued to work in exactly the same fashion on the center's board. He attended quarterly board meetings and our annual Public Service Awards dinner in Washington, D.C., gave and raised money, and quickly responded to any request for involvement. He was a rare exception among film- and entertainment-industry people, who typically will agree to make an appearance or write a check but have little sense of the substance of policy and politics. Mainly they welcome the public exposure—or the feeling of moral satisfaction—that involvement in politics or a cause may give them.

The Center for National Policy went from zero to high effectiveness in probably as short a time as any such organization has done. Our publications and monographs were substantive, solid, and topical. We successfully mobilized thinking Democratic-leaning leaders in all parts of the country and from a spectrum of opinions. Our work was directed toward officeholders, policy analysts, and opinion leaders. Our monographs and reports were not partisan indictments of Reagan policy but, instead, serious analyses of major public issues.

Typically, we would publish three sets of analyses, with accompanying proposals, in a monograph exploring an issue such as health-care reform, industrial competitiveness, or U.S.-Soviet relations. We did not endorse one perspective over another. The aim was to build a gradual consensus around an updated, coherent agenda which could replace the stale, interest-group-dominated agenda discredited by Reagan's definitive victory. Short-term partisan attacks could emanate from the DNC, from Congress, and from labor, environmental, consumer, and other critics of Republican policy. We meant to develop a longer-term base of support for alternative policies. But in the context of a powerful and popular Reagan presidency, we made barely a dent.

Reagan truly defined the political terms of reference during his eight-year time in office. Like FDR, he probably could have been elected again, had presidential term limits not been in place. As it was, his impact was such that his vice president, George H. W. Bush, was to succeed him in office—something incumbent vice presidents have a hard time doing.

After Reagan's resounding defeat of Mondale in the 1984 presidential election, I could feel enthusiasm begin to drain from the Center for National Policy's sponsors. A Democratic return to the White House was at least four years away. Money became harder to raise. At the beginning of 1985, Ed Muskie succeeded Cyrus Vance as the center's chair (Vance had succeeded Terry Sanford two years earlier). I had favored Bob Rubin and Jane Harman, both younger and more vigorous, as cochairs to succeed Vance. But Vance felt that Muskie would lend greater weight to the chairmanship. I liked and felt comfortable with Muskie but suspected that he would not want to become personally involved in fundraising, as Sanford and Vance had been willing to do. That proved to be the case. I also was becoming tired and felt my effectiveness waning. Like many others in similar roles, I was spending far more time raising money than thinking about the policy issues the center had been founded to address. I had been devoting far too little time to my wife and children and limiting my income to that which a nonprofit entity could afford, while paying Duke tuition for our two sons. In mid-1985 I resigned from the center to reestablish the consulting firm I had operated in the 1970s. At the last minute Charles Curry, a board member who had his own independent foundation, proposed that he and others endow the center. But I had already decided to move on. When I did, Curry withdrew his endowment proposal. A month earlier, in May 1985, I had turned down an offer of generous financial support from another source. On the last day of a visit to Moscow, during a World War II fortieth-anniversary observance, I was walking through Gorky park with a KGB officer, who suggested that a several-hundred-thousand-dollar gift to the center could be arranged through Occidental Petroleum's Armand Hammer, long rumored to be a Soviet agent. "We have supported other American think tanks that way," he said.

A search committee at the center hired as my successor Kirk O'Donnell, who had been Speaker O'Neill's chief of staff. He had strongly supported the center's activities since its founding, and I felt pleased that it would be in good hands. He would later be succeeded by Madeleine Albright, a Muskie protégé who had joined the center's board under Muskie's sponsorship when he became chairman. She subsequently would use the center presidency as a stepping-stone to her appointment as U.N. ambassador and then secretary of state. The Center for National Policy still exists, but it is only one of several such institutions generally oriented toward the Democratic side of the political and policy spectrum. If I had known, on the center's founding, that financing would be a long-term problem, I would have argued more strongly with Sanford and Vance on behalf of the mergers that Chuck Manatt and Pamela Harriman had proposed. Nonetheless, I take pride in the work that the center did during the four and a half years I led it and, if faced with the same challenge, no doubt would accept it again.

Another organization, the Democratic Leadership Council (DLC), had been formed in 1985 with a somewhat different orientation than the Center for National Policy's. Whereas the center had attempted to bring about consensus, through involvement of all factions and viewpoints important to Democrats, the DLC staked out an avowedly "moderate" position for itself, and purposely left out of its activities the labor movement and the then-chairman of the DNC, Paul Kirk. Al From, the DLC's president and principal founder, invited me to join the DLC board and become an active participant. I was in general agreement with the DLC in its emphasis on economic-growth-oriented policies and the need to break the Democratic Party free of domination by single-issue and single-interest groups. But I disagreed with its decision to leave large segments of the party—including some of its core constituencies—out of its work. I still believed in an "everybody in, nobody out" approach that engaged as many groups and people as possible in something so fundamental as a political party's rethinking. I therefore declined From's invitation. The DLC, to its credit, has had a continuing impact. Some of its leaders, including Bill Clinton, Al Gore, and Joe Lieberman, have used it as a source of ideas and political support. But I continue to feel uncomfortable about the absence of major labor, minority, and liberal involvement in its activities.

After President Clinton's departure from office in 2001, a new Democratic-oriented think tank, the Center for American Progress, was founded, with John Podesta as its president. It has been more strongly funded than the Center for National Policy was, and has been able to finance in-house scholars and policy specialists. But its work, too, will inevitably be overshadowed by the main-tent debate taking place between the White House and Congress.

President Reagan was a classic out-box president: he had a small number of agenda items he would place in his out-box and then pursue vigorously. In that regard, he was like Franklin Roosevelt, Eisenhower, Truman, Nixon, and Johnson, and unlike notorious in-box presidents who responded to events and issues as they developed day by day. There is no necessary correlation between an out-box presidency and a successful outcome for the country. An active, focused president, if he has the wrong priorities, can do great damage. A reactive, scattered president often will do little good or harm. My own preference, of course, is for a positive, wise out-box president. But they are not that easy to find.

Reagan, in the White House, was reportedly lazy and often distracted. A member of the White House support staff told me during his presidency that Reagan as often as not would leave the Oval Office in the late afternoon, change to pajamas, and have a 6 PM TV dinner with the first lady, watching movie reruns. This, of course, was in sharp contrast to predecessors such as Lyndon Johnson, who lived to govern, and would set priorities, then rigorously pursue the fine print. If you thought as Reagan did, however, and were uninterested in the fine print, it made good sense to lay out the broad strokes of policy and then leave it to trusted specialists to fill them in. Reagan also recognized that, as the so-called Great Communicator, he could persuade millions with carefully staged mass-media appearances rather than dissipate his energies trying to manage his government.

Reagan told us what he wanted to do, and then set policy in a direction to do it. To a degree that few Democrats foresaw, he was successful. He said he would generate prosperity and did—although with borrowed money. He said he would reduce tax rates and did. He said he would reduce the role of the federal government, but in that area he had less success than he foresaw. He did, however, change the context of political debate and place large-government advocates on the defensive. Within his own Republican Party, he moved emphasis from Main Street, hardware-store, balanced-budget economics—comfortable for Republicans such as Gerald Ford and Bob Dole—to supply-side, take-risks-for-growth economics. Most dramatically, he said he would not accept communist domination of Eastern Europe and did not. Along with the Polish pope John Paul II and AFL-CIO president Lane Kirkland, he openly supported the Polish Solidarity movement when the policy establishment scorned such initiatives. He characterized the Soviet Union and its satellites as "an evil empire" and challenged Soviet prime minister Mikhail Gorbachev to "tear down" the Berlin Wall separating West Germany from East Germany. Conventional wisdom in both U.S. political parties held that the Soviet Union would control Eastern European countries into perpetuity. No one except a dwindling band of pre–World War II émigrés believed that the Soviet Union itself might cease to exist. Most policy and political professionals, myself included, believed that the best course to world peace and stability was the encouragement of a reform-minded Gorbachev regime in the Soviet Union which gradually would open its institutions and sphere of influence to liberalizing political and economic policies.

Reagan's point of entry to political discourse, however, had been the 1930s and 1940s, when ideology had a central place. He had come of age viewing both fascism and communism as destructive, evil creeds to which there could be no accommodation. His message to Gorbachev, thus, was not "help us help you" but "Mr. Gorbachev, tear down this wall!" He also set in motion U.S. defense spending increases intended to break the Soviet economy if Moscow tried to match them. When I visited the Soviet Union in 1985, as a guest of its government, I found Soviet officials in a state of near panic about Reagan's Strategic Defense ("Star Wars") Initiative (SDI) to construct a U.S. strategic-missile defense system. Many American analysts, myself among them, regarded the SDI as a non-starter, a money-eating pipe dream. But the Soviets took it quite seriously, believed the U.S. capable of producing and deploying it, and felt themselves helpless to match it with their own defensive system and/or new offensive systems that might penetrate it. The threat

of SDI played an important role in forcing the Soviet Union into a fundamental reassessment of its defense priorities and capabilities.

During the same 1985 visit, soon after Gorbachev's ascendancy to power,
I found his new government also absorbed with trying to rescue a domestic
economic system that was in shambles. I went to the government's central
document-distribution site in Moscow (akin to the U.S. Printing Office) and
obtained copies of the initial public statements of Gorbachev and his senior
ministers. All focused on internal reform; few even gave lip service to international politics or traditional Marxist formulations. Crumbling infrastruc-
ture, shoddy construction, and widespread public drunkenness were symptoms
of decay. At the Moscow airport, awaiting my flight back to Frankfurt and
the West, I gave my remaining rubles to my U.S.-Canada Institute escort
officer so that he might buy some of the pitifully few consumer goods on sale
at the airport. He immediately joined Soviet general officers, relatively well-
dressed bureaucrats, and a handful of foreign visitors in a long line waiting
to buy cheaply made Italian shirts, all of the same purplish color. Earlier during my visit, the same escort officer had asked me to purchase for him English-
language books which were unavailable to even Communist Party members
such as himself. I visited a bookstore open only to foreigners; its titles were
a pathetic collection of party-line junk.

Post-1945 estimates within the U.S. government consistently had attributed greater capabilities and performance levels to the Soviet and Comecon/
Warsaw Pact (Eastern European) defense establishments and economies than
reality should have dictated. Our principal global adversary and its satellite
states were, in fact, Potemkin villages collapsing from within. Whether Reagan knew all this—or simply believed it because he wanted to believe it—we
will never know. The outcome was the same. As the Berlin Wall came down
and Germany reunified, other Eastern European and Baltic states broke free,
and the Soviet Union itself ceased to exist, most American and Western European politicians and analysts were stunned. I thought back to my 1961 military recall to the Pentagon, after the Berlin Wall had been erected, and thought
it remarkable that in a thirty-year period the entire nuclear-armed, threaten-
ing enterprise had collapsed inward on itself. Would it have done so without
Reagan's belief that it could be made to happen? Maybe. But maybe not.

It can be argued, of course, that over the long term world peace and stability would have been better served in a relatively stable two-superpower
world—in which the lesser superpower, the Soviet Union, was in a state of

gradual liberalization—than in the current one-superpower world in which chaotic, Book of Revelations–type events appear to loom regularly on the periphery. Had the Soviet Union not collapsed, this argument goes, then the nuclear weapons and materials within its former borders might not have been subject to transfer to rogue states and terrorist groups. Similarly, a more stable and longer-lived Soviet Union might have given the European Union greater time to integrate and fully develop internally, rather than being forced to admit former Soviet satellite states generally unprepared for absorption into EU institutions. It is quite true that the situation has forced the EU to become a loose confederation of states, as favored in the 1960s by Charles de Gaulle, rather than a federal United States of Europe as favored by Jean Monnet and other early supporters of European unity. Yet who could do anything but welcome the rapid and unforeseen liberation of millions of human beings within the former Soviet Union's orbit from defunct and dysfunctional economic and political systems that limited their freedom and growth?

Reagan may have been no more than a simplistic and even simple-minded movie actor playing a role from a patriotic World War II black-and-white film. Yet what he did, internationally, likely will place him in the top ranks of American presidents historically.

In the 1984 presidential campaign, the earnest, serious Walter Mondale was little more than a sacrificial lamb against Reagan. There was a revealing moment in their televised campaign debates in which the much older Reagan declared that "I will not use my opponent's age as an issue against him." Mondale, on camera, could not but laugh at Reagan's joking dismissal of the age issue that opponents had tried to use against the aging incumbent. Mondale, talking straight to his Democratic convention and national television audience, conceded in his nomination-acceptance speech that he would raise federal taxes—thus confirming voters' fears and Reagan's warnings that liberal Democrats always wanted to raise taxes. Mondale's defeat was just as one-sided as George McGovern's had been twelve years earlier. Reagan's victory was much greater than Richard Nixon's in 1972, however, because it signified a fundamental ratification by voters of a new policy paradigm. That strong-defense, low-tax, less-government approach still outweighs in U.S. politics the more diffuse and confused message of the Democratic Party.

During the second Reagan term I busied myself with my consulting practice, continued writing periodic essays, and also became immersed in the financial world for the first time. My friend Mark Meagher had moved from the

Washington Post to *Financial World* magazine. I began writing periodic back-page columns for the magazine when regular columnist (and former *Newsweek* editor) Kermit Lansner did not, and then also began writing a regular "Washington Watch" column in the magazine. In both columns I wrote about public policy trends that might affect financial markets. Early in 1987 I began a new biweekly newsletter and advisory service for institutional investors, called *Washington Intelligence*. The newsletter covered developments in the executive branch, Congress, the Federal Reserve, and regulatory agencies that would be important to financial markets. Clients subscribing to an expanded service received periodic briefings in their offices from me and from public- and private-sector experts on various policy areas. During this time my consulting clients came to include the government of Tajikistan, newly free of the USSR; the government of New Zealand; the Japanese External Trade Organization (JETRO); property and casualty insurance companies, some also involved in managed health-care services; private foundations involved in public philanthropy; general aviation manufacturers; the National Association of Manufacturers, run by my friend Jerry Jasinowski; and the trade association of the pharmaceutical industry. All of these assignments gave me insights into new policy areas.

One consulting assignment, on behalf of the Prudential Insurance Company Foundation, involved monitoring and helping recipients of the foundation's grants. One such grantee was the Children's Defense Fund (CDF), founded by my friend Marian Wright Edelman, who was married to Peter Edelman. The fund was a highly effective advocate of children's issues but needed a stronger research capability. I worked with fund staff to establish it and, while doing so, I got their feedback regarding CDF leadership. Staff regarded Marian Edelman with affection and respect. But her hand-picked chairman, Hillary Rodham Clinton, was seen as rigid, egomaniacal, and thoroughly unpleasant. I filed their opinions in a mental back corner.

I also was pleased to pursue an assignment for the government of New Zealand that struck a blow against what I regarded as Reagan administration bullying. Strong antinuclear sentiment in New Zealand, running through both principal political parties, had led the government to ban U.S. nuclear ships from New Zealand harbors. The Reagan administration had reacted by criticizing the New Zealand government publicly. A particularly outspoken attack appeared on the front page of the *New York Times*. New Zealand was painted by the Reagan State and Defense Departments as an out-of-step, goofy country and an unreliable ally. I counseled successive New Zealand ambassadors to Washington not to take the administration's bait and become involved in a public debate they could not win. Instead, I took them and the country's ministers to meet congressional leaders of both parties who sat on foreign affairs and armed services committees. These U.S. politicians readily recognized that the domestic political climate in New Zealand made it impossible for any prime minister to change policy on the nuclear ships, and that New Zealand remained otherwise a reliable ally and trading partner. The administration, unable to secure congressional support for its negative view, decided to lay off the issue.

I noted in this book's preface that it is not appetizing to see baloney made in a sausage factory. The same is true of just about every public- and private-sector pursuit. It certainly was true of the financial community, with which I was starting to have more interaction. I found my *Washington Intelligence* subscribers and clients to be thirsty for news of relevant public policy. But I also found some of them habitually ready to make billion-dollar investment allocations on little more than street rumor. Many also had a tendency to believe almost any information that seemed favorable to the investment climate. In the late 1980s and 1990s, there was a growing belief—nearing certitude—among investment houses that Social Security would be fully or partially privatized, thus providing a bonanza of new monies flowing to them. I found my own representations to the contrary being met with skepticism and disbelief among money managers who considered themselves realistic and hardheaded. One client withdrew after I told a group of its brokers that Social Security privatization was bad policy and, moreover, would be bad for the investment industry. The industry, I said, would face a negative public backlash as Social Security recipients found their net worth diminishing during periodic market downturns.

During the eleven-year life of my *Washington Intelligence* service, I developed a high regard for chief economists, investment strategists, analysts, asset managers, and retail brokers of many institutions. I particularly respected those at Oppenheimer Funds, Merrill Lynch, TIAA/CREF, the Boston Company, and U.S. Trust. But I also reached a decision to make my own investment judgments. I continue to watch prices of listed securities bounce back and forth without regard to their fundamental strength or weakness. It is a truism in the financial community that, over the long term, prices reflect the underlying value of stocks, bonds, derivatives, commercial and residential real estate, currencies, precious metals, and other assets. That is so only over the truly long term. Speculative bubbles and unaccountable ups and downs prove the point that prices at any given moment reflect many factors—but not necessarily the genuine worth of the assets.

The ordinary investor may not realize that his broker usually is relying on his firm's research unit, which in turn may be relying on information provided by a third party hyping a particular investment. As was made clear during the late 1990s, many major firms had outright conflicts of interest, touting to their customers stocks in which they had a direct financial stake. Brokers, too, have incentives unknown to their customers to sell them one particular investment instrument over another. Generally unregulated hedge funds solicit money not only from wealthy individuals but from banks and other institutions whose customers have no idea that their funds are being put at risk in these funds. Major corporate scandals and collapses over the past several years have caught the investment community napping. An Enron, Tyco, or Refco can be a "strong buy" recommendation one day, and the next day be in the tank.

There also is a tendency for even the most professional investors to regard their clients' money with less seriousness than they would their own. Attending a conference of mutual-fund chief investment officers in Palm Beach, shortly after the severe stock market downtown of October 19, 1987, I was shocked to hear Fidelity's CIO relate to his colleagues that, on the day of the crash, he returned to Boston from out of town to find his managers buying for their clients but selling furiously out of their own accounts. The other CIOs laughed—they'd had the same experience.

What I learned: Watch your own money closely and make your own investment decisions. If you do invest with professionals, question them closely about their recommendations and sources of information. Markets, it is quite true, are driven by fear and greed. But, as often as not, it is the fear and greed of professionals rather than of ordinary small investors.

My consulting assignments with insurance and pharmaceutical clients caused me to conclude that they, too, bear watching by consumers and regulators but that they are far from the villains often portrayed by their critics. Insurers, by and large, are neutral entities whose rates are based on actuarial risk. Pharmaceutical companies, it is quite true, reap huge profits on a few of their products. But it also is true that they invest huge research sums in products that never gain Food and Drug Administration approval or get to market. They must make money on their winners before their patents run out.

Utilizing a team of economists, my consulting firm in 1993 studied the development of new drugs in all major Western countries. It was only in the United States, we found, where major innovation was taking place. Other countries typically were producing a small number of tried-and-true drugs; there was no incentive there to do more. In a related study we found that price controls on pharmaceutical products, as on all products, quickly lead to shortages, black markets, and/or real or de facto rationing.

Much as we might like to believe it, sinister corporate and industry forces are not working in collusion to screw taxpayers and consumers. Some companies and their managers are bad apples—just as some labor unions, consumer groups, nonprofit institutions, and other entities are corruptly or badly led. By and large, people and companies in the private sector are trying to provide a product or service at a profit, and to do it within legal and regulatory boundaries. Where they break the rules or overreach, they must be policed.

By far the greatest threat to the general welfare from companies and entire business sectors comes from their continuing quest for favored treatment in the tax or regulatory codes or in receiving government contracts or subsidies. They are not alone in doing this. States, localities, nongovernmental organizations, and charitable groups seek them too. New, budget-straining favors can be found at the end of each congressional session, sponsored by senators and members of Congress for interests from their home states—most favoring one entity at the expense of the rest of the economy. The same favored treatment is sought at state, county, and city levels as well.

General tax reform, built on the removal of favored treatment for anyone, is the logical step toward recapturing "tax expenditures" extended to favored recipients and toward creating a more efficient economy. The experience, historically, has not been encouraging. The last big reform push, led by Senator Bill Bradley in 1986, removed loopholes and reduced tax rates and brackets. But now, twenty years later, the tax code is more complex and ridden with special-interest provisions than even before the 1986 reforms. Moreover, to tighten the code effectively, ordinary citizens would need to sacrifice. Special tax treatment given to home-mortgage and medical-expense deductions, for example, would have to be reduced or removed—as in the cold-turkey removals proposed at the 1972 Democratic convention by Senator Fred Harris. The home-mortgage interest deduction alone, if repealed, would yield the federal treasury $76 billion annually; the capital-gains tax exclusion for home sales, $36 billion; the state and local property tax deduction, $15 billion; the medical expense deduction, $9 billion. Each of these provisions benefits millions of taxpayers. Working politicians, for the most part, consider such reforms not worth the political pain associated with trying to implement them.

The special-favor syndrome has become more pervasive as political parties have weakened and been supplanted in influence by sources of political campaign money and votes. Most officeholders and candidates turn first for support to entities with the money and power to put and keep them in office. In return for their support, the donors get what they want. It is a two-way courtship, with the politicians being just as much the aggressors in the relationship as the beneficiaries of it. In my home state of Washington and hometown of Seattle, for example, Microsoft, Boeing, Weyerhaeuser, Amazon.com, Starbucks, and billionaire Paul Allen's enterprises have little trouble mobilizing federal, state, and city officeholders on their behalf. Their interests and the public interest are, often mistakenly, seen as synonymous, and these big companies are seldom challenged by local media or other enterprises that suffer when favored treatment is given to the politically powerful.

My own Democratic Party's national candidates have habitually attacked insurance, drug, and other companies since Bill Clinton made them handy scapegoats in his 1992 presidential campaign. Al Gore in 2000 and John Kerry and John Edwards in 2004 attempted to position themselves as comparable populists, even though as officeholders they regularly went to bat for home-state enterprises seeking government help. Part of this positioning flowed from Democrats' reflexive memory of President Roosevelt's 1930s assaults against "economic royalists" and the class-warfare rhetoric that often issued from their labor-union base. Much of it came from political consultants' advice that populist messages could be successful. But it came across as strained and irrelevant when voters could see for themselves that both major parties court business support and that, in a competitive global economy, "you can't love employment and hate employers," as 1992 Democratic candidate Paul Tsongas put it.

As 1988 neared, Democrats' chances to regain the presidency seemed strong. President Reagan could not seek a third term. His vice president, George H. W. Bush, was not a galvanizing figure, and moreover, vice presidents have generally not done well in trying to succeed the presidents they served. The Democrat with the best chance to win the White House seemed my old McGovern-campaign colleague Senator Gary Hart. Hart, who had challenged Mondale for the 1984 Democratic nomination, had name recognition; knew the nominating process as both an organizer and candidate; favored a post–New Deal agenda stressing economic growth, individual liberties, and a modernized defense establishment; and, perhaps most importantly, was generally free of ties to organized interest groups.

Many of his 1972 campaign colleagues had not been Hart boosters by the end of the campaign. Two years later, when Hart launched a U.S. Senate primary campaign in his home state of Colorado, most McGovern campaign alumni in Washington, D.C., including both Frank Mankiewicz and myself, endorsed his opponent, former Robert Kennedy assistant Joe Dolan, and held a fundraising event for Dolan in the capital. After winning a Senate seat, however, Hart concentrated earnestly on trying to rethink public policy. Although he knew that I had supported Dolan against him in the Colorado Democratic primary, Hart held no grudge—as I held no grudge about what I regarded as his sometimes self-serving conduct in the 1972 McGovern campaign. He supported my efforts in founding the Center for National Policy and made appearances on its behalf. Later he periodically invited me to sit down with his staff to discuss issues; we did the same informally between ourselves. I thought he aspired to serious public service.

John Holum, the former McGovern legislative assistant who was then working in a Washington, D.C., law practice, had committed to a Hart presidential candidacy and asked me to commit as well. I hesitated, but after talking with Hart, decided to do so. A *Fortune* magazine writer had interviewed me about candidates and issues in the Democratic Party, and I had told him that Hart had no real competition in developing alternative ideas. I agreed to cochair his policy advisory committees, to review and edit his principal policy papers, and to stay in regular contact with his policy staff in Denver.

Upon formally announcing his candidacy for the nomination, Hart immediately took the lead in national polls ranking prospective Democratic nominees, and he also ran strongly in matchups against Bush and other possible Republican nominees. Yet his broad public popularity did not immediately translate into support inside the Beltway.

Lobbyists and ambitious operators in the capital are notorious for rushing to front-runners with money and offers of help. I thus was surprised when a fundraising event at the Madison Hotel in Washington was only sparsely attended. Former 1972 campaign comrades John Holum, Eli Segal, and Harold Himmelman were there, but perhaps only 100 others. A front-runner's opening event should have drawn an overflow crowd. The absence of insiders, I thought, was not all bad, as it reflected Hart's independence from many organized interest groups.

As Hart's campaign proceeded, it made operating stumbles I would not have expected. During an appearance in Los Angeles, Hart was picketed by Democrats who had made loans to the campaign and had not been repaid. His staff botched its response, and Hart went before TV cameras to deal with the matter. His explanation was unconvincing and he was flustered. The next morning our mutual friend Warren Beatty, who was with Hart in Los Angeles, called me in Washington, D.C., to ask that I fly out to join Hart, and remain with him for the duration of the nominating campaign. I told Beatty that my family would just plain go on strike if I left them again for months of airplanes, hotels, and phone calls home on the run. I also had a business to run. I told Beatty that I had tried to reach Hart several times in recent days to express concern about economic-policy statements he had made. He had not returned the calls. "If you are with him, he will do what you say," Beatty said. An internal instinct told me to decline.

Rumors began to surface that Hart was actively womanizing. I had no knowledge that this was true. There had been similar rumors in 1972, but as far as I knew, in 1988 Hart was bearing down on his Senate duties and presidential candidacy. A *Washington Post* reporter arrived at my office one Friday afternoon. Would I speak frankly with him about the matter without fear of quotation? I told him that, on or off the record, I had no knowledge that Hart was womanizing. As a matter of fact, I had on my desk at that moment an economic-policy speech draft that had just been faxed by his staff from his Denver campaign headquarters. I would be working on it over the weekend, and I presumed that Hart would be doing so as well. He was running a serious candidacy, and I doubted he had time for hanky-panky—the speech was to be delivered in New York the following week. That same afternoon I put in the mail a letter to several hundred Democratic foreign- and domestic-policy types, asking them to serve on various Hart task forces and enclosing a form with which they could respond.

That weekend, Hart's relationship with model Donna Rice became public. Hart had challenged reporters asking about rumors of his womanizing to follow him and see if they could find any evidence of it. They did and they did. Within a few days, Hart had withdrawn from the nominating race. During the same period I began receiving responses to my ill-timed mailing to former Democratic appointees and policy specialists. Many agreed to serve on Hart task forces, leading me to conclude they either had not been reading their newspapers or had been traveling in remote areas cut off from news of the outside world.

I promised myself and my family that I would put presidential campaigns behind me. I attended the Democratic Party's 1988 convention in Atlanta, but was content to participate in panels and seminars, off the convention floor, and watch others stride the main stage. After Hart's abrupt withdrawal from the primary race, Massachusetts governor Mike Dukakis marched to the nomination. I knew him to be a serious and responsible officeholder who was genuinely interested in the content of policy. I also liked him personally. He came across publicly, however, much as Fritz Mondale had four years earlier—not as a star but as the star's sober and colorless best friend. I also feared that, like Mondale, he would be perceived as a traditional interest-group liberal rather than as someone who could set forth a more independent vision, as Hart might have done.

Atlanta convention attendees exchanged jokes about an overly-long convention speech by Arkansas governor Bill Clinton. The convention floor became restless and noisy as Clinton ran well beyond the time allotted to him on the podium. Then, as he neared his peroration, the convention-floor din subsided. In a moment of silence, a female voice from the Massachusetts delegation could be heard throughout the hall: "My Gawd, isn't he done yet?"

Major-party nominees traditionally gain a "bounce" of several points in opinion polls after the television exposure they get from their national conventions. Dukakis appeared even stronger than anyone foresaw coming out of the Atlanta convention. He held an 18-percentage-point lead over Vice President Bush. Once campaigning began, however, Dukakis's lead began to erode. He replaced his initial campaign manager, Susan Estrich, with a more seasoned professional, John Sasso. Although Sasso's appointment stabilized the campaign organization, it did little to reverse the dynamic between the candidates. In any political campaign—but especially in a national campaign where broad media exposure outweighs organizational activity—the first imperative for a candidate is to strongly define himself or herself for the electorate. The picture must be drawn clearly so that opposition attacks will be unable to distort it. Any candidate who fails to do this inevitably becomes defined by his opponent's terms of reference—as Senator John Kerry, for example, was defined by opposition Swift Boat Veteran television commercials during the 2004 presidential campaign.

Although Dukakis entered the 1988 campaign with a big lead in opinion polls, he remained largely undefined except as "another Massachusetts liberal." Two early campaign wounds were inflicted on Dukakis that defined him disastrously. The first came from a Republican television commercial depicting him as the Massachusetts governor who had allowed on furlough a black convict, Willie Horton, who had then committed murder. The second came from television news film depicting Dukakis, wearing a helmet, in the turret of an Army tank. In this staged event, intended to underscore Dukakis's defense credentials, he looked like a ridiculous elf about as far from a commander in chief as seemed imaginable. Finally, in a televised debate with Bush, Dukakis gave a decidedly wrong answer to a question to both candidates as to what each would do if his wife were murdered. Bush reacted emotionally and with horror at the question itself. Dukakis responded with an antiseptic discussion of the death penalty. None of the above factors should have mattered in the selection of a president. But they proved decisive in Dukakis's defeat.

Televised candidate debates, in particular, are not rational, intellectual exercises to be judged on the basis of the candidates' substantive responses to questions—unless the responses seem decidedly wrong, as with President Ford's 1976 mischaracterization of the relationship between the Soviet Union and its Eastern European satellites. Rather, as long as candidates do not commit some obvious gaffe, debates more often are decided by the candidates' demeanors and body language. Radio listeners to the 1960 Kennedy-Nixon debates, for example, largely judged Nixon the winner. Television viewers, on the other hand, thought Kennedy won. Voters seeing, rather than just hearing, the debates saw Nixon with a five-o'clock shadow, sweating, his collar too loose around his neck, and displaying defensive body language. Next to him they saw Kennedy, handsome and clean-cut, flashing humor, well tailored, and looking assertive from behind his podium.

It is regrettably true that form rather than substance usually determines campaign-debate winners. Candidates preparing for televised debates must, of course, absorb all the substantive and political arguments contained in their briefing books, lest they display ignorance or fumble a policy matter. They also must know that most viewers will not be able to distinguish one policy argument from another but will be able to recognize if one of the candidates is nervous, fearful, or uncertain. They will watch to see who is in command, who defensive.

In 1992 Arkansas governor Bill Clinton won a pivotal debate with President Bush in large part because Bush twice glanced at his watch during the course of the debate, leading voters to wonder: "Is this guy bored or what?" Bush's nervous watch-checking gave substance to the Democratic campaign theme that it indeed was time for him to leave.

I was just one more Democrat on the sidelines during Dukakis's general-election campaign. I sent Dukakis and his campaign chairman, Paul Brountas, several memoranda about campaign strategy and themes, and I wrote a series of essays in the *New York Times* and the *Los Angeles Times* suggesting ways in which Dukakis might rekindle campaign momentum. But I recognized that all of this was marginal. When it was over, I felt badly for Dukakis, as I had for Mondale four years earlier. Both were good men and good public servants who would have been good presidents. But Reagan's popularity in 1984 and the Dukakis campaign's bumbles in 1988 had kept the White House comfortably in Republican hands.

Late in 1988 I observed firsthand President Reagan's formidable political skills. I was serving at the time as a member of the board and executive committee of the Roosevelt Institute, which confers the annual Four Freedoms Awards and supports the FDR Library in Hyde Park, New York. We had often heard Reagan's tributes to Franklin Roosevelt and knew that he had been an active supporter of FDR and the New Deal until undergoing a political conversion in the 1950s. After considerable internal debate, we solicited Reagan's help for the Roosevelt Institute before he left office. He agreed to host and speak to a fundraiser event during his last days in office, and suggested that the event be held at the National Archives building on the Washington Mall. Thus the outgoing Republican president was placed in the position of addressing a wholly Democratic audience to raise funds for an institution honoring a Democratic president. Our invitation list included all major donors to Dukakis's 1988 campaign, as well as members of the Roosevelt family, New York Democratic governor Mario Cuomo and Democratic senators Kennedy, Mitchell, Sarbanes, Moynihan, and others. Reagan would be literally the only Republican in an otherwise Democratic sea of faces. The guests arrived at the archives at the appointed hour. We all were restless and a bit ill at ease. The president was running late. Then, when he arrived, we found ourselves being herded quickly into a line to have our photos taken, one by one, with Reagan. Reagan gave all a firm handshake, smiled, and posed for the camera until guests had passed through the line into the luncheon room.

As lunch was served and eaten, a mood prevailed that could only be described as restrained. Finally, over dessert, Reagan rose to speak. He smiled expansively: "Look," he said. "I know what you are thinking. But I'm the only person in this room to have voted four times for Franklin Roosevelt!" Reagan then launched into a series of hilarious anecdotes about Roosevelt, his own Hollywood career, and even his early days as a radio sportscaster. By the time he was done, he had us all. He closed with a fundraising pitch that resulted in a generous return to the institute.

Weeks later, after Reagan had left office, I ran into Ken Duberstein, who had been his White House chief of staff, and mentioned the archives luncheon. Duberstein told me that the event had been very important to Reagan and that, when he had received the request to help the institute, he had directed immediately that the luncheon be scheduled while he remained in office and could choose an appropriate public facility for it. At about the same time I received in the mail a grey envelope with no return address. When I opened it, I found inside the color photo with Reagan taken at the luncheon. It was personally inscribed. The next day I saw Ted Kennedy and mentioned receipt of the grey envelope and photo. "Yes, I got mine too," he said.

13

STORM CLEANUP AND A NEW STORM

President Bush the elder, succeeding President Reagan in January 1989, was in the difficult position of not only following a popular president but also having to clean up the debt burden his predecessor had created. Reagan had cut federal taxes but, after his bargain with House Speaker O'Neill, had not cut federal spending accordingly. As a result, in his eight-year presidential tenure he generated more debt than had been accumulated by all prior American administrations. Reagan had played the role of the charming uncle, staying with his family for an extended visit during which he regularly brought home gifts and treated the family to expensive vacations and meals. Bush found himself playing the sober nephew who, after the uncle's departure, discovered that all the largesse had been charged to the family credit card.

Bush's four-year presidency thus was doomed, at the outset, to being one of storm cleanup. Yet, during the campaign he had repeated, "Read my lips: No new taxes." He soon found himself having to renege on the pledge. This, in turn, enraged devotees of Reaganomics who believed in cutting taxes no matter what the surrounding economic situation. Deficit reduction was made even more difficult by Bush's decision to intervene militarily to block Iraq's invasion of Kuwait, which, it was anticipated, might extend to an invasion of Saudi Arabia.

The U.S. had an ambivalent relationship with Iraq and its leader, Saddam Hussein. No one contested the fact that Saddam Hussein was a tyrant and a rascal. But he did seem to fit the description President Franklin Roosevelt had for Latin American dictators of comparable character: "They may be SOBs. But they are our SOBs." The greater threat in the region, in the 1980s, seemed to be the theocratic government of Iran, which was actively hostile toward the United States and was underwriting terrorist groups in the Middle East. Thus the U.S. had provided weapons and other assistance to Saddam during his bitter eight-year (1980–88) war with Iran, which resulted in at least a million casualties in the two countries.

Saddam's August 1990 invasion of Kuwait, however—and the threat to next-door Saudi Arabia—could not be tolerated. Both countries were closely tied to the United States; both were major sources of oil for Western and Asian markets. The question for American policymakers was how best to force Saddam's withdrawal from Kuwait: by use of direct military force, preferably multilateral; or through a blockade and embargo which would take longer, but in time would strangle the Iraqi economy and force Saddam to back down.

Most congressional Democrats, chastened by the American experience in Vietnam, leaned toward the isolation strategy—at least until it proved unworkable. Former Secretary of State Cyrus Vance and I shared the view. We had remained close following our work together at the State Department and the Center for National Policy, and Vance often used an office in my consulting firm in Washington when he was visiting from New York. Vance's public image was that of a straight-laced establishmentarian, but in private he was personally warm and generous. He greatly enjoyed chatting on the telephone and exchanging tidbits of Washington and New York gossip. He was devoted to his family. I would help him periodically with drafts of speeches and articles. Characteristically, he always would suggest that any articles include both of our bylines. But I was able to convince him that an article bearing only his byline, as former secretary of state, would be more effective in influencing opinion. I could write my own articles with my own byline.

We both became active in supporting the embargo/isolation strategy toward Iraq. Vance articles advocating the approach appeared in several daily newspapers. I helped with drafting of testimony that he delivered to both Senate and House committees. Then, as a vote on the issue approached in the Senate, we called on key Democratic senators together and provided them with a white paper (which Bob Hunter had also helped to write), setting forth both the strategic and legal bases for the isolation strategy.

On the eve of the Senate vote, Senator Al Gore Jr. remained undecided on the issue. He flew from Tennessee in time to meet us for breakfast in the Senate dining room before casting his vote later that day. His aide, Leon Fuerth, accompanied him. Gore's questions for us centered on many of the legal issues associated with the isolation and military-intervention options. Vance and I were impressed with his depth of knowledge on the issue and the region. As Gore left us, we were pleased that he had spent so much time in discussion, and we were convinced that our arguments no doubt had swayed him in our direction. However, although most Senate Democrats—especially those with possible national ambitions—cast their vote our way, Gore voted for military intervention. We regarded it as a vote of conviction, as the easier political path would have been to choose the option we recommended. He had weighed the information and reached an independent conclusion.

The Persian Gulf War of January–February 1991 expelled Iraq from Kuwait and devastated Iraq's armed forces and war-making capabilities. Vance, afterward, concluded that "President Bush was right and we were wrong," and that we had been mistaken in believing that anything short of outright military intervention would have forced an Iraqi retreat from Kuwait. He delivered a speech soon after the intervention advocating the formation of permanent United Nations peacekeeping forces that could position themselves on the frontiers of nations in conflict, to forestall any outbreak of war. Had such forces been stationed on the Kuwaiti frontier during Saddam's threats of invasion, he said, the whole episode might have been averted.

In addition to my business and family, I also devoted myself during this period to various pro-bono activities, including serving on the four-person board of Health Care for America, a nonprofit organization launched by Senator Kennedy to educate citizens about the need for health-care reform. At the time, he and others were sponsoring various incremental proposals to increase health-care coverage nationally; it was conceded that comprehensive universal coverage was not politically viable. Then our family was hit by our own health-care crisis. My wife, Jean, was diagnosed in March 1991, near her fifty-eighth birthday, with multiple myeloma, a cancer of the bone marrow. As we took evening walks near our home, Jean had been suffering fatigue and leg aches. Her physician told us matter-of-factly that scans revealed she was already in the third stage of the disease, for which there was no known cure, and had perhaps eighteen months to live.

Kennedy's health care committee staff quickly looked up clinical research trials then taking place at the National Institutes of Health and elsewhere. None fit. We made independent inquiries about all the treatment options available to her. In the meantime, Jean continued directing the art department at Primary Day School, a private school near our home in Maryland which both our daughters, Terry and Sue Ellen, had attended. Her oncologist put her on a standard regime of chemotherapy, which data indicated was useful for some patients, useless for others. Some patients failed to respond to any therapy, he explained, and were gone quickly. Fortunately, in Jean's case the therapy stabilized the disease. Our research led us to conclude that only a high-risk, aggressive therapy could increase Jean's life expectancy. A specialist at Sloan-Kettering, New York, told us that if she were in a comparable situation she would see Dr. Bart Barlogie, who performed controversial double marrow-transplant procedures for multiple myeloma patients at the Arkansas Cancer Research Center in Little Rock. (Sam Walton, the Wal-Mart billionaire, had suffered, and eventually died, from multiple myeloma. In fighting his own illness, he had moved an entire team from the M.D. Anderson Cancer Center in Houston to Little Rock and funded their work.) Some patients, she said, had survived two or more years longer than expected because of Barlogie's treatment. We contacted Senator David Pryor of Arkansas, an old friend, who in turn arranged for Jean an assessment by Dr. Barlogie. Jean underwent a series of tests to see if she was a suitable candidate for a transplant. She was a borderline candidate because of her age and the progression of the illness. We asked Dr. Barlogie if he recommended alternative therapies. There were such therapies, he explained, but he did transplants. He gave Jean a sheaf of consent forms to sign for the surgeries.

During our time in Little Rock we stayed at a motel-like facility that housed only multiple myeloma patients. In the evenings they gathered to discuss their illnesses and offer each other support, and during the day they were shuttled by bus to the cancer center for treatment. Jean and I attended a couple of the evening support sessions but were depressed by them, as we were by the entire environment. The patients were weak and trying last-ditch therapy. Their illnesses were the only topics discussed. If Jean were to undergo the double-transplant therapy, we would be spending two periods of several months each in this environment. Transplant recipients' immune systems were quite vulnerable during the transplants, and some did not survive. Even if the first transplant succeeded, Jean knew, she would have to return for a second one. It was possible that she would end up spending most of whatever time was left to her in the Little Rock motel and hospital, in physical distress and far from her children, school, and friends. She returned the consent forms unsigned to Dr. Barlogie, who seemed taken aback by her decision. During our final appointment he asserted that establishment oncologists on the eastern seaboard often scorned his therapy, and that he did not receive proper recognition for his work.

We learned during Jean's illness that there was a national support group of multiple myeloma specialists and patients who maintained an information network and convened once a year for discussions. We received its newsletter, and on occasion spoke by telephone with doctors specializing in the disease, while Jean's D.C. oncologist continued to administer chemotherapy. At one meeting, held in Falls Church, Virginia, we encountered a young dentist in his forties suffering from the disease. He and his wife, they told us, were going to Little Rock for the double marrow transplant. A few weeks later we read his obituary. He had died during the first attempted transplant. Jean felt validated in her decision to just keep on living as close as she could to a normal life until the illness claimed her. A year after her diagnosis, Jean felt well, was keeping a normal teaching schedule, and refused any concession to the cancer. I also kept normal working hours, but cut extracurricular and out-of-town business activities to a minimum. Under the shadow of her illness, we spent more time together than we had since we were newlyweds, and we traveled frequently to see our children and grandchildren.

It was at this juncture that I unexpectedly, at Jean's urging, joined another presidential campaign. The 1992 Democratic presidential nominating race was expected to include Senator Gore, who had run well in 1988, New York governor Mario Cuomo, and perhaps other well-known national candidates. Arkansas governor Clinton entered the race for the same reason he had sought a speaking assignment at the 1988 Democratic convention in Atlanta—to get national exposure prior to launching a serious presidential candidacy in 1996. John Holum, who had urged me to support Gary Hart in 1988, similarly urged me to support Clinton in 1992. I received a couple of self-typed notes from Clinton asking my opinion about his national service and other proposals. I responded. But I told Holum that I intended, because of Jean's illness, to sit out the campaign. (I also believed, privately, that Clinton was a talented campaigner but far from ready for the presidency. Moreover, rumors in the political community had it that he was an indiscriminate and often reckless womanizer. It was baggage, I thought, that the party did not need in its nominee.) Senator Bob Kerrey of Nebraska was another possible 1992 aspirant. I thought highly of him and periodically received visits from his staff, seeking input and ideas. Former senator Paul Tsongas of Massachusetts, a cancer survivor, also signaled his candidacy, and issued a booklet setting forth his ideas for renewal of the domestic economy. I knew him but not particularly well. Both Kerrey and Tsongas appealed to me as independent-minded figures who might be willing, as Hart had been in 1988, to break free of the interest-group mindset that plagued the party.

As it turned out, Gore, Cuomo and several other well-known figures declined candidacies—Cuomo only a few hours before he was to file for the

New Hampshire primary. Thus Clinton, Kerrey, Tsongas, and California's Jerry Brown remained as the only credible candidates in the field. Just prior to the New Hampshire primary, Clinton was beset by reports of a long-standing affair with cabaret singer Gennifer Flowers and of other peccadillos in Little Rock. Tsongas, from next-door Massachusetts, won the primary, although a fast-talking Clinton dubbed himself "the comeback kid" for finishing second and made many in the media believe he thus was some kind of winner. As Jean and I watched the New Hampshire returns, I was annoyed by Clinton's brazen claim, and felt sympathy for Tsongas, whose staff could have stopped the Clinton false boomlet by simply pointing out that Tsongas had won, Clinton had lost, and a couple more such "comebacks" by Clinton would have him out of the race. Kerrey ran weakly in New Hampshire and withdrew his candidacy. He later told me that he was furious with himself for taking the advice of his professional campaign consultants (the same ones who later would manage the 2000 Gore and 2004 Kerry campaigns). Their fees chewed up most of the money he had raised. Their campaign commercials, portraying him as a protectionist resolved to keep out foreign goods, presented an entirely false picture of him. Kerrey was a proponent of free trade.

A few days after the New Hampshire primary, Jean and I attended a dinner in Washington, D.C., with our friends Peter and Judy Kovler, at which Tsongas spoke. He mentioned briefly his cancer of several years before, but spoke at length and with real conviction about his tax policy and other plans to reduce the residual Reagan budget deficits and generate domestic growth. His policy booklet, which he had written himself, stood in contrast to the booklet issued by the Clinton campaign, which was much praised by the media but was really nothing more than a mishmash of collected notions from many sources. He also exhibited a self-deprecating humor that contrasted with Clinton's continuous self-aggrandizement. My heart went out to him for his ideas and for his underdog status. Later, as we drove home, Jean said: "You should help Paul Tsongas." She clearly had read my reaction to Tsongas's appearance that evening. She also felt drawn to Tsongas because of their shared cancer experience. "I am feeling fine right now," she said. "I would feel even better if you helped Tsongas. Do it for me and for the country."

I thus volunteered to help Tsongas. To begin, I flew one morning to Chicago to join him on a campaign swing and to assess his performance and staffing. I arrived at his hotel carrying that morning's *Washington Post*, which by chance carried on its front page a photo of Clinton with a story enumerating his and his wife Hillary's alleged conflicts of interest during his time as Arkansas governor. As it happened, a three-way televised debate was about to take place among Clinton, Tsongas, and Jerry Brown. Back at the hotel, Tsongas spotted my copy of the *Post*, tucked it under his arm, and carried it to the television studio with him. We had discussed it only briefly. Tsongas placed it on the podium in front of him. He stood between Clinton and Brown as microphones were being attached to all three. Brown saw Tsongas's *Post*, with its front-page photo of Clinton, and asked if he could read it, then handed it back to Tsongas. As lights went on and the debate began, Brown without warning took the newspaper from Tsongas's podium, waved it in front of the cameras, and launched a fierce attack against Clinton for alleged corruption in his governor's office. Clinton was furious. His face reddened. He chastised Brown as someone "wearing $1,000 shoes" who dared to question what he had done as a poor boy in a poor state like Arkansas. The debate was televised only in Illinois but, had it been seen nationally, it would not have shown either Brown or Clinton in a positive light. Tsongas, standing between them, was surprised and amused by the exchange.

After the debate ended, I walked behind Tsongas as he left the studio, then stopped a moment to chat with Brown, whom I had known since his student days. As I turned to rejoin Tsongas, I found myself face-to-face with Clinton. The veins in his neck were swollen, his face puffed and red, his eyes angry. I thought he might be in a steroid rage. The thought suddenly occurred: Clinton thinks I set this whole thing up between Tsongas and Brown. Clinton continued to glower, then moved on without speaking. Thus was my first day spent as a Tsongas volunteer.

Observing Tsongas, I quickly developed affection for him. I also had immediate concern for his health. His cancer was not just in remission, he said, but firmly behind him. But he clearly needed rest time between appearances. I wondered whether he would be able to make it through the taxing campaign schedule lying ahead. His campaign manager, Dennis Kanin, and his policy director, Steven Cohen, were serious and honest people. I found his other staff, supporters, and eventual convention delegates to be the same. The Tsongas campaign, like Tsongas, was characterized by good humor, hard work accepted easily, and a general refusal to take itself too seriously. Tsongas had a quality I particularly admire in people playing for big stakes under big pressure: he took time for real conversations with people along the way, whether they be staff members, supporters, or ordinary citizens he encountered along his path.

The campaign quickly ran into money problems. Thus, even though Tsongas was running second behind Clinton in overall delegate totals, he withdrew his active candidacy for the nomination just prior to the New York primary. Yet a strange thing happened. Tsongas kept piling up respectable vote totals in states where he remained on the ballot and, consequently, kept amassing convention delegates. At the end of the nominating process, he thus ran a respectable third behind Clinton and Brown in delegates.

As Tsongas considered whether to continue an expensive active candidacy in New York, he had received a phone call at his home in Lowell, Massachusetts, from former president Jimmy Carter. Clinton had authorized him, President Carter said, to offer Tsongas any Cabinet or other position he wished in a future Clinton administration, if he would withdraw. Tsongas thanked him for passing along the offer but said he would prefer to act as if it had not been made. As it turned out, Tsongas did withdraw, but because his campaign funds were low. "Funny thing," he said after the fall election, "I never did hear from Clinton or Carter after the election offering me any big jobs."

Tsongas's treasury was low, we discovered later, because his finance chairman, a lifelong Tsongas friend, had stolen $1 million from it. (Clinton, we learned later, was just as broke, but had kept campaigning with Arkansas bank loans.) When he learned of the theft, Tsongas made no comment about his erstwhile friend but simply shrugged and accepted it.

I took on the task for Tsongas, as I had for others, of representing him in the platform committee drafting process. Tsongas's campaign was more about his economic agenda than about himself, and thus the party platform, formally declaring the party's agenda, was important to him. The drafting committee's meetings were to be held in Santa Fe, New Mexico, home of Representative Bill Richardson, who was chairing the drafting process. At a closed-door caucus, before the committee began formal business in front of television cameras, Steve Cohen and I were surprised to hear Democratic National Chairman Ron Brown, a former Ted Kennedy staff member, explain the ground rules for the process. In all prior drafting processes in which I had participated, planks were introduced, formal debate and votes held, and final language worked out among candidate representatives. This time, Brown said, there would be discussion of various planks, but a vote would be taken only on major sections as a whole. As a practical matter, this would ensure ratification of the Clinton draft with little or no change.

I knew Brown, and most others in the room, quite well. I had supported his candidacy for the party chairmanship, over those of my friends Mike Barnes and Jim Jones, because I thought it was high time for the Democratic Party to have a black chairman. He had invited me to his installation as chairman and placed my name on the invitation as a member of a host committee. I spoke directly to the procedure he had outlined. It was unacceptable, I said, and had never been followed in recent platform processes. It resembled the process by which documents had been drafted and approved in the Soviet Union. Unless fair play was evident and normal procedure followed, I would step outside and on Tsongas's behalf denounce, before network TV cameras, the whole exercise as a sham. Cohen, participating in his first platform drafting process, was shocked that I would lay down such an ultimatum. It was preferable, I whispered to him, to issue it on the inside rather than to take it public. Sure enough, Brown conceded, a more normal process could be followed. In fact it was—although we had to check language closely, after each plank was debated and voted, to be sure it actually reflected agreements made at the table. John Holum was serving as drafting-committee secretary. I worked with him and with Senator Joe Lieberman, Stuart Eizenstat, Sandy Berger, and Bill Richardson, all Clinton supporters but comrades from prior causes, to ensure that Tsongas's input and the language approved in the drafting committee appeared in the final draft to be submitted to the platform committee as a whole at its upcoming meeting in Washington, D.C.

A majority of members of the drafting committee, and all of its staff, were Clinton supporters. Cohen and I were there for Tsongas, and worked with his and other delegates. Yet Jerry Brown, with the second largest block of delegates, did not until the last minute designate his own representative to the proceedings. A Jerry Brown–supporting college student showed up. He did not speak. He sat to the left of Cohen and me and took his cues from us. Then, in the late morning of the second day, Brown himself showed up. There was always a celebrity aura around Jerry Brown, and as he arrived cameras and reporters flowed to him. He held a noisy ad hoc press conference outside the meeting room that made it difficult to conduct business. Then he entered the room and asked that he be given time to address the drafting committee. His remarks, for the most part, had nothing whatsoever to do with the document being developed, but were quotable sound bites designed to attract evening news exposure. Ron Brown, a Clinton loyalist, was steaming. Stuart Eizenstat and Sandy Berger, sitting to my right, nudged me to call attention to the fact that, as Jerry Brown took a seat in the drafting committee, Ron Brown placed a name card in front of him on which his name was printed in letters about one-third the size of those on the name cards in front of the rest of us.

After his remarks Jerry Brown invited me to join him for lunch while the drafting committee continued its deliberations in the meeting room. Madeleine Albright, another Clinton supporter at the session, overheard Jerry Brown invite me to lunch and asked that I introduce her to him. I did, but I was unsure what that was about. After chatting with Madeleine, Jerry led me to a table in the dining room where, it turned out, we were alone. There was no table service—the luncheon was a buffet. Brown kept rising, going to the buffet, then returning to the table without food. He was suffering from adrenaline overload. I finally walked to the buffet table with him and stood with him while he filled a plate.

I had first met Jerry Brown in 1968, when he was in his twenties. He had been an avid supporter of Eugene McCarthy for the Democratic presidential nomination. His father, California governor Pat Brown, was a lifelong friend of Hubert Humphrey's. After Humphrey's nomination as the Democratic presidential candidate, Pat Brown enthusiastically stumped for him in California, but his son Jerry had kept his distance. Then, in October, when Humphrey was scheduled for campaign stops around the Los Angeles area, Pat Brown arranged to ride with him in his campaign limousine and to bring along his son Jerry. I was the fourth passenger in the limo. The campaign day began early and lasted until nightfall. Humphrey would make a hard-hitting rally speech, get back into the limo, ride an hour to the next stop, make another speech, then ride an hour to the next, and so on. During the long rides between campaign stops, Humphrey and Pat Brown, much alike in personality, told jokes and campaign stories. The material was of *Saturday Night Live* quality. Humphrey, Pat Brown, and I laughed and enjoyed it all immensely. Jerry Brown, however, sat silently and sullenly in his window seat. Finally, at the last stop of the day, the two Browns stood watching as Humphrey roused a labor audience with old-time Democratic rhetoric, imitating Richard Nixon, mocking his refusal to debate, and making the whole thing a light-hearted happening. "Well, son," Pat Brown said, turning to Jerry, "what do you think of Humphrey now that you've spent a day with him? Isn't he a great guy?" "I still think he's a shit," Jerry responded.

Jerry, in 1992, had come a long way from the young man of 1968 who had scorned not only Humphrey but also, much of the time, his own father. He had become California governor in his own right and had been forced to move from political existentialism to presentation of budgets and legislative proposals. Yet, even so, he had governed untraditionally, living in a small apartment in Sacramento rather than in the governor's mansion, and was famous for hours-long political and philosophical bull sessions with visitors. While running the Center for National Policy, I took care to include him in our programs. I invited him on one occasion to take part in a seminar in Bonn, Germany, cosponsored by the center and the Friedrich Ebert Foundation. Meeting with newly elected Green Party parliamentarians, Brown—famous for being unprogrammatic—questioned the Greens closely about their agenda and political approach. Finally, he interjected: "You need a plan and a program. Where are they? You will get nowhere without them." On another occasion, during the same conference, we dined with our German hosts at a historic hotel on the Rhine River, which was flooding. Charter buses taking us the several miles to the hotel drove through hubcap-deep water; we entered the hotel walking on boards suspended above flooded pavement. Hours after the dinner, I encountered Brown entering the lobby of our downtown Bonn hotel. His suit trousers were soaked to the thigh. He had somehow missed the buses returning from the dinner and had walked back to our hotel through the flood.

A year or two later, while I was visiting Los Angeles, Jerry invited me to a party he was giving at his home for his parents. Afterward, I needed a ride back to my hotel. Jerry's secretary, who was driving a Rent-a-Wreck car, offered to give me a lift. The junker died while entering a freeway exit. I found myself pushing it the remainder of the way off the exit, convinced another car would hit us from behind at high speed. I was going to be killed on an L.A. freeway exit, I thought, as the price of my involvement in a Jerry Brown Production.

At our 1992 lunch in Santa Fe, Brown asked for my reaction to his drafting-committee remarks. I told him they amounted to irresponsible grandstanding. If he were serious about the process, I said, he would have designated a qualified person rather than a college student to represent his views to the committee. He conceded that was true. But he had no one he could trust to represent his views, he said, and he had not had time to formulate finished views in writing. I pointed out that, ten years earlier, he had been the principal advocate of a North American Free Trade Agreement (NAFTA), yet, in 1992, he was opposing it. Brown said he had forgotten entirely about his earlier NAFTA advocacy. He was, as usual, winging it, counting on his energy and intelligence to carry him day by day through his campaign. A

Jerry Brown candidacy, I knew, was never about a conventional agenda but about Jerry Brown. Yet I knew he had a serious and genuine respect for ideas.

Brown sought general collaboration of some kind with Tsongas going into the summer New York City convention. I told him we would welcome Brown's support of Tsongas's economic proposals; we would support any Brown platform and credentials proposals that seemed sensible. As far as engaging in any "stop Clinton" movement, we would have to play it as it came. If, between then and the convention, Clinton were damaged by ethics or other charges from Arkansas, it was conceivable that the party would have to turn elsewhere for a nominee. On the other hand, if he remained relatively undamaged, there seemed little point in mounting strident platform, rules, and credentials challenges, which would hurt both Clinton and the Democratic Party's chances in the fall election. Clinton was a skilled campaigner and generally likeable. He was not someone posing a menace to the party who needed to be stopped.

At the very end of the Santa Fe deliberations, something took place that shocked me but seemed to faze no one else. Pennsylvania governor Bob Casey was one of the strongest and most important of the party's national leaders. As a Catholic, he opposed abortion, and he had sent a letter to all drafting committee members expressing a view that the abortion issue should be raised and discussed. But none of us had received our copies of the letter, which had been sent through the Democratic National Committee. As the meeting broke up, and we were leaving the table, Ron Brown casually distributed the letters to us. We opened them after leaving the conference room. The meeting had adjourned and it was too late to consider the Casey communication; not having been discussed in the drafting committee, Casey's views thus never made it to the overall platform committee or to the convention floor. Tsongas was pro-choice. So was I. But I was taken aback that such an important party leader as Casey would be brushed off so cavalierly.

Later, at the meetings of the platform and credentials committees in Washington, D.C., the Tsongas campaign followed the general plan of collaboration with Brown that we had discussed at luncheon in Santa Fe. Brown, this time, was there to represent himself. Most of his delegates supported Tsongas's economic planks; we supported a handful of Brown's platform and credentials planks. The rest mainly were notions lacking a constituency outside Big Sur. The Tsongas planks did not command a majority of platform committee votes. But they did receive enough votes to be considered as minority planks at the upcoming national convention in New York. We decided to push hard in New York for the adoption of two Tsongas minority planks that amounted to the core of his campaign message. They called for economic macropolicies based on free trade, federal deficit reduction, and growth- and employment-oriented tax policies, and regulatory proposals that would stand in contrast both to Reaganomics and to increasingly protectionist, inward-looking notions gaining ground in the Democratic Party.

We took the Tsongas minority planks to caucuses of state delegations and to delegates representing all candidates. I spoke to a caucus of Brown delegates at a run-down auditorium on West 34th Street, covered in a marijuana-smoke haze, and wasn't sure they were listening. Later in the day we learned that they had voted unanimously to endorse the Tsongas proposals. As the final vote was tallied on the majority (Clinton) and minority (Tsongas) economic planks, we found that all Tsongas and Brown delegates, and fully half of Clinton delegates, had cast their vote with us. Tsongas had, with the content of his arguments, won the battle of ideas. Clinton, safely nominated, couldn't have cared less. He embraced the Tsongas planks as if they were his own.

Both Brown and Tsongas got their prime-time television moments at the convention. Both spoke only briefly. Brown used his time to offer a loving tribute to his father, Pat Brown, then gravely ill, whom he characterized as a great man. Jerry Brown, I thought, was a prodigal son finally home. Dick Tuck, the Californian political prankster who had worked for both Browns, stood next to me on the convention floor. Tears glistened as he listened to Jerry's speech. Tsongas used his time to talk about his economic ideas, and got a ringing ovation. Before he spoke, he did something that candidates seldom do: he went out of his way to thank a supporter who had no electoral or other current power. Tsongas saw me standing on the Madison Square Garden floor and detoured on his way to the podium to give me a long hug for benefit of the television cameras. He knew that Jean, a fellow cancer victim, and my children would be watching the speech at home. His embrace signaled to them that my time on his behalf had not been wasted. After Clinton's acceptance speech, the convention floor was authentically buoyant. All of the delegates danced, marched, waved their candidates' signs, and celebrated together the honest democratic process they had shared.

Later that evening there was a reunion across town of 1972 McGovern campaign alumni. It, too, was joyous. Several hundred former McGovern campaigners celebrated the nomination of Clinton, also a 1972 campaign staff member, and his running mate, Al Gore, who had campaigned actively for

McGovern in Tennessee. George McGovern hailed their nomination and predicted their election. "Too bad," he said off-microphone, "that neither bothered to show up here."

Most Democrats did feel positive about the Clinton-Gore ticket, its chances in the general election, and its possibilities in the White House. Clinton at times was a fast-talking, smile-and-a-shoeshine hustler of the border-state school, but he also was intelligent, had seen the outside world, and was likeable in part because he so clearly wanted to be liked and approved of in return.

Clinton, in the campaign, proved to be Jerry Brown without asceticism, Jimmy Carter with warmth. As with Brown, his was a one-man show. Like Carter, he lacked any clear ideological grounding, but projected a general populism and could make an argument on behalf of just about any pragmatically taken position. Clinton formed a campaign team in Little Rock made up mainly of men and women I had known in prior Democratic national campaigns. Eli Segal served as campaign chief of staff. Mickey Kantor, a Californian who had served in Sargent Shriver's 1972 vice presidential campaign, was chairman. Warren Christopher, a Johnson and Carter administration alumnus, directed presidential transition activities. But Clinton, and to a lesser degree his wife Hillary, called the shots on just about everything. I sent any input by fax through Clinton's secretary, Nancy Hernreich. In one memo of general campaign-strategy recommendations, I expressed confidence in Segal and Kantor. Clinton must have shared it with his senior staff—to my surprise, I received calls from both Segal and Kantor thanking me for commending them to Clinton. It was clear that Clinton kept even his closest campaign aides at arm's length and unsure of their status.

Prior to the campaign season, Sandy Berger, who had worked on our McGovern campaign speechwriting staff, had approached me to ask that I recommend him to either the Clinton or Kerrey presidential campaign. He knew neither candidate well. Now he was serving as Clinton's national security advisor, billed as "an old and close friend from McGovern campaign days."

Godfrey Sperling of the *Christian Science Monitor* conducted regular breakfast meetings at the Sheraton-Carlton Hotel for political journalists at which guests discussed topical issues. I had been a frequent guest over the years at these so-called Sperling breakfasts. Shortly after the platform committee had finished its work, Sperling invited me to appear on Tsongas's behalf at a breakfast. Lieberman, Eizenstat, and Richardson would be there for Clinton. Midway through the breakfast, Clinton entered the room. He was in the capital, had heard of the meeting, and could not resist the temptation to participate. I thus found myself on the short end of a four-to-one matchup, with Clinton himself among the four. Sperling apologized for the mismatch; I thanked him for it, as it provided an underdog status I welcomed. I thereupon attacked some of the arrangements, grossly favoring Clinton, being made for the New York convention by party chair Ron Brown. After breakfast, I lingered to urge Clinton to take an accommodating posture on Tsongas's platform planks. I told him that, after his nomination, both Tsongas and I would help however we could in the general-election campaign.

Tsongas expected to help but was never asked. My own help was informal and marginal. It consisted of exchanging occasional faxes with Clinton and of talking once or twice a week with campaign staff when they sought advice. On a couple of occasions I spoke by phone with Berger as he stood beside Clinton at campaign events. I had confidence in and felt affection for Clinton campaigners I had known since their entry into politics. I was disquieted, though, by the approaches taken by James Carville in developing Clinton campaign themes and television commercials. Carville was a Louisiana political consultant clearly accustomed to practicing a gamey, say-anything brand of politics; friends within the campaign told me they found Carville to be outwardly charming but also superficial, profane, and unscrupulous. Clinton's campaign reflected his two sides. There was the Bill Clinton who had gone to Georgetown, Oxford, and Yale, enlisted in the peace movement, and cultivated liberal Democrats and media. There also was the Hot Springs, Arkansas, Bill Clinton who could become a low-road, piney-woods mini–Huey Long when circumstances made it convenient.

I was publishing my *Washington Intelligence* newsletter throughout the general-election season. I frequently heard from national journalists who were running down reports of corruption and conflicts of interest during the Clintons' time in Arkansas. I largely discounted them but was concerned that fire might lie behind some of the smoke. One report had it that a famous $100,000 commodity-trading profit made by Hillary Clinton, in a Tyson Foods managed fund, was nothing more than a cash payment by Tyson for Clinton services rendered in the state house. (Hillary Clinton's first explanation of the commodity-trading profit was that she had grown up at her father's knee examining financial tables in newspapers. Presumably she had learned enough there to emerge a winner in the risky world of commodities trading.) There were reports connecting Clinton to drug traffickers who gave him political money.

Conservative and alternative media were the only ones to pursue the reports aggressively.

Reports of Clinton's promiscuous sexual behavior while governor made their way into mainstream media. I had always believed that candidates should be judged on the basis of their performance in the public sector rather than on occurrences in their private lives—and should never be judged on the basis of unverified rumor. But if private behavior involved a breach of public trust or affected public policy, that would be another matter. The Clintons, in any case, were able to deflect and hold off inquiries that might have damaged the presidential campaign. Often they used the tactic of attacking their critics in an attempt to undermine their credibility. Many of the reports, Hillary Clinton declared, flowed from a "right-wing conspiracy" determined to undermine them.

Facing President George Bush, Clinton was the superior candidate. He was vigorous and aggressive, and therefore set the campaign's terms of reference. In many ways the campaign seemed a rerun of the 1960 campaign in which an equally vigorous and youthful John F. Kennedy had overcome a Richard Nixon who was seen as a mere understudy to the larger figure of Dwight Eisenhower, as Bush was seen as a lesser understudy to Ronald Reagan. Bush in 1992, like Nixon in 1960, also fell victim to the circumstance of a stagnant economy. Most incumbent presidents take steps in an election year to assure that tax cuts or spending increases prime the economic pump. Bush did not. Clinton also benefitted from the third-party candidacy of Ross Perot, who took 19 percent of the total vote, mostly at Bush's expense.

In 1960, thirty-two years younger and much more innocent, I had been thrilled to the core by JFK's victory over Nixon. In 1992 I was hopeful but not thrilled about Clinton's victory. His general-election campaign had seemed to me excessively glib and expedient. I had not liked the populist attacks on various sectors of the economy and the fierce and immediate counterattacks against political and media critics. Moreover, although the media praised him as a "policy wonk" who knew substance as well as politics, I recognized that on policy he often was making it up as he went along. He certainly knew more, entering the fall campaign against Bush, than a blank-slate Jimmy Carter had known before facing President Ford. But it was apparent that his knowledge was of the cram-the-night-before-the-test kind. I also could see that he routinely brushed aside staff and advisors. Part of this, I knew, stemmed from his experience as Arkansas governor, where he had in fact been smarter than most of those around him. If rumors were correct, in Arkansas he also had stepped near or across ethical lines which he would cross at his peril in the presidency. I tended to see Clinton as many others did at that juncture—as a bright but sometimes willful person of great promise but not yet fully mature. A day or two after the election, I phoned friends at the Arkansas campaign headquarters to congratulate them on their success. None, it was clear, had any idea what jobs they might have in the Clinton administration. Eli Segal, a solid and serious person, had served as campaign chief of staff in Little Rock and, he expected, would fill some similar role in Washington, D.C. Instead, he found himself running the National Service Corps—a challenging assignment but far from the center of power. Clinton named as his White House chief of staff Mack McLarty, an Arkansas business executive lacking any national-policy or political experience. The appointment seemed similar to President Carter's appointment of Hamilton Jordan as his White House chief of staff. Warren Christopher attempted to run an orderly transition process, but it soon became apparent that Clinton, like Carter, was making ad hoc appointments of people he barely knew. Hillary Clinton, it appeared, was being given latitude to select female Cabinet members at Justice and Health and Human Services. Clinton interviewed as a possible secretary of state Lee Hamilton, the respected chair of the House Foreign Affairs Committee. Former vice president Mondale was thought another possibility, and then was rumored about to be appointed ambassador to the United Nations. Then Christopher himself was named secretary of state, and Madeleine Albright, a party activist and fundraiser but hardly a foreign-policy heavyweight, was named U.N. ambassador. On the eve of her appointment, a group of female activists had held a press conference in Little Rock decrying the lack at that point of senior female foreign-policy appointees. Albright then was named for the United Nations job. Former Arizona governor Bruce Babbitt, himself a onetime presidential candidate, sat in a Little Rock hotel room awaiting word as to which one of several Cabinet-level positions he might fill. In the end, he was made secretary of the interior, a position where he potentially faced conflicts of interest because of his family's Western landholdings. Ron Brown was named commerce secretary. Mickey Kantor, a Los Angeles attorney and lobbyist, was named U.S. trade representative. He had aptitude for the position, but no background of experience in the field. Donna Shalala, regarded in the Carter administration as an eccentric upstate–New York political character who had stumbled into a federal appointment, was named secretary of health and human services. Two female attorney general nominees were discarded because of ethics questions, before Florida prosecutor Janet Reno was given the appointment. One of her first actions would be to authorize the bloody FBI attack on the Koresh compound in Waco, Texas.

Clinton, it was reported, was seeking a woman appointee in a key economic policy post. The logical choice would have been Alice Rivlin, a Brookings macroeconomist with long national-policy experience. Instead, Laura Tyson, a young and attractive Berkeley economist associated with quasi-protectionist "industrial policy" proposals, unexpectedly was named chair of the Council of Economic Advisors, a position formerly held by such economists as Walter Heller, Arthur Okun, and Charles Schultze. Tyson normally might have been considered as a possible deputy assistant secretary of commerce or labor, specializing in sectoral policy.

Before the campaign, many appointees, as well as the Clintons, had attended so-called Renaissance Weekends in South Carolina—a commercial-hotel promotion that staged seminars for the benefit of ambitious baby boomers seeking to network with others who might benefit their careers. Senior career diplomats and several distinguished private citizens were passed over for the vital position of U.S. ambassador to London. Historian Arthur Schlesinger Jr., for one, had expressed interest in the appointment. I sent a note about it to Warren Christopher. Christopher responded that he liked the Schlesinger idea. The appointment went instead to Admiral William Crowe, who had endorsed Clinton, and then in Clinton's second term to Phil Lader, coordinator of the Renaissance Hotel promotion. The whole enterprise was shaping up as Carter déjà vu—except that, in seeking Cabinet members, Carter had at least tried to appoint people recommended to him as competent. Clinton appeared to be treating the whole business with offhand carelessness.

Here I should add a word about how the Executive Branch works and why key appointees can make a huge difference in the well-being of the country. Once elected, a president almost immediately begins limiting his attention to the key international and domestic issues that have highest priority for the country and for him personally. Any president spends most of his time with key big-issue advisors—that is, the secretaries of state, defense, and treasury, the White House national security advisor, the director of the Office of Management and Budget, and his two or three most senior White House staff members and advisors. The vice president may or may not be one of these. Any president also has a high stake in the identity of his attorney general. The attorney general oversees a host of legal and law-enforcement issues vital to the presidency. Normally, he or she also would be a close political confidant of the president—as Robert Kennedy was with John F. Kennedy or John Mitchell with Richard Nixon. Janet Reno, clearly, was not such a person. Webster Hubbell, Clinton's old Arkansas friend, would fill the role of presidential confidant in the Clinton Justice Department. It may be indelicate to say so, but a president wants a trusted friend as attorney general so that, among other things, he does not find himself surprised by indictments, legal actions, or other embarrassing matters involving either himself or his political allies. Since 9/11, the Department of Homeland Security and intelligence agencies have been added to the list of inner-circle players. Presidents look to other Cabinet officers, at Commerce, Labor, Interior, and Agriculture, for instance, and to heads of independent agencies to keep their operations running trouble-free and to pacify their various public constituencies. These appointees seldom see the president except at formal Cabinet or interagency meetings. Other than that, they are likely to spend time with the president and his senior staff only when a delicate problem comes into view at their department or agency. The White House would prefer to keep them out of sight and mind.

For example, public and media attention became focused on the Federal Emergency Management Agency in 2005 after its performance was found lacking during Hurricane Katrina's passage and the aftermath of flooding in New Orleans and adjacent areas. How could a president have let FEMA bumble so badly? The fact is, FEMA traditionally has been a bureaucratic backwater largely staffed by political hacks. Most presidents would be unable to tell you the identities of the people who ran the place—until or unless they really let the ball drop.

It is easy to see, after the fact, that damage was done in the Kennedy and Johnson administrations by the appointments of Secretary of State Rusk, Secretary of Defense McNamara, and National Security Advisors Bundy and Rostow, and that President George W. Bush and the country were badly served by Vice President Cheney and Defense Secretary Rumsfeld. So-called "inner Cabinet" appointees, in particular, can do harm to decision making in governments led by presidents relatively inexperienced in foreign affairs. Their damage can last for years afterward.

Internal decision-making processes, too, are vital. The famous Cheney energy-policy task force, in the early days of the George W. Bush presidency, apparently took most of its advice from energy-industry representatives and operated in secret. The health-care task force headed by Hillary Clinton in 1993–94 similarly operated behind closed doors and included only people with compatible views. Both were disasters.

Clinton made astute choices in 1992 by naming Senate Finance Committee chairman Lloyd Bentsen as treasury secretary, New York financier Roger Altman as deputy secretary, and Goldman Sachs vice chair Bob Rubin as director of a new White House National Economic Council. And he maintained continuity, and the trust of the financial community, by leaving the Federal Reserve in the hands of Chairman Alan Greenspan. Later in the administration, after Bentsen retired and Altman had resigned after controversial congressional testimony, Rubin was to become a highly successful treasury secretary, trusted not only by Wall Street but also by the international community and the Congress. A few years earlier, when he had served on the founding board of the Center for National Policy, I had known Rubin to be both honorable and able and—what is rare in the financial community—devoted to the well-being of society's have-nots. He once invited me to lunch at a downtown Manhattan private club complete with mahogany wall paneling, sailing-ship paintings, and a central-casting service staff. He had received his first Wall Street job interview there and been rejected, he said. Moreover, he later learned that there were no Jewish club members. He therefore took pleasure in dining there as a senior Goldman Sachs executive and in the company of Jewish and non-WASP members. Rubin, it would turn out later, was to be the captain whose wise economic and financial policies would provide a calm sea in which the Clinton political ship could remain afloat even as its engine room flooded.

The initial foreign-policy team of Warren Christopher, Secretary of Defense Les Aspin, CIA director Jim Woolsey, and National Security Council advisor Tony Lake and his deputy, Sandy Berger, was not fated to last. Aspin and Woolsey departed quickly. At the end of Clinton's presidency, only Berger remained, having become NSC advisor after Lake's nomination was submitted as CIA director, then withdrawn. Through shake-ups at all the foreign-policy agencies, the Clinton team's fundamental approach changed only as events forced it to change. It generally shared Carter-era terms of reference—that is, an overoptimistic view about the results that solely peaceful means and multilateralism might yield in a world still populated by leaders and nations quite willing to proceed by force and outside the rules. A fuzzy Wilsonianism—recurring in American policy over several generations—led it to seek propagation of Western values and institutions throughout the world. But its Wilsonianism differed greatly from that of the present Bush administration, for example. Whereas the current administration has proved ready to utilize military force for Wilsonian ends, the Clinton administration took office sometimes talking tough about its commitment to these goals but avoiding use of tough policies to pursue them. It exhibited from its outset a tendency toward "speaking stickly but carrying a big soft," as Carter-era policies once were characterized. The only tough guy on the eventual Clinton foreign-policy team was Madeleine Albright, who succeeded Warren Christopher as secretary of state. A child of pre–World War II Eastern European émigrés, she knew that history could be cruel and that international bullies must be resisted. Yet she was more a careerist than a thinker or strategist. Both during her service at State and since, she has shown a surprising readiness to speak as a political partisan rather than as a stateswoman. Clinton would be his own strategist, and would generally improvise policy case by case, more often than not on a basis of realpolitik.

I was determined, as Clinton's inauguration neared, to put aside disquiet about reports of Arkansas ethics-skating and womanizing and my disappointment at the ragged appointments process. I hoped that Clinton's "good side" would prevail and that his considerable intelligence and political aptitude would help him grow quickly in office. I attended several meetings of inauguration planners, and prevailed on several of my consulting clients to sponsor the inauguration financially and attend its events. Jean, still feeling strong, and I bought a table at the inaugural dinner attended by Arkansas Clinton supporters, and we greatly enjoyed their happiness. Talking with Democratic senators, members of Congress, and capital regulars at other inaugural events, however, I could find few who felt any real enthusiasm about the president-elect. Most, like me, were hopeful and waiting watchfully.

Soon after Clinton took office, I was speaking by phone with Arkansas Senator David Pryor about a legislative issue. Pryor, whom I had known since his days as a first-term congressman, asked if I would have dinner the following evening with Skip Rutherford and two other Arkansas advisors of Clinton, to discuss the reported string of Arkansas ethical misadventures that were harming the new president's credibility before he could get started. Would I provide advice regarding handling of these issues? Would I perhaps consider accepting responsibility to manage them for the president? As it happened, I would be in New York the following evening, and, besides, I would not be interested in managing the problems, I told him. Among other things, as Pryor knew, I was committed to spending as much time as possible with Jean during her fight against cancer. But I would be pleased to offer advice to Rutherford or anyone else. The advice would be simple, I said. First, don't get bogged down in explanations of pre-presidential problems. Second, launch White House initiatives strongly and as if the Arkansas problems did not exist. Third, don't do anything in the White House to create new problems. If there were special circumstances that would preclude such a strategy, I said, I would be happy to discuss them with the appropriate Clinton advisors. I have no idea if Pryor passed along my advice or how it might have been received. In any event, he never called to reschedule the meeting.

Soon thereafter, I became concerned that responsibilities given to Hillary Clinton might cause problems for President Clinton. Though she did not hold an official Cabinet or other position, she was attending Cabinet and other senior-level White House meetings. She was not HHS secretary, or appointed formally otherwise, yet it appeared that she was being given responsibility for formulation of an administration health-care policy proposal. I saw substantive, political, and procedural problems that might come of this. I phoned the president's secretary, Nancy Hernreich, and asked for an appointment to discuss this and other matters with Clinton. She called back a day or two later to request that I meet instead with Mack McLarty, the newly appointed chief of staff, and talk with him as candidly as I would with the president. When I arrived for the appointment, I saw McLarty walking briskly out of the West Wing carrying a briefcase. I was met in the lobby by Mark Middleton, a young Arkansan who introduced himself as a former member of Clinton's gubernatorial staff now working with McLarty. McLarty, he said, had been called on short notice to New York to represent the president at an event there. Could I share my thoughts with him? As I began to outline them—including my thoughts about Hillary's developing role—he quickly put up his hands. "Wait a minute," he said. "You need to talk directly to the president or Mack. I can't deal with any of this." He asked that I call to reschedule an appointment with McLarty. When, after a week, I had received no return call, I simply put my thoughts into a memo for Clinton and faxed them to Hernreich. I never got a response. I mentioned the matter to Chuck Manatt, the former Democratic national chairman, when I encountered him shortly thereafter. "I know," he said. "I have had the same experience and so have others. It is very hard to get through to anyone at the White House. We'll see if things change."

There were more warning signs. I had met Michael Kelly, a *New York Times* reporter, at the McGovern-campaign reunion at the New York convention. We had talked periodically thereafter. Kelly had been assigned by the *New York Times* Sunday magazine to do a cover story on the new president. It explored, among other things, events in Clinton's Arkansas childhood and teenage years as well as the years before and during his governorship. The article appeared informative and balanced to me. A few days after its publication, I had lunch with Kelly. The Clintons had been fiercely attempting to discredit the article and him, Kelly said. He was surprised at this, because in researching the article, he had run across information that could have damaged Clinton seriously, but lacking corroborating sources, and not wanting to be unfair to a new president, he had omitted it from his article. He related some of what he had heard. It mainly involved episodes from the personal lives of Clinton and his family and was rather depressing. But it made me feel more, rather than less, sympathetic to Clinton than I had been before. It went a long way, I thought, toward explaining Clinton's nonstop campaigning. Much of his life had been a continuous search for praise and approval. He had to keep moving, and focusing on the external, lest he be forced to slow down and face inward. His seemed to me a classic story of a child growing up with alcoholism, conflict, and periodic violence in his family. Many Americans had undergone similar experiences and risen above them. Few had risen to the presidency.

14

A NEW JACKSONIAN ERA, PART ONE

President Jimmy Carter had started his presidency by resuming an old feud with the U.S. Army Corps of Engineers—an interesting exercise but hardly a worthy first priority for a presidency. President Bill Clinton began his by having to withdraw his nomination of Zoe Baird as attorney general, by becoming embroiled in a controversy over gays in the military, and by getting bogged down in an attempted purge of the White House travel office. Then he became entrapped in a favorite idea of Vice President Al Gore's, a BTU (energy) tax, and in his naming of Hillary Clinton to develop a health-care plan that would preempt a number of plans which had been developed by Democratic senators and members of Congress.

He did, however, heed the advice of his principal economic- and financial-policy advisors to bite the bullet of federal deficit reduction. The tax increases and spending cuts associated with his budget plan were not the easy political way out. But they were better addressed during the new president's traditional "honeymoon period," when he enjoyed much goodwill, than later when they would be more difficult to enact. He later would confide to a business audience that he regretted the tax increases in his plan. Whether he truly did or did not, the plan provided exactly the right medicine for the economy at the proper time.

One of the White House staff members involved in the travel office fiasco was Deputy Counsel Vince Foster. Foster had been a partner at the Rose Law Firm in Little Rock and was reputed to be Hillary Clinton's best friend there. Rumors during the campaign had suggested that Foster and Hillary were more than friends and that, while Governor Clinton womanized, Hillary had found a stable alternative relationship with Foster. But Foster was a family man known as a straight arrow, and Hillary was focused on her husband's career and her own, and on their daughter, Chelsea. The rumors seemed doubtful. Yet, when the Clintons came to the White House, Foster spent a disproportionate amount of his working time attending to matters principally involving Hillary's interests. These included her health-care task force, which she proposed to shield from public oversight. Foster, along with Associate Attorney General Webster Hubbell, another former Rose partner, was featured in an unflattering *Wall Street Journal* article. (In March 1994, Hubbell would be forced to resign from the Justice Department because of investigations into his activities at the Rose Law Firm as well as his role in the Whitewater, Arkansas, real estate venture in which the Clintons also were involved.)

On July 20, 1993, Foster's body would be found at Fort Marcy Park in suburban Virginia, just across the Potomac River from Washington, a revolver in hand. It took only a few days before hard-edged conservative media were speculating that Foster's body had been rearranged after his death, that law enforcement officers had engaged in some kind of cover-up, and that he could have been murdered to keep him from disclosing damaging information about the Clintons. I did not believe any of it. What was interesting, however, was that Hillary Clinton had Foster's White House office immediately sealed and his files removed. Several months later, when media inquiries forced public release of the list of files taken, they included files on the travel office, the health-care task force, and the Whitewater real-estate scheme which had followed the Clintons to the capital.

Clinton's first big foreign-policy crises came in October 1993, when old-line Kremlin and military leaders attempted a coup to dislodge Russian president Boris Yeltsin, and when forces aligned with a local warlord killed a number of U.S. troops in Somalia, where Clinton had maintained an involvement begun in the prior administration (the latter episode was to become the subject of the film *Black Hawk Down*). During the same period an American ship carrying civil advisors and U.S. Army engineers was unable to dock in Port-au-Prince, Haiti, when an angry mob threatened it from the pier. The ship turned around. The United States had sent the advisors and soldiers as part of a UN-sponsored attempt to reverse a military coup that had deposed President Jean-Bertrand Aristide.

I regarded the commitments in Somalia and Haiti as mistakes. The Somalia venture had begun as a humanitarian mission and had evolved into a peace-keeping mission on behalf of the United Nations. The U.S. involvement in Haiti, I thought, was dubious at best. The desperately poor country had undergone coups and counter-coups throughout the century, and our military presence there could at best make only a marginal and temporary difference unless we were prepared to take over Haiti and thus become responsible for it. The fate of the Yeltsin government, however, was of prime importance to the

United States. We had to do whatever was necessary to resist the reestablishment of an old-style Soviet regime.

I was disgusted by the debacle in Somalia and worried that it would sour the American people on a wide range of foreign-policy commitments that were far more important. I sent a memo to the president expressing the view that the commitment in Somalia should be ended. I listed at least a dozen high-priority foreign policy/national security tasks that could be jeopardized by a public backlash against our Somalian involvement. I told him I had been to Mogadishu and could assure him that no vital U.S. interest was at stake there. I sent copies of the memo to Warren Christopher, Les Aspin, and Tony Lake. A few days later I was surprised to find a White House envelope, delivered by messenger, awaiting me at the reception desk as I came to my office. Inside was a letter from Clinton, indicating that he agreed with my assessment and would end the U.S. involvement in Somalia as soon as the din subsided over the killing of the U.S. troops in Mogadishu.

I was pleased to hear that Clinton shared my view. But I was surprised by two things. First, I was taken aback that he would be so candid about his intentions, before he acted on them, to someone outside government. I did not leak the letter to the media or discuss it with anyone else. Nor did I use my knowledge of it in my *Washington Intelligence* newsletter, still being published and widely distributed. But many others, on receiving the letter, would have done so and thus prematurely betrayed the president's intentions. I had a second surprise a short while later when Lake sent me a note on another subject, adding a postscript that my Somalia memo had triggered a lively policy discussion within the administration. It made me conclude that neither Clinton nor his foreign-policy team until that time had been paying sufficient attention to what they were doing. It should not have taken a memo from an outsider to make them focus on so chancy a venture as the U.S. involvement in Somalia.

Clinton did extricate the U.S. from Somalia, but stuck with and deepened his commitment in Haiti, largely in response to political pressure brought by the Congressional Black Caucus. Predictably, the U.S. presence there cost billions but in the end made little difference in Haiti's fundamental situation. The Yeltsin government was sustained, although principally through Yeltsin's own tactical skills. The rush of October events, however, served to focus Clinton on foreign-policy issues that had not engaged him in the first nine months of his presidency. I came to think of the period as Clinton's October Evolution.

Clinton, like other presidents before him, had too greatly trusted the advice of foreign-policy and national-security types whose recommendations should have been received with greater skepticism. George W. Bush, in making a major U.S. military commitment in Iraq, also accepted bad advice. New presidents—especially those coming from statehouses and previously inexperienced in foreign policy—can enter the office not even knowing the right questions to ask their advisors when major initiatives are proposed. After the Somalia and Haiti debacles, Clinton involved himself directly in major foreign-policy issues, not only because they affected the U.S. national interest but because they also affected his own political viability.

It was at about this time that I was exposed to Clinton's "other side" as well. I had written an editorial-page essay for one of the national daily newspapers, questioning some aspect of administration policy. A few days later, James Carville attacked me by name, in a prepared speech delivered to political consultants in Washington, D.C., as a corrupt advisor to the insurance and pharmaceutical industries. Then Richard Cohen, a favorite Clinton columnist at the *Washington Post*, wrote a column dismissing my criticism and belittling me. I did not know either Carville or Cohen. I did not respond to either of them but, instead, wrote a note to the president saying that he knew me well enough to know that my opinions were honestly expressed: I would praise him when I thought he deserved it, criticize him when I thought otherwise. However, if the White House intended an orchestrated personal attack on me, I would have to respond to it. The attacks stopped and did not recur over the remainder of Clinton's presidency—even when, in 1996, I wrote a *Wall Street Journal* essay endorsing for the first time in my life a Republican presidential candidate, Senator Bob Dole.

Late in 1993 the president was successful in enacting the North American Free Trade Agreement. During his 1992 campaign, seeing that he was struggling to cope with the issue (opposition to NAFTA was strong in upper-Midwest industrial states and unions whose votes he needed), I had sent him a fax setting forth the substantive and political pluses and minuses of the prospective treaty. Both the benefits and downsides of the treaty were being grossly exaggerated, I said. It was, in one sense, anti–free trade, as it would create a North American trading bloc from which Caribbean and Central American nations, among others, would be excluded. Moreover, it was a risk to meld two advanced and open economies, such as those of the United States and Canada, with one such as Mexico's that was still developing and protected. However, NAFTA had become a somewhat inappropriate litmus test for whether political leaders were internationalist and enlightened or inward-looking and protectionist. I suggested that, on balance, he was best served to endorse NAFTA even though there were quite respectable internationalist arguments against it. He had thanked me for my fax, said it was helpful, and endorsed the treaty. But, on final passage of the legislation in the House in 1993, only a bit more than a third of Democrats voted with the president. Republican votes resulted in its passage by a narrow margin.

The year to come would be remembered mostly for the failure of the Clinton health-care plan. Democrats in Congress had been trying for many years to enact incremental health-care plans, even though a near majority, if asked, would tell you they really favored a comprehensive national scheme. But they quickly would add that the existing structures of the health-care and insurance industries, as well as the procedures in place in Medicare and Medicaid, would make such a transition a practical impossibility. Thus they kept working at the margins. Hillary Clinton, when given the health-care assignment by the president, decided to undertake a first-principles review of the existing system, and then introduce a new scheme that would resolve the matter once and for all. Some years before, she had undertaken a similar review of Arkansas's public education system and presented proposals to the state legislature. Arkansas Senator David Pryor had told me at the time that her effort was impressive in all respects.

Hillary Clinton's health-care task force made an early decision that responsibility for health-care coverage should lie principally with employers rather than individuals. But during the early 1990s the economy was changing rapidly. Major employers, such as those in the automobile, steel, and other traditional industries, were laboring under employee and retiree health-care costs that were reducing their competitiveness drastically. The new economy, moreover, increasingly was one of entrepreneurs, start-ups, small businesses, partnerships, and independent operators. People were moving more and more among different companies and industries, and often striking out on their own. As they moved, they could be left without health-care coverage or with coverage greatly inferior to what they had enjoyed at their original employers. The task force also proposed creating a series of regional bodies, subject to control of state governors, that would serve as de facto managers of the new system. Anyone with practical experience could foresee that the bodies would become centers of political patronage and abuse.

By the time it had been fully developed, the Clinton health-care plan's outlines could be drawn on a chart. That was a big problem. The chart disclosed it to be a hopelessly incomprehensible and bureaucratic remake of an entire sector of the economy. Industry and political opponents had a field day displaying the chart and raising doubts about it, most of them legitimate.

The Clinton health-care proposals met resistance not just because of their substance but because of the procedure by which they were reached. I had seen President Johnson succeed with Medicare and other health-care proposals by drawing a wide range of public and private players into dialogue about them. When any major policy or institutional change is contemplated, it is imperative that some kind of prior consensus be formed behind it. But the Clinton health-care task force went out of its way to be exclusionary. Hillary Clinton and the task force's director, Ira Magaziner, known previously as an eccentric "idea man" of the boomer generation, mobilized several hundred people for participation in the exercise. But they mainly were like-minded policy types. Industry representatives purposely were kept at bay. Even relevant congressional committee members and staff were unable to gain full access to what was going on. Only favorably disposed media were given insights into the project's progress; others were kept on the outside. By the time a fully developed proposal was ready for presentation to Congress, a huge contingent of the excluded and distrustful was prepared to oppose it. Even President Clinton's economic policy team and several Cabinet members weighed in with substantive criticisms and warnings of looming political disaster. But, because the first lady was involved, they went unheeded.

By the middle of 1994, the Clinton health proposals had been discredited and were withdrawn. It all happened within a few weeks of the November 1994 election and left a strong impression on an electorate making decisions about congressional candidates. At the time of the collapse I asked House Democratic leader Dick Gephardt how many votes he thought the Clinton plan might have gotten among House Democrats. "No more than 125, tops," he said. Voters, the debacle fresh in their minds, gave Republicans their first majority in the House of Representatives in forty years. It could have been worse. A number of close House races turned at the last minute toward incumbent Democrats. Had they not done so, and the Republican victory been even larger, surviving Democrats in the House would have mounted an outright public rebellion against the president. They also might not have been disposed to save him when a later impeachment process got underway. At the end of 1994, the Clintons found themselves largely alienated from their own party on the Hill.

Jean's cancer slowly had progressed. She now walked with a cane. She had read in the *Washington Post* about a Christmas-season folk art exhibit at the White House that she badly wanted to see. Her physical condition would make it impossible for her to stand in line for hours with tourists, in winter weather, in order to take a public tour of the exhibit. The Clintons, beset by troubles, had begun to adopt a bunker mentality and I was hardly their strongest supporter. I doubted I could get private access to the exhibit for Jean, but was determined that she not be disappointed. I called John Podesta, then an assistant at the White House and not yet Clinton's chief of staff, to make the request. He called back only a few minutes later to say that the president had learned of the request and wanted us not only to see the exhibit but to spend some time with him personally. The president had suggested we join him that Saturday morning as he made his Christmas radio broadcast to the country, and then to visit for a while in the Oval Office. We were welcome to bring any of our children with us.

Thus, on the Saturday morning before Christmas 1994, Jean and I, with two of our four children and their partners in town for the holidays, came to the West Wing. As we stood briefly in the reception area, a senior State Department official emerged from the Oval Office. "I have just spent the most unpleasant hour of my life in that office," he told me. "And I've got to come back this afternoon for more." I worried that Clinton would be sour and Jean's visit spoiled. But that was not the case. We were taken on a tour of the exhibit and then ushered back to the Roosevelt Room, adjoining the Oval Office, where a Christmas tree stood and where a small table was set up with a microphone for Clinton's broadcast. Clinton entered, speaking to my family although not to me. "I'm just going to broadcast a simple Christmas message," he said. "I am sure it will not be substantive enough to suit Ted." His eyes watered in allergic reaction to the tree.

After the broadcast, he took us into the Oval Office for small talk. Jean told him she had gone to the Arkansas Cancer Research Center for treatment. He replied that his mother was also receiving cancer treatment there. After a few minutes, a photographer arrived. Clinton asked us to join him in a photo. My family stood next to him, but some unconscious reaction held me back. "C'mon, Ted," he said, "get in the picture." I stood at the end of the group rather than next to Clinton. As we left the office, I turned in the doorway to offer a last, encouraging word to Clinton during his hard times. But he already was behind his desk and did not look up. Jean would see only one more Christmas. But in the remaining months of her life, she felt a bond with Clinton and with his mother and urged me to be as generous in my judgments of him as I could.

The new year dawned with the political initiative having passed from a still-new Clinton administration to House Republicans, led by Speaker Newt Gingrich, who had issued a ten-point "Contract with America." The contract mainly was a reaffirmation of Reagan Republican principles and policies in both domestic and foreign policy. One of its points: Welfare reform should be enacted. Debate about the contract was interrupted, however, by the unexpected weakness of the peso in neighboring Mexico.

Collapse of the peso would have ripple effects in our own and other economies. On the other hand, a U.S. intervention to bail out the peso carried many perils. What if, after an intervention, the peso's fall continued? What if other currencies became threatened? Would the U.S. have an obligation to bailouts elsewhere? I noted in my *Washington Intelligence* newsletter that the peso crisis followed the exit of an outgoing Mexican government. Mexican presidents and their associates traditionally had looted the national treasury of billions when they left power. Did the U.S. have an obligation to finance the thefts? An intervention carried enormous risk. On the other hand, an even greater risk lay with inaction. Treasury Secretary Bob Rubin, newly appointed to his job, argued for an intervention while explaining its possible downsides. Clinton took Rubin's advice. It was the right decision and showed that the president was prepared to act decisively and to risk unpopularity when he considered the national interest to be at stake. Had he not undergone his painful October Evolution in 1993, I thought, he might not have made the proper call this time.

In the meantime, House Speaker Gingrich had driven to passage nine of the ten items in his Contract with America. House Democrats mostly urged Clinton to challenge the contract head-on. I had encountered several Clinton aides and advisors in the lobby of the Mayflower Hotel shortly after the contract's introduction. Most of the provisions, it seemed to me, were superficially popular but could be attacked and discredited effectively. Moreover, I thought, an effective presidential counterattack could remobilize congressional Democrats who had lost confidence in Clinton. The Clintonites said they agreed. But, after an internal White House debate, Clinton decided he had more to gain by seeming accommodating, and buying time, than by taking on directly an agenda that appeared to have initial public approval. During the same period, the bombing of the federal building in Oklahoma City diverted public attention and gave the president a chance to exhibit leadership in a domestic crisis. On his return to domestic and budget debate, Clinton continued to take a moderate policy line. Yet, in November, he drew a hard line in budget negotiations with Republican congressional leaders and called their bluff when they threatened to shut down the federal government if the president failed to come to what they regarded as a satisfactory budget agreement with them. Republicans were surprised when Clinton failed to compromise. They did shut down the federal government, and subsequently found public opinion turning strongly against their tactic.

During the same period Clinton took another big gamble by sponsoring negotiations in Dayton, Ohio, among the Bosnian, Serbian, and Croatian presidents toward an agreement on a division of Bosnia that would stop several years of rampant ethnic killings there. At the end of November, when the talks appeared near failure, a deal was made. However, Clinton was left with the necessity of sending 20,000 U.S. troops to the Balkans to help maintain order. He pledged to the American public that the commitment would last only a year, but it was to last for many years. Whatever the longer-term implications of Clinton's Balkan commitment, the Dayton agreement and the face-off with Gingrich and Republicans over the government shutdown boosted his public-approval ratings: from a low point in early 1995, they had become quite strong entering the presidential-election year of 1996. He began that year by declaring in his State of the Union message that "the era of big government is over." The declaration had no basis in reality, but because it was delivered by a Democratic president, it seemed a dramatic departure and was generally well received by voters.

It was presumed during this period that Clinton's reported womanizing had ceased on his assumption of the presidency. Several prominent Democratic women had told me, though, that during White House social events or visits to their cities, he had touched their breasts or made otherwise suggestive approaches. Then gossip indicated that the president might be having trysts with staff members or other women who were regularly at the White House. One, it was later to turn out, was an intern named Monica Lewinsky, who was giving oral sex to the president while, among other things, he did official business over the telephone. (When the Lewinsky relationship later was publicly disclosed, a prominent Democratic senator remarked to me that "Clinton may turn out to the first president literally blown out of office.") The Lewinsky relationship, however, would not become public until much later.

In the late summer of 1996, Clinton made a controversial decision that would help him win that fall's national election but which was divisive within his party and administration. He had spoken of "ending welfare as we know it" during his 1992 presidential campaign. But no one regarded the pledge as anything but superficial political rhetoric playing to a middle-American constituency disillusioned with the welfare system. In mid-1996, however, a welfare bill emerged from congressional conference committee that Clinton had either to sign or to veto. It called for the end of a system that had provided a safety net for the poor ever since the New Deal. It was opposed by all within his party except Democratic Leadership Council types. Treasury Secretary Rubin, Labor Secretary Bob Reich, Health and Human Services Secretary Shalala, and then–White House chief of staff Leon Panetta opposed it. Marian Wright Edelman of the Children's Defense Fund publicly urged a veto, as did her husband, Peter Edelman, an HHS assistant secretary.

After temporizing, Clinton signed the bill. Peter Edelman promptly resigned. Not surprisingly, the action enjoyed majority support throughout the country, and Clinton's poll ratings rose again. The long-term effects of the welfare change remain to be seen. The nation has not, since 1996, suffered a dramatic economic downturn that would show us its net effects on the poor. But it positioned Clinton even more clearly as a pragmatist willing to reverse course on bedrock Democratic commitments dating back to Franklin Roosevelt.

15

A NEW JACKSONIAN ERA, PART TWO

The president's 1996 reelection campaign against Senator Bob Dole was a mismatch. Clinton was the younger and more aggressive and articulate candidate. Dole was laconic, and at times could seem downright uninterested in the audience or subject matter before him. Yet I feared that lurking political time bombs might detonate during a Clinton second term. I was depressed by Clinton's constant focus on short-term tactical politics. Moreover, I had watched Dole evolve from the angry, partisan figure of his 1976 vice presidential campaign into a universally respected congressional leader committed to bipartisan problem-solving. A war hero who had been severely wounded and handicapped during World War II, he had genuine and special concern for those in society who were poor, hungry, disabled, or otherwise harmed by forces larger than themselves.

A Clinton electoral victory seemed certain. Nonetheless, I was moved to speak out in a *Wall Street Journal* essay in which I endorsed Dole for president. I thought in particular of my father, of his faith in the country and in Franklin Roosevelt, and of his abiding commitment to a Democratic Party that had always stood up for "the little guy." Dole, I thought, had genuine concern for the hurt and the left out, whereas Clinton's principal concern was with himself. I thought another four years of the Clinton presidency would change the character of my party.

Clinton's first CIA director, Jim Woolsey, also endorsed Dole. But few other Democrats, whatever their private feelings, had done so. The Dole campaign, following publication of my *Wall Street Journal* essay, asked me to become more actively involved in their effort. I responded that I had said my piece in the essay and would leave it at that. I received a large volume of mail in response to the essay. I heard from no one in the Clinton administration or presidential campaign, but I did hear from a number of Democrats in Washington, D.C., and throughout the country. My friend Harry McPherson, President Johnson's counsel who had helped me form the Center for National Policy, wrote a long and serious letter asking what could have caused me to endorse a Republican presidential nominee. I responded that I feared in particular that Clinton's free-wheeling conduct in Arkansas and during his first term could come home to hurt him in a second term and make governance next to impossible. (As it happened, Dole, after his defeat, would join McPherson's law firm.) A surprising number of Democrats wrote to laud my *Wall Street Journal* essay. Among them was Sargent Shriver, the 1972 Democratic vice-presidential nominee.

Clinton, after his reelection, spent a desultory year talking but doing little tangible about public education, improved race relations, and other poll-tested issues. But he was well served by his economic- and financial-policy advisors, who began his second term as they had his first: successfully negotiating a bipartisan budget deal on Capitol Hill which by year's end would reduce the federal budget deficit to zero. He was to benefit, as other presidents had before him, from a generally positive economic climate in the country.

His newest chief of staff, Erskine Bowles, had taken the lead in the budget negotiations. Other changes had been made in the president's supporting cast. U.N. ambassador Madeleine Albright had been given her United Nations appointment because of the active intervention of women's groups in Clinton's first-term transition process. History would repeat itself four years later when Albright was chosen, over former Senate majority leader George Mitchell and Balkans negotiator Dick Holbrooke, to be Warren Christopher's successor as secretary of state. The same women's groups, backed by Hillary Clinton, mobilized on her behalf. Tony Lake, never fully comfortable with Clinton, would step aside as National Security Advisor in favor of his deputy, Sandy Berger. It was never certain whether Lake's nomination as CIA Director was a means of moving him out of the White House or of rewarding him for his sometimes trying devotion to his duties during the first Clinton term. In any case, the nomination ended badly.

Media and Republican critics charged that Lake, fresh from the Clinton White House, would be insufficiently independent at the Central Intelligence Agency. I regarded the charge as ridiculous. I had known Lake since the early 1960s. I regarded him as excessively Wilsonian and a bit soft in his approach to hard national-security issues, but I respected his intellect, his dedication to public service, and, above all, his independence. As a National Security Council staff member, working for Henry Kissinger, he had resigned in protest over Vietnam policy. It was a chancy thing for a young Foreign Service officer to do and could have ended his career. I noted that neither the White House nor congressional Democrats were mounting much of an advocacy for Lake. Thus I wrote an op-ed essay defending his nomination and submitted it to a national daily newspaper that often published my articles. The essay was rejected. I sent the essay to another paper where I frequently published. It was rejected again, and then, a third time, by another publication. I was puzzled by the response. I was known as a sometime critic of the Clinton administration, and I was now defending one of its nominees. The issue was topical. What was happening? I then called a friend, a columnist for the *New York Times,* to discuss Lake's nomination. "Don't talk to me about Tony Lake," he said. "I don't trust him and won't write anything favorable about him." I called another columnist and got a similar reaction. It then dawned on me that the publications and columnists were becoming edgy about the Clinton presidency and using Lake as a surrogate target. A short while later, Lake's nomination was withdrawn and he returned to academia.

Meanwhile, issues associated with Clinton's dark side were surfacing. His old Arkansas ally, Webster Hubbell, had after his resignation from Justice been found guilty of stealing hundreds of thousands of dollars in false billings from Rose Law Firm clients. In the period before reporting to federal prison, however, he received other hundreds of thousands in "consulting fees," including $100,000 from an Indonesian group that was under scrutiny for having made illegal foreign contributions to the Democratic National Committee and Clinton's 1996 reelection campaign. Close Clinton associates were found to have solicited the fees on Hubbell's behalf—they appeared to amount to hush money. Public reports also surfaced regarding huge contributions to the DNC and the Clinton campaign by the Indonesian consortium and other Asian sources which also might have been illegal. Some, it appeared, were directly tied to Chinese intelligence agencies. John Huang, a Commerce Department official and Democratic National Committee fundraiser, and other Asian fundraisers were found to have channeled millions of dollars to Clinton-associated political entities. Another operative named Johnny Chung was found to have visited the Clinton White House some fifty times and to have handed a $50,000 check to one of Hillary Clinton's staff members. A Chinese restaurant owner from Little Rock, Charlie Trie, had contributed $460,000 in money orders—all completed in the same handwriting—to a fund to be used in the Clintons' Whitewater legal defense. Roger Tamraz, a Lebanese-American businessman seeking White House support for a Caspian Sea oil pipeline project, was found to have visited with Clinton and to have contributed $177,000 in campaign money. Clinton had invited for coffee and a chat a New Jersey swindler tied to organized crime. Literally dozens of campaign contributors and favor seekers, it turned out, had overnighted in the Lincoln bedroom. A handwritten note from Clinton to DNC chair Terry McAuliffe had specifically instructed McAuliffe to exploit the White House mansion for political fundraising purposes. Huang, Chung, and others were to plead guilty to campaign-finance violations. The Clintons took only glancing damage. But the picture, in its totality, portrayed the Clinton White House as soliciting and receiving big money from often tawdry and questionable sources. Why had Clinton done this? For the same reason, I thought, that he later gave as the reason he had sexually exploited a young White House intern: "Because I could."

The second Clinton term would include a notable Middle East peace summit, deeper involvement in the Balkans, and Rubin's and Clinton's successful management of U.S. policy during the late-1997 Asian financial crisis, which, like the earlier peso crisis, had the potential to bring down the global financial system. But it would be remembered mainly for Paula Jones's charges of Clinton's sexual misconduct in Arkansas, Monica Lewinsky, Special Counsel Ken Starr, perjury, impeachment, and the polarization of opinion regarding the Clinton presidency which became pervasive in the Congress and country.

Should Clinton have been impeached? The president's conduct, in particular his perjury to a grand jury, invited impeachment. A more politically astute person than Starr might have seen, however, that an impeachment seemingly focusing on circumstances surrounding the president's sexual misconduct might be regarded by the public as a less appropriate measure than, say, a formal censure. Republican congressional leaders should also have recognized that any impeachment they brought should have related to the president's role in Whitewater, Asian campaign contributions, or other matters—not on a matter relating to sexual conduct, even if the president had lied about it under oath. If a sufficient basis did not exist for an impeachment relating to other issues, there should have been no impeachment.

Clinton and his allies characteristically waged a no-holds-barred counterattack, impugning the motives of Starr and Republican critics and depicting the president as once again the target of "right-wing extremists" determined to bring him down because of his progressive economic and social policies.

I was no longer living in Washington, D.C., at the end of the Clinton presidency. I had left the capital to return to the West Coast at the end of

1997. As I watched Clinton's travails, I had decidedly mixed feelings. I had foreseen what might happen and had therefore endorsed Dole for president in 1996. On the other hand, I did not regard Clinton as I had come to regard President Jimmy Carter—that is, as someone unsuited to the presidency. Clinton was a political natural, intelligent, quick on his feet, with potential for big achievement. Carter had not been up to the job in the first place.

My heart sank as I watched Clinton's final actions in the presidency: 177 pardons and commutations extended to cronies, the politically influential, his own half brother, and Susan McDougal, who had gone to jail rather than testify against him in the Whitewater investigation. He pardoned fugitive financier Marc Rich, whose former wife had given more than a million dollars in Democratic political contributions during the eight years of the Clinton presidency. The Justice Department, FBI director Louis Freeh later would report, had not been consulted regarding any of the last-minute pardons and commutations.

Clinton, after an initial post-presidential period in which he seemed lost and uncertain, has reverted as an ex-president to his earlier patterns of conduct—without, one would hope, the compulsive womanizing. He has taken in several million dollars annually in lecture fees for speeches to business and international groups. He has reentered the limelight with selective appearances at times and places that associate him with humanitarian causes. He clearly savors his role in advising and helping Senator Hillary Clinton develop her 2008 presidential campaign. He is still seeking attention, still talking, still seeking affirmation and approval. Those are not bad things per se. They characterize a high percentage of successful people, especially in the performing arts, to which politics partially belongs. Bill Clinton, after all those years of striving, and after two terms in the presidency, still labors under the burden of unrealized potential.

While in office, President Clinton appointed wise economic and financial policymakers and took their advice. The country's economy remained strong under his stewardship. He resisted an increasingly protectionist tide in his own Democratic Party, although at the end of his term he appeared to side with demagogic anti-free-traders at a failed World Trade Organization meeting in Seattle. He came to office with the first terrorist bombing of the World Trade Center in New York and left before the more devastating attacks of September 11, 2001. In between, he failed to recognize the threat of Al Qaida and take strong actions that might have ended its existence as a formal organization. His intervention in the Balkans, made necessarily without UN Security Council approval, was problematic. He came close to brokering a comprehensive Middle East peace agreement and deserves credit for the attempt. The jury remains out on his welfare-reform initiative; it will not be fully tested until the country experiences a truly serious economic downturn. His failed health-care initiative set back meaningful reform efforts in that sector by more than a decade.

On substance, principally because it brought prosperity, the Clinton administration deserves a passing grade. But Clinton's brand of politics—the never-ending campaign—did not serve us well. It owed less to Franklin Roosevelt, Adlai Stevenson, Hubert Humphrey, the Kennedys, and George McGovern than to Huey Long and, yes, Andrew Jackson. Policy and politics go together and depend on each other. Lyndon Johnson, for one, understood back-scratching, tactical politics. But he used it for higher policy aims. With Clinton it was all politics, all the time, with the prime agenda at most times being his own viability. Democrats today revere a President Clinton who never was. History is less likely to treat him with respect or gentleness.

On the final day of the 2000 Democratic National Convention in Los Angeles, I wrote an essay for the *Los Angeles Times* editorial page headlined "He Moves out from the Shadows and into the Light." In the essay I urged Vice President Al Gore, the party's presidential nominee, and his running mate, Senator Joe Lieberman, to repair the damage done to the Democratic Party during the preceding eight years. The column expressed my feeling about the harm done to the country, the political process, and the Democratic Party by Clinton's conduct in the White House.

> With Vice President Al Gore's formal nomination for President last night, and his selection last week of Sen. Joseph I. Lieberman as his 2000 running mate, the Democratic Party may finally be coming out on the other end of what it later will see as its eight-year degradation by a President who polarized and lied to the country and who was guided by little more than his personal and political self-interest.
>
> Leaving this legacy behind will open the way to a Democratic victory this fall.
>
> The party and most of its elected leaders still are unable to recognize what the Clinton years have done to them. But perspective and distance will clarify President Clinton's tenure. The policy reversals, the sellouts of

his Congressional party, the refusals to embrace bipartisan solutions to the thorny Social Security and Medicare issues, the hopeless botching of the chance to enact comprehensive health-care reforms, the stinking campaign finance scandals and the casual and open-ended commitments of troops and tax dollars to dubious involvement in Haiti and the Balkans—all were offenses to the country and Democratic Party far more serious than any casual sexual dalliance in the White House. It was never about governance. It was always about political expediency. And, in defending the President against impeachment and other charges, Congressional Democrats themselves fell too easily into the same expediency.

We Democrats need to get it straight. The President's troubles were never the result of some right-wing conspiracy or vendetta by prosecutors. They were the result of his own conduct.

Sen. Al Gore, before he became President Clinton's vice president, was a measured, thoughtful and intellectually independent person. Most of all he was a person of integrity. Yet, as I saw my old boss Hubert Humphrey change during four years as Lyndon Johnson's vice president, I saw Al Gore change during eight years as President Clinton's understudy. Surrounded by the hyper-political, manipulative culture of the Clinton presidency, Gore became, as Humphrey with Johnson, a cheerleader for actions and policies that he himself often would not have pursued.

Watching the Vice President last week as he proudly presented Lieberman as his running mate, Gore seemed more open and liberated than at any time during this campaign year. Now that he has been nominated in his own right, his liberation can be complete.

There is no doubt that Gore and Lieberman are men with moral compasses. Their personal and family lives are beyond reproach. Their word is good. As Senators, both often worked with colleagues across party lines to find solutions to public problems. Both were unafraid, when necessary, to face up to interest groups in their own party when they disagreed with them.

In the coming campaign, we can expect the two men to draw sharp differences with the Bush-Cheney ticket. The country needs and deserves that. But we need not see the confrontational campaign tactics we sometimes saw in the Vice President's nominating contest against Bill Bradley. Those were Clinton tactics; they should not be Gore-Lieberman tactics.

George W. Bush and Dick Cheney, just as Gore and Lieberman, are honorable and public-spirited men. They should be treated as such in the upcoming campaign.

But Bush and Cheney have espoused policy positions on Social Security, taxes and spending, education and defense that would create a different kind of America than that which would be created by the Gore-Lieberman proposals. Thus it is a campaign, above all, on those issues, and not on personalities, that the country deserves and that Democrats can win.

Clinton is often given credit for a successful Presidency. It is quite true that peace and prosperity have been prevalent during these years, just as they were prevalent, for instance, during the otherwise empty and scandal-ridden term of President Warren Harding. But given the gift of peace and prosperity, Gore and Lieberman have the chance to demonstrate that there is a large-minded, publicly moral Democratic Party that can put petty politics, name-calling and "spinning" aside and return to its historic role of high public leadership. We can again be true to ourselves, beginning now.

16

ESCAPE FROM THE CAPITAL

My productive time in Washington, D.C., really ended in the months preceding Jean's death on April 24, 1996. I continued my consulting business and *Washington Intelligence* advisory service and otherwise attempted to proceed as usual. I turned down a meeting with associates of Russian president Boris Yeltsin to discuss my spending weeks in Moscow to advise his reelection campaign. From the beginning of 1996, when it became evident that Jean's brave battle against bone cancer was nearing its end, I spent most hours, day and night, at her side.

When she departed, the funeral chapel was filled with fellow teachers and administrators from Primary Day School, parents of the children she had lovingly nurtured, and others whose lives she had touched. My children, grandchildren, and I buried her in a suburban cemetery, as she had requested, near my parents' grave. My name was placed on the headstone, next to hers, in anticipation of our reunion later.

I was not fully myself for the next year and a half I spent in the capital. I continued to work and to write. I traveled twice to participate at conferences at Oxford University sponsored by one of my clients, Oxford Analytica. But, evenings and weekends, I found myself sitting alone in our big house in Potomac, gazing at the empty chair Jean had occupied in her final months. I divided most of our belongings among our four children and gave most books and clothing to charity. Our daughters Terry and Sue held a yard sale to dispose of remaining items. I sold the house and moved what remained into a two-bedroom apartment in Maryland at the District of Columbia line.

I badly needed something to bring me back to life and make me feel useful. In mid-1997, after Clinton's reelection, I sent a private note to Sandy Berger, his national security advisor, expressing a willingness to take on some important but seemingly insoluble task confronting the administration. I reminded Sandy, in my note, that I had endorsed Dole for president the previous fall and, moreover, had supported Tsongas rather than Clinton for the 1992 Democratic presidential nomination. Berger, to my surprise, responded immediately and enthusiastically. I was badly needed, he said. Anyone who knew me understood my Dole endorsement. He would get back to me promptly suggesting a foreign-policy-related option or two.

A short while later I received a second note from Berger saying he had encountered unexpected (by him) resistance to the idea—I presumed from Clinton. However, if I wanted him to do so, he would actively try to overcome the resistance. I responded that he should use none of his internal political capital on my behalf. It had probably been a bad idea in the first place. It was. I recognized that escape from grief and depression was not the right motive to seek service in the administration of a president whom I doubted. (Later, as Clinton's second-term troubles fully flowered, I could see how truly bad the idea would have been.)

Then, as had happened so often in my life, change came from an unexpected source. During my time at Weyerhaeuser, nearly twenty years before, I had worked with Donald Straszheim, who subsequently had left the company and become chief economist at Merrill Lynch in New York. He had been an early subscriber to my *Washington Intelligence* service.

In 1997 Straszheim left Merrill Lynch to become president of the Milken Institute, a nonprofit economic policy think tank in Santa Monica, California, founded and chaired by Michael Milken, the brilliant and controversial financier who had spent time in prison in the early 1990s for securities-law violations and had subsequently turned to philanthropy. Straszheim was an economist and knew financial markets, but he had no prior experience in public policy or in running a policy institute. I had both. I thus took on a consulting role in which I helped him organize the institute and frame its agenda. I met and enjoyed working with Milken, who was prohibited by law from pursuing his former profession in the securities industry. Despite his great wealth, he and his family continued to live in the San Fernando Valley neighborhood where he had grown up. His closest personal staff and advisors were fiercely loyal to him; he had known many of them since boyhood, and they were, without exception, straight-shooting, open people. I found that the political, business, nonprofit, minority, and other communities in Southern California continued to embrace him, despite his legal troubles, without reservation. His family's foundations emphasized public education, prostate-cancer research, and, in the case of the institute, economic policy research.

Shortly after his release from a California federal prison, Milken had been diagnosed with prostate cancer. He attended, incognito, a seminar in Texas to learn what he could about the disease. Afterward, he told me, he sat alone in his hotel room to consider his fate. Fined nearly a billion dollars by the federal government and sentenced to jail, he had been released to learn that he had perhaps months to live. His father, an independent accountant in the San Fernando Valley, and seven other close family members had died of cancer. Characteristically, Milken decided not to yield but to undertake independent prostate-cancer research, on behalf of himself and of others, and to contribute as much as he could to positive causes.

At the beginning of 1998, I accepted Milken's and Straszheim's proposal that I move to Santa Monica and become executive vice president and chief operating officer at the Milken Institute. The change was good for me. I bought a condo on the Santa Monica beachfront within walking distance of the Milken foundations' headquarters building. I purchased, for the first time in my life, a convertible. Santa Monica's morning fog and fresh air were like Puget Sound's. My friend Ted Sorensen, in New York, when he learned of my move, wrote what he thought was a tongue-in-cheek letter saying that he imagined I was now "living on the beach, driving a convertible, going tieless, and wearing sunglasses much of the time." In fact, he was correct on all counts. I renewed my old friendship with Warren Beatty, and probably spent more time at his family's dinner table than his wife, actress Annette Bening, appreciated.

I was particularly attracted to the notion of building and running a policy institute that, unlike the Center for National Policy, would not have to be constantly seeking operating funds. Milken contributed $12 million annually in operating funds to the institute. We could concentrate on hiring quality staff and undertaking independent work. Donors' interests need not dictate the projects we took on.

The 1997 Asian financial crisis had just blown over. I proposed an annual Global Economic Conference, which would examine all aspects of current financial and economic trends worldwide, and whose first session would be devoted to the aftermath of the Asian crisis. Leading national and international authorities, including several Nobel Prize winners recruited by Milken personally, participated in the conference. We also formed various policy task forces, hired several new staff economists, and published their independent work. I recruited Peter Passell from the *New York Times* to edit the *Milken Institute Review*. He formed an economic-establishmentarian advisory board for the magazine.

My further immersion in economic and financial issues at the Institute reinforced my belief that globalization makes it impossible for any country or sector to isolate itself from events elsewhere and that an open global system is the only viable option for the American or other economies. The free movement of goods, capital, services, and, to the degree possible, people is a process that causes dislocations but in the end serves everyone best. In this age of terrorism, of course, movements of people and goods do not represent what they once did. National borders must be protected from people, devices, and materials that could cause harm. But otherwise, the rule still holds.

Study in particular of the 1997 Asian crisis reinforced my belief, as well, that second- and third-world countries as diverse as South Korea and Indonesia would truly prosper only when their business and financial markets were liberalized, when rules of law and transparency were established internally, and when the United States, other donor countries, and the United Nations, International Monetary Fund, World Bank, and regional development banks insisted that their aid be conditional on adoption of rational policies by recipient countries. I had formed that opinion strongly during the time I led the 1977 Carter administration's international-development review exercise; had renewed it during 1992 service as a member of a presidential commission on foreign assistance appointed by President George H.W. Bush; and saw events of 1997 as further evidence in its favor.

I also concluded that Milken's controversial high-yield-bonds financing strategy had indeed enabled the creation of dynamic new companies. It represented the "democratization of capital" that he claimed it did. But, I often thought, it could be disastrous in a riskier, slower economic environment.

Milken, as a person and personality, ranks among the most fascinating figures with whom I have worked. Ranked by *Time* magazine as one of the three leading financial figures of the twentieth century, he almost single-handedly changed the face of American capitalism over the course of a few years. His pioneering of high-yield, or "junk," bonds provided access to capital for many new-economy companies that otherwise would not have had funding. A San Fernando Valley Jewish kid, he had started out working for a white-shoe investment firm in Philadelphia, Drexel Burnham; after moving up through the company's ranks, he moved the business with him to Beverly Hills. He quickly became the bane of big, establishmentarian firms on Wall Street and elsewhere that regarded him as a cheeky upstart poaching on their exclusive preserves.

Despite his prostate cancer, Milken's energy level was like Hubert Humphrey's. Even when no pending business required it, he would rise at dawn, begin telephone calls, and bounce ideas off his colleagues. As a widower, living alone, I found myself frequently receiving calls at 6 AM on weekend mornings from Milken, suggesting that I drive from the beach to the Valley to have breakfast with him and discuss important pending business. Upon my arrival, though, it often would turn out that there was no pending business—or at least none that could not have been disposed of quickly at the office on Monday. By the time I arrived, Milken usually would have consumed his *New York Times* and *Los Angeles Times*, and he would be pacing the floor, impatient to discuss the trends and events reported in their pages. Straszheim and/or I would be summoned on other occasions to discuss his ideas for institute activities. As is the case with most creative leaders, some of his ideas were good, others completely inappropriate. Milken was always generating new things to do, always running late. On one occasion, as I passed his open office door, I was surprised to see him sitting quietly on a sofa, doing absolutely nothing but gazing out his window at palm trees beyond. I said, almost involuntarily, "Mike, what are you doing?" "I'm having a reflective moment," he answered. "You should try it some time."

Milken, like Clinton, constantly sought approval and an audience. Institute staff meetings attended by Milken were difficult—they tended quickly to become Milken monologues. I encouraged him to sit in on presentations made by staff economists on studies they were undertaking and to listen rather than talk. That usually did not work. However, on one occasion, during a long presentation by Hilton Root on prospects for liberalization of the South Korean economy, Milken said absolutely nothing. Later he confessed that he had missed the main points and remained silent so as not to expose his own lack of understanding.

Milken's mother, Fern, widowed twice, was a person of high good humor and spirit. Knowing I was a widower, she made it her personal business to scout new lady friends for me. Most turned out to be widows closer to her age than to mine. On one occasion, while I was on institute business in New York, my hotel-room phone rang at 2 AM (11 PM Pacific time). "This is Fern," a voice said on the other end, "the woman who gets you girls." She had found a younger prospect for me, she announced. When I met this latest candidate, she turned out to be Mike's cousin. Mike Milken also had the engaging, little-boy habit of sharing small triumphs and excitements. He would phone to talk about meeting a famous personality or about receiving favorable media mention.

Things at the Milken Institute changed early in 1999. After a family meeting, Milken announced to Straszheim and me that he thereafter intended to fund only 50 percent of the institute's budget rather than 100 percent. We would have to raise the rest. He also wanted a shift from independent policy research to contract research commissioned by private businesses and financial institutions. That and other changes in emphasis at the institute made work less satisfying for me than it had been during the period when we were defining and building the organization. Milken urged me to stay, but I left at midyear and found myself pleased to withdraw from responsibility for running anything.

Until a few days before my departure from the institute, Milken acted as though I had not resigned. He continued to be as communicative and generous toward me as previously. However, as my last day loomed, communication stopped. Milken's secretary, Karen Vantrease, informed me that a planned farewell luncheon could not be scheduled. I received well-wishing e-mails and phone calls from Milken's longtime friends and personal staff. But I heard nothing from him. A few days later I was at dinner with several of Milken's old colleagues from Drexel—all made rich by their involvement in his deal making. They remarked on my departure from the institute. "What did Mike say when you left?" one asked. "He apparently did not like it," I said. They all laughed. "Listen," another told me, "Mike never fires anyone and no one ever quits. He takes it personally." I could understand. Milken had treated me as a friend and confidant, and felt betrayed that I would leave his benign sponsorship. But, unlike his colleagues at Drexel, I was not making millions in his service. I was being paid a good salary—but not enough to hold me in a situation that had changed from what I originally agreed to. Although I did not tell Milken, I also did not want the institute to be my last port of call. It was comfortable. But I remained cursed with the need to feel that I was making a real difference—something I thought was no longer possible there. I left with almost wholly positive feelings about Milken, though. He had strengths and weaknesses, but beneath it all, he had a good and big heart.

I spent the balance of 1999 and 2000 as a senior fellow at the UCLA School of Public Policy and Social Research and teaching a public-policy course to doctoral candidates at Claremont Graduate University's School of Politics and Economics. I served as author of the international trade-policy proposals contained in the RAND Corporation's official presidential transition document presented to presidential candidates Bush and Gore. I had reached the age of sixty-six but still felt I was treading water until the next real challenge turned up. I had attended and seen many old friends at the 2000 Democratic national convention in Los Angeles. On the final day of the convention, the *Los Angeles Times* had published my essay suggesting that national nominees Al Gore and Joe Lieberman break from Clinton's tactics and return to the higher, larger agenda that had served the party well in the past.

I had known Vice President Gore as a moderate, serious public servant, driven in part by a desire to meet his father's expectations. On one occasion, before he declared his 1988 candidacy for the presidential nomination, I had attended a meeting called by his father, former senator Al Gore Sr., at his Washington, D.C., apartment near the Supreme Court building. Al Jr. appeared painfully uncomfortable; his father was an oppressive presence. Midway during Al Jr.'s remarks to the gathering, Al Sr. interrupted him to introduce Armand Hammer, a benefactor of Al Sr.'s, who had just arrived. On another occasion I was invited to sit at Al Jr.'s table during a Democratic dinner. I had met with him occasionally to discuss public issues. I had been impressed by the commitment and courage he displayed as he stayed by his son's bedside over many weeks after his son had been struck by a car while both were crossing a street after a Baltimore Orioles game. I had observed him and his wife, Tipper, after Gore's withdrawal from the 1988 presidential nominating campaign, while attending a fundraising event at the Children's Museum in D.C. that was intended to help pay off the Gore campaign debt. Losing candidates can be treated cruelly and cynically by capital regulars; on this occasion, the treatment was unusually cruel. The museum had been prepared and decorated for the event. Eager young Gore staff members were on hand to extend hospitality. But, over the course of the evening, only a bare handful of guests came. I chatted with the Gores, somewhat uneasily, hoping that more people would arrive to give them a better feeling after their loss. But few came. Yet neither Al nor Tipper Gore betrayed disappointment or uneasiness—they met the situation with grace. I regarded them as serious and good people.

After Paul Tsongas's withdrawal of his active candidacy for the nomination in 1992, I had asked Gore if he might be prepared to offer his own, compromise candidacy at the national convention if fresh scandals might cause Clinton's candidacy to collapse before he was formally nominated. I thought Tsongas, Jerry Brown, and many Clinton delegates would find it easy to support Gore. He said he would think about it. Five minutes later I received a call from his chief of staff, Peter Knight, suggesting a meeting on the subject. But then he called back to say that Gore wanted to hold off. As it turned out, of course, Gore would be Clinton's running mate.

Senator Joe Lieberman had been attorney general of Connecticut before becoming a U.S. senator. I had to come to know him in the Democratic Party and as he represented Clinton in the 1992 national platform process. He was balanced and thoughtful, had a wonderful sense of humor, was a committed family man, and shared Gore's moderate instincts on most matters of policy. Lieberman, like Tipper Gore, had dared to criticize Hollywood and the entertainment industry—bastions of Democratic financial support—for their degradation of cultural values. I knew both Gore and Lieberman to be personally uncomfortable with Clinton's personal recklessness and freewheeling conduct of his office. My *L.A. Times* essay had been a personal message to each of them as much as a general message to the party.

The omens were good for a 2000 victory by Gore and Lieberman. Democrats would benefit from a climate of general peace, prosperity, and domestic calm. They would not have to carry the baggage left over from Clinton's impeachment and related troubles. Voters correctly saw Gore and Lieberman as upright people unlikely ever to be involved in personal or public scandal. Beyond that, Lieberman would bring special strength to the ticket in Florida, where Jewish voters in the southern part of the state could make the difference between winning and losing.

Sure enough, Gore and Lieberman won the national popular vote. But, along the way, anticipated tactical victories failed to materialize. Gore, a skilled debater, failed to do much better than a draw in nationally televised debates with Texas governor George W. Bush. Lieberman and Republican vice presidential candidate Dick Cheney also fought to a debate draw. Gore failed to carry his own home state of Tennessee. He lost West Virginia, solidly Democratic since FDR. He failed even to carry Clinton's home state of Arkansas. The electoral contest thus would be decided by late-night results from Florida. But savvy Democrats knew it should never have come to that. Gore and Lieberman had not done as well as they might have, in part, because Gore never could come to terms with Clinton or how to employ him in his campaign. Instead, the Gore campaign generally shunned him. That should not have been necessary. Others besides me had counseled the candidates to separate from Clinton's "never-ending campaign" tactics and to reassert the party's traditional leadership on difficult national issues. There was no need for Gore or Lieberman to defend Clinton missteps or excesses. They simply needed to point to peace, prosperity, and domestic stability and to underscore their own moderation and rectitude. Clinton, for his part, should have been asked to campaign in states where he remained popular, including Arkansas and West Virginia, and among minority and other constituencies which he could energize. He also could have been used to raise money nationally. But the nominees handled the "Clinton problem" by removing the outgoing president from sight not only in places where he would hurt but also where he would have helped the ticket.

The dispute over the 2000 Florida electoral result is still being felt. The take-no-prisoners legal and political tactics on both sides contributed to the red state–blue state polarization that remains in the country. Normally, such a dispute would have been resolved through legislative processes. That is, the Florida legislature would have declared a winner; the U.S. House of Representatives, with each state delegation getting one vote, would then have ratified or overturned that result. Because Republicans controlled both houses of the Florida legislature at the time as well as a majority of U.S. House delegations, Governor Bush's looming victory seemed apparent, even though Gore had outpolled him in the national popular vote. The Florida Supreme Court, with a Democratic majority, unexpectedly intervened, however, overriding the Florida Legislature's decision. As rhetoric and feelings rose in intensity, the U.S. Supreme Court took jurisdiction.

I expected the Supreme Court to kick the matter back to normal legislative channels for resolution. Had the Court done so, however, it would have been many weeks before a decisive vote was taken in the U.S. House. Instead, the Supreme Court in a narrow decision opted to shorten the process and declared Bush the winner. Most after-the-fact criticism of the process centered on the supposed partisan vote in the court. My feeling, then as now, however, was that the Supreme Court deliberately proceeded to spare the country additional weeks of acrimony after which, in any case, the U.S. House also would have declared Bush the winner. It acted pragmatically to relieve building pressure on the system.

Many sighs of relief, in any case, were heard from House members of both parties, as they were spared the task of resolving the dispute. Imagine the pressures that would have been felt by representatives whose state votes would have gone for Bush or Gore although their own districts voted otherwise. Only later did some congressional Democrats begin to question the

Supreme Court's intervention. Gore, to his credit, accepted the decision grace-fully, as Richard Nixon had done after his close 1960 defeat.

Latter-day partisans, however—fed by veterans of Clinton's never-ending campaign—have chosen to argue that the 2000 election was "stolen" by Republicans and that President Bush's legitimacy thus should be questioned. The country has never fully calmed after the dispute. Had leaders of both political parties acted earlier to change the national electoral process so that presidents would be elected by overall popular vote, rather than a majority of state electoral votes, the dispute might have been averted. Most had for years seen such a dispute coming. None acted to avert it. Still, these years later, we remain complacently committed to the Electoral College system, awaiting the next crisis.

Our entire national electoral process is due for a thorough scrubbing. Gerrymandering—or redrawing of congressional-district boundaries to assure reelection of incumbents—has become so flagrant that there are, at most, no more than thirty-five to forty truly competitive congressional districts in most national and midterm elections. The House of Representatives, intended constitutionally to be the body most responsive to changing national opinion, thus does not turn over as it once did, when 100 or more seats and control of the House would change in response to big national or international events. The House, instead, has become a bastion of continuity. The Senate, intended to be the more deliberative body, has become more competitive. But since no more than a third of its seats are contested in any two-year cycle, a change of control is difficult there too.

In recent years control of both houses of Congress, whether by Democrats or Republicans, has been narrow. Because a growing number of senators and representatives owe their elections to liberal or conservative single-issue or single-interest groups, the bodies have become more polarized ideologically. Issues that inflame hard-liners on either end of the political spectrum—abortion, gun control, school prayer, court nominations, immigration, gay marriage, and "values" issues—have tended to overwhelm what used to be debate primarily about economic-, domestic-, or international-policy questions affecting the broader national interest. Moderation, these days, attracts few votes or campaign contributions from organized blocs. Compromise, consensus legislative outcomes are difficult to reach. The legislators who would need to reform gerrymandering are the ones who benefit from it, so the outlook for change is not good.

The presidential nominating process can be changed by the two parties themselves. The fact that caucuses in Iowa and a primary in New Hampshire became over the years decisive in winnowing Republicans' and Democrats' presidential-nominating fields was absurd. Neither is populous. Neither is particularly representative of the country at large. By the time the nominating process moved to big states such as New York and California, it often had been effectively decided. We cannot and should not turn back the clock to the time when a handful of power brokers at state conventions, at party caucuses, and in smoke-filled rooms determined who would or would not be a national convention delegate and who would or would not be the parties' nominees. A nationwide primary election, as some have proposed, could risk favoring the best-financed candidate and those with an appealing but short-term demagogic message. Both parties have created a new problem for 2008 by sanctioning big-state primaries, which in effect will create a national primary deciding their nominations a full nine months ahead of the general election.

By far the best course would be a system of four or five regional primary contests in which candidates' regional advantages would be equalized. If staged over a several-week period, the regional contests would give the national electorate a chance to observe the candidates and weigh their messages. Perhaps most important for public policy, candidates from various parts of the country would be forced to learn about and address issues in other regions—for example, northeastern urban candidates would be force-fed knowledge about the south, and southerners knowledge about the Pacific coast. By the time of their parties' conventions, delegates would have a far better sense than they do now of the characters and competence of their candidates for the presidential nomination. The game will be over in February 2008, before voters have really gotten to know the candidates. Just like the Electoral College system, the current nominating system amounts to a dangerous game of roulette.

The campaign-finance system has been reformed and re-reformed constantly over the past half century. The most recent reform legislation was the McCain-Feingold Act, which facilitated formation in the 2004 national campaign of so-called "527 committees"—independent, unpoliced entities separate from the political parties themselves and therefore not subject to control of the parties or candidates (and named after section 527 of the tax code that regulates tax-exempt organizations)—which were free to say and do anything they pleased. The infamous "Swift Boat" television commercials attacking Senator John Kerry's military record were put out by a 527 committee. The McCain-Feingold Act enables billionaires ranging from George Soros, on the ideological left, to Richard Mellon Scaife, on the right, to spend unlimited amounts of their own money to deliver whatever messages they please. Altogether, 527 groups spent more than $400 million in the 2004 election. To pretend that these committees operated with total independence, and without contact or coordination with candidates or their campaigns, is ridiculous.

One rule of thumb always has been true in politics: money will find its way.

Spending limitations and reporting requirements can be instituted. Candidates can be required to approve messages contained in their own advertising and literature. Political action committees, independent committees, and other entities can be placed in separate categories and made subject to different rules and regulations. But, in the end, money will flow from interested parties—whether their interests be economic or ideological—to candidates and campaigns in one way or another. Where labor unions and business organizations are prohibited from contributing general funds to candidates, those entities will form political committees or resort to "bundling"—that is, soliciting from members or employees individual contributions at the legal limit which then are delivered, together, to candidates or their campaigns. The same corporation or organization that makes a $5,000 contribution through its political-action committee can, for example, bundle another $100,000 in individual contributions to the same candidate. It is difficult to prove that such bundling took place—unless the checks are all in alphabetical order, as once happened with heavy Boeing contributions from employees whose last names ran from "A" through "M."

Before reporting requirements and spending limitations were in place, there was nothing to prevent a Nelson and Happy Rockefeller, for example, from making six-figure contributions to the 1968 Humphrey-Muskie campaign, as likely happened, or to any other campaign. Nor could Max Palevsky be kept from rescuing George McGovern's 1972 campaign with a large injection of cash prior to the New Hampshire primary. Nor could Stewart Mott, in 1972, be prevented from conducting with his own money what he called the Muskie Accountability Project, in his attempt to block Muskie from the Democratic nomination that year.

Far more sinister transfers are possible and are hard to detect. I related earlier in this book the offer I received from a KGB agent to effect a major fund transfer to the Center for National Policy through an American donor. Early in 1968, after Vice President Humphrey had met with the Shah of Iran, George Carroll, the CIA officer attached to the vice president's office (and who had served in Iran during the coup that had installed the Shah in power), suggested that he could arrange for "a million dollars" to be transferred from the Shah to bolster Humphrey's political ambitions. I told Carroll to forget it. But, had we decided to accept such money, there would have been a thousand ways to make it appear to have been contributed by American sources. I had little doubt that if Carroll had made the suggestion to a Nixon aide rather than to me, it would have been promptly accepted.

Heavy Asian contributions to Clinton campaigns have been documented. It would take hundreds of investigative reporters, with sophisticated forensic backgrounds, to illuminate the thousands of trails that could bring political money into the American system from points around the world. There is never a way, of course, to trace or regulate cash delivered in suitcases to candidates or their representatives. The only constraint on candidates is their fear that they might be caught receiving it.

Over time I have concluded that the only foolproof way to police campaign spending is to place hard caps on the amount of paid media spending allowed to candidates. These expenditures are hard to hide. The rates are set. Opposition campaigns will watch closely to see that the caps are not being exceeded. But, although broadcast and print advertising are vital components of any major campaign, they are less central in this alternative-media age than they once were. Other expenditures are more difficult to track—especially if they are crowded into a campaign's final days and not reported until long after the election has taken place.

In my version of campaign-finance reform, all raising and spending of money would be undertaken by the major political parties rather than by individual campaigns. It would be fully reported. Presidential-campaign spending, in the general election, would be wholly publicly financed, and the two major-party candidates granted an equal amount of money. Even under that arrangement, however, there would be many ways that candidates and their allies could hide the raising and spending of huge amounts of money—albeit illegally. Would a presidential-election winner be impeached, months after his or her inauguration, if it were found the campaign had raised illegal campaign money? Unlikely.

Money, regrettably, will continue to find a way in politics. Our only reliable antidote to campaign-finance corruption is to vote for candidates we believe to be unwilling to act corruptly.

17

A NEW CENTURY

The presidency of Bush the younger was to be one of "compassionate conservatism" and incremental domestic reform, led by a former Texas governor who had reached across party lines to govern successfully in his home state. Instead, it will forever be defined by September 11, 2001, and by the intervention in Iraq.

Bush's cornerstone Social Security reform proposal—based on the same partial privatization notion so beloved of the 1980s and 1990s investment community—has come and gone. His proposed Pentagon reform program had to be deferred in favor of crisis actions in Afghanistan and Iraq. His Medicare prescription-drug benefit, seen as a concession to Democrats, is now perceived mainly as one more thing deepening federal deficits, which, despite having apparently been closed by the end of the Clinton years, have exploded since 9/11. Congressional Republicans and Democrats alike have compounded that problem by joining in an irresponsible spending spree that will place the country in the same budget box in 2008 that it was in at the end of the Reagan presidency in 1988. Some $10 trillion in deficits are now projected by 2015. Genuine long-term solutions to Social Security and Medicare financing have not been addressed. Bush's No Child Left Behind education initiative is meritorious, but has had an uphill slog in a fiercely partisan environment.

Lyndon Johnson in 1964 expected the Great Society to be his legacy. George W. Bush no doubt expected his presidency to be a relatively quiet, transitional period of moderate populist change. Both were trapped by and will be marked by questionable foreign interventions.

Between Bush's 2000 election and 2001 inaugural, I moved from Santa Monica back to Seattle, where I always had intended to end up. I had written a long article on the electoral aftermath for a Sunday "Focus" section of the Seattle *Post-Intelligencer*. Subsequently, after discussions with Roger Oglesby, the *P-I*'s editor and publisher, I came home in semi-retirement to write a regular editorial-page column for the paper. My beachfront condo was hard to leave, but I settled into a Seattle waterfront high-rise with a sweeping view and within walking distance of the Public Market, downtown shopping, Pioneer Square, and sports stadiums. Writing a column for the *P-I* involved "coming home" in more ways than one. As a Bellingham High School senior, in 1950–51, I had written a regular *P-I* Saturday sports column about prep-school sports in northern Puget Sound. It had carried my photo. As I began to write my editorial-page column early in 2001, I was instructed to go to the photo studio for a head shot to be carried in the column. I told my editors that they could simply pick up the old photo from fifty years earlier (which of course they did not).

Seattle had changed greatly since my time growing up in the area, and even since my brief return in 1978–80. A region previously dependent primarily on Boeing, Weyerhaeuser, and a few other huge employers had become diverse. New companies such as Microsoft, Amazon, Starbucks, Costco, and a wide array of high-tech and biotech firms had broadened the local economic base and made it less vulnerable to cyclical swings. The city's culture had become vibrant. World-class art, architecture, and performing arts were now embedded in the city's daily life, as were the popular-music and arts scenes. The Gates Foundation had become a philanthropic powerhouse.

The city's demographics had changed, however, in an even more marked way than in other big cities. The Seattle school board had voluntarily instituted compulsory busing for racial balance in the late 1970s at precisely the time that other communities around the country had given up on it. As kids were bused from their neighborhoods and instruction levels suffered during the transition period, thousands of parents moved with their school-age children to the suburbs or enrolled them in private schools. Students remaining in the public-school system were disproportionately poor or members of minorities. Dropout, truancy, and delinquency rates shot up. In addition, school system mismanagement created a huge funding gap. Public schools that a generation earlier had been at the center of Seattle neighborhood and community life became marginalized. I recalled Seattle's Memorial Stadium being jammed with students and parents for Friday night high-school football games. By 2001 the games were being played before scattered handfuls of spectators. The city had fewer school-age kids than any other big city in the nation except San Francisco.

The middle class had fled the city not only because of the schools. It also could no longer afford housing in Seattle. Home prices—bid up in part by high-tech instant millionaires—had risen to the highest level of any city north of San Francisco and west of Washington, D.C. Working families and senior citizens already owning homes found their property taxes rising beyond their means. They could sell their homes at a profit, but afterward could afford to buy only in lower-cost suburbs.

I was most surprised to find that the populist, feisty politics of the city—historically associated with practical liberals such as Senators Warren Magnuson and Henry Jackson—had changed as well. The city remained solidly Democratic. But its nominally nonpartisan city offices were no longer graced with the periodic Republican mayor or City Council members who had helped provide balance. Preponderant opinion on national issues appeared to fall somewhere between Ralph Nader and Dennis Kucinich. Howard Dean would be a favorite of city Democrats, and endorsed by the party's state chairman, during the 2004 presidential nominating process. Yet the city governance conducted by the same people was less Ralph Nader than Benito Mussolini. Seattle mayor Paul Schell, a real-estate developer and cultural liberal, had been unseated after one term for his failure to deal effectively with 1999 WTO and Mardi Gras violence in the city. He was succeeded by Greg Nickels, a lifetime political worker, who narrowly defeated moderate Democrat and city attorney Mark Sidran. Nickels promptly instituted major subsidies for developers—including an estimated $500 million to $1 billion subsidy for Microsoft cofounder Paul Allen's commercial real-estate development on South Lake Union. He endorsed multi-billion-dollar public works schemes including monorail and light rail systems that proved to be far more costly than alternative bus and bus-rapid-transit options. Nickels's and City Council members' ties to developers such as Allen and the rail projects brought them reelection campaign money from the network of law firms, consultants, contractors, subcontractors, unions, architects, financial institutions, and engineering firms involved with the projects. It proved a handsome bargain for the donors, who could provide thousands in campaign money and, in return, receive hundreds of millions in public money approved by mayor and council. Local business and media establishments generally accepted the situation uncritically.

While citizens amused themselves at Bumbershoot, a music and arts festival; Hempfest, a city-sponsored marijuana festival; Seafair, a celebration involving hydroplane races, Blue Angel flyovers, and boosters in pirate costumes; the Gay Pride parade; boating, skiing, camping, climbing, and whale-watching, the public business was being run as in one of those towns in black-and-white Hollywood Westerns—the ones where local big shots profit and call the tune, public officials eat at their trough, and the townfolk eat dirt and pay the bills. Low voter turnout and high public complacency seemed likely to keep the situation as it was. At the state level, nominally liberal governors and legislatures had blown huge holes in the revenue base with "tax expenditures"—subsidies and loopholes extended to favored industries and companies—while raising taxes on consumers, small business, and homeowners.

I also remembered Seattle as having been a lively and competitive newspaper town. When I was growing up, the *Post-Intelligencer*, *Times*, and *Star* had competed for daily readers. On my return, only the *Post-Intelligencer* and *Times* remained, existing under a joint operating agreement whereby the *Times* was responsible for circulation, advertising, and printing functions, and the *P-I* maintained only an editorial staff. Both had become morning papers; the Sunday edition was wholly the *Times*'s except for a shared editorial-page section. Both papers' circulations had been shrinking, the *P-I*'s more sharply than the *Times*'s. Seattle, in fact, remained the smallest American city with two competing morning newspapers. A renegotiated joint operating agreement appears likely to keep both papers alive but unprofitable.

The plight of Seattle's newspapers was not unlike that of newspapers in other cities. Alternative media, the Internet, and cable news channels are becoming the news sources of choice for many citizens; traditional newspapers and conventional network news programs are losing their audiences. Local television news broadcasts in Seattle, as elsewhere, had in any case long since abandoned any attempt at serious, hard-news coverage and had shifted to weather, crime, and lifestyle stories more to the tastes of a shrinking base of viewers.

Washington once had been a swing state in national politics, capable of going for either major party's national nominees. Liberal Seattle always had been balanced by independent and more conservative voters in the suburbs and the eastern part of the state. But by the time of my return, not only had Seattle become a true-blue bastion of political correctness, but its suburbs and much of the Puget Sound area had moved more strongly toward the Democratic column. Only the more lightly populated farming and ranching eastern Washington remained reliably Republican. While George W. Bush had won the 2000 national electoral vote, Washington had been carried handily by Gore (and would be carried just as easily in 2004 by John Kerry). In 2004, moderate Republican gubernatorial candidate Dino Rossi would lose to Christine Gregoire only after three ballot recounts and a dispute over lost and mishandled ballots in liberal King County. But his victory would have been an upset in what had become a Democratic state.

I found, further, that my home state's governors and legislature, and Seattle's mayors and city council, had fallen into the California habit of bucking difficult political issues to the electorate for resolution, rather than dealing with them at the state capitol or city hall, as they presumably were elected to do. Initiatives and referenda had become vehicles for tax increases and rollbacks; teachers' pay increases; construction of cost-ineffective rail systems; looser marijuana-law enforcement; and a host of other matters. These ballot measures, used primarily in Western states, had been seen at the beginning of the twentieth century as direct-democracy checks on powerful mining and railroad interests that had used their power and money to corrupt and control state and local elected officials. But now they were being used by powerful interests to short-circuit normal policymaking processes. A well-financed, organized interest group could sponsor a ballot measure to satisfy its objectives and prevail over diffuse, disorganized, or unfunded opposition in situations where it might not have been able to do so through a deliberative legislative process. This was particularly true if the measures were on the ballot in low-turnout, off-year elections in which disciplined and motivated supporters could more easily dominate the process.

Away from my home state and city, I had thought of them as progressive, clean-politics oases in an often arid national political landscape. On my return I found that they maintained high-road pretensions, but in practice were just as fumbling and often corrupt as anywhere else. Seattle was not exceptional. It had undergone the same changes that had swept other regions and cities.

* * *

The thing I found and continue to find missing in my home city's, home state's, and national politics is a way of thinking that was second nature to those involved in them from the New Deal period through the mid-1980s. There were three fundamental questions always to be asked by political leaders and their parties as they framed their agendas:

- What are the people's most pressing needs?
- How do we propose to meet those needs?
- How can we persuade a majority of voters to accept our proposals?

That was the basis on which historic civil rights legislation, Great Society proposals, arms control initiatives, environmental legislation, and the Reagan Revolution were framed. Whether they be liberal, conservative, or in-between, political leaders proceeded from those questions. When it came to the last question—how can we persuade a majority to accept our proposals?—it was a generally accepted proposition that leaders of any persuasion would need to reach across party and ideological lines to make anything significant happen. If you suggest such an approach to most working politicians today, you will get a quizzical, what-are-you-talking-about response. Those no longer are the terms of reference.

During the first national campaigns in which I participated, pollsters and campaign consultants played only marginal roles. Today they mainly are in charge. An often-recounted episode from John F. Kennedy's 1960 presidential campaign illustrates how things once were. Pollster Louis Harris was presenting polling data to the candidate and his principal advisors. Harris then began to interpret the data and to offer suggestions for campaign strategy. Kennedy cut him off: "Just give me the fucking numbers, Lou. I'm smart enough to figure out the rest."

The same general climate prevailed in the 1964, 1968, and 1972 campaigns in which I served. Consultants were at work, but, as Humphrey used to say, "always on tap; never on top." The 1976 Carter campaign, based not on an agenda but on Carter's marketing appeal as an outsider, marked a real point of departure.

Now, regrettably, most candidates do not review data and, in JFK's words, "figure out the rest," but instead place themselves in the hands of mercenary consultants and pollsters who often carry the same strategies and messages from one campaign to another—and are paid handsomely for giving the same advice many times over to different candidates. Democratic presidential candidates Al Gore, in 2000, and John Kerry, in 2004, pursued populist themes at a national level that they had not pursued as regional candidates earlier in their careers. The reason: the same campaign consultants gave the same (mostly bad) advice to the party's nominees in both electoral cycles. The fault, of course, lay with the candidates themselves, who should have known better than to accept advice and pursue themes out of sync with their previous records and instincts. One thinks of Gore, having dressed and comported himself a certain way over a lifetime, suddenly emerging with new mannerisms and a new earth-tone wardrobe as a presidential candidate. Even worse, presidential candidate Gore, known to his Senate colleagues as a sensible, moderate worker for consensus, emerged on the 2000 campaign trail as a scornful, class-warfare-preaching partisan.

Kerry, from Massachusetts, always had a more liberal voting record than Tennessean Gore. But his personal demeanor always had been balanced and restrained. I had come to know him well during my years in the capital, beginning with his time as a cofounder of Vietnam Veterans against the War during the McGovern campaign, and had endorsed him for the 2004 Democratic presidential nomination in my *P-I* column. But in playing catch-up in the nominating race to the anti-Bush-raging Howard Dean, Kerry adopted a persona only slightly less agitated than Dean's and pursued many of the same empty class-warfare themes used four years earlier by Gore. Both Gore and Kerry, whether they recognized it or not, became someone other than themselves.

It has been interesting to see, on the Republican side, the effect that pollsters and consultants have had on Senator John McCain as he has mounted a 2008 presidential campaign. McCain, prior to 2000 a conservative with strong ties to Arizona developer Charles Keating and the alcoholic-beverage industry, remade himself in Republican primaries that year into a "straight-talking" independent alternative to Texas governor George W. Bush. He subsequently went out of his way to further establish his independence by identifying himself with bipartisan congressional initiatives. But, as 2006 began, he began moving rapidly back toward his prior conservative posture, even praising fundamentalist religionists he had denounced in 2000. Someone clearly had told McCain that he could not win Republican primaries wearing an independent wardrobe. Then, as his 2007 poll ratings sagged, McCain returned to an independent posture. McCain does not recognize that he is drawing a picture of himself as neither conservative nor moderate but as opportunist and cynical.

There is another big problem in relying too greatly on pollsters and campaign consultants. Few among them know anything about substantive policy. They are remarkably value and substance free. Thus you have a candidate staffed on one side by policy specialists and advisors and on another by professional campaign consultants—as though the two functions were separate and unrelated.

The policy breakthroughs of the years between the mid-1930s and the mid-1980s could never have been achieved if national leaders had heeded pollsters or political consultants. One can imagine a conversation between one of today's pollster/consultants and any of the brave leaders who pressed a progressive agenda forward during the politically barren 1950s:

> *Consultant:* The numbers are not promising on this civil-rights thing. A majority of voters favor something called equal opportunity, but, when you get down to specifics, just about every major voter group in every major region has a problem with it. Needless to say, the issue is sure death south of the Mason-Dixon. You should pursue other issues.
>
> *Liberal 1950s leader:* Get the hell out of my office.

Most elected officials and candidates do not want to ask the fundamental questions that once were the entry point of political discourse. The answers to those questions, for the most part, entail the assumption of political risk by politicians who are risk-averse. It is far easier to embrace positions and express opinions that will bring money and votes from groups and people animated by a narrow economic or intense ideological interest. When such people and groups rule, the result is what we have now: angry polarization, deadlock, and a failure to address and resolve big issues.

18

NOT THE SAME COUNTRY

Most of my career has been spent in and around public policy and politics. But I began and am finishing as a journalist. I always have revered the profession as a place where independent, objective reporting and analysis could help protect our society from the excesses and mistakes of the powerful in both the private and public sectors. Recent surveys have shown the media to be falling steadily in public esteem, down around personal-injury-attorney territory. It is not without good reason.

Just as politics has changed substantially since the mid-twentieth century, so have the media. From my time as editor of my junior-high-school newspaper, the *Whatcom Next*, in 1940s Bellingham, Washington, until the 1980s, daily newspapers, newsweekly magazines, and the three commercial broadcast networks dominated news coverage. The people running news in those organizations could have been interchangeable. NBC News's Reuven Frank, for example, could just as easily have been editing the *New York Times*, and *New York Times* editor Max Frankel could have been running NBC News. Peter Lisagor, the Washington, D.C., columnist for the *Chicago Daily News*, could have been editing a newsweekly or doing daily television commentary. Their values and outlooks were similar. All came to their work with the same print-journalism orientations. All had viewpoints but strove, above all, for fairness and objectivity.

The Vietnam War and Watergate gave rise to a new generation of journalists more skeptical and scornful of establishmentarian institutions than their predecessors. By the 1980s the new generation gradually was taking over leadership of the media. Like other baby boomers, they often valued personal expression over a concept of objectivity many thought unattainable anyway. They presumed that leaders of major institutions were either corrupt, lying, or hiding something. So-called "gotcha journalism" became prevalent. Whereas earlier-generation White House correspondents and national columnists and commentators, for instance, knew that President Franklin Roosevelt could not walk on his own and had a mistress, and that President

Kennedy was a compulsive womanizer and in dubious health, they chose to avoid those subjects as not being relevant to their conduct of the public business. No such constraints bound the oncoming wave of boomer journalists.

It was not, of course, as if earlier journalists all had operated without bias and according to strict rules of fairness and objectivity. President Roosevelt's 1936 victory over his Republican opponent, Governor Alf Landon, came as somewhat of a surprise, as most major newspaper publishers—in that pre-television era—had endorsed Landon and predicted his election. Roosevelt worked around the publishers with his radio "fireside chats" to the people and his informal sessions with favored White House reporters.

When I arrived in Washington, D.C., in 1961, I soon learned that many media figures were anything but objective. President Kennedy was known to have several media pals, including the *Washington Post/Newsweek*'s Ben Bradlee and columnist Charles Bartlett, who received favored treatment. While working with the European Communities, I discovered that columnist Joseph Kraft had been paid by the EC to write a book favorable to the development of an Atlantic Partnership between the United States and Western Europe. Then, working for Hubert Humphrey, I learned that nominally objective journalists played favorites all the time. On one occasion, during Humphrey's vice presidency, I drew up a long list of questions and answers for his use in preparation for a weekend broadcast interview. Afterward, he remarked that it was a shame that only one or two of the questions had been asked and the material would go to waste. I thereupon arranged with the bureau chief of a major national newspaper for the prepared questions and answers to run in his paper as "an exclusive interview." There was, of course, no interview—only the questions and answers I had written beforehand.

When opposing candidates were scheduled for broadcast interviews, I often would receive calls from interviewers friendly to our campaign, seeking embarrassing questions and information with which to challenge their guests. When I received no such calls, I often initiated them. I cannot recall a time during either the 1968 or 1972 presidential campaign, for example, when I did not talk in advance with and provide material to broadcast interviewers of President Richard Nixon or Vice President Spiro Agnew. I knew that the interviewers' less friendly colleagues no doubt were conferring in advance of Humphrey or McGovern interviews with my counterparts on the Republican side.

During the entire span of my national political involvement, there were also frequent instances in which print or electronic journalists would suggest a private drink or meeting. They then would step outside their journalistic roles and offer political or policy advice—or pass on information they had gleaned while covering the opposition. I presumed that other journalists, of other persuasions, were doing the same in similar settings. These lines should not be crossed. But they are.

During the sensitive Vietnam War period, I experienced particularly unpleasant incidents involving CBS News. In one, Mike Wallace, accompanied by the CBS Washington, D.C., bureau chief, Bill Small, interviewed Humphrey at length. When the interview was broadcast, however, it had been severely edited to the point that Humphrey's views became unrecognizable and distorted. I promptly called both Small and CBS News president Richard Salant. Neither apologized or admitted error. When broadcasting-industry trade magazines subsequently called with questions about the interview, I told them straight out what had happened. Neither Small nor Salant seemed to mind. They remained friendly, and Small invited me to be his guest at an upcoming White House correspondents' dinner.

On another occasion, CBS News anchorman Walter Cronkite made on-screen comments about Humphrey and the Vietnam War that were factually incorrect. When I called him to discuss his statements, he responded: "I don't care what I said. I think this war is dreadful and I am going to do and say everything I can to stop it." I shared his view on the war but rejected his apparent belief that it justified abandoning truthfulness. Later, at the end of the 1968 Democratic convention in Chicago, Cronkite would from his anchor booth conclude that Humphrey's nomination had been forced down delegates' throats by police tactics on the streets and in the convention hall. Roger Mudd, his coanchor, thereupon remarked that he saw no way that Humphrey could be connected to the disorders. Cronkite was so enraged by his comment, Mudd later told me, that Mudd had difficulty getting prime-time exposure for months afterward. Viewers had no way of knowing that the avuncular Cronkite, shown by polling data to be the "most trusted" man in America, could be so willful and biased. Unfairness and subjectivity were indeed present more than it may have seemed, but still, such instances were seen as exceptions—and they were.

Today's cable-news networks—increasingly the principal source of Americans' daily news—barely try to maintain appearances of objectivity. Fox News programming clearly tilts to the Republican and conservative side; CNN clearly to the Democratic and liberal side. This extends not only to the kinds of questions asked by interviewers but to the identities of the guests and even to the biased "crawl" lines displaying headlines across the bottom of the screen. The biases are so clear, however, that no viewer could claim he or she was being misled by the network. They wear their allegiances on their electronic sleeves.

There is a far greater danger in the all-news networks than bias, however. It is in the general ignorance of most on-air correspondents. CNN political analyst Jeff Greenfield, a former Robert Kennedy staff member and a balanced and knowledgeable observer of politics, was asked during the 2004 presidential campaign to give his assessment of most of his cable-news colleagues. "Most of them just plain don't know anything," he said, going on to explain that they had no practical knowledge or experience relating to politics. Most simply repeat questions and comments channeled through their headphones by producers who, themselves, know little.

Conservative and liberal talk-show hosts are, for the most part, entertainers and propagandists rather than knowledgeable commentators. Bloggers serve a useful purpose in spotting and exposing sloppy or erroneous mainstream-media reporting, but they otherwise purvey a lot of emotional, uninformed, and sometimes purposely misleading content.

Readership of newspapers and general weekly magazines is down. Attempting to build their circulation, most of those publications have moved to ever softer news and feature coverage. Many consumers use their websites rather than reading the publications in hard copy, but, at least until now, no major newspaper or magazine has found a way to make its website truly profitable.

One thing has not changed, however, from the mid-twentieth century until now: the editorial pages of three major national newspapers continue to play a pivotal role in opinion making. They are what other members of the media read before they begin their own professional workdays. Almost invariably, an opinion expressed on the *New York Times*, the *Washington Post*, or the *Wall Street Journal* editorial pages will find its way, a day or two later, into print, broadcast, or online commentary.

The quality of these editorial pages has been influenced to an enormous degree by the leaders of those publications. The *Washington Post*, once thought the most liberal of national newspapers, has under Donald Graham become more balanced and careful. Editorial-page columnists David Broder, Anne Applebaum, David Ignatius, Bob Samuelson, Sebastian Mallaby, and Jim Hoagland, in particular, can be counted on for old-school let-the-chips-fall objective analysis of political, economic, foreign-policy, and national-security issues. The *Times* editorial page, by contrast, has moved away from the careful balance pursued under former publisher Arthur (Punch) Sulzberger to undisguised partisanship under his son, Arthur (Pinch) Sulzberger. Token conservative columnist David Brooks pursues a moderate Republican line. Nicholas Kristof is liberal but scrupulously professional. But columnists Paul Krugman, Frank Rich, and Bob Herbert—none with a background in politics, foreign policy, or national security—express unremitting Bush Rage about those topics on a daily basis. Unsigned editorials pursue a similar line.

Paul Gigot runs a straightforwardly conservative but substantive and fair editorial page at the *Wall Street Journal*. Regular staff columnists are featured, but in addition a wide range of outside columnists present perspectives ranging from Old New Deal to neoconservative. It remains to be seen how the paper's new ownership will affect the character of the page.

Changes in the media, overall, reflect changes in a United States whose society has become more and more "vertical" and less "horizontal." Just as citizens are more likely to identify with a narrow interest group than with a broad political party, they have become more likely to seek information from specialized websites, single-interest magazines, and other focused sources than from the national newspapers, newsweeklies, and commercial television networks that once dominated the flow of information.

Surveys in 2006 found that, even after being subjected to weeks of nonstop media coverage of southeastern-state and New Orleans flooding, a high percentage of Americans had no idea of the geographic locations of Louisiana or New Orleans. Another survey established that a near majority of citizens believed that the attacks of 9/11 somehow were an "inside job" undertaken with complicity of U.S. government officials. Yet another found that, a full three years after it was established that weapons-of-mass-destruction programs had been abandoned by Iraq's Saddam Hussein prior to the U.S. invasion there, almost half of Americans believed that WMD were present in Iraq.

This ignorance clearly cannot be blamed solely on failings of media coverage. Such dumbing down results from failings in our educational system, an increasingly Know Nothing popular culture, and reliance on unreliable online sources such as bloggers. But some of it must be laid to the failure of mainstream media to present information on a timely and reliable basis.

Media critics such as *U.S. News* and syndicated columnist John Leo, the *Washington Post*'s Howard Kurtz, and Ken Auletta, who frequently writes media-related essays for the *New Yorker*, are trying to maintain the integrity of the profession. So are ombudsmen appointed by many media organizations to act as internal watchdogs. But they are fighting an uphill battle in an industry that increasingly appears unable to distinguish news from entertainment or fact from opinion and, what is more, appears to care less about it than it once did.

Many other American institutions have changed enormously and under the general radar screen in recent years. The military establishment is one. Before and during World War II, the U.S. armed services had as much racial discrimination and injustice as the country at large. But today they constitute the most diverse and open major institution in the United States. They have provided equal opportunity and upward mobility to millions of young men and women who otherwise might not have gotten it. They are grappling with gender and sexual orientation issues, but are likely to resolve them before other institutions in our society. In the meantime, our all-volunteer forces have performed in Iraq and Afghanistan at a level of discipline and professionalism unmatched in our history. Yet faculty and students at some American colleges and high schools oppose allowing military recruiters on their campuses. Would they likewise ban recruiters seeking government interns, doctors, nurses, police officers, firefighters, and emergency workers? Similarly, many commentators and editorialists have reflexively fallen back on Vietnam-era, My Lai stereotypes—false even then—in characterizing behavior by U.S. forces in Iraq, Afghanistan, and elsewhere. Contrary to media emphasis, military abuses since 9/11 have been far fewer than those in previous conflicts. This perception deficit is due partly to the fact that, since the end of the military draft, most Americans have had no personal experience with the military, nor, for that matter, have they known someone serving in the military. One little-known phenomenon: Nearly 60 percent of Americans aged fifteen to twenty-one presently are unable to qualify for military service because of either health or educational deficiencies. Without a draft, that reduces substantially the pool of young men and women from which the military can draw. Our military constitutes a quite thin red line often having too little contact with the society at large.

Another institution that has undergone big change is the labor movement. The labor unions of my father's time fought for the basic right to organize and represent workers. They sought better wages, benefits, and working conditions. During the years of my entry into politics they were committed to economic, social, and international agendas beyond the labor movement. The AFL-CIO, United Auto Workers, and United Steelworkers lobbied strongly for passage of President Kennedy's landmark 1962 Trade Expansion Act and liberalized global trade. The AFL-CIO formed the backbone of the Civil Rights and Poor People's Marches on Washington, D.C., in the early 1960s and of the movements behind the Civil Rights Act, the Voting Rights Act, Medicare, Medicaid, and federal aid to education. AFL-CIO president Lane Kirkland led an often lonely battle to help break the Iron Curtain, backing the Polish Solidarity movement when the policy establishment viewed it as an annoyance.

Today's labor movement is notably absent from debate about big issues, except for its general opposition to the liberalized trade it once championed. Auto and steel unions are among the most protectionist. Striving masses led by heroes in flannel shirts are long gone. The movement itself has splintered into contending factions, each led by a former president of the same union. Service industry, teachers', and public employees' unions have supplanted traditional industrial unions as the most influential in the movement. They constitute half the delegates at most Democratic national and state conventions. A late-2005 report filed by the National Education Association revealed that more than half its 600 staff received six-figure salaries, as compared with the $48,000 earned by the average teacher. Member dues accounted for $295 million of the NEA's $341 million in total receipts over the year. The union spent more than $90 million of teachers' dues money on political activities, lobbying, and related grants to advocacy groups—as allocated by NEA staff rather than by rank-and-file members.

Numbers underscore the changes that have taken place in both the military and the labor movement in the United States. In 1970, nearly 20 percent of Americans eighteen and older were military veterans. In 2006 the number was 12.7 percent, and their median age was 57. The percentage of unionized American workers has shrunk from 35 percent a half-century ago to 12.5 percent today. Half of those are taxpayer-paid. More than half of state legislators in Washington State are present or former public employees. That is a common pattern in many states.

Another big change has crept up on us. More foreign-born people are present in the country than at any other time in the past 100 years. Some 12 million, particularly Latinos from Mexico and Central America, are undocumented and living technically outside the law. Most are filling important gaps in the American workforce. But they also have created huge strains on the country's education and social-service systems. California quite soon will become a Latino-majority state. No country, especially since 9/11, can afford to lose control of its borders. The United States is struggling to find a balance between its traditional open-door, Statue of Liberty tradition and the practical necessity of putting limits on access to the country. Immigration also has brought new tensions and political dynamics internally—for instance, black Americans in many communities have seen their power wane as Latino and Asian immigrants have flooded their neighborhoods, outnumbering them and competing for public resources, jobs, and college admissions.

Most of all, the society has become more narrowly oriented. Both the globe and our country have been flattened by financial, economic, and technological changes which, together, have more greatly empowered individuals—and the specialized, narrow groups to which they adhere—while devaluing the roles formerly played by broader organizations. This is true "narrowcasting."

A Depression kid like myself can feel nostalgia for simpler, clearer times. The Great Depression and World War II made us stick together, share in sacrifice, and focus on the fundamentals. In the 1960s, led by the Greatest Generation, which had fought Depression and war, we addressed fundamental wrongs in our society and set them right. Then political assassinations, Watergate, and Vietnam bred cynicism and disillusion in a society previously marked by resilient optimism. The boomer generation now running things can seem to my own Depression/Korean War generation to be insufferably self-involved and incapable of sacrifice. In January 2006, the first official baby boomers—those born between 1946 and 1964—reached 60. Self-analyzing articles, written mainly by boomers, examined the values and outlooks of that enormous cohort of 76 million.

It is true that the boomers will cause enormous strains on Medicare, Medicaid, Social Security, and private retirement systems. Moreover, they have not been savers; they have been spenders and borrowers. What is more worrisome, however, is the boomers' habitual "values posturing," as author and philanthropist Pete Peterson puts it, and their preachiness about issues of race, poverty, and peace when in fact it was others who made the sacrifices in those fields before most of them reached maturity. The boomers' only real claim to personal sacrifice comes from the tiny percentage of the generation which saw service in Vietnam. But most of those who served in Vietnam—mainly draftees, the poor, and minorities—have little in common with the college-educated elitists who do the preaching to the rest of us. The boomers in leadership and opinion-making roles are for the most part the sheltered children of generations that made real sacrifices and have every right to do some preaching—but do not. It remains to be seen if boomers will ever live as they talk. They continue to adopt postures of moral superiority while at the same time trying to "have it all" through self-gratifying acquisitions of material goods and creature comforts.

To oversimplify, the difference between earlier generations and the boomers might be seen as those between, in the media, the serious Punch and callow Pinch Sulzbergers and, in national politics, George H. W. Bush, a genuine World War II hero, and George W. Bush, who spent time as a sometime no-show National Guard pilot. Or between Bob Dole, Michael Dukakis, and Walter Mondale, all of whom saw service as Army enlisted men, and Bill Clinton, Dan Quayle, and Dick Cheney (whose behavior makes him an honorary boomer), who found ways to duck.

What once were known as "intermediary institutions"—that is, political parties, civic groups, and other organizations that helped our society form consensus—have withered. Organized religion has made a comeback as people seek institutions to which they can adhere. The education and skill levels of our citizens have been eroding. Popular culture seems particularly degraded and coarse. The quality of our public discourse, especially surrounding such issues as the Iraq intervention and domestic social issues, has become often unthinking.

It would be nice to think there are previously obscure leaders about to emerge and set us a higher course. There are not. The people presently on the national political scene are the ones who will succeed the current president and congressional leaders. They are quite reflective of the society they represent.

19

WHO WILL LEAD?

Anyone reading this book could easily conclude that great men and women are difficult to find. Contrary to their often glamorized media depictions, those holding and seeking high political office often having glaring weaknesses, just like the rest of us. Those I have respected most—those who put public interests above self, and who could inspire and elevate those around them—have not always been winners. Readers of this book will not be surprised to find that I would not exchange one Hubert Humphrey, George McGovern, Ted Kennedy, Walter Mondale, Mike Dukakis, or Paul Tsongas for two Jimmy Carters or Bill Clintons, although the latter two served three presidential terms between them. Carter and Clinton were driven principally by personal ambition; the others, though presidential-campaign losers, were animated principally by agendas larger than themselves. Looking ahead to the presidential election of 2008 we have candidates in both parties who might be characterized as either agenda- or ambition-driven. No one seeking the presidency, of course, is a shrinking flower. The role requires an enormous ego and type A personality. But candidates can be characterized generally as falling into one camp or another.

On the Democratic side, senators Barack Obama and Chris Dodd and New Mexico governor Bill Richardson are identifiable as agenda-driven. I have known and observed Dodd and Richardson over many years. Dodd, the son of former Connecticut Senator Thomas Dodd, has a long career of effective senate service and was a former chair of the Democratic National Committee. He is hard-working, articulate, and not self-obsessed. The same could be said of Richardson, a former congressional aide, chair of the Congressional Hispanic Caucus, Energy Secretary, and U.N. ambassador. Neither Dodd nor Richardson speaks without thinking. Each knows his own mind and is not susceptible to manipulation by pollsters, campaign consultants, or handlers. In debate over the past four years concerning Iraq, the war on terror, and related issues, both Dodd and Richardson have been critical of administration policy but have stopped short of making the accusations of bad faith and lying that have characterized more fevered critiques of Bush policy. In short, they are mature people interested in moving beyond partisanship to arrive at constructive solutions serving the national interest.

Obama—mistakenly identified as Osama bin Laden in a National Press Club speech by his colleague, Senator Ted Kennedy—also clearly falls within this category. His law school classmates, who mainly went for big money, report that Obama was special and apart even in his student days. He was universally respected for returning to Chicago, after receiving his degree, to be in low-paying community service. His relatively short state and national legislative experience cannot match in years that of several other candidates seeking their parties' nominations. Yet those who have served with him praise his integrity, intelligence, and diligence. Circumstances have thrust him into a presidential candidacy earlier than he might have wished. But he has not been overmatched in the role. His foreign and domestic policy views are evolving, but his instincts clearly are superb. He has a quality shared by few politicians: Those who see and hear him instinctively trust him. He has shocked, in particular, New York senator Hillary Clinton—the candidate with the longest and closest ties to party organizers and donors—by matching her fundraising totals. He has raised as much as Clinton but from many more donors, indicating that his base of support is broader and bottom-up. He is the only post-boomer-generation candidate in the race and also has an appeal that cuts across racial, ethnic, gender, and partisan lines.

Senator Clinton and former Senator John Edwards are also strong Democratic candidates. But you would be hard-pressed to say that they are motivated by agenda rather than ambition. Edwards, a rich former trial lawyer, is generally given low marks by his former North Carolina constituents as an absentee senator who did little for his constituents while pursuing his national ambitions. He deserves sympathy for the loss of his teenage son, in an accident, and his wife's gallant battle against cancer. These experiences can only have deepened him. Yet, as during his 2004 campaign as John Kerry's running mate, his presentation of himself seems programmed and limited. You have the feeling that, somewhere in the background, pollsters and advisers told him that a protectionist economic message would attract disaffected labor-union and middle-American voters and that a generalized message about two Americas, rich and poor, would pull at the heartstrings of traditional liberals as well as discontented populists. Edwards has had the courage to present a health-care reform plan with an expensive price tag attached. But

I sense, and suspect that most voters will come to sense, that beneath the into-the-camera Edwards sincerity there is not a lot of depth. Would voters have confidence in him in a war-and-peace situation? That is doubtful.

Hillary Clinton no doubt would protest being categorized as being driven more by ambition than by a public agenda. She has, after all, been a strong advocate of women's and children's issues. She makes much of her exposure to public issues she experienced while serving as first lady. Yet her time in the White House was characterized by a terrible botching of her health-care assignment and, moreover, by the rigid, absolutist way in which she pursued it. Clinton is highly intelligent. She has surrounded herself with capable— some would say callous and ruthless—political managers and operators and in the senate attempted to establish herself as a more moderate, collabora- tive, and congenial person than voters perceived her to be during her first lady years. Yet how much is real and how much is calculated? In a real pol- icy crisis, foreign or domestic, how would she react—if polling data and focus groups did not provide her with a politically acceptable way to proceed? Hillary Clinton might well have the capacity for high achievement in the presidency. It would be good for the country to have a woman president. But there is much in Clinton's background to give voters serious pause: the commodities profits and other dubious transactions in Arkansas; the petty attempt to fire White House travel office staff; the lost documents which showed up in her sewing basket; the low-politics "right-wing conspiracy" themes she pursues under pressure; the quick jabs at Obama early in 2007 as his campaign became competitive; and, of course, the health-care fiasco. All of these things (except possibly the health-care mess) relate to power and ambition rather than to a selfless desire for public service.

On the Republican side, the principal candidates—former New York mayor Rudy Giuliani, Senator John McCain, and former Massachusetts governor Mitt Romney—are less easy to categorize. Giuliani proved a tough and inspiring leader during New York's 9/11 agonies. As district attorney and mayor, he took on both organized and street crime, and, in most cases, suc- ceeded. Yet he has had some dubious professional and personal associations and seems unable to recognize their inappropriateness. His personal life has been a mess. His political strength in 2007 has flowed from the national mem- ory of his 9/11 toughness and courage. It has enabled him to generate sup- port even in border and southern states, where his New York views on social issues might otherwise be thought disqualifying. Is he agenda or power driven?

More of the latter, I suspect, but we will know more as his party's nominating process tests him.

Most in the media would categorize McCain as being agenda-driven. I would disagree. McCain's story is interesting, but through it runs one common thread: He takes the main chance. I listed on page 265 some of the twists and turns McCain has taken to position and reposition himself politically.

Romney, as Giuliani, still remains to be fully defined. As a Republican governor in a heavily Democratic state, he took positions which gained bipartisan support but also skepticism in his party's more conservative states. He has raised much campaign money—more than either Giuliani or McCain by early 2007—but has not risen commensurately in the polls. He comes across as telegenic and articulate. Is he agenda driven or ambition driven? Just as with Giuliani, the balance will become more clear as the 2008 campaign season proceeds.

Should former House Speaker Newt Gingrich enter the Republican race (which he had not at this book's publication date), he could be categorized as being principally agenda-driven. His 1994 contract, although based in large part on polling data, nonetheless provided a substantive platform that House Republicans previously had lacked. And it brought them success. Alone among Republicans, he seems genuinely stimulated and engaged by discussion of public issues. Clearly they are not to him just a means to a political end.

Late-entering former Senator Fred Thompson can only be classified as opportunistic. In the Senate he was notorious for laziness and a lack of legislative achievement.

My own preferences are no secret. I would prefer an Obama-Richardson or Obama-Dodd Democratic ticket in 2008. Either ticket would present the country with trustworthy, serious leadership devoted to the public interest. As a Democrat, I would prefer weak Republican opposition. But as an American I would welcome a Republican candidacy either by Giuliani or Gingrich. I could not vote for either, but either could be expected to wage an intelligent, issue-oriented campaign worthy of the country.

In mid-2007, New York Mayor Michael Bloomberg announced that he was considering an independent presidential candidacy. Such a candidacy would represent an insurgency from the center and conceivably could result not only in his election but also in an historic national political realignment. It is too early to make a judgment but, depending on the identity of the major-party nominees, Bloomberg not only could win but could organize a new, moderate national party.

Will we be able to find common ground again in this socially and politically polarized country?

In the past, it has taken a depression, a major war, or, briefly, a major terrorist attack to bring us together. Let us hope we experience none of those things in the immediate future. Otherwise we must count on new leaders, and on ourselves, to make a fresh start, putting, as Jean Monnet used to say, our problems on one side of the table and ourselves all together on the other.

20

THE DEMOCRATIC MESSAGE

Syndicated columnist Michael Kinsley, a Seattle resident, asked me recently if I was prepared to saddle up again for service with a presidential candidate or new national administration. I will turn seventy-four before the 2008 national election. That is too old for the intense twenty-hour days that can come with such service. But I surely will be watching and writing about everything going on in that period. My children and grandchildren are not that far behind me, and will be living in the country that will be led by our next president and the ones after that.

Though now practicing journalism, I remain a lifelong and forever-committed Democrat. I am a hereditary Democrat and an intellectual Democrat—although some would allege, in this cynical time, that "intellectual Democrat," or, for that matter, "intellectual Republican," are oxymorons. I also am a visceral Democrat.

Republicans, and Republican business leaders in particular, would dispute this characterization, but I have found over time that they are far less interested in the political process and in actual governance than Democrats are. Many appear to see government per se as an undesirable institution that Republicans, from time to time, must seize in order to straighten it out. Most Democrats, and certainly my generation of Democrats, see the political process and government as central to the country's well-being.

The same Balkanizing pressures and "narrowcasting" have taken place within the Democratic Party as within the rest of society. Since my time of entry into politics, I have seen the party's agenda move from broad economic, domestic, and international issues to narrower and often more emotional social issues. In 1960, for instance, no serious politician would have imagined that abortion or gay marriage would in the future sometimes outweigh debate in the party about jobs, economic policy, or national security. Nor could it have been predicted that our party of ideas—the party whose agenda had transformed the society from the 1930s into the late twentieth century—would

have become in the early twenty-first century such a shrill, reactive, and oppo-
sitionist entity.

Especially since the contested 2000 presidential election, I have been dismayed to see Democratic Party communications and talking lines filled with
vituperative charges against the integrity and truthfulness of the incumbent
Republican administration. The administration has been bumbling and
inept in both making and executing policy. Should that not be enough?

I grew up believing in a "tough on issues, soft on people" approach to
partisanship. But, since 2000, my party often has taken an opposite view. The
syndrome took root during the eight Clinton years, when the party's incumbent president quite literally was fighting day to day for his political life. Clinton alumni have continued the practice. I was surprised, early in 2001, to begin
receiving direct-mail communications from the Democratic National Committee signed not by a former president or respected congressional leader, as
previously would have been the practice, but by slash-and-burn partisan consultant James Carville. This represents a kind of reverse evolution. Such communications have been filled with such phrases as "Bush Lies" or "They Lie,"
often without citing specific examples. I also have been dismayed by the dis-
missive characterization by many Democrats of people of faith as "religious
extremists." I also resent many Democrats' too easy use of the race or gender cards—reflexively charging opponents with bias.

All of this not only lowers the level of public discourse today, but has
made it difficult to reach bipartisan solutions in Congress. It will also ensure
that, should Democrats regain the White House in 2009, we will be on the
receiving end of the same bitter, personal attacks from an opposition Republican Party. It has helped create the public polarizations that cripple the process.
Weren't Democrats once the party of tolerance? How have we now become
so intolerant?

Democrats' 2006 retaking of congressional majorities should have helped
them escape their negativism. They will, until 2009, share policy-making responsibility with the administration. But thus far they have continued to see themselves as shrill critics.

If the Democratic Party's 2008 nominee were to give me one last task,
I would want to draft his or her nomination-acceptance speech to the party's
national convention. It would launch a campaign against a Republican Party
nominee named neither Bush nor Cheney and unlikely to be directly associated with administration policies of the previous eight years. It would set

a tone for the upcoming national campaign and, at the same time, set forth in unmistakable terms a direction for the party and country from 2009 onward. Here is what it might say.

A NEW BEGINNING

We have waited together for this day. Now it is here. It is the day of a new beginning both for our party and for our country.

We should start by stating who we are and why we are here. We Democrats are the party of the people. From the time of Franklin Roosevelt forward, we have stood without apology for the striver, for the newcomer, for the powerless, and, yes, for the innovator and the creator. To paraphrase Roosevelt, we have stood with those who had too little rather than with those who already had enough.

It was our party, and our party's courageous leaders, who fought for and achieved Social Security, Medicare, Medicaid, civil and voting rights for minorities, health care and nutrition for those who otherwise would have lacked them, women's rights, gay rights, a minimum wage. Civil rights. Civil liberties. These are old words, but I say them proudly because we believe in them. Freedom and justice for all in this new country in a New World.

Our party has been absent from the White House for eight years. Right now, right here, we begin our campaign to take it back—not for power's sake but for the sake of what power can do.

The Bush-Cheney era will end in a very few weeks.

I do not need to tell you what their eight years of stewardship have done to this country. Our resources have been squandered, and our strength dissipated, in unwise military interventions in places not vital to our national interests. We are weaker, not stronger, than we were eight years ago. We are less, not more, safe in our homeland than we were on September 10, 2001.

Our domestic economy and financial system have been imperiled by overreach. Billions in American IOUs are in the hands of foreign creditors who can decide, at any time, to help or harm us.

We have been guided by an administration and party believing in some mythical invisible hand that will in the end bring prosperity and well-being to our country.

We Democrats believe, too, in the power of individual initiative and entrepreneurship. We do not want state ownership or control of our economic or financial systems. But we know that no invisible hand will properly educate, train, or prepare American kids for the tasks of this twenty-first century. Nor do we believe that this invisible hand will care for those left out from even a general prosperity. It will not provide health care to those presently unable to afford it. Nor can we allow our Social Security system to be corrupted or risked by putting its resources into the hands of private investment firms.

We believe in a free economic system. Our economy can be a powerful engine generating private growth and public revenue for the overall good. But the economy is not an end in itself. It is a means to an end. The end is to create a society not only of prosperity but of greater equity and justice. That is where we differ from our opponents and will always differ. These are fundamental differences.

We have since 2001 been engaged in a war on terror and in a costly and continuing responsibility in Iraq. The war in Iraq was a mistake. Others may charge that President Bush lied to draw the United States into Iraq. I do not say that. The Clinton administration and most international analysts also believed that Saddam Hussein continued weapons of mass destruction programs which were ongoing when he expelled United Nations weapons inspectors. But the intervention in Iraq was a strategic mistake going well beyond the question of whether special weapons were or were not present there in 2001.

President George W. Bush's great mistake was not in fearing Saddam Hussein's possible weapons but in buying into the vision of Richard Cheney, Donald Rumsfeld, Paul Wolfowitz, Richard Perle, and others— a vision that saw American troops marching into flower-strewn Baghdad streets in scenes like the 1945 liberation of Paris. Their vision saw governance flowing seamlessly from Saddam's fascist legions to a new, democratic central government in which all ethnic and religious factions willingly would participate. While the transition took place, public and private institutions would continue to provide essential goods and services to the Iraqi people. Then, within a short time, Iraq would become a beacon of political democracy and economic liberalization in a region notably lacking both. The Middle East would become transformed.

The problem with this vision—promulgated by supposedly hardheaded realists—was that it was divorced from the reality of the time and place. These visionaries sought stability. Instead they have created greater instability. All Americans have paid the price for their mistake. Their time is up. The Bush theorists must leave their positions of responsibility in America. They must not be replaced by others like them.

The Cold War is over. But the balance of terror in the Cold War has been replaced by multiple and dangerous threats all over the globe—threats of international terrorism; of nuclear, biological, and chemical weapons in the hands of both rogue states and terrorists; of climate change; of instability and uncertainty in societies threatened from within and by predatory neighbors; of disease, famine, and poverty.

We cannot afford to squander American lives and money on a thousand ventures around the globe. We must know what is vital, what is not vital, where we can make a difference; and where we should not try.

Our Democratic Party traditionally has been the party of peace, of international cooperation, and of peaceful development. But the world must know that, in 2009, we will stand and defend our interests, by whatever means necessary, where we believe the American people's safety and well-being truly are at stake. No hostile leaders or persons elsewhere in the world, watching or hearing this speech, should doubt that statement. They should not test it.

The safety and security of the American people must be and will remain our first priority. The Constitution requires it.

There is another aspect of national security, however, not usually considered in that realm. It is the strength and cohesion of our American society. National security depends not merely on twenty-first-century armed forces and weapons systems:

It depends on a sound, balanced full-employment economy.

It depends on a well-educated, well-trained workforce.

It depends on the health and nutrition of our citizens.

It depends on our environment being protected rather than exploited.

It depends, most of all, on a link between our country's leaders and our country's citizens that is built on mutual trust and shared belief. The phrase "consent of the governed" must mean something.

In all these realms the Bush-Cheney administration has ill served our national security. We pledge to set this right.

I will carry the Democratic banner in this fall's campaign and, if elected, will serve proudly not only as a Democratic president, but as president of all the American people. Everyone in this hall is a Democrat. But, above that, we are Americans.

There must be an end to the petty partisanship and so-called blue state–red state divisions in our country. If elected, I will work with congressional leaders from both sides of the aisle—to get the public business done. I will seek in my campaign not only Democratic votes but the votes of Republicans and independents who want an end to the polarizing and paralyzing disputes that are holding us back. I will get the public business done.

There will be many occasions in the months ahead to speak of specific issues—of party platforms and legislative proposals. There will be ample time to critique the ideas of the Republican Party's nominee. I will be pleased to meet the Republican presidential nominee in open, public debate—as many times as he can stand it. I will campaign relentlessly.

My message tonight to America is this: The Democratic Party is back. It has a nominee. We offer a new beginning to our country. We have faith in the American people—all our people, regardless of their partisan affiliation. We pledge that, if given power, we will not abuse it. We will use it wisely and on your behalf. We will treat the lives of your sons and daughters as precious. We will hold you in respect and regard your support as something that must be earned anew each day.

Now, a personal word. I have since my childhood wanted to serve my country. I have tried my best in public service to serve honestly and effectively. I have been given a mandate by my party to lead. I now seek that mandate from all the American people.

I pledge to you that I will give every ounce of my being to the presidency, if you will grant it to me. My faith in this country is boundless. Whatever happens, we will persevere and we will prevail.

Tomorrow morning is a new morning and the first in the rest of our country's history. Let us begin our work then and be sure it never ends.

EPILOGUE

As I age, I recognize in myself daily habits of thought and mannerisms that I once noticed in my parents and grandparents. I see the same in my four children, who reflect my late wife Jean's side of the family as well as my own. They work hard, are devoted to their own children, and share the Van Dyk impatience with hypocrisy and dishonesty. I never knew my grandmothers. But I still see in my mind's eye not only my parents but my two grandfathers, both sturdy, uneducated men in plain clothing wearing handlebar mustaches. My grandfather Williams, shortly before he died at ninety-three, told me of walking as a boy through the Civil War battlefield at Wilson's Creek, near the family farm in southwest Missouri, and seeing the Union and Confederate bodies on the ground, not a tree or tree limb left standing after the exchanges of fire. The Williams family came from Wales to Tennessee to Kentucky to Missouri to Canada and then back to the United States, in constant search of both freedom and opportunity. That was the case, too, with the Van Dyk family, moving from the Netherlands to South Africa to South America to Canada and to the United States in search of the same things. There is something in all of us, no matter our origins, still seeking that more open and just society in a New World.

Even in disquieting times such as these, there is an American idea that has been passed from one generation to the next—from the descendants of those who came on the Mayflower, on slave ships, at night across the border, or, as in my father's case, in a freight car.

I root now, as I always have, for the strivers at the bottom. They bring us new energy and leaders who will be impelled to generate change. I beware leaders who think they can create Des Moines in Baghdad or Singapore. We must do what we can to push history in a generally progressive and benign direction. But we would do best to perfect democracy in our own country before decreeing it elsewhere.

I distrust those with hard, absolute views of any persuasion. I particularly distrust those who rage and hate. I value the heterogeneity of our society. It makes us less susceptible to the extreme ideologies and views that are most easily implanted in places where everyone looks and thinks the same.

I would like to think that we are not deadlocked in America but simply pausing a bit, thinking things through, and regaining our balance before we move forward again toward perfection of the American idea.

Looking back, I feel fortunate to have worked with men and women of high idealism and purpose, and to have been part of large events. The moments I most value have been those in the company of people motivated by something beyond themselves. I think of House Speaker Tip O'Neill, a wonderful public servant in his own right, recounting his last conversation with Hubert Humphrey before Humphrey's death. Even after being stricken with terminal cancer, Humphrey remained an active senator. He and O'Neill, along with a handful of other congressional leaders, met weekly with President Carter to advise him on legislative strategy. On this occasion, O'Neill related, he and his wife were seated at their kitchen table the night before a scheduled White House meeting with Carter. The phone rang. "It's Hubert Humphrey," Mrs. O'Neill said. "It can't be," the Speaker replied. "I understand he's very sick in Minnesota." "I tell you, it is Hubert Humphrey," she insisted.

O'Neill picked up the phone. It was Humphrey. His voice was weak, but he still spoke in his unmistakable staccato. "Tip," he said, "I am under the weather and cannot make tomorrow's meeting. But I want you to be sure to tell President Carter the following things." He then gave O'Neill a list of items to discuss. "I certainly will do that," O'Neill replied. "I'll tell the president it came from you." "I'll be back there in a jiffy," Humphrey went on. "Hold the fort until I return." A few days later the O'Neills heard the radio news at their breakfast table. Humphrey had died.

I think often of President Lyndon Johnson and of the 1965 legislative meeting in the White House dining room where he exhorted his party's congressional leaders to get Great Society legislation moving. I think, too, of the worn and frayed man he had become by the time he left office in January 1969. Our political process is cruel. A president can one day be everything, the next nothing. We have no "safe seat" refuges for our fallen leaders. In 1999 I attended a Johnson White House reunion and seminar held at the University of Texas and at the LBJ Ranch. At the final event, a barbecue in a tent on the banks of the Pedernales River, Mrs. Johnson presided over an irreverent afternoon at which tapes of Johnson White House conversations were played aloud for those who had served him. Everyone howled to hear

LBJ cajole and give "the Johnson treatment" to everyone from senior senators to a tailor from whom he was trying to wheedle a free pair of slacks. I
imagined that Johnson would be happy to know that there were those who
respected and even loved him. He certainly had left a wonderful legacy of
achievements on behalf of his country's have-nots.

I remember George McGovern, doggedly trudging through snow-filled
streets in New Hampshire in late 1971 and early 1972, given no chance whatever of gaining the Democratic presidential nomination and outrightly derided
by the handful of media paying any attention to him. He pushed on with
equanimity and faith in his cause, which was to end the Vietnam War. He
never lacked a small joke or self-deprecating comment. But I could see that,
inside, he was hard as steel.

I recall sharing a flight from Washington, D.C., to New York in early
1985 with Walter Mondale, who had just lost a one-sided electoral contest to
President Reagan. Almost all on the flight must have seen him as they entered
the plane—he was seated on the aisle in the third row from the entry door.
Yet no one spoke to him. Finally, just before he deplaned at LaGuardia, a
flight attendant thanked him for choosing the flight and for his public service. As we shared a taxi to downtown Manhattan, I remarked that politics
was a tough game, and losing hard. "It's not just this defeat," he replied. "It's
the whole twenty-five years—of giving up your family life; of coming to meetings where no one showed up; of receiving pledges of campaign contributions which never were made; of just giving everything." This good man, I
thought, had deserved better. He would, of course, serve later as U.S. ambassador to Japan. His public career had not ended.

I think of Senator Ted Kennedy, at the peak of his legislative prowess,
facing a long period in which Republicans would control both sides of Capitol Hill. "Majority or minority," he told me one evening, "I am not going to
let it make a difference. I am going to keep getting up each morning and
working hard for things I think are important—whether I'm alone or have
an army behind me." Beset by frequent tragedy and illness in his family,
Kennedy has just kept on coming. He again chairs key committees and can
make things happen.

I think of Paul Tsongas on a speaking tour we did together, several years
after his 1992 presidential campaign. As we went from city to city, I could see
his energy flagging, until, at our last stop in New York, he nearly collapsed at
the podium and was forced to sit down. I finished his part of the presenta-

tion. Afterward we rested for a time at a coffee shop. "I think my cancer is back," he said. "I've got to get home." But, the next moment, he was telling a story about a mutual friend and an incident in a Boston bar. Some passers-by recognized him and engaged him. He asked about their children and how they were doing in their daily life. Tsongas, I thought, was a man who left something with everyone he met. His life was too short, but he lived it well.

I recall a dozen brave Freedom Democrats, standing together on the Atlantic City Boardwalk in 1964, calling on the Democratic National Convention to desegregate the Mississippi delegation to the convention. They won a small victory that day. Later they would prevail in a far larger way.

I think of the countless, nameless volunteers I have seen working long hours in political campaigns and the many dedicated people I have known in public service. All have been animated by strong, good motivations. As I began this book, I thought of listing by name those who I believed deserved special recognition. When the list reached the hundreds I knew there were too many to enumerate. They more than overbalance the self-seekers and emotional cripples who often pursue power and fame through politics.

I think often of the GIs I saw in Vietnam and of their memorial in Washington, D.C. During my years in the capital I made a point of visiting the Mall at least once yearly to make a tour of all the monuments. My next-to-last stop was always the Lincoln Memorial. President Lincoln's powerful, sad face seemed to know and see everything. I always felt in his presence a sense of overwhelming calm. My last stop, after its construction, was the Vietnam Memorial. The memorial's design caused viewers to see their own reflections in the stone. In the early years there always were Vietnam veterans, in uniform and often wearing their medals, standing nearby—not ready, it seemed, to leave their buddies. There also were the wrenching childhood photos, baseball gloves, and other memorabilia placed at the base of the memorial by the families and friends of the 58,000 whose names were listed above. Each, I often thought, represented at least one broken heart. I often wondered if former secretary of defense Robert McNamara or former secretary of state Henry Kissinger had personally visited the memorial. I doubted it. They either could not face what they had done, I thought, or were too insensitive to recognize it. After the memorial honoring the military nurses in Vietnam was constructed, I always stopped there, too. Their empathy seemed to radiate from the sculpture.

I smile as I think of wonderful moments, in the 1960s and 1970s in particular, when I joined my colleagues in Democratic administrations and national campaigns at the ends of long workdays which sometimes had gone well, other times badly. We would laugh uproariously at the absurdities that had beset us and would look forward to the next morning. I could feel in those moments "the spirit of public happiness" that President John Adams described as flowing from knowledge that one was engaged in the service of the people. Both Hubert Humphrey and Eugene McCarthy often spoke of that spirit.

Always I think of my parents, and those like them, who had nothing, worked hard, never complained, loved their country, and would do anything for a friend, neighbor, or stranger in need. I recognize now that everything I have came from them and that, through my life, everything I did was for and about them.

INDEX

Abrams, Creighton, 72
Abzug, Bella, 135
Adams, Brock, 168
Afghanistan, viii, 258, 259, 272
AFL-CIO, 190, 273
Agency for International Development
(AID), 170, 171, 172, 173, 174
Agnew, Spiro, 115, 150, 268
Agronsky, Martin, 98
Albright, Madeleine, 188, 213, 220, 224, 238
Alliance for Progress, 41
Altman, Roger, 223
Ambassador Hotel, 70, 72
Americans for Democratic Action
(ADA), 32, 48, 106, 114, 160
Anderson, Jack, 15
Andreas, Dwayne, 53, 102, 103
Apple, R. W. (John), xi, 92
Applebaum, Anne, 270–71
Aspin, Les, 223, 229
Astrachan, Anthony, 54
Auletta, Ken, 271–72

Babbitt, Bruce, 220
baby boomers, x, 221, 267, 274
Bagley, Smith, 154, 184
Bagley, Vicki, 154
Bailey, John, 87
Baird, Zoe, 227
Ball, George, 20, 40, 85, 86, 87, 101–2
Barlogie, Bart, 207

Barnes, Michael, 155, 183, 184, 211–12
Baron, Alan, 153
Bartlett, Charles, 268
Beatty, Warren, 80, 184, 186, 199, 247
Beckington, Herb, 55
Bellingham Herald, 6
Bellingham (Washington): Van Dyk's
family roots in, 3, 4–5; Van Dyk's
growing-up years in, 6, 7–8, 9, 260, 267
Bening, Annette, 247
Bennet, Doug, 140, 173
Bennett, W. Tapley, 42
Bentsen, Lloyd, 223
Berger, Sandy: as Clinton's National
Security Advisor, 223, 238, 245–46;
and 1972 presidential campaign,
130–31, 141, 147; and 1992 presiden-
tial campaign, 212–13, 217, 218
Bergland, Bob, 184
Berlin Crisis, 12–14, 15
Berman, Edgar, 87
Berman, Mike, 167
Beveridge, Albert, 174
Bloomberg, Michael, 279–80
Blumenthal, Mike, 184
Bode, Ken, xi, 114
Boggs, Hale, 39
Bond, Julian, 159
Bosch, Juan, 42
Bourne, Peter, 160
Bowles, Erskine, 238